WINNING the MONEY GAME

WINNING the MONEY GAME

No-nonsense Answers
For You and Your Money

---

by TAMA McALEESE, CFP

World of Money Books
Summit Financial Products, Inc.

© 1998 by Tama McAleese

All rights reserved, including the rights of
Reproduction in whole or in part
In any form or by any means.

First Edition

Parts of this book were adapted by the author
from:
Get Rich Slow (Third Edition)
By Tama McAleese
Career Press, 1995

**Library of Congress Cataloging-in-Publication
Data**
McAleese, Tama.
Winning the Money Game/ by Tama McAleese.
p.   cm.
World of Money book
ISBN 1-889692-16-6 (paper): $16.99

World of Money Books
Summit Financial Products, Inc.
19590 E. Main Street, Suite 108
Parker, Colorado 80134

Disclaimer

This book was designed to provide accurate and authoritative information of a general and current nature only. It is published under the express understanding that neither the writer nor the publisher has the specific background to or is engaged in rendering legal, accounting or other professional services. Any information, therefore, should be evaluated in the context of each individual's particular and unique financial circumstances. The services of competent legal and accounting professionals should be sought and consulted before implementing any strategies outlined here.

It is also assumed that tax taws and economic dynamics change on a constant basis, and other uncontrollable factors may limit or even prohibit the use of certain investment options or financial planning strategies.

Since a basic financial education is desirable and helpful to begin self-reliance and empowerment toward financial independence, this book was developed as a helpful tool and basic building block upon which to develop additional personal money management, financial planning and investing skills.

Contents

Preface   **7**

Introduction
Winning the Money Game   **9**

Chapter 1
Financial planning: not just for the rich   **11**

Chapter 2
It's a jungle out there   **18**

Chapter 3
Remember the golden rules   **32**

Chapter 4
Show me the money   **42**

Chapter 5
Your piggy bank   **55**

Chapter 6
Credit cards: friend or foe?   **66**

Chapter 7
Insurance: cover your ass-ets   **76**

Chapter 8
Will the real financial planners please stand up?   **114**

Chapter 9
Home is where your money pit is   **129**

Chapter 10
Your child and money   **158**

Chapter 11
Using your kids for a change   **165**

Chapter 12
The hassle of the tassel   **173**

Chapter 13
The perils of partnerships: not married   **186**

Chapter 14
When you are alone   **197**

Chapter 15
On a clear day you can see retirement   **209**

Chapter 16
Pensions, profits and pitfalls   **221**

Chapter 17
IRAs: New and improved   **232**

Chapter 18
Estate planning: You can't take it with you   **243**

Chapter 19
Myths, legends and truths of investing   **252**

Chapter 20
Turning investment-ese into investment-ease   **270**

Chapter 21
Investing strategies: short-stop vs. marathon money   **278**

Chapter 22
Mutual fund-amentals   **290**

Conclusion   317

Appendix: Worksheets
I know it's in here somewhere   318

Preface

Once upon a time, a Russian czar commanded his advisors to seek out and bring back the sum of all knowledge so he could rule as the wisest potentate in history. The advisors spread out across the globe, investigating every civilized society they could reach.

One year later, they returned to their country, carrying voluminous books of information and data. The czar threw up his hands in frustration—it would take 10 lifetimes just to sort through the reams of documents they offered. He demanded they compress this into something smaller and more digestible.

In time, the advisors presented a shorter version to their czar. Still, it seemed too long to be of immediate use. So the czar instructed them one last time: Be abrupt, if necessary, but get to the point, the bottom line.

One advisor finally appeared in the throne room. In his hand was one single piece of paper. The czar, visibly relieved, was even happier when he saw only one sentence on the page. Satisfied that he had found the secret to ultimate wisdom, he rose and read it aloud:

There are no free lunches.

Introduction

Winning the Money Game

The number one retirement plan in America today is winning the lottery. Shouldn't you have a Plan B?

The average worker doesn't need a raise as much as he or she needs to better manage and invest the hard-fought-for paychecks he or she currently earns. Many financial consumers spend more time packing underwear for weekend getaways and summer vacations than they do planning their financial futures.

Most of what consumers are taught regarding their money comes primarily from vested interests and well meaning incompetents. Therefore, much misinformation is spread. Most folks are taught that, though smart enough to earn their paychecks, they are not savvy enough to manage them. That, the financial industry warns, should be left to the "experts."

Nothing could be further from the truth. Either you watch carefully over your own money or other people gladly will—always at their profit—perhaps at your expense. But you can take control and manage your investments as well as the pros—perhaps even better.

You have nothing more important to do than to take charge of your own financial destiny. You also have the greatest vested interest in seeing that your money remain healthy.

When your latest car costs more than your first home, you need inflation fighting strategies to outpace the deadliest money killer of them all over long periods—inflation.

Are you racing toward retirement faster than your retirement savings (even faster than you may know because of downsizing or rightsizing)?

If you are already retired, concerned that the victories of medical science may actually allow you to outlive your shrinking retirement nest egg, it's time to become fiscally fit.

Sit tightly on your wallets and pocketbooks as you skillfully outmaneuver the self-interested financial community. Carefully navigate the rocky terrain and seek objective and competent information that often flies in the face of tradition. Keep a watchful eye toward Congress, currently sizing you up as its source of an unlimited budget after the next election.

But never, my friends, never sit on your "thinking machines." If you calculate the time and effort to gain a financial education as too costly, please consider the alternative: continued ignorance regarding how the real rules of the Money Game are stacked against you. Succinctly put, at all times you must *cover your ass-ets*.

Happily, this book is written in the same English language we all learned in high school and for those who hate money management guides because they are dull, boring and intimidating.

Winning The Money Game is a financial survival guide for the "yachtless," a primer for folks born, through no fault of their own, to nice but middle class families with no winning lottery ticket in their immediate future, no rich Uncle Harry to count on and no trust funds on their horizon. They have, however, tremendous challenges ahead: funding college for their children, desperately attempting to retire successfully on a fixed income and sometimes just keeping their financial heads above water.

Why should you read this book from cover to cover? Because *learning* about your money is as vital as *earning* it.

Chapter 1

Financial planning: not just for the rich

Two men on a hunting trip encountered an angry bear with little tolerance for intruders in her territory. While one hunter turned to run for his life toward the nearest tree, the second man sat down on a rock and began tightly tying his shoelaces.

"What are you doing?" called the first man over his shoulder, panting heavily. "You can't outrun that bear."

"I don't have to outrun the bear," answered the second man. "All I have to do is outrun you."

Like our intrepid hunters, you are already well into the longest and most serious race of your life—winning your Money Game. Inflation may be outpacing you, while the financial industry is outthinking and outmaneuvering you. Banks and insurance companies are outsmarting you, and your government is outvoting you. Everyone else, it seems, wants your money for him- or herself.

Perhaps you are lulled into a false sense of security, wanting to believe that some winged angel is standing guard over your hard-fought-for dollars, or that some legal agency will protect you from misinformation, deceptive sales practices or mismanagement of your assets.

In the story about the bear, the intended prey knew he was in serious danger and needed his ingenuity and wits. Real life financial victims work hard for their money yet succumb to mismanagement of their assets or fall for clever marketing gimmicks designed to separate them from whatever they have managed to squirrel away. Most people know more about greening up their lawns, lush vacation spots and last night's TV sitcom than about how to take charge of their money. With little time to actively manage their personal lives, let alone their financial affairs, they seldom know where their money is, who is taking care of it and how well it is doing.

There are three economic consumer classes in our country today: the rich, the poor and the middle class, the last bearing an increasing portion of future tax burdens and social entitlements. The rich can well afford expensive advisors, tax experts and other consultants to protect them from common money mistakes, taxes and the greed of the financial community. The poor have little money to manage. The middle class, then, is the group with the most at risk.

The basic rules of the Money Game are simple: Either you work your money or someone else gladly will. The object is to grab as many dollars as possible within a limited period of time you set for yourself. When the game is over, the players with the most dollars win. The losers are nearly broke. They never developed an emergency fund, a college fund, a definite financial or savings plan or put away enough to retire in comfort. They probably will, however, live long enough to outlive the small pile of cash they did manage to build up. Perhaps they hope their kids will do well and will support them for a change.

Take Back The Power

If the basic rules of the Money Game are so simple, why are so many people playing it poorly? Because the real rules are in the fine print and folks don't notice, let alone read, the small print—not on their monthly credit card bills, not on bank statements and not in the contracts they trustingly sign for the goods and services they purchase. They believe what they are told. They also believe that someone somewhere must somehow be protecting them.

Some dreamers are still searching for that winning lottery ticket to solve their financial challenges, hoping for a "free lunch." It is time consuming to take back the power over your financial life, to determine financial priorities, to research and compare, to scrimp and save, to set priorities and limits on spending, to live beneath your financial means, to give up today's immediate satisfactions for the sake of tomorrow's goals, especially when everyone else seems to be doing so much better with less effort. **If you like where you are, keep doing what you are doing.**

Most folks don't plan to fail—they simply fail to plan. And those who seek advice are often led to believe that a **<u>financial planner</u>** is primarily a product seller. So the average citizen buys financial promises and products instead of seeking real life solutions—purchasing a little of this and that until her or his portfolio resembles a full plate at a reunion buffet table. The pieces (products) aren't designed as a part of the whole, like a finished puzzle. Savers continue to throw money at future goals, picking blindly among a wide variety of financial products that may benefit the salesperson better than the customer. They understand little except the sales pitch, ignoring the fine print (the actual contract limitations and exclusions). Depending on projections and illustrations from salespeople motivated by generous commissions, they buy from those who can't tell the future either. Not an effective method of ensuring financial security!

When financial goals come too close to be solved by effective planning strategies, some people panic, going even deeper into debt. They console themselves with the thought that things will get better. Unfortunately, things tend to become worse.

Financial planning: not just for the rich

Too many personal financial balance sheets look like the Titanic, except that the ship had a band. A child may be graduating from high school while the college fund—alias emergency fund, savings account, Christmas or vacation fund—will stretch until Thanksgiving—of the student's first semester.

Based on statistics, whether we admit it or not, most of us are living from paycheck to paycheck or living life on the installment plan. If your primary breadwinner were out of a job for three months, would you lose your good credit rating? If he or she remained unemployed for six months, would the family car be repossessed? After a year without work, I'll bet there goes the mortgaged home.

Long term financial planning in many homes today consists of attempting to stretch one paycheck until the next one comes in the door. **Too many families, at the end of the month, have more month left at the end of the money.**

You will probably never win the lottery. But, in your lifetime, you will earn a small fortune. Americans are making more money than ever before. Why, then, is the middle class standard of living declining? Because it's not what you make that counts, but what you can keep after taxes, inflation, and redistribution of your income by your government and financial middlemen.

If clever salespeople can talk you into spending your dollar, that money will grow and compound. . .for them. The more you spend, the more memories you will have of pizza, designer clothes and romantic summer cruises, while some business minded stranger will have your dollars compounding in his or her favor.

Maybe you believe Papa Government will give you a handout if you fail financially. But where will it get enough money? When Social Security began, 42 workers supported each payee. Currently, only three employees contribute for one retiree, disabled worker or dependent receiving benefits. You should already realize that, if you continue to rely on Uncle Sam, your government will be standing in the same soup line with you many years from now.

We are the government. It is our pockets that are continually picked for every benefit, tax, social or entitlement program, subsidy or pork barrel project. Your government can manage your money for you. Simply hand it over, so the government can redistribute it back to specific individuals and special interests (minus administrative costs).

I have never attended a charity ball for anyone but the poor. If you manage to save a little, just not enough, you may be too rich to enjoy any government subsidies, but too poor to be comfortable. In this country we don't let people starve if we can subsidize them. So, if you manage to save carefully, invest well and store away enough for your own retirement, guess who will be at your front door, demanding that you share some of your reserves? You are saving for two, yourself and a poorer stranger which makes your uphill task even more challenging.

I won't insult your intelligence by promising to send your children to college free, to cut 80 percent off your current insurance premiums, to show you how to buy real estate with nothing down or to pretend that you can become rich without taking any risks. If this is your goal, you don't need advice from me. You need a #900 psychic investment phone hotline or Rumplestiltskin to spin straw into gold!

If anyone could actually substantiate such claims, do you believe she or he would sell such powerful information for $20? Or $2,000? And what do these **"experts"** really know? If they are so good at predicting the future, why aren't they secretly investing for themselves from some exotic and warmer climate instead of selling via TV and radio, or delivering advice to your mailbox? **Don't look for a soothsayer; search for a truthsayer!**

Monthly consumer financial publications claim that, in exchange for a small annual subscription fee, they will be your personal financial guru. If they are so capable, why are they firmly entrenched in the publishing business instead of the investing business?

They don't invest their corporate profits in the products which they recommend to you. Their funds come primarily from full page colored advertisements and your $29.95 annual check. Instead, publishing companies employ journalists whose upbeat writing style is supposed to convince you they are financial wizards or, at least, have schmoozed with money gurus.

The rich can better afford sloppy money management. They can also afford to lose money if they (or their advisors) are wrong. You cannot. The less money you have to work with, the harder that money must work for you.

When in a swamp dress like a frog

Good money management has changed little in the past 50 years. You can utilize real diversification to reduce risk, and use the KISS (Keep It Simple, Stupid) theory of money management.

Financial markets—insurance companies, banking institutions and brokerages—may market anything they believe you can be seduced into purchasing, no matter how risky to your investment principal, illogical the basic concept, expensive the price of the product or inferior the underlying investment concept. How? They proceed with the secure knowledge that if they sell you only the sizzle, instead of the steak, you will happily sign on the bottom line of their product applications.

Marketing blitzes and glitzy ad campaigns use greed and fear devices to encourage emotional buying, leaving common sense out of the sales picture.

Customers are whipsawed from product to product and company to company, never understanding what they originally purchased or the contractual benefits and limitations of their new acquisitions. From each sale, a new commission to the salesperson comes right off the top of the sales price.

If you became seriously ill, you would undoubtedly visit a physician for a diagnosis. If, however, your doctor advised that one of your most popular body parts be removed in a hospital setting at once, would you quietly comply? You would certainly seek a second opinion, perhaps even a third.

But the same folks who know that even experienced physicians are not infallible often perform self taught financial surgery, implicitly trusting living room TV, self-styled money gurus, radio personalities or telephone solicitors. The same smart shoppers who ordinarily search and compare supermarket and clothing outlets for the best deals, let financial vendors take control over their money as a reward for an Oscar-winning sales presentation. Blind faith is absolutely no basis for any long term financial relationship and no foundation on which to build a successful well oiled financial machine. **Learn to trust yourself!**

When consumers purchase a "lemon" of a car, toaster or refrigerator, they soon discover their plight, either returning it to the manufacturer in exchange for a new one or selling it off to an unsuspecting secondary buyer. Either way, their previous problem now belongs to someone else. But if they buy a financial "lemon," they may not know it is defective until the time comes to use it—at death, disability, the college years or during a medical catastrophe—then it is too late.

It doesn't require a rocket scientist to understand basic money management and simple investing options. You must, however, learn to translate the fine print, eliminate the salespitch, and develop a perspective on how all this theory works in the real world. **A cheap compound interest calculator can be a powerful friend in the heat of a sales presentation.**

There are no magic solutions or simplistic answers to the complex decisions in your financial future. But you can maintain a healthy skepticism, keep your "thinking machine" tune, and rejuvenate your money genes to control your own financial destiny.

Objective information is even more valuable than money. With the right information, money can ultimately be made. Good news to those with no winning lottery ticket or trust funds on their immediate horizon.

Use time and the magic and miracle of compound interest as your transportation. A savvy financial consumer cuts through the sales pitches (the sizzle), determines the value or real benefits of various options (the steak), and selects the optimum bottom line for his or her own unique financial path.

Women And Investing

Women have been labeled as mattress stuffers, procrastinators who rarely get in on the hottest deals, and unwilling to take the kind of risks that make big money in the investing arena. In my opinion, these very attributes create successful and prudent investors!

Women can't tear a phone book in half with their bare hands, but any woman who can manage today's tight fitting budget demands or who live successfully on a fixed income may be more capable than some CEOs to manage a major American corporation. Women come with money managing genes, which means that they are CAREFUL!

Women are information diggers, yet they often lack confidence in their own ability. As caregivers for much of their lives, they are generally less assertive about their convictions and more apt to allow spouses or other family members to handle their financial matters.

Women, whether married or single, need to manage their own financial resources. Suddenly single through death of a spouse or divorce, they must learn basic investing fundamentals and how to prudently outpace inflation with their precious funds. All women need to empower themselves <u>NOW</u> to take charge of their money matters, even if they are currently married.

Women belong in the home, in the workplace, and, especially in the investing arena. By using the KISS principle of money management, they can structure their portfolios for comfort, not for speed. They already know the value of "paying themselves first" because, as home managers, they know how to stretch one paycheck until the next one is earned.

Moms have jobs too

With small children you have a lot on your mind. How much should the tooth fairy bring? How to schedule dancing, Scouting, athletics, T-ball, Little League, swimming, and other enrichment classes? How much to spend on Charlie's birthday party, and for holiday and graduation gifts? How to get that vacation fund spruced up?

Wait a minute! Who is watching your money? If your financial life is on auto-pilot because being a Mom is more than a full time job, take a breath and ask: are you working for them at your own financial detriment? Can you do both? Look at your chore list again. What item is more important than doing something for your money this week? One chapter at a time you can digest and implement the common sense strategies in this book.

Where's The Beef?

Buying quality products is like buying oats. If you want nice, clean, fresh oats, you must pay a fair price. However, if you can be satisfied with oats that have <u>already been through the horse</u>. . . well, those comes a little cheaper.

Financial planning: not just for the rich

Question before you buy any financial product. There are no fair or friendly contracts. Don't fall for sales pitches and promises made in the heat of a commissioned sale. The bold print giveth while the fine print can taketh away just as quickly. Buy the steak instead of the sizzle.

Understand what you are buying. If you can't, don't buy it. When it sounds too good to be true, it probably is. There is no free lunch. So, when the song comes for free, watch out for the accompaniment. It's not what they promise but what you sign that counts.

At all times cover your ass-ets. Sit on your wallet and pocketbook but never on your thinking machine. Money may calm the nerves but it also attracts the vultures.

Learning about your money is every bit as important as earning it. Invest some time in a competent and objective financial education. Experience is one thing you can't buy on the easy payment plan.

Information is the key to your financial independence. Although money can't buy happiness, it does allow one to be miserable in a better neighborhood.

Take back the power over your financial destiny. **PAY YOURSELF FIRST!** LEARN TO LIVE BENEATH YOUR FINANCIAL MEANS. If you waste your money you can change your habits. But if you waste your time no one can turn back the clock.

You have the power to control your own financial life. Live only for today and you will pay for it tomorrow...and tomorrow...and tomorrow. Start today and take control of your own money!

Chapter 2

It's a jungle out there

Every morning in Africa, a timid and frightened gazelle wakes. She knows she must run fast that day or she will be eaten. At the same time, a powerful lion also awakens. He, too, must run fast—faster than the gazelle—or he will eat nothing and ultimately starve to death.

Whether you picture yourself as a courageous lion in control of your financial destiny, or as a gazelle carefully picking your trail over the rocky financial terrain, when that sun comes up you had better be running. It's a jungle out there. The financial industry wants to seduce you, impress you with its large buildings (for which you pay) and mega advertising blitzes (for which you pay), and sell you the sizzle instead of the steak (for which you may pay dearly).

The financial community spends billions of dollars each and every year to schmooze you, to establish credibility it may not deserve, to push your hot buttons (greed and fear), and, most of all, to share your money with it. While you struggle to amass college, retirement or other savings, the financial pros have similar goals. But in order to achieve their objectives they must capture your money. The salesperson gets the commission and you get the future risk if the investment goes bad. Sound like a fair deal to you?

Most of what folks learn about money management comes from two sources: vested interests of the financial community and, perhaps even more dangerous because they come with built-in credibility, well meaning incompetents—your friends, colleagues, fellow workers and family.

Empower yourself with the tools and skills to get rich slowly but surely. Don't just grow older this year—grow wiser. Take some time to assess how fiscally fit you are. The biggest barrier to financial success is not the lack of time but the lack of direction and action.

Time flies! Retirement gets closer every day. Children grow older and closer to those college tuition years. Time can be your financial friend—or your real enemy. Time is money.

Once upon a time there was a man of great faith who believed that God was an integral and vital part of his life. Every day he endeavored to live as he felt God desired him to.

Financial foreplay: getting started with your education

The man lived in a town next to a river that irrigated the town's crops during the growing season. One spring the rains came. But instead of bringing new life to the fields, they turned into torrents, overflowed riverbanks and threatened to sweep both buildings and people away.

Most of the citizens quickly packed what they could carry and escaped in whatever transportation they could find. But the man of faith stayed behind, sneered at the menacing storm and assured himself that God would save him, though his neighbors implored him to leave.

As the water rose higher, the man was forced to ascend to a second floor vantage point. Peering out of his bedroom window, the villagers begged him to join them and leave while he still could. The man ignored them. He knew God would help him.

The water eventually rose so high that the man was forced to climb onto his roof. The villagers paddled by in boats, urging him to leave his roof before the water rose further. But there he stood, his hands in the air, stretched towards the gray skies, waiting for salvation.

Nothing happened.

Only the last cries of the villagers beseeching him to save himself could be heard.

The man looked up to the heavens, clasped his hands and yelled, "God, I have been faithful to You. I have lived according to Your laws and have been grateful to You for all things. Why have You forgotten me now?"

There was a period of silence, then a thunderous answer from above. "My son," the voice rumbled, "who do you think sent all those villagers and boats?"

Many people assume the bills will somehow get paid, their child will receive enough financial aid for college, or the government and their employer will come through with a comfortable retirement pension.

They pass on traditions that don't work and listen to (and even trust) propaganda that the financial industry churns out. The mistakes in this chapter (I've given you a baker's dozen) are examples of the most destructive and sinister.

1. Spend now, plan later

Capitalism and the search for the American Dream have done much to encourage consumers to spend, to enjoy today. They have done less to get people to save and invest and to let the magic of compound interest work over time.

Are you in better or worse financial shape than you were five years ago? Is your percentage of assets over debts increasing or decreasing? Have you planned to protect yourself against losing 6 percent (or more) of your yearly earnings due to invisible creeping inflation? What are your contingency plans if your company flies south with the geese next winter? What story ending will be written if you fall off the roof next weekend, become disabled, and lose your job trying to save the cost of a professional roofer?

Achieving your financial goals does not depend on luck and good intentions. Success lives at the intersection of Hard Work and Smart Work Avenues. In the race for financial security, you must be a marathon runner—which means taking it slow and steady. And you can start today.

2. The "Miss Scarlett" approach

Individuals procrastinate. This is probably not the first money book you have read. What happened to the last set of good intentions to trim the budget, cut the consumer debt and get started on a disciplined monthly savings plan? Let me guess. The next crisis came along. Or perhaps you talked yourself into a vacation, a new car or an addition on the house, ridding yourself of any guilt by promising to start again on that intended savings plan...first thing tomorrow...next month...next year.

Maybe you decided you were young enough to have some fun first. You may have concluded that next year's raise would be a better time to start saving. Christmas is certainly no time to start any compromising. It's even possible that, once you took a good look at the financial hole you'd dug for yourself, you gave up altogether.

3. Paying yourself last

How do you budget your monthly income? What is the **first bill** you pay each month? What is the next? Are you paying yourself last? Before you pay for anything next month, put away something for yourself. Make the first bill you owe each month a bill to yourself. Even $25 per month in a savings or investing plan will become a significant lump sum after just a few years. Pay yourself first, easy to remember; even easier to achieve through an automatic payment plan.

If your parents were starving, could you buy $25 worth of food for them? Of course you could! Aren't you as valuable? Do you care as much for yourself and your family? Then you have the responsibility to pay yourself first. Think of that payment as a bill you owe yourself. In 10 years, the memory of bygone pizzas or entertainment will not be as valuable or keep you as warm as a significant nest egg for a new home, a college education or your retirement.

Nearly everyone fritters away $25—or more—a month. Once you start disciplining yourself, perhaps through a payroll deduction or automatic checking plan, you won't see the extra money and, therefore, you won't spend it.

4. No problem, I've got a pension

Quick! What's the primary job of the CEO of your company? The answer? Raising the price of the shareholders' stock, not guaranteeing the health and welfare of an aging work force. Workers depend on others for their financial security—Social Security, company pensions, insurance companies, lending institutions—and lose control of the use of their money. By turning over all of your savings to others, you deny yourself the basic financial decisions every person should make.

Few workers today still believe they are putting Social Security taxes into their own account. Ask your kids about their future prospects for Social Security. Chances are they believe they have a better chance of seeing Elvis or a UFO than of getting future benefits. They realize their premiums will eventually be mailed to a retiree's home for immediate use. Do you believe Social Security will be there when you retire?

Put Social Security aside. Trust in your pension? Maybe not when you need it. Workers used to believe that the responsibility of a company was to nurture and protect its employees. Not so today with fierce international price competition. If moving its operations will increase a company's profit margin, it may retire to a warmer climate or terminate (downsize) employees before they can say "take this job and shove it".

A 47-year-old worker (or executive) who loses his or her job faces age discrimination in the workplace, though they may not be able to prove so. If you were a CEO, would you hire an aging health risk and an immediate pension liability? Could you pay $10 or $20 per hour per employee while competing with international companies who pay their workers as little as $2 per day? Even if you wanted to, how would your shareholders vote?

Many people rightly worry whether their company will be in business five years from now, let alone at retirement. And if it is, can (or will) it pay out the promised pension benefits to all retirees?

5. Learn the Golden Rules

Consumers don't understand the basic rules of the Money Game: The magic of compound interest, the Rule of 72, the time value of money, opportunity cost, and loaning your money to others versus owning your own investment products. These are critical strategies to consider when putting together your action plan. These ideas have been hidden from you by the financial industry for good reason—they work!

The insurance industry owns assets totaling more than $7 trillion! Banks are worth more than $4 trillion! How well do those numbers stack up against your portfolio? Whose money was used to create those dynasties? You loan banking and insurance institutions your money so they can invest it at a significant profit for themselves. **How decent of you.**

6. Custer's last command: Charge it!

Americans are caught in a credit crunch. Everyone wants everything now. When you want that truck, be assured that some stranger (whom you will make rich) will befriend you. At least until you can sign the purchase order. Neither governments nor individual families can borrow themselves into prosperity. Your government has a back-up plan: you. Where will you turn when you are "out of financial order?"

A credit card can be a valuable tool, like a hammer to a carpenter, if it is properly utilized. Using plastic can establish an initial credit history when you are ready to purchase a car or a home. It can allow you to use a company's money free for up to 30 days every month **if you pay off your monthly balances on time.** It can also be an emergency card if your car needs towing or breaks down away from home.

But it will be the greatest financial enemy you will ever know if it encourages you to feel richer, to live beyond your affordable means and to fool yourself into believing you will be able to pay it off with future income. Keeping up with the Joneses who may be keeping up with the Rockefellers is financial suicide.

The credit crunch is destroying lives because people are borrowing against their futures to support stratospheric consumption levels. In fact, you are not spending at all. You are simply signing your name to a greater commitment to future obligations with money you don't have and may never earn. If you cannot afford to pay off what you owe now, what in the world are you doing borrowing more plastic money?

It takes marketing genius to convince people to pay more and more for an item that becomes worth less and less as each day passes. The average consumer rarely considers how much his or her total debt is, but, rather, asks what the monthly payments will be. How many of your seed dollars will you fork over for your home? On a 20-year loan, over twice the amount originally borrowed. On a 30-year loan, nearly three times the original mortgage debt.

7. Listening to Madison Avenue

Advertising achieves three results: 1) it **sells**! 2) it costs you, the consumer, to get the advertiser's next customer to the sales counter; 3) it guarantees absolutely **nothing**—nothing about the real value of any goods or service you will purchase. It wasn't a Harvard MBA who put Joe Namath in panty hose and made a fortune—it was a Madison Avenue ad campaign marketer. Remember the bunny whose batteries never wore down? That's marketing at its best!

Slogans are test marketed to deliver the emotional appeal necessary to induce you to buy. In fact, I'll bet your next tuition payment that in 60 seconds you could recall at least a dozen advertising slogans, tunes or logos (trademarks) embedded in your brain that are intended to part you from your cash.

In reality, companies are composed of highly stressed and ulcer ridden management. They must confront constant change, competition from all corners, hostile takeovers, angry shareholders, and still maintain a singular mercenary sense of purpose—

to increase their stock price. Stockholders are fickle and will grumble, revolt, and even sell at the first sign of financial trouble.

If your friendly neighborhood thrift or bank were on the brink of insolvency, would the president give you a call to advise you to pull out your deposits? Even if you asked, could they tell you the truth? If your investment company discovered that the accountant disappeared with the entire year's profits, would you expect to receive notice to withdraw your money before they declared bankruptcy?

Unless you are the CEO's mother, you would probably hear the bad news on CNN like everyone else. Instead, you would be at work or involved at home, self-assured that you are in good hands with someone whose expensive ads have made you feel secure.

8. Read the fine print

Buyers don't read the fine print. The old saying, "The bold print giveth, and the fine print taketh away," is true. Every word in a contract you sign is important enough for the company's lawyer to have included it in the contract. It should be just as important for you to understand. Too many people believe what they are told. You must look further.

Look at the following sentence: "I didn't say he stole that money." See how easily it can "read" differently:

1. I didn't say he stole that money.
2. I didn't say he stole that money.
3. I didn't say he stole that money.
4. I didn't say he stole that money.
5. I didn't say he stole that money.
6. I didn't say he stole that money.
7. I didn't say he stole that money.

By emphasizing or accenting different words, I have made one sentence imply seven entirely different meanings. So, the next time you are ready to sign your name to the dotted line, take the time to read the **fine** print—and make sure that what you're committing to can't be interpreted in any way that could be harmful to you.

A better idea: take the whole contract home unsigned (in spite of the gasps of salesfolks in the show room), brew a cup of strong coffee, and carefully translate what the "legaleze" means.

9. A 20% return and no risk?

Unsophisticated consumers may believe unrealistic promises and extraordinary expectations of return. If it sounds too good to be true, it probably is. Remember: No one is ever going to pay you any more than they must to induce you to hand over your fistful of dollars. Not the U.S. Government, not private industry, and not your neighborhood lending institution. The more they pay you, the less they have left.

When you listen to "get rich quick" promises you are treading on dangerous ground. Many products today offer increased yields by raising your risk of losing principal. The salesperson gets the commission. You get the risk if the investment later goes south. Sound fair to you?

10. Taming the taxbeast

Some folks will do nearly anything to escape the wrath of the tax beast. They will purchase poor quality investments to acquire tax deferral. They will buy illiquid investments with restrictions on their money and large surrender charges for early withdrawals. They will pay huge internal costs that reduce their overall returns, and they will run like lemmings toward a hot tax strategy before examining the inherent risks to investment capital. **Never let the tax tail wag your investment dog.**

Tax deductible, tax deferred and tax exempt are magic marketing monikers that put billions of dollars into insurance company coffers. Such investors never stop to research the risks of the underlying investments or contemplate how well they will work in other types of investment weather.

Your money can do more good around your house than around Uncle Sam's. However, with tax changes occurring nearly every year, it is vital that you learn what solid and enduring strategies can reduce your tax bite and which tax angles make good, common sense decisions.

Tax planning doesn't begin on April 1st, just before tax time—it begins on January 1st of the same year, when there is time to plan how to keep more of your income. Tax planning should remain a part of your financial life, not the major focus of every investment transaction. **Become tax smart, not tax driven.**

11. Passing on the family tree

Generations pass on traditions that do not work. The last generation didn't drink or gamble their money away. They simply loaned it to others who smiled and said comforting things, like "safe," "guaranteed," "high yield" and "trust me."

Today's retirees, in general, learned little about investment options. They bought a home, put some money in low interest bank accounts, bought U.S. savings bonds, and handed the remainder to the insurance industry through the neighborhood house-to-house debit agent. That is the primary reason so many of them stay home on the third of each month nervously waiting for their Social Security checks so they can finance next month's living expenses.

The only elderly retiring in comfort today (except for lottery winners) are those who watched over their own money, owned their own investments (like mutual funds and stocks), understood money management principles, and made their money work harder than inflation through the years.

12. Inertia

Consumers utilize outmoded vehicles and give up flexibility and liquidity to move with the times, and as their financial lives change. Some are too tired to watch changing interest rates or to move a bank CD down the street for a better interest rate. Others may feel that standing pat is the safest route. This concept implies that where you are now must be safer than where you might move because nothing bad is happening to you right now. Read your newspapers and digest the events of the day. Companies go broke, employees get laid off, pension plans are raided, and insurance companies fail. With so many options today, it is not necessary to let your money depreciate.

Don't expect your banker to suggest moving to a better paying vehicle. Their paycheck depends on earning the most for their employer; not for you, the customer.

With thirty-day, even seven-day CDs, NOW accounts and money market mutual funds, even your short term cash can earn competitive rates. Banks have money sales, and savvy financial consumers shop for low interest rates like they do for sales on linens and groceries.

13. At last, a free lunch!

Before you jump into an attractive looking product, ask what hidden costs are involved, especially if you leave in six months, one year, or five years. Many products have severe penalties for withdrawing—deferred charges, backloaded expense fees, early distribution charges and pre-retirement penalties. If I sold you a car and told you it was free if you drove it for seven years, would you believe me? If I told you I was sacrificing my family's well being for you, a perfect stranger, would you buy my salespitch? There is no Santa Claus (except for Virginia's), no tooth fairy, and no such thing as a free lunch. There are, however, gullible customers who buy such bunk. When the song is sung for free, watch out for the accompaniment.

A long time ago, a king was auditioning court jesters. One candidate came forward and announced to the king that he could, within one year, teach the king's horse to talk. Everyone was astonished. The king immediately named the candidate Court Jester and gave him and his assistant access to all the pleasures of his kingdom.

As the new jester and his associate left the throne room, the assistant whispered to him that he, too, was astonished to find that his friend could accomplish such an unusual feat.

The jester just smiled. "A year has 365 days and nights; each day has 24 hours," he explained. "A lot can happen in so many hours. The king could die. I could die. The horse could die. The kingdom could be lost in a battle. And, who knows, the doggone horse might even learn to talk. In the meantime, we have a nice life for a year!"

Make sure any promises made in the heat of a sale are backed up on paper. Are you sure you would never fall for a talking horse?

Let's review common money mistakes

1. We depend on *others* for our financial future (Social Security, company pensions, insurance companies and banks) and lose control of the use of our own money.
2. We don't understand the basic rules of the Money Game, such as compound interest, time value of money, renting versus owning our own investments, and funneling money through financial intermediaries that take the largest portion of profits.
3. We get caught in "loanership" positions (through credit card debt and home equity loans).
4. We don't understand which perils to insure and which risks to retain (insurance needs principles).
5. We buy insurance products for the wrong reasons, *without understanding our contracts*, and put our savings inside these products to work for those corporations.
6. We develop unrealistic expectations of return for products we do not *really* understand. We buy the sizzle instead of the steak.
7. We pay ourselves last, whether through procrastination or inertia.
8. We overpay on taxes because we don't understand the benefits of tax-sheltered vehicles such as IRAs, SEP-IRAs, KEOGHs, 401(k)s, TDAs and UGMAs/UTMAs.
9. We follow tradition and utilize outmoded investments which restrict our flexibility to move as time changes.
10. We compromise *liquidity, flexibility of investment goals and higher rates of return* for products that sound good but have time-loss factors and surrender costs.
11. We perpetuate investment myths such as buying a home, hoarding gold, purchasing collectibles, or depositing savings in mediocre vehicles, that *do not keep pace with inflation*.

12. We set no firm financial goals or the means to reach them. (Financial dreams do not happen—they are carefully selected, monitored, and re-evaluated over time.)

Financial opportunities may not be limited, but your precious dollars certainly are.

Caveat emptor (Buyer beware)

Warranties are not guarantees. Do you need that extended warranty? When the original guarantee runs out, your options may not. Many manufacturers offer some type of special warranty program **without** extra cost. Auto makers routinely notify owners regarding defects, and repair them at little or no cost. Your local dealership may also have a vested interest in keeping its customers happy.

Whether you purchase a "lemon" of a toaster, a bedroom set or any other product or service, you should expect value consistent with the price you paid. The squeaky wheel often gets the grease, and consumerism means standing up for your rights. Companies value your next sale, and pressure from consumer groups and regulatory agencies are mandating that more manufacturers pay for out-of-warranty repairs.

Warranty companies may not be affiliated with your manufacturer, instead, marketing their own service by phone or mail. Such an extended partnership may be useless if the company goes out of business before you need them.

Even warranties sold through manufacturers can be misleading or have few teeth after a year or two. Some offer free parts but charge indecent rates on labor, while others offer only reduced prices on repairs. Many will offer to repair your product but won't trade you for a new one. You may end up with a scratch-and-dent special that has been repainted, restained or restored in some other way instead of a brand new item that you paid full price for. You must understand the contract you are purchasing.

If the company pushes a warranty along with a new product sale, is it implying it's selling you an inferior product that may fall apart once you take it home? If not, then why would you need extra protection today? If a product fails before I believe it should, I take it back, expect a repair, a refund or exchange, or receive some other type of accommodation. And I am prepared to take my complaint to the top of the company, if necessary.

When I pay a fair price, I expect full value. Most warranties are not needed, and the few that are may cost you for labor. Products become obsolete so fast that by the time you use the warranty, the company may not produce or be able to fix the style of product you bought. Many consumer publications advocate less expensive methods of getting what you pay for.

To track down a hidden warranty, talk to the customer service representative of the company whose name appears on the product. Reward companies who guarantee satisfaction and boycott those who make their profits with inferior merchandise and refuse to back it up. Look for retailers who put the customer first.

The Rule of 250

Everyone has bought a "lemon" at one time or another. How you approach the company for an exchange, refund or other solution has a lot to do with the outcome. Consumerism works as long as customers demand value in the marketplace (patronize companies whose quality standards are high) and pay a fair price for goods and services. When you receive less than what you paid for (an impaired value), there are numerous options.

First, take the item back to the store. Don't expect a clerk to make a decision. Find the store's manager and politely, but firmly, explain your dilemma. Expect a positive solution. Honey attracts flies; vinegar may impede negotiations. If this fails, prepare for more aggressive measures.

Many retail distributors want happy customers and will gladly accommodate upi if they can. If the store will not help, contact the manufacturer directly if the product is made in this country. The consumer service department is the usual starting point.

Be prepared to carry your case to anyone who will listen. TV stations and newspapers often have consumer complaint departments. You may also find the Better Business Bureau helpful, although its basic allegiance is to its customers, good and proper businesses who pay membership fees.

If your problem is serious, your elected officials may be able to assist or direct you to the appropriate channels. **When one door closes, find another one higher up to knock on.**

A letter to the company president generally will not be ignored. Executives have authority to make special dispensations. If Bill Gates wants to help you, not much is going to stand in his way.

Sometimes you get bogged down and no one seems to care that you flushed money down the drain. If so, try the Rule of 250.

Find the most powerful manager you can contact, then explain your problem and the desired solution. If this doesn't get results, explain the following Rule of 250:

"Everyone, whether he or she realizes it or not, knows at least 250 people, a sphere of influence to whom he or she is credible. When experiences go well, there is often not much time to reminisce, even to offer gratitude and praise. But when life turns upside down, folks tend to turn to everyone they can find, commiserating every sordid detail to friends, dwelling on the negative, blaming those they believe are responsible. Perhaps you can live without me as a future customer. But can you afford to lose the business of the 250 people I will repeat my story to, and the 250 times 250 potential customers they will tell? The best advertising in the world is word of mouth. I want to be a satisfied customer. But, first I need your help."

Keeping fiscally fit

Why bother to learn about your finances at all? Because you still remember that last sales presentation when you felt like a mushroom, kept in the dark and fed propaganda.

Because Ed McMahon has not notified you that you are a $10 million winner. And Super Lotto still hasn't called.

Because, like most of us, you were born into a nice but middle class family with no Uncle Harry to leave you his millions when he dies.

Because you have a humongous financial challenge waiting if you intend to fund even a public college for your children.

Because the responsibility for accumulating a supplementary pile of retirement dollars nearly as large as a third world country's gross national product is resting squarely on your shoulders.

Because you will watch over your money more carefully than any institution or paid individual.

Finally, because you can do a better job of conservative investing than anyone else.

Today's emphasis on physical fitness is a positive sign that consumers are taking charge of their health over the long term. However, to be able to enjoy those extra years of healthy living, you must also be fiscally fit.

What every consumer should do now

1. **Complete a written financial plan** to identify both short term and long term goals. Complete the **Financial Goals and Objectives Worksheet** in the Appendix. Then organize your financial life using the checklist, **Do You Know Where These Documents Are?**
2. **Compile a budget** detailing where you are now and in which primary direction your paycheck dollars are flowing. Research areas where you can conserve costs or find better value for dollars spent. A budget does not take time; it saves time. It does not prevent you from getting what you want; it assists your financial desires and creates a good financial roadmap to follow. Complete the **Monthly Budget and Expense Sheet** in the Appendix.
3. **Stash the cash** to develop an emergency fund for three to six months of your take-home pay. If this is impossible before tackling long term goals, attempt to have a least a two-month reserve. These funds should be put into a liquid investment with no risk to your principal. Complete the **Net Worth Statement** in the Appendix and add to it as you accumulate financial assets.

4. **Reduce the hassle of the tassel** and start funding college early even with $25 or $50 per month in a growth oriented mutual fund. Initiate a systematic monthly investment plan either through payroll deduction, your checking account or a credit union deduction. This is long term money that must outpace inflation. So avoid fixed income vehicles (savings bonds, bank CDs, insurance products). Seek prudent growth of your investment capital. The **College Cost Worksheet** appears in the Appendix.
5. **Look for tax advantages** without restricting your primary investment objectives: 1) the purpose for the investment, and 2) the best investment vehicles within the time your money has to work. **Don't purchase investments for tax benefits first.**
6. **If you are receiving a large IRS refund**, increase monthly deductions and set up an automatic payment plan that removes the savings before you see your paycheck. **Pay yourself first.** Repeat this slogan again and again to yourself. Businesses who want your money do.
7. **Prepare for retirement today**, especially if you are young. Time coupled with the magic of compound interest are your best weapons against inflation and outliving your retirement nest egg. It takes less seed money to create that large pot over time than if you wait until you are older. **The Retirement Planning Worksheet** in the Appendix can assist your retirement planning.
8. **Live *beneath* your means.** As your paycheck increases, increase your investing resources instead of your spending lifestyle. Know the difference between your "want to" and your "can do."
9. **It's the bottom line that counts.** It's also what purchasing power you can preserve from the ravages of inflation. Keep track of the real inflation rate, not government propaganda published to convince the elderly that smaller Social Security cost-of-living increases are sufficient. Learn to spot GIGO (garbage in, garbage out). Design your investment portfolio to outpace inflation while controlling risk to principal.
10. **Insure breadwinners properly with "death" insurance.** A family with small children and a mortgage needs $350,000 or more in insurance death benefits while the wage earner is young, the financial risk of dying too soon is great, and before significant assets have been accumulated. Buy **term insurance** for the cheapest death benefit and start a separate investment plan to provide retirement dollars when your problem becomes living too long.
11. **Understand your company health, death and retirement benefits.** Group insurance certificates are merely temporary coverage. Your company could discontinue its contract tomorrow. Premiums are outrageous when you convert to an individual cash value policy. Premiums increase depending on the average age of the insured group. Use these as basic coverage only. You probably need additional protection.

12. **Create an estate plan** by titling your assets to avoid probate, if desired. Have a durable financial power of attorney drawn up in case you become disabled. This gives someone you choose now the ability to manage your financial assets later in case of disability. Include a living will and/ or medical health directive to make medical decisions clear if you can't (if appropriate in your state). **The Estate Organizer** in the Appendix can help organize this process.
13. **Create a comprehensive will** to transfer your additional assets, name the guardianship of your children and the trustee of their assets. Modify your documents each time your health, personal life or financial circumstances change significantly. The most dangerous estate planning mistake is default planning; in other words, procrastinating.
14. **Calculate long term college tuition needs and retirement fund needs** by using the Rules of 72, 116, and 144. These calculations provide ballpark figures to determine how well you are doing toward accumulating those needed funds at the appropriate time. These Rules are explained in Chapter 3.
15. **Pay off your consumer credit card debt** while still contributing to your emergency fund. A budget will help determine how much extra you have for both projects. Dial for dollars by phoning current card companies, threatening to leave unless they lower their loan shark interest rates. If you get no response, transfer old balances to lower interest rate cards. Pay highest interest rate balances off first, paying only minimum monthly payments on the remaining cards. Retire each card in the same fashion. The **Credit Card Management Strategy** in the Appendix can turbocharge your financial freedom plan.

When you have completed these steps, complete and check off the **Current Status Financial Goals and Objectives** review in the Appendix. You should be fiscally fit. Make steady progress for a strong foundation upon which to build your financial dreams and objectives.

Chapter 3

Remember the golden rules

Some things should be fuzzy—like teddy bears, newborn chicks and the top of a baby's head. And some things shouldn't. Your financial future should be clearly marked, and your pathway mapped out for both short term and long term goals and objectives.

The affluent aren't any smarter than you. They can, however, afford to hire full time experts like accountants, investment managers and lawyers to protect them from money mistakes and from the greed of the financial industry. They can also afford to lose money on lousy investments.

The less money you have, the more vital it becomes to manage it efficiently, to access the best advice available and to place great emphasis on protecting your money from others.

Compound interest: 8th wonder of the world

It has been said that Albert Einstein was once asked to recount his most notable discovery. His answer? Compound interest—the miracle and magic of compound interest.

Whether or not the story is true, it's a powerful motivator. The business person most familiar with compound interest is not the CEO of a large conglomerate or a corporate accountant working daily with cash flow charts. It is the grocery store owner in your neighborhood. Poor man. His markup on shelf items is usually only one-half of 1 percent per sale. Most large corporations would have become extinct on such a puny profit margin.

But how long does that can of soup or bottle of milk stay on the shelf? The store owner may make only a tiny profit per item, but he does it over and over in a relatively short amount of time, and each time the profits are converted into new inventory for sale.

Because of constraints on space, personnel and limited markets, no business can increase profits indefinitely. But your money has only two restrictions: the rate of return you receive and the time the money can work for you before it is needed. If you give money enough time to work, and make sure you have the most competitive rates of return, it will produce the profits you need to fund what you desire most.

How powerful a concept is this? Consider the man who applied for a one-month term of employment. His new employer allowed him to choose the form of his salary:

$300 per week for the next month or 1 cent the first day, that amount doubled the second day and each day's pay thereafter doubled again for the entire month. Which option would you choose?

A penny may not seem like much in comparison to $300 (which is 30,000 pennies), but compound interest can make it powerful. If you took the penny salary option, at the end of 30 days you would have accumulated a total salary for the month of $10,737,418.23.

No real employer would offer such a deal. But it effectively illustrates how awesome compound interest can be.

I can think of no better example of compound interest coupled with the aid of time than the story of twin brothers—Bill and Bob, 23 years old. Bill decided to take care of retirement early and invested $2,000 a year, paying himself first in a retirement IRA account for seven years, a total of $14,000. Then he stopped and moved on to other financial goals, letting his money continue compounding at an average annual rate of 10 percent per year.

Bob, however, was more interested in fast cars and an even faster lifestyle. He saved nothing for the first seven years. But as he grew older, he began to worry more about retirement. So at age 30, soon after Bill stopped contributing to his IRA, Bob began putting $2,000 per year into an IRA account at the same rate of return, 10 percent per year.

By retirement at age 65, each twin had accumulated nearly $600,000.

This nest egg cost Bill only $14,000 because he started earlier, but Bob was forced to invest $2,000 for 35 years—a total of $70,000—to accomplish the same goal. Would you rather spend $14,000 or $70,000 to make approximately $600,000?

The Rule of 72

Everybody can figure out that the higher the rate of return (interest) you receive on your money, the faster it will grow. But how fast? And how can you predict what you will actually have at any given time?

The Rule of 72 is a ballpark method of determining how quickly money will grow at a certain interest rate. Just divide the number 72 by the rate of return you expect to receive. The answer tells you how many years it will take to double your money. The following examples should help:

At 3 percent per year, your money will double every 24 years (72 divided by 3 equals 24).

At 6 percent per year, your money will double every 12 years (72 divided by 6 equals 12).

At 8 percent per year, your money will double every 9 years.

At 9 percent per year, your money will double every 8 years.

At 12 percent per year, your money will double every 6 years.

Always use the number 72. It's a fairly accurate and simple way to predict future returns.

Winning the Money Game

Age	Bill's Investment	Bob's Investment
23	$2,000	0
24	$2,000	0
25	$2,000	0
26	$2,000	0
27	$2,000	0
28	$2,000	0
29	$2,000	0
30	0	$2,000
31	0	$2,000
32	0	$2,000
33	0	$2,000
34	0	$2,000
35	0	$2,000
36	0	$2,000
37	0	$2,000
38	0	$2,000
39	0	$2,000
40	0	$2,000
41	0	$2,000
42	0	$2,000
43	0	$2,000
44	0	$2,000
45	0	$2,000
46	0	$2,000
47	0	$2,000
48	0	$2,000
49	0	$2,000
50	0	$2,000
51	0	$2,000
52	0	$2,000
53	0	$2,000
54	0	$2,000
55	0	$2,000
56	0	$2,000
57	0	$2,000
58	0	$2,000
59	0	$2,000
60	0	$2,000
61	0	$2,000
62	0	$2,000
63	0	$2,000
64	0	$2,000
Total Investment	$14,000	$70,000
Amount at age 65	$586,548	$596,254

Let's examine how this principle applies to real dollars. As an example, I have figured the interest on a $2,000 investment (a typical IRA contribution). Taxes were not considered for this illustration, and the money was contributed at the beginning of the first year.

Contribution	$2,000	$2,000	$2,000	$2,000
Percent return	6%	8%	9%	12%
After 12 years	$4,024	$5,036	$5,625	$7,792
After 24 years	$8,098	$12,682	$15,822	$30,357

Two points are critical. First, the higher the interest rate, the larger the account value over time. More importantly, doubling the interest rate *more than doubles the return* over longer periods of time. Look at the 6-percent and the 12-percent columns. After 13 years, the difference between the 6-percent and the 12-percent yields is more than double. And the gap continues to widen—at the 24-year mark, there is a difference of almost four times the return between the 6-percent and 12-percent investments.

Now let's see what happens to your money when you loan it out to institutions such as banks and insurance companies. According to the Rule of 72, at 15 percent, money doubles every 4.8 years. At 20 percent, money will double in 3.6 years.

	Your Return		**Their Return**	
$2,000		@ 6%	@15%	@20%
12 years		$4,024	$10,701	$17,832
24 years		$8,098	$57,250	$158,994

If you feel this comparison is unfair because no one could possibly be making that kind of return on your money, check out your credit cards, finance company rates, and the 30-year indentured servant plan you refer to as your mortgage.

Now that you understand how important the Rule of 72 is to your financial future, strive to get competitive returns on both short term and long term savings. The Money Game teaches one very sobering lesson. **Use it or lose it.**

Perhaps you are muttering to yourself that this concept is great for your children, but it comes too late to keep the wolf from *your* door. The concept remains the same, whether you are 5, 35 or 55. The only difference is that the less time you have, the harder your money must work. Since your time is limited, you have no time to lose.

Sit down tonight and explain the story of Bill and Bob to your children. That may even be a better idea than sending them to medical or law school. Our children can use time more effectively because the longer their money can compound, the greater the future lump sum will be. Money gains momentum over time like a snowball rolling downhill.

Einstein's theory of relativity may have great benefits to science, but in the race to beat inflation and provide those dreams and goals you have promised yourself and your family, the theory of compound interest has greater "relativity."

The Rule of 116

How long will it take to triple a sum of money? Divide the number 116 by the expected future annual return. The answer will tell you how often your investment fund is expected to double. By adding regular payments to your existing investment fund, your money can work even harder as you will see when you apply the Rule of 144.

The Rule of 144

Many investors make regular annual investments, say $2,000, per year into an IRA. How many years before the total amount of money invested doubles?

This rule works the same as the rule of "72." But it is used for annual investment payments rather than for a single lump sum investment.

Assume you contribute $2,000 each year to an IRA Account that earns 8%. In approximately 18 years you will have $72,000 in the account: $36,000 from IRA contributions, and an equal amount of $36,000 from accumulated interest (144 divided by 6= 24).

Inflation: the silent but deadly money killer

An astronaut, returning to earth 30 years after his flight into space, rushed to the nearest public telephone and dialed home to greet his family. After assuring them he had landed safely and that he would soon be home, he called his broker to see how his investments had done during the time he was in orbit.

His broker congratulated his client for leaving the money in his hands, as his account had grown several times. Then the operator interrupted the conversation:

"Please deposit $300 for the next 5 minutes."

If I told you that, as one of my best clients, I would offer you a special investment opportunity that was worth $1,000 in 1945, had steadily declined in value each and every year since then and was now selling at $228, would you be so anxious to purchase it? That is what 3-percent annual inflation has done to the American dollar! Because inflation erodes money away quietly, it is mostly ignored by the consumer, but not by the institutions and corporations who borrow your savings or lend you money.

Webster's has a lofty definition of inflation: "An increase in the currency circulation or a marked expansion of credit, resulting in a fall in currency value and a sharp rise in prices." Phooey! Inflation is not some boring theory of interest only to economists. It represents a real loss.

Ignoring inflation is a serious mistake, much like turning your back on an aggressive pooch. If inflation is trotting along at 6 percent per year, you must earn 6 percent (after taxes) on your money just to stay in the same place you were at the beginning of the year. If inflation is greater than 6 percent, you must receive an even higher return just to continue treading water.

Let's look at the effect of inflation on savings. Assume you have $10,000 working at 5-percent interest with a 6-percent inflation factor working against you.

How inflation hurts you

$10,000	Savings at beginning of year
$500	Interest @ 5% (before taxes)
- $140	Taxes on interest (28% bracket)
<u>- $600</u>	Inflationary loss of money (6%)
$9,760	Real purchasing power at end of year
<u>$240</u>	**Total loss in <u>one</u> year**

Carry these losses long enough and the bottom line will reach zero. The longer your money works below inflation, the more principal you use up. Each year you gain less interest, because there is less money to receive interest on. If you're an elderly couple needing to live on the income your seed money generates, it's easy to see why the greatest financial danger most retirees fear is outliving their nest egg.

The effect of inflation on wages is even more unsettling. If it takes $30,000 per year today to keep your family and home going, in 10 years at 6-percent inflation you will need $53,725 per year to retain the same purchasing power. In 20 years it will cost you $96,214 per year. Where are you going to find that kind of money? Are you planning to get those kinds of raises at work? Have you told your boss?

The Rule of 72 can work against you when it robs you of purchasing power over the years. Using the Rule of 72, if the average rate of inflation is 6 percent, your money will shrink in half every 12 years (72 divided by 6= 12). After 24 years it shrinks in half once more. A $100,000 nest egg today will reduce to $25,000 when inflation spits it out after 24 years. This is why those bank CDs won't keep a roof over your head and three meals in your stomach. You must research other financial life forms and learn how to manage the various risks inherent in all forms of investing.

No matter what your age today, you must beat inflation with your future retirement money. Learn to seek higher returns and prudent growth on your long term money.

Some people are so frightened to move out of anything that is not guaranteed that they are incurring real losses after inflation is factored in. Of all the guarantees you may hear about, the one no one advertises is the guaranteed loss of purchasing power. Fixed income vehicles have not generally kept pace with inflation over time.

Inflation can be more deadly to your financial health than high blood pressure or heart disease is to your physical health—nothing can cure the ravages of inflation after its symptoms appear.

Inflation and college

In my lectures, I always include the effects of inflation on higher education, and young couples immediately start thinking about limiting the size of their families.

A good public university currently costs up to $10,000 per year. That won't keep your kids in pizzas, but it will pack enough educational skills into them so that they can ultimately find another source of revenue than you.

Present college costs are escalating at 8 percent to 10 percent per year. So let's assume education expenses will increase at 8 percent per year.

If Debbie is starting college next year, your total cost will be $45,061. You'll have to lay out $71,506 for 12-year-old Bruce. And cute 6-year-old Zelda will cost you $113,471. No wonder she smiles a lot. She knows she's going to do some sales job to coerce you into handing over that much money.

If you are debating whether to add one more child to your cozy family, future college costs may change your mind. Can you lay your hands on an extra $180,065? That's the projected price tag of college in 18 years at an 8-percent increase per year. For that kind of money you would think you could have the school named after you (or at least a gymnasium). Of course, we have been talking about state universities. If the Ivy League is your goal, you may need to double or even triple these numbers. (See Chapter 12 for a more detailed discussion of college funding.)

A rose may be a rose, but 5 percent is not always 5 percent

Financial institutions realize that many consumers have learned to search for the highest interest rates on their savings and investment dollars.

But they also realize that most customers have little idea how to use the concept of compound interest to compute annual yields, if they compete with different ways of figuring interest (simple or compound) combined with different periods (semiannually, quarterly, monthly). Some investments like money market mutual funds may even compound daily.

Is a 4.5-percent yield for nine months better than a 5-percent return for 12? How about a six-month deposit at 3.75 percent compared to a seven-day CD yielding 3.95 percent? By mixing interest rates with a variety of maturities, institutions can baffle even the savviest customers.

You can be sure of two things. No one—not your bank, not a large corporation, not your insurance company and certainly not the government—is going to pay you any more for the use of your money than it absolutely has to. We can also assume that it will charge a borrower (you) as much as it can to allow the use of "its" money.

Deposit $10,000 into a passbook savings account earning 4 percent at your local bank and you will fall asleep watching it compound. Now, borrow that same $10,000 from the same bank, and you will be looking at 8-percent interest or more...compounded in a different manner. You work your money at 4 percent compounded quarterly. They work it at 8 percent compounded monthly. Considering that it may be your own money that you are borrowing, that's some partnership!

Since compound interest works harder the more frequently earnings are compounded, let's analyze the effect of various compounding on a lump sum with an advertised rate of return of 5 percent.

$10,000 @ 5% for 1 year

Simple interest	= $500 profit
Compounded semi-annually	= $506 profit
Compounded quarterly	= $509 profit
Compounded monthly	= $512 profit
Compounded daily	= $513 profit

The more often the money is compounded, the greater the profit over a specific time period. Over longer periods of time, this relatively small difference will provide a much larger nest egg.

As long as you know the annual effective yield and how often (quarterly, monthly) the money is compounded, you can compare rates. This skill is essential, as it will allow you to compare apples to apples (or lemons to lemons).

For those of you who fear any small box remotely resembling a calculator, there is an easier method of comparing rates. Before giving your money to any institution, ask the teller, "If I put my money in your hands for one year, how much profit will I have at the end?" Compare his or her answer with those of at least two other institutions.

If the representative cannot give you an answer, ask to see the manager. If he or she cannot quickly calculate an accurate response, run with your money out the front door as fast as you can. Any novice with a compound interest calculator can figure out the answer. Do you really want to leave your hard earned dollars in a place where they can't even calculate compound interest?

I'd hate to think that every time they conducted a transaction they had to count it out on their fingers and toes in the back room. Of course, they have computers that do all the work. But whenever I call, the computers are temporarily down. Still want to leave your money alone with these folks?

Financial institutions know the customer is willing to shop around at first but soon gets tired of watching his or her money. Some institutions advertise great yields on short term CDs, knowing that after one or two weeks, those high advertised rates will drop right through the floor.

Although it is impossible to continually move your deposits from place to place as interest rates change (you would lose your profits to telephone calls and gasoline, not to mention losing your sanity), I advise clients to check short term rates every month with their institution. If you feel you can do better, move your money. Lenders need the stability of time deposits to loan out money on a long term basis. If enough customers show resolve in this area, companies will stop these games.

Just remember: Without you, they'd have no money to lend! So find a lender that is willing to respect you. And respect can be easily defined: whoever offers you the best return on your money respects you the most. Financial institutions may have begun to understand they must compete for your money, but don't expect them to comply freely or not to try to confuse you in the process.

This is serious business. Every fraction of a percent you forego now will decrease your future dollars. If the institutions make poor decisions, poor loans (remember the Savings and Loans fiasco?) or mismanage assets, there are government entities that will indemnify them (or find ways to get us to indemnify them through increased taxes).

Who will cover the losses you suffer because you mismanaged your own portfolio?

The first step to achieving anything valuable is to institute a plan of action. Whether you are planning a revolution, the entrapment of your favorite guy or girl (or someone else's guy or girl) or a defense worthy of an Oscar when that state patrolman stops you for speeding, every goal needs a fail safe plan of action.

Financial planning is no different. Most people already have their own kind of financial plan. Stored away casually in their heads, it sounds something like this:

"We would like to buy a house sometime in the future. Can't save up much now because I don't make very much yet. Besides we need that vacation away from the kids next summer..."

"And speaking of kids, they have been pestering us to get a pool like the Millers next door..."

"The car has been acting up lately. I really need a new one, with air conditioning..."

"Sure, we want the kids to go to college—I think we will be all right on that one—I can start to save in a couple of years. Besides Joey is pretty smart—he'll probably get a scholarship..."

"Retirement? Oh, I'm all set—my company has a pension plan, and I have Social Security. After the kids are out of college, I should be able to start to save some extra for retirement—since the house will be paid off, we'll be rolling in bucks..."

"If I'm laid off? I've got unemployment and a few bucks saved up—should be enough—besides I can always get a job with my brother-in-law if I want..."

"If I get sick? The company has some kind of health policy on me, and my wife can work if we need the extra income. Right now, it's all we can do to keep ahead of the bills—the credit cards, you know—they can sure add up before you know it. We just got another one so we have plenty of credit, if we need it..."

"I'm sure things will get better and then we'll be able to save for the future."

If you're not sure where you're going, as an old saying goes, "Any road can take you there." Vague ideas founded on little else won't solve your financial challenges. Solid financial planning, using the strategies in this book, are the solution.

RETIREMENT GOAL OF $100,000 AT AGE 65

Age	Needed/Month	Rate of Return	Value at 65
25	$16	10% for 40 years =	$100,000
35	$44	10% for 30 years =	$100,000
45	$131	10% for 20 years =	$100,000
55	$484	10% for 10 years =	$100,000

Time can be your friend

Assume your goal at age 65 is to accumulate a lump sum of $100,000, and you expect you can earn 10 percent a year on any money you invest.

If you start at age 25, you will need to contribute only $16 per month.

Wait until age 35 to start saving, and you will need to fork out $44 per month.

Starting at age 45 will cost you $131 per month.

If you follow the most common retirement plan, you will wait until you're 55, at which point you'll have to sock away $484 per month.

The same rate of return over longer periods of time makes the difference. By letting time and compounded interest do most of the work for you, you can achieve your $100,000 goal much more easily and with less money.

Maybe you're not 25 any longer. If you wait much longer, your problem will get even larger, your goal even more unreachable.

There will never be a better time, a cheaper time, or a more convenient time to start than today. Time can be your friend or your enemy. The time to start saving is always *now*! Invest today for a successful tomorrow.

The enemy of any plan, financial or otherwise, is procrastination. (There was once a town so full of procrastinators, they vowed to start a procrastination club. Naturally, they never got around to it.) By systematically setting aside even a small amount of money each week, each payday or each month (it's called "paying yourself first"), over time you will have accumulated a significant nest egg. If, however, you let a stranger talk you out of your money, that egg will be hatching in someone else's nest.

Chapter 4

Show me the money

You always said you'd start planning for the future when you got your first job. Then it was when you got married. Then when you had kids. So what's the plan?

The purpose of developing a financial road map is to plot the most direct route toward your monetary goals, with comfort stops along the way so you can monitor your progress. As you determine your financial goals and objectives, keep in mind some questions in order stay on track.

What are your short term priorities? What are your long term financial goals? Are they realistic? Can you make the long term goals by achieving the short term ones?

Are both types of goals working in tandem with each other? How much time have you allotted for each goal? Do you have breathing room in case unexpected life challenges interfere with your optimum plans?

What is your debt picture? Will your goals allow you to live within your economic means? Will they strengthen your future? Do you need the cooperation of others?

Before you can assess where you're going and how you're going to get there—or work with a financial planner to help you find those answers—you need to know, in detail, exactly where you are. Completing and analyzing the following are essential:

1. Your short term financial plans.
2. Your long term objectives.
3. Your current income and expenses.
4. Your total net worth.

The worksheets in the **Appendix** will help you compile this information.

Financial spring cleaning

Did you ever wish life came with subtitles? Down to earth answers in plain English? With a little humor stirred in to balance a bad hair day?

Whether you are hooking up your computer for the first time, managing your finances, investing in your first mutual fund, or even choosing the right wine with dinner and friends, the right information will guarantee success. You don't produce financial success over night. But you can over time.

Pulling your life pieces together can be treacherous if you don't become organized. Throughout your life you have left footprints and accumulated many documents, written evidence of property ownership and paramount events such as marriage, the birth of children, etc.

Do you find yourself rustling through sorted piles, mumbling "I know it's in here somewhere?" Why not do some financial spring cleaning? Use the checklist in the Appendix titled **Do You Know Where These Documents Are?** to organize your financial history.

Spock to the bridge

Developing a financial plan involves shutting off the TV (you may have to pull the plug) for at least one night and having a family council. Use your discretion whether to include your children. If they will work with you as part of the team, this will be a big help, as they should be taught basic money management skills, too.

Through experience I have found that the first session occasionally revolves around one of two basic themes:

1. He has made all the money and he gives her his entire paycheck, which he never sees again. She, in turn, spends every lousy cent and then some, which is totally the reason they are in this sad financial shape at present.
2. She has tried 1,151 recipes to disguise hamburger as fish, quail or even mousse, and she can't remember the last time she got a new dress, possibly when she promised her husband she would have a baby boy.

These roles may be reversed, the script may be different, but the outcome is usually the same—you and your spouse have different financial attitudes. If you feel that no valuable benefit can come from the two of you being left alone at this point, either bring in a stranger who isn't partial to either side, or use a financial planner as a mediator. Umpires aren't the answer; dialogue is. Don't procrastinate any longer—it's time to get your financial house in order. Singles can more easily host a quorum to conduct the following financial business.

Step 1: Establish your goals

Start with the **Financial Goals and Objectives** worksheet in the Appendix. Based on your family discussions, decide what is and isn't important right now. List all your specific objectives under each of the major categories: retirement, estate, educational, income and other. Fill in the **Attitudes** section.

What are the family's most important short term goals and long term goals? Short term goals may include establishing an emergency fund, reducing consumer debt, purchasing a new car, a summer vacation, or financing college (if it's just around the corner). Long term goals may be adding to retirement savings, starting a college fund, beginning a small business or purchasing a first (or new) home.

For a single parent, the sole breadwinner, careful planning becomes even more vital. Make your goals more specific than "keeping your head above water," "staying above the national poverty level" or "becoming filthy rich."

Step 2: Create a spending plan

Multiply your annual take-home pay by the number of years you have been working. Then look at your savings and investment plan. Are you working for a living or for a life? Whom are you making rich? Probably everyone else in town.

The next step is to create a cash flow statement, which will show you what money is coming in, how much of it is going out, and to whom.

Creating an environmental plan to save the ozone may be easier than coercing some people to write down their monthly expenses. It is time consuming. It is boring. It may be depressing. It is also the most necessary part of your entire plan!

If you proceed without this step, you are tying your shoelaces together before attempting to run a four-minute mile. You must see real numbers on a piece of paper in front of you to evaluate your current financial position. And until you know where you are, there's no way to figure out how to get where you'd like to be.

Look at the **Monthly Budget and Expense Sheet** in the Appendix. At the top is a line for net take-home pay. This figure should reflect your monthly income based on a regular work week, and not including overtime unless you can depend on the extra funds month after month. Gather your pay stub or employee earnings statement, and use the figure from a normal work week.

If you are paid weekly, multiply your take-home paycheck by the number 52, then divide by the number 12. If you are paid every two weeks, multiply the net take-home by 26, then divide by 12. Both methods give a monthly income.

Do **not** calculate using your gross income figure—this is not the amount you actually have to manage; gross is merely what your employer sold you on when you interviewed for your job. You don't see gross in your paycheck. You don't manage gross. You manage *net*.

Next, go through each expense category and write down what you spend per month—as realistically as possible. Utilities, for example, vary each month. Average the bills for the winter months, the highest of the year. Avoid a monthly juggling act because the paycheck won't stretch far enough.

Items such as clothing, entertainment, car maintenance and house maintenance are more difficult to estimate. Be as realistic as you can. When in doubt, estimate higher.

A new car will require less upkeep than an older one, but tires, oil changes and other incidentals add up each year. Older vehicles need water pumps, temperature gauges and radiators, as well as tires and oil changes.

Children's clothing costs increase as they grow. Shoes, winter coats, jeans, and a dress or suit will expand those expenses. Review last year's charge card statements and checkbook for a rough idea of any clothing binges that have increased debt levels. Budget in the future for those items, and pay for them with cash.

Auto and homeowner's insurance premiums, real estate taxes and medical expenses may be paid on a semiannual or annual basis. Even though the money does not leave your account monthly, divide the payment due by the number of months the payment will cover. For example, semi-annual property taxes should be divided by six so that the money can be accumulated by the time the actual payment is due. In the meantime, this cash will be earning interest for you, and your juggling days will soon be history.

Include a category for Christmas—or other annual gift giving events. Many people overspend, then take nine months to pay off presents from the previous year. Children need a college fund more than the latest toy or designer jeans. Decide beforehand on a maximum spending limit and either set aside money each month for the upcoming holiday or purchase gifts out of "miscellaneous" throughout the year.

Though Christmas clubs usually pay an abysmal interest rate, I would recommend them for those who find it otherwise impossible to defer current spending. This method will act as a temporary way station—cash that is not easily available until the holidays arrive. If all else fails, use the envelope system to organize such special categories.

Total all monthly expenses and put that amount at the top of the page after "Monthly Expenses."

Subtract your net expenses from your monthly income.

Most consumers are amazed at the amount of money coming in compared to the cost of expenses. There is usually a large amount of money missing, what I call "fritter" money. Fritter money is unconsciously spent, does little long term good, and must be recaptured and put aside for savings, college or other future goals, such as retirement. A significant percentage of these lost funds should be prioritized at the top of your monthly expenses, and a pre-set figure should be the first bill you pay each month. This is one bill you pay to yourself.

This payment to yourself can increase your emergency fund, start a college fund or add to retirement goals. It is not important what vehicle (savings account or credit union) is utilized at this point. The main idea is to put something away each and every month. As your income increases and your debt level decreases, increase your monthly savings payment instead of your spending lifestyle.

Occasionally, the difference between what comes in and what goes out is a *minus* number—you are spending more than you make, month-in, month-out. This requires immediate attention and extra effort to plan how to reduce those expenses as quickly as possible. Borrowing is not the answer. That's why you already have a debt "overload."

Plan with today's income. Do not use expected future income in your calculations. Attempt to stay within the general percentage allowance for each category of expenses listed. If possible, the first 10 percent of net income should flow into savings of some type. The mortgage payment (including property taxes and homeowner's insurance) or rent should be kept to no more than 22 percent of take-home pay. Consumer debt (including car payments) must be kept under 18 percent. Disposable income expenses (food, clothing, utilities and other costs to keep you alive and comfortable but that do not possess any long term intrinsic value) will likely require 50 percent of your income, maybe more if you are raising and educating children.

It may be necessary to throw in overtime pay so as not to destroy the confidence you might have built up for this project. Add in the value of next month's grocery coupons, any coins you find under the furniture cushions and the current recycled value of aluminum for pop cans, whether opened or not, which you can imagine as salvage.

Once the cash flow statement has been completed, look at each area and star any category that can be reduced. Insurance premiums—auto, homeowner's and life—can be reduced by shopping for more competitive rates. Though some overhead expenses are fixed (mortgage or rent payments, utilities, gasoline and food), other areas can be marginally decreased (telephone, clothing, vacations, dining out, entertainment, gifts, and miscellaneous).

Step 3: Develop a working budget

What is the first bill you pay each month? If you answered the mortgage or rent, think again. The first bill you pay is to Uncle Sam, who takes your money and redistributes it to strangers. You can be more mercenary and establish an IRA, a 401(k) plan at work or a SEP or KEOGH plan if self-employed.

How do you budget each month? Most folks pay bills in the following order: the mortgage or rent first, then utility bills, car payments, food, and last, a scramble to cover the monthly minimums on credit cards, time payments and miscellaneous expenses. Medical bills usually go to the bottom of next month's pile because we know that doctors are filthy rich and couldn't possibly need our money as badly as we do.

Let's try a different approach to monthly budgeting. Assume that you have found some small light between what comes in and what must go out. Then *pay yourself first*. Even if you can't save 10 percent of your net income—the amount I recommend as a target—saving *something* now is vital. "Paying yourself first" is the most underrated way to accumulate wealth over time.

The second bill becomes the mortgage or rent. Then, as you prioritize them, all other necessary expenses will be paid. What you have done by paying yourself first is recover the fritter money that flowed through your fingers to make it work hard for you.

"Paying yourself first" will automatically help you become frugal with your spending habits because the usual bills will be paid, including the bill you owe to yourself each month or payday.

An emergency fund or rainy day money fund can be a lifesaver for unexpected bills. It should provide three- to six-months' income should you get sick or lose your job. If you are a seasonal employee (in construction or other uneven employment), you may desire a more generous backup fund.

Once you have built up a reasonable emergency fund, do not be discouraged if it occasionally dwindles. The primary purpose of the fund is to provide money for unplanned expenses you previously bought on credit or at the expense of your other financial goals.

Add to this fund on a regular basis. Eventually, you will reach a comfortable level. Then tackle your long term goals by reallocating that monthly payment to another investment goal.

Step 4: Identify your net worth

Finally, list your assets—long term savings, Series EE bonds, employee retirement plans, other securities, etc.—on the Portfolio Planning worksheet in the Appendix.

If these pages remain nearly blank, funneling money into one of these areas should be a priority. Keep this record and add to it over time. It will give you a quick and complete estimate of your net worth now and in the future.

Income taxes have not been included in this process because they are taken out before you receive your take-home pay. If you are receiving a large refund after tax season, then you are giving an interest-free loan for an entire year to the U.S. Government. At the end of the tax year, Uncle Sam gives it back to you (with no interest, of course).

Could I make this kind of deal with you? How about giving me an extra $75 or $100 per month (before you ever see your own paycheck) so I can work it for my own benefit and give it back to you with no interest in April of the following year? The most common justification is that if the money were available, it would be spent on nonsense during the year. At least this way there is a check in one lump sump that can be used for some beneficial purpose.

If you are using this method as a forced savings plan, instead establish a monthly amount that you are overpaying in federal taxes and have it withdrawn from your paycheck and transferred into some type of weekly or monthly investment. Then you will have your money working throughout the year for you. It will be withdrawn from your paycheck before it gets to you, you won't see it and, therefore, you won't spend it foolishly.

Reduce your deduction at work so that you receive no more than $200 or $300 back after the tax year.

But be careful not to be too generous to yourself—if you wind up owing Uncle Sam money, you could be penalized.

Step 5: Commit to your plan

When you have completed your financial plan and committed both checklists to memory, it is vital that any major expenditure be within your new budget. A facelift may not get a majority vote at this time, and the annual hunting trip with the boys may be out for another year.

Put your budget up on the refrigerator so it can be seen daily. It will be a good reminder of the commitment your family has made. Don't be afraid if friends drop in and discover it. They will probably be relieved to find out that you aren't doing any better than they are. Now that everything is out in the open, they can spend less money to impress you and start on a savings program themselves.

Review your plan at least once a month. Hold another family council to pass around the credit (or attach blame). Attempt to make each member of the family responsible for some part of the plan's success. For example, if your teenager has decreased the number of times she has called a casual friend in Venezuela, you will want to offer some positive reinforcement.

Make up your mind to stick to the plan. Reevaluate it from time to time if it can be improved. If temporary emergencies occur that make the plan impossible to stick to, start it again as soon as possible. (Emergencies do not include getting your hair bleached so you can be seen again in public or buying new golf clubs because you are entertaining your boss on the links.)

The most important point is to use your money wisely. When you have mastered control over your everyday financial life, you will feel a real sense of accomplishment and self-satisfaction. Once you are on your way, the rest of your attitudes about money will change and you will begin to view money in a new light.

Develop a working monthly budget

1. Start today.
2. Include your spouse, hopefully also your children in financial planning discussions.
3. Calculate monthly expenses for all listed categories on the **Monthly Cash Flow Statement** in the Appendix.
4. Estimate monthly variable expenses such as utilities, clothing, medical bills and maintenance.
5. Divide occasional bills such as taxes and insurance premiums into estimated monthly payments on the budget.
6. Multiply weekly expenses such as food and gasoline by 52, then divide by 12 for a monthly average figure.
7. Develop a strategy for accumulating gift funds before the holidays.
8. Don't include income taxes unless you receive a large IRS refund each year. In that case, reduce overpayments to Uncle Sam by increasing exemptions and using the money for your own benefit.
9. Review all categories to reduce outgoing expenses (auto, homeowner's and other insurance, entertainment, vacations, miscellaneous).
10. Total all expenses and list in the "**Monthly Expenses**" space.
11. Calculate only dependable take-home income; do not include unreliable overtime.
12. List all net income in the space for net take-home income.
13. Subtract expenses from income. Divide the result in half. Use half to pay down consumer debt and the other half for a savings or investing goal.
14. Pay yourself first.
15. Pay all other bills in order of their priority.
16. Keep remaining funds set aside for future payments in an interest bearing account.
17. Develop an emergency fund.

18. Remember what the word "emergency" means.
19. Compile current assets on the **Portfolio Planning Worksheet** in the Appendix.
20. Sign up for an automatic checking or payroll deduction plan to develop dependable savings for future financial goals.
21. Discuss and negotiate every major capital expenditure. Be patient.
22. Keep the budget on the refrigerator (and credit cards in the freezer) as a reminder and commitment of your fitness plan.
23. Stick to your plan—re-evaluate it on a regular basis.

Keep more cash

Get rich quick schemes all involve easy ways to make money. An important component of winning your money game is to keep more of the money that you have already worked so hard to make. Here are some critical yet simple ways to do that:

1. Cancel your brokerage account. Take possession of stock and bond certificates. Better yet, sell your individual securities and utilize mutual funds for maximum diversification and as "set and forget" investing.
2. Wait to pay bills while you earn interest on the money in an interest bearing checking account.
3. Set up a regular automatic investment plan for a future financial goal.
4. Drop one credit card, the one with the highest annual percentage rate. Then pay off the one with the next highest rate until you get rid of most of your plastic. Paying for revolving credit at loan shark rates is just too expensive.
5. Don't prepay low interest loans. If the interest is low enough, your money should be working harder for you in your investments.
6. Don't overpay income taxes during the year. You should not be Uncle Sam's rich uncle or his banker.
7. Increase your current life insurance policy by your outstanding mortgage balance—then discontinue credit life mortgage insurance. Buy term insurance for the cheapest death benefit.
8. Switch regular checking accounts to interest bearing ones. Checks purchased by catalog may cost less than through your bank's check vendor.
9. Review club memberships with annual dues.
10. Seek out the maximum interest on your emergency fund. Check several local lenders' rates on short term, interest bearing accounts.
11. Reduce safe deposit fees by purchasing your own fireproof lock box safely stored near an exit in your home. Burglarproof the box by taping the key where it can be seen. Since it is too heavy to easily steal, the burglar will likely unlock it, search for cash, then flee the scene with your TV and favorite figurine. Store copies of savings bonds, stock certificates, etc. elsewhere.

12. Defer income and accelerate deductible expenses if the underlying economic purposes are sound. Don't borrow to get tax deductible write-offs unless the loans make good economic sense and you can repay them if they are called in.
13. Quit smoking, and use cigarette savings for a special financial goal.
14. One year later contact your life insurer and request a rating upgrade to a non-smoking policy, three years later to upgrade to a preferred rating.
15. Get paid to save money. Phone companies will pay big bucks for your short term loyalty. Call for discount long distance provider rates or just stay home during dinner time. A discounter will surely call you.
16. Don't switch personal credit lines to home equity loans for tax deductions unless you're positive you can repay them, even if you lose your job. Remember you are putting your home on the auction block if you default.
17. Review homeowner and auto insurance. Comparison shop. Maintain high limits of liability and high deductibles.
18. Consider refinancing your mortgage if current percentage rates justify it.
19. Drop single disease or accidental death insurance policies. When shopping for car insurance you don't purchase a separate policy for each car part. You need all-purpose catastrophic major medical coverage.
20. Shop for a used car instead of a new auto. A nearly new vehicle lets you escape high first-year depreciation costs.
21. Shop for clothing at new-to-you shops. Major film stars brag about their name brand bargains. There is no status in overpaying.
22. Utility and rental security deposits are often forgotten in the flurry of moving. Request your deposit refund plus market interest on the funds for the time the company has been investing in its own interest.
23. Eliminate one magazine subscription, one club membership, and one weekly car trip.
24. Purchase tax-efficient mutual funds that don't distribute all profits during the year as taxable income.
25. Dial for dollars. Call all credit card companies and demand a lower interest on unpaid balances. If they balk, switch to lower interest rate cards while you pay off your plastic.
26. Take full use of community adult education courses by requesting payment from your company benefits department. Many employers allot such funds even if the course has no work purpose.
27. Feed your children before grocery shopping. Make lists prior to mall shopping trips. Impulse purchases can ruin a family budget as quickly as the orthodontist bills mount up.

Secrets of a successful financial plan

Arrange a system for handling money and make certain that other family members (if you are not living alone) understand the system. Then, once you have the day-to-day money matters worked out through a budget, start thinking about a more long-term financial plan.

Set both short term and long term financial objectives and goals. List them in order of the time horizon until the funds are needed. The shorter the time period, the more dollars should be diverted to those specific objectives.

Limit spending to purchase of greatest value. Don't waste dollars on impulse or emotional binges.

Make your spending and savings plan suit an affordable lifestyle. Your budget will differ from others' plans.

Where you are now on your road to financial independence is not as important as in which direction you are traveling.

Bankruptcy: the 10-year mistake

When debts are overwhelming, bankruptcy can look like the fastest way out. But the process, the toll on your self-esteem and the financial aftermath aren't as painless as you may believe.

Job discrimination, lost friends, family conflicts and the loss of credit far into the future are byproducts of walking away from debt. A lawyer can maneuver the legal process for $500 to $1,000. But you may pay dearly in costs not explained beforehand.

Since you must pay taxes owed to the IRS (if you want to avoid a jail term), a payment plan can usually be arranged.

If debt is becoming too heavy to handle, stop spending at once. Get to a consumer debt counseling service and assess your options. Cut up your credit cards, then write credit card companies to cancel charge privileges and discuss a payback plan.

Get a balanced presentation regarding the pros and cons of bankruptcy from a legal advisor before starting the process. There may be options for repayment you have not considered. You are walking away from a debt you voluntarily purchased, leaving your creditors in the dust. Even with rebuilt credit, bankruptcy never goes away entirely. The emotional turmoil lingers. You may get a fresh start, but you will pay a high price.

Bankruptcy is a very serious issue. Get as much information beforehand and professional guidance as you can.

Parents with parents

Are you part of the sandwich generation? Parents of teenagers with the double challenge of caring for one or more aging parents of your own?

Today medical science is allowing folks to live longer, perhaps even to outlive their retirement nest eggs. This is a new phenomenon and few have much experience to offer solid guidance.

They say it's not the years in your life but the life in your years that makes life worth living. However, convincing Dad, who is still driving but probably shouldn't be, that he is a menace behind the wheel, or pulling the family together for Mom who needs assisted living can generate more than migraine headache unless you have a plan.

Here are some tips for supporting your parents and a checklist while you support those who took care of you for so many years:

Health Issues

_Complete physical scheduled
_Eye examination
_Dental appointment
_Nutrition review/ kitchen tour
_Medications review with doctor
_Medications organized for easy intake
_Highest level of independence encouraged
_Assessment of outside activities
_Support of friendships to avoid isolation
_Emotional/ psychological problems
_Emergency illness plan
_Communication alert

Financial planning objectives

_Current written summary of assets and location
_Compilation of legal papers
_Financial power of attorney
_Medical power of attorney
_Medical living will
_Fireproof box for documents
_Safety deposit box location and key

Insurance review

_Homeowner insurance update
_Auto insurance review
_Liability umbrella policy
_Life insurance policy benefits
_Insurance beneficiary update

__Long term care/ nursing home insurance analysis

Estate planning

__Burial arrangements
__Current will and location
__Review of real estate titles
__Investment registrations/ titles to avoid probate
__Documents organized and accessible to family members

Stop the world, I want to get off

You just bought 5 routers, four servers, 5 ISDN cards, and rerouted your LAN. Now your E-mail doesn't work, you can't access your FTP, BBS or website. Your ISP just went out of business and your B-O-S-S wonders what you spent all his M-O-N-E-Y on. Makes you want to stop the clock, doesn't it? At least for a while.

Most of us have felt this way. However, few get the chance to follow their personal dream, to enjoy a respite from the corporate world, to go back to school, to raise our children while they are young, or to care full time for aging parents or other family.

If you yearn to shut off the alarm one morning and snuggle further under the toasty covers, or ignore wintry weather alerts knowing you won't face slippery highways and traffic gridlock, here is a financial fitness checklist to review before you compose your letter of resignation:

1. Stash your cash. Be sure you have sufficient cash reserves so you can focus on the new priorities in your life without financial hardship. Six month's expenses in guaranteed accounts is a minimum even if your spouse can support all household expenses on one income.

2. Prepare for medical costs.

If your spouse has a medical plan, ask to be added. If you are single, short term catastrophic health insurance is available at affordable rates. If you are uninsurable, however, request a leave of absence or other leave program that will maintain your health coverage, even if you have to pay the monthly premiums during your absence.

3. Understand your employee benefits. Know how your 401(k), profit-sharing or other savings and investment programs will be affected and what your re-entry rights are if you change your mind and return to work. Union members may find these terms in their negotiated contracts. Other workers may request company policy booklets from their benefits department.

4. Make a family budget. Review dependable income sources. Have a backup plan in case the working spouse becomes unemployed.

5. Keep structure in your life. Plan your day just like before. Rise and shine. You have only 365 days per year. So make special use of each one. This may be a great time to join a health club to stay in shape or start a new hobby.

6. Rollover company pensions/savings unless you think you may return to work soon. This way you can control your own investment decisions. Convert some assets to income if needed, but don't ignore future growth to outwit inflation. Do not spend funds frivolously.

7. Use credit wisely. Avoid using credit as an income source because paybacks can cost you big interest dollars later. Don't purchase anything you can't afford to pay off in full when the statement comes next month.

8. Maintain your self-image. Occasionally people believe if they are not working in the traditional sense, they become less valuable. Use this period to add value and enrichment to your life.

Chapter 5

Your piggy bank

"We are a good natured bunch of saps in this country. When a bank fails, we let the guy go start another one."

—Will Rogers

This little piggy went to market

The Federal Reserve (the Fed) determines indirectly what banks will pay for borrowing money (the discount rate), what banks charge their best customers (the prime rate) and what the banks must pay into the FDIC kitty for reserve requirements.

Without you, banks have no money to loan, but since no one reminds you how indispensable you are, you may be intimidated when entering the local shrine where they keep the big vaults and (supposedly) the large piles of dollars.

When the Fed needs to stimulate the economy, it can lower the interest rates banks must pay for reserves, and expect that the lenders will then lower their rates to all bank customers because they will still make a decent profit spread.

But nobody explained these rules to the bankers. When the Fed reduces the discount rate, bankers rejoice because their costs go down. It never occurs to them to pass these savings to their customers. Why, that would shave off some profits!

In fact, in some areas like credit card debt (with a captive audience) they can increase the annual percentage rates. Knowing that consumers cannot pay off balances until their paychecks get larger, lenders can charge nearly any rate their mercenary policies dictate.

This little piggy stayed home

Instead of reducing mortgage rates, car loans, home equity loans or credit card interest, they *advertise* sales. Then they mark down the mortgage rate a bit but jack up the points and closing costs enough to offset most of the reduction in the mortgage rate. Realizing that most folks don't pay the points with up-front cash, they roll those costs into the refinanced mortgage, tack on disability, credit life, private mortgage insurance (PMI), and the banks make their loan figures for the month on higher points and closing costs for many years.

Why have a sale when the merchandise is selling like hotcakes without one?

To hear bankers complain, there is little profit in banking these days. They don't need consumer hostility, or customers clogging up the bank lobby asking to process transactions with "real tellers" and "human beings." So we had better stop maligning them so they can get back to counting dollars in their back rooms or they may raise their monthly bank charges, ATM fees, or other monthly costs to depositors even higher.

Banks don't always want to loan out money. They also don't want to pay you a lot for it while it gathers dust around the neighborhood branch. It's the same principle that other suppliers follow today—"just in time" delivery. It costs to keep inventory on hand that isn't going out as fast as it is coming in.

It is not feasible for your local bank to send a courier around the neighborhood calling for deposits because there is a customer sitting at the loan desk, waiting for a pickup. So it will take in your money now, and attempt to cut costs by decreasing your interest rate until the dollars are bought (loaned out).

I get no respect

Rodney Dangerfield made this line famous, but there are millions of Rodneys firmly ensconced in passbook savings accounts paying less than fish food rates, while these same consumers complain about rising inflation or worry when the Social Security check is late, vehemently maligning doctors and others for charging escalating fees. Laziness and inertia keep money in accounts at embarrassingly low yields.

Banks haven't competed for your dollars for years. They don't have to. They sit in neighborhood shopping malls, between the eggplant and the lettuce at your favorite supermarket or at the end of your street waiting for you to drop by. You demand convenience, not rate of return. You have better things to do with your valuable time than shop interest rates.

There is a place for short term bank CDs in your total portfolio. But don't assume your loyalty is returned because you gave your bank all your past business. Learn to comparison shop for the best money store. Because S&Ls and commercial banks are both backed by the promises of the FDIC, it makes little difference whether you patronize one or the other. Generally, S&Ls offer higher time deposit returns than their commercial counterparts.

Don't buy brokerage CDs or credit card solicitations for CDs at out of state institutions. Invest your CDs in your own neighborhood, where you will hear any gossip that may alert you to financial troubles. Brokerage CDs may pay more. But you don't know what's happening if your account is creating loans for Alaska uplands, California rehabilitation projects or Texas cow country.

Most bank customers understand basic products such as savings accounts, NOW liquid interest-bearing accounts and Certificates of Deposit (CDs). Although packaging varies between bank institutions, most deposit accounts are guaranteed by a federal agency of the U.S. Government, the Federal Deposit Insurance Corporation (FDIC). But always ask anyhow, just in case the certificate you are being solicited is a claim on the piggy bank only instead of the FDIC. Technically, the FDIC is *not* the U.S. Government itself instead, just one of its agencies. But it is widely assumed that Washington would step in and refill empty bank coffers should a local bank disaster occur.

However, if bank failures occur on a broad basis, it may take some time to sort out options. So diversification of your savings into several institutions is wise. A little cash stashed at home (small bills only) is also warranted in case your daily bills (food, gasoline, utilities) won't wait until your government gets its act moving. Even a short term bank closing could crimp your living style.

CD strategies

During periods of falling interest rates, it may be wise to lock in longer CD maturities. When interest rates are on the rise, however, the opposite strategy may work better. Short term maturities of 30 days or less allow depositors to reinvest at higher rates when interest rates are climbing. Predicting the direction of interest rates is a losing game, even for the experts. But it is often easy to see a trend developing, which can tip you off whether to "go long" or "go short."

"Laddering" bank CDs used to allow investors to win, no matter which direction interest rates were headed. With a $10,000 investment, a depositor might have purchased five different $2,000 CDs in six-month series. They might buy separate 6-month, 12-month, 18-month, 24-month and 30-month CD accounts. At the end of each six-month period, some of the initial investment money could be reinvested at a higher rate if interest rates had climbed. If rates had fallen, however, the investor still had a large portion of his or her funds invested in higher yielding CDs.

Today, short term interest rates are so volatile that I recommend most depositors keep their CD maturities at <u>one month or less.</u> As interest rates fluctuate and banking institutions merge or develop financial trouble, investors may want immediate accessibility to their funds without a penalty.

Don't lock up your savings in long term time deposits unless a banking institution allows you an emergency escape hatch *in writing* (like allowing your IRA CD to be withdrawn without penalty after age 59½) or shows you greater respect than at today's long term rates.

Interest bearing checking

So many hybrids have been created by banking marketing departments that it is impossible to list them here. Request a brochure with options for short term competitive interest savings products and cost effective checking options.

Money follows the golden rule: the one with the gold controls the rules. Banking institutions are your financial adversaries. They are working in their own self-interest. Employees are paid to earn profits for the bank, not impart banking secrets to the customer list. They used to smile and chat to get your money in their accounts. Today you rarely see a human being, and many you do encounter are overworked, underpaid, and occasionally downright hostile.

Don't trust a teller's suggestion regarding which products are best for you. Bank personnel may get commissions, referral fees or other rewards for selling certain bank products. Some staff even have sales quotas to meet each month, like stockbrokers do. You may have a bounty on your head before you step into their lobby. Don't let a friendly teller or manager talk you into something that may be better for their bottom line than for yours.

Compare the various products for yield and liquidity (not for convenience). Bank solvency and competitive interest rates should be your major concerns. Convenience, friendliness, or ATM machines should remain secondary objectives.

Although consumers carry pocket money that collects no interest, financial institutions have their interest clocks ticking every minute, all day, all night—even on weekends. Look at a recent checking statement and locate the "daily investable balance." This is the amount of your money they can loan out to others and collect interest with on a 24-hour basis. You must receive a competitive yield on short term emergency funds as well as on time deposits. Check a number of lenders and compare their rates.

Beware of high yields that sound too good to be true. An institution may be experiencing temporary solvency problems, advertising for short term funds for operational expenses. Remember there is little money in the bank. It has been loaned out to strangers (whose names you do not have) in the hope they can maintain a job long enough to pay it back with interest.

Choose the most solvent institution first, even if its returns are a bit lower. Prudent investing by the bank institution may bring in a slightly less yield. But you are interested only in sleep-tight money. Then search for competitive yields. The last consideration should be convenience and personnel attitude. What a shame a bank customer can't expect all three.

Weigh the costs of service charges on a "regular" checking account against free checking combinations that require you to keep a minimum amount in your checking or savings account. Minimum balance requirements may cost your bottom line more with the "freebies" due to lower interest rates on required savings. Compare charges on a regular checking account with the opportunity cost (lost profits you could be making at higher yields with your funds) to secure the "free" checking privilege. If you can make more by paying service charges and banking your savings elsewhere, do it.

Don't accumulate extra funds in required minimum balance accounts than necessary to qualify for the "free" service or benefit unless the yield is competitive.

Ask how the bank's minimum monthly balances are calculated so you are not charged a penalty for an under-funded account. If your account value varies a lot, you could get cut out of a benefit because it dipped below the minimum for just one day. Marketing departments stay up nights creating clever financial traps for customers to raise their profit margins.

My rate is better than yours

Einstein would have scratched his head trying to compare the yield on today's bank products. Advertisements offer various figures with differing maturities. How can you find the best yields?

You can't calculate the annual effective yield or the annual percentage yield without a compound interest calculator. (You could ask for one for Christmas, however.) Instead, ask the teller (who may not know) to ask the manager (who may not know) to ask the downtown main office (who had better know) how much money will be in your account at the end of one year. This puts all offers on the same footing because they are compared to the same time period.

Some time deposits will be quoted for a whole year even though their maturity is less than one year. If the new interest rates are down when you must reinvest, you will receive less interest than you originally expected. But for our basic computations compared all potential time deposits using a one-year compounded return.

Secret bank CD rollovers

Some banking institutions are less than forthright about communicating CD maturity dates to their customers. Some will send a letter stating your withdrawal rights, while others silently hope you don't remember your original CD statement date until the seven-day maturity withdrawal period has safely passed.

You have some moral standing in this matter. If you want your money back after the grace period, you should scream loudly on Saturday morning in the crowded lobby. Tell other customers your money has been kidnapped, until someone in power offers to shut you up by releasing your funds with apologies that they really thought you meant to leave them there.

Bank money market accounts: the old gray mare

Bank money market demand accounts (MMDAs) provide you with instant accessibility to your money or to certain withdrawal privileges at certain times during the month. Most bankers don't like this "hot money." So they price their MMDAs unattractively. A lower rate encourages customers to choose other bank instruments the institution can better utilize for profit purposes.

Don't confuse bank money market accounts with similar sounding money market mutual funds that have become so popular. Bank money market demand accounts are insured by the FDIC. You pay for the protection through a lower yield. Consider diversifying your liquid cash into **both** a bank money market with check writing and a U.S. Government money market mutual fund, also with check writing privileges.

As safe as money in the bank?

Not all Certificates of Deposit are backed by the FDIC. Private corporations can create debentures (IOUs) or "certificates" which are backed only by the bank's assets. A higher advertised yield may be one clue. Ask if your CD will be insured by the FDIC. Though no one will lie, some bank vendors may not volunteer this important information. Look for the FDIC sign on the institution's exterior doors or near the teller's window.

Package banking

To catch a mouse, one must make a noise like a cheese. Banks advertise many services and wrap programs to attract seniors, young adults, newly married couples and parents. Personally, I would rather have higher CD rates, shorter lines, longer hours, and friendlier tellers. Advertising only guarantees passing the cost of their marketing programs onto you, the customer.

Bank checks may cost more than those offered by catalog chains. Reduce safe deposit fees by purchasing your own fireproof lock box.

Watch for user fees on accounts below certain levels, on check writing accounts, on ATM cash withdrawals and other freebies you once took for granted. Once a year, add up all the costs for your banking needs and compare with other local institutions.

Account services for customers age 55 or over are very popular. Read the fine print and know what you may be giving up in opportunity cost by not investing somewhere else. Some banks advertise club memberships and charge one monthly charge for several service options. Packages aren't always better deals. You may not use those privileges enough to make the service beneficial for you.

Bank IRAs and rollovers

Individual retirement accounts (IRAs) are long term money which must outpace inflation. Instead, CD/IRAs represent "certificates of *depreciation*" which attract inflation and will not make you rich.

Lenders spread the news about the IRA account. But they never told customers about better inflation fighters such as mutual funds. IRA Accounts must preserve future purchasing power. Consider transferring those dust catchers into conservative mutual funds so the tax deferred benefits of the IRA label can work even harder through your retirement years.

Maybe you should leave home without it

Major lending institutions offer credit cards such as Visa and MasterCard. Each lender has a specific agreement for its particular card. So interest rates and terms vary significantly. Shop for the best credit card on a national basis, and resist buying one from your local lender unless its rates are competitive.

Personal loans can often be cheaper through credit unions or other preferred lenders you have a relationship with. When shopping for money, request the compounded annual percentage interest as well as the simple interest rate figure they would rather quote you since it is lower.

Most of us realize our money isn't gathering dust in the vault. It has been loaned out to others based on confidence they can keep monthly mortgage payments and interest flowing back into the bank in a timely fashion. Balance your greed factor, FDIC insurance promises, and the potential feeling in the pit of your stomach, should you hear on the evening news that tomorrow will be business as usual but your lending institution is taking a short vacation.

Collateralizing a CD for loan purposes

Suppose you want to buy a car for $10,000. You stop at your lender to withdraw your $10,000 CD—you're ready to pay cash for the car. Your lender discusses another option with you. If you take out your CD, he says, you will lose the future interest (at 6 percent) that you could make on that investment. If, instead, you used your CD as loan collateral, he would gladly loan you money for financing your car at 9 percent— only 3 percent higher than your CD is paying. A 9-percent personal loan minus the 6-percent interest from your CD equals a 3-percent loan: it's almost like stealing from your lender. Would you take that deal?

Let's examine what's going on:

The formula for compounding the annual effective yield on your CD is probably quarterly, while the annual percentage rate of a loan at 9 percent is compounded monthly. So the difference between the interest on the CD and the interest you pay on the loan will be larger than 3 percent.

It should also be apparent that you will borrow at a higher rate (9 percent) than you will invest your CD (6 percent). You are financially better off paying cash for the car rather than to finance, even though you will use your CD.

Since collateralizing means that your CD is hostaged anyway, you can't have your CD money until the full loan balance is paid off. What's the use of investing it at a lower rate while borrowing at a higher rate when you can't even have your funds if you need them until your loan is complete paid off?

This strategy is typical of the banking industry. The lender keeps the time deposit on which other loans can be made, talks you into an additional loan and now has protective custody over the time deposit for a longer time.

Pay cash for the car, become your own banker by investing the payments you would have sent to the lender into your own account and you will be far ahead at the end of the proposed loan period.

How can I charge you?

Let us count the ways. Instead of gratitude for all that interest on your home mortgage, home equity loans, credit cards and auto payments, some banks are creating even more methods of nicking you.

If your bank charges fees for services you believe should be free, complain to management. If your complaint falls on deaf ears, vote with your feet to another institution that respects your patronage—and the dollars you share with it.

Good financial consumers shop for money as carefully as for other products and services. You want your bank to respect you, not just your last check.

Never open an account to get death (life) insurance or some other dubious financial benefit. These policies are generally accidental death insurance or disability products that pay off less frequently than you may believe. The premiums are cheap because their underlying benefits are so limited.

Loose lips sink ships

Your banker may be sharing your private financial affairs with other department employees, insurance or investment companies. When a bank employee spots a healthy bank account or CD resting quietly, they are taught to flag the account and call in the troops. Then a salesperson will solicit you for insurance annuities, mutual funds, wrap investment accounts, health, disability or long term care insurance.

Bank customers should expect privacy of their financial matters, and this dateline should make you very angry. If solicited by phone or through a friendly bank teller to visit the "investment specialist," decline the offer to further profit from your money and, instead, complain to the CEO of the banking institution. Banks get away with a lot because customers allow such treatment.

This little piggy now has roast beef

To compete many banks have entered the insurance and investment business big time with their own insurance annuities and other CD-like investments. The operable phrase here is "CD-like." No CD-like investment is backed by the FDIC. This is marketing hype.

Watch out for this kind of sales pitch:

*"We are _____, and although we're not really the Bank, we are very closely associated with the Bank, and maybe even owned by the Bank. We would like to show you our CD alternative we sell here in the bank building. It is not insured by the FDIC, but we have really researched this and feel that this company is very **safe** for your money or we certainly wouldn't be showing it to you.*

*"It has a **much higher return** than Bank CDs can offer, and look at all this **tax free** income you'll accumulate every year until you take it out. And if you never take it*

out, the money will keep compounding tax free until it goes to your heirs, **probate free.**

"You certainly qualify for tax relief plus the higher interest rate.

"The choice is up to you, and we certainly don't want to push you into anything. We especially don't want to limit you to the bank's **low yielding, taxable** *CDs."*

Most customers are going to remember three things from this pitch: safe, high yield and tax free. Wrap it up. Take it home.

Bells should be clanging. Why is "the Bank" suggesting you send your money anywhere else? What is the motive for this sudden lack of bank employee loyalty?

If solicited in this manner, tell the manager that as soon as your current CD matures, you will be off to some bank down the street.

There is a large insurance industry crisis afoot, in case your insurance agent hasn't notified you. This is no time to be taking a leap of solvency faith. If banks want to compete for your dollars, I have a suggestion for them: Try raising CD rates.

Investments sold on bank premises are not backed by the bank or by the FDIC, even if they are stamped "U.S. Government" 47 times on their brochures or mention words like "safe" and "guaranteed." *No mutual fund, insurance annuity, bond or stock is FDIC insured, though some may have gobs of government insured securities inside them.*

Do not be misled into believing that because you are being solicited on bank premises every product must be backed up by your government. Just because it is sold on bank property, by a bank employee, sitting on furniture belonging to the bank, purchased on forms provided by the bank, managed by a company that may be even wholly owned by the bank, with the bank getting part of the product commission, doesn't mean this is strictly bank business. (How could you make such a mistake in the first place?)

The investment expert

Your banker wants to manage your money. Banks have envied the profit centers of mutual funds and brokerage houses, and they want annual management fees too. Some are marketing managed accounts and wrap free programs, while others are peddling their own in-house mutual funds, insurance annuities, and individual securities.

Most bankers have little investment experience, certainly not the expertise of veteran mutual fund managers, and are not only vested interests pitching products for commissions but may also become well meaning incompetents. Separate your banking and investment needs. It takes more than a desk inside the bank, a passing grade on a Series #7 securities test, and a sales pitch to know how to manage money.

Rating piggy bank safety

Though FDIC insurance may allay any fears over potential bank troubles, many consumers have a keen instinct telling them the government promises things it can't always produce. It is important to check out how prudently your banking institution is investing and its current asset position.

Banks do *not* have to "mark to the market," which means disclosing today's current values on some assets they hold. So figures on a balance sheet may not reflect current values of real estate or other investments that have dropped in value.

There are agencies that, for a small fee, will send you an analysis of any bank you request. But this report is only as good as the information the agency has gathered. Reports may even contain favorable comments due to a business relationship or conflict of interest not disclosed.

Request an annual company report and turn to the balance sheet. Calculate the acid ratio (short term assets, such as money on hand, accounts receivable, minus inventories, divided by short term liabilities such as loans, taxes due, and salaries under one year). If your answer is greater than 1, the bank can pay its short term obligations. If its debt is greater than its short term funds, vote with your feet (and with your wallet) and find an institution that manages its wealth as they should yours.

Utilize two or three banking institutions who pass muster, and stash a little "green" at home in case your bank temporarily closes its doors.

Customer wish list

Bank profit margins have soared again this year. Yet customers still languish in submerged savings and deposit accounts that would have starved Ghandi. If banks want your business, here is a checklist to follow. A reputable piggy bank should:
1. End the mortgage confusion with understandable loan applications and user friendly cost disclosures.
2. Loan originators should disclose the real interest rate the bank intends to charge after adding in points, closing costs, unpaid interest due, and associated fees **before** the customer signs a truth in lending statement. Adjustable rate mortgage (ARM) projections should show highest interest rate scenarios and be accompanied by fixed rate illustrations.
3. Raise the interest rates on savings and bank deposits. Consumers can teach bank owners and shareholders whose money keeps the bank open and stockholder profit margins up by shopping carefully.
4. Establish ethics in credit card deals and use one fair method to calculate monthly charges on outstanding credit balances.
5. Lower service fees and offer real services, such as free checking, like we used to get.
6. Allow us to conduct business with real employees, not androids by phone or computer monitor.
7. Treat us with courtesy and respect though our names are not Perot or Rockefeller.

8. Remove those CD penalties. With rates so low, how can they justify taking any more out of our pockets?
9. Inform us when our bank deposits are about to mature. Secret CD rollovers is kid behavior and deceptive.
10. Raise returns on short term accounts so we can keep them with you longer.
11. Stop using terms like "simple interest loan" when such loan balances are compounded on a monthly basis just like our credit cards.
12. Remove fancy titles on loans secured by our homes. A home equity loan (ELOC) is a mortgage. Disclose these products for what they really are: second or third mortgages with adjustable interest rates and immediate demand payment clauses in case we lose our jobs or get sick and miss a few regular payments.
13. Provide understandable written disclosure on CD rates that calculate the annual effective yield (rates). Ditto for loans disclosing the compounded annual percentage rate.
14. Give our loan applications the prompt attention *they* would want, not leave our forms inactive on desks due to a short-handed workforce.
15. Give small business owners the same treatment offered to the rich. We don't have fancy attorneys and accountants to advise us how to default under Chapter 7, 9, 11 and 13. We figure if we owe it, we should pay it back.
16. Back up billboard advertising by "walking the talk" when we transact business.
17. Let us talk to a human being without paying service fees.
18. We know the meaning of the term "float." We understand why they hold our deposits for days before coding them into our accounts.
19. Workers don't keep bankers' hours. Structure hours around us and we will show our gratitude.
20. Stop acting like a full service brokerage wire house and multiple lines insurance company. Drop investment and insurance products from their business products. If we wanted to take risks on our principal or talk to a long term care insurance agent, we would take our money somewhere else.

Chapter 6

Credit cards: friend or foe?

"When a dog has a bone he don't go out and make the first payment on anything. First payments is what made us think we were prosperous, and the other 19 is what showed us we were broke."—Will Rogers

On a lazy summer afternoon two men were reunited by their twenty-fifth college reunion. They found they still had much in common. Both had been honor students, and now each was married with three children. Even their personalities were similar: bright, personable, optimistic about the future. Surprisingly, both were even working for the same multi-national company, though in different areas of the country.

There was, however, one significant difference. One man was the manager of a small department. The other was the company's Chairman and CEO.

What made that spectacular difference? Not ambition, native intelligence, or even persistence. The difference lay in what information each one had gathered and how he had made use of such knowledge.

Imagine for a moment that you could purchase only one item at a time through credit. You could buy nothing else (except with cash) until you had finished paying off your credit balance. What would you purchase first?

If you answered your home, how would you get to work every day?

If you said your car, where would you live?

What about Christmas presents or other gifts, clothes, vacations, pools, furniture, appliances, hospital and doctor bills?

Is it difficult to imagine your lifestyle without credit? Is it impossible to imagine any form of life without it?

Those nice credit card people

The credit card is the financial industry's quick fix for everyone who can't stretch that paycheck as far as his or her high lifestyle. And it's so convenient! Buy now, pay later. Buy a lot now, pay just a little...for a lot longer. Live life to the fullest. You deserve it. Why wait? You could be gone tomorrow.

Credit cards: friend or foe?

Before you consider nominating credit card companies for a "Humanitarian of the Year" award, let's take a closer look. Credit cards, in a nutshell, are permission to buy something you really don't need right now at a price you really can't afford right now with money you don't have right now.

A credit card can be a valuable convenience. But it will become the most dangerous financial nightmare if it makes you feel richer than you really are and encourages you to spend beyond your current income.

Neither countries nor households can borrow themselves into prosperity. Too many individuals and families are borrowing themselves into poverty, committing years of future income that may not materialize to finance current levels of overconsumption.

What do you really owe?

The average consumer really doesn't know how much in debt he or she is...and is not anxious to total up. He or she only remembers the size of each monthly payment.

The more debt you buy (you are really buying money at a price), the more it affecta your future goals. A high debt level can affect the next five to 10 years of your life. An astronomical debt level can lead to long term disaster.

The consumer debt of the average family—including car payments, credit card loans, time loans and other items bought on credit (excluding your home)—should consist of no more than 18 percent of your take-home pay.

But I'm paying every month!

If your consumer debt level is greater than 18 percent of your take-home pay, you must trim it immediately. Paying monthly minimum payments endears you to the credit companies because many cards are designed never to pay off as long as you continue to use them. In fact, some companies' minimum monthly required payments are less than the interest due for that month.

For example, assume the minimum payment this month is $20. If you looked at the interest column, you may discover that this month's interest is $25. If you pay only the minimum, there will be an extra $5 of interest left unpaid. This $5 will be added to next month's balance, which will charge you interest on the loan and on the unpaid $5.

With this payment schedule, you will sink deeper into debt, even though you stop charging and continue making payments. You could conceivably pay on this type of credit card for 20 years, never charge again and watch the unpaid balance increase each month.

Presuming you're not ready to pay everything off tomorrow, how can you avoid some of the games the credit card companies play? Even get them to play by your rules?

Make a list of all of your credit cards and monthly installment loans or obligations. Include appliances, cars and anything else you have bought on installment payments, excluding home equity loans. (Use the **Credit Card Management Strategy** in the Appendix.)

This will enable you to find out, once and for all, what you are really paying for the privilege of buying now, paying later and losing along the way. If there is a marketing benefit in one column (such as an abnormally low interest charge), the credit card company will find a way to make up its loss in another column (the annual fee or the way it computes the interest). Fill out all of the columns, then compare each card with the others.

Card games with a fixed deck

The annual percentage rate (APR) on your credit card statement is derived by multiplying the monthly interest rate by 12 (months in a year). For example, if the monthly interest rate is 1.5 percent, the annual percentage rate is 18 percent.

But this is not an accurate figure. It's faulty arithmetic. If you carry a balance on a card over an entire year, you will pay more than 19 percent for the use of borrowed money.

How could that be? Let's examine what happened to the interest you paid during that year. Each month, after crediting your payment, the company charges 1.5 percent on the remaining balance. The following month another 1.5 percent is charged on the remaining balance. At the end of the first year, because of the effects of monthly compounding, you really paid 19.561 percent, not the 18-percent simple interest you have been led to believe you are paying. Compound interest, in this case, works against you.

Keep your eye on monthly disclosures that come with your statement. Sneaky companies may keep the interest rate the same but change the way they figure it, divulging this chicanery in the fine print they know few will read. The result? You're paying more interest every month; you just don't know it.

Hey, our card is free!

Many credit cards charge you an annual fee for the privilege of overspending. Some don't. Are these bargains? Not necessarily. A company that charges no annual fee may have higher interest rates. Some companies advertise no annual fee for six months or a year, then tack one onto your monthly balance when the initial period is finished.

They told you in the original contract you received when you were approved, or they sent you a disclosure in your monthly statement, that piece of paper with words so small that an amoeba would have a hard time reading the print.

And only .0001 percent interest!

A company that advertises an attractive, low initial interest rate may already be planning to raise that rate in two or three months. It knows you don't keep track of the small changes on your statements and that it will be several months (if ever) before you figure out you are paying more.

Some low interest credit cards charge from the point of sale (from the moment you purchase your item), and have no grace period whatsoever. By the time you receive your bill at month's end, you already owe interest. You will never use these companies' money free, not for one minute.

Most credit cards charge on a variable interest scale. Heads you lose, tails you lose. If interest rates spike, you suffer an immediate interest hike. If interest rates drop, it takes substantially longer for the average institution to drop its monthly rate. Competition in the credit card market brings costs down.

Be careful with cash advances!! The interest clock generally starts ticking from the moment you receive the money, not from your closing statement date or the date you receive your monthly statement.

Credit card traps

Watch for these rules in the fine print designed to separate you from more of your money:

* reduced grace period and strict enforcement of payment due dates;
* higher interest rates (from 2% to 10%) as a penalty for late payments;
* termination of your account resulting from infrequent use;
* increased penalties for over-the-limit purchases until your balance falls under the maximum credit limit;
* rising interest rates on variable rate cards;
* penalty fees for transferring balances greater than your maximum credit limit;
* double cycle billing where the issuer calculates interest retroactively on the previous month's balances on top of the current charge period;
* higher interest rates for cash advances and balance transfers than you pay for credit purchases;
* transfer fees and other costs on balance transfers from other issuers;
* user fees for services that were once free;
* promotion selling marketed to look like spending awards;
* "freebies" designed to lure you away from the competition.

Tucked in among the bills may be a replacement credit card from a gasoline company or local department store, or so it appears. You pocket the card and use it, and in the process get more than you bargained for: a full service Visa or Mastercard. Or perhaps you receive what you believe is an annual credit card updated replacement. However, the new "platinum" card comes with a brand new set of rules without you understanding the new contract you have unwittingly accepted.

Another pitfall to avoid is the "free from monthly payment" ploy. At Christmas, when you are pressed to find money to buy presents for a host of people, it becomes more difficult to continue your monthly payments. Then, just in the (Saint) nick of time, the credit card company comes to your rescue and offers to defer your monthly payment until next year. It, too, has a big heart.

Don't kid yourselves. The credit card company didn't stop computing interest during that time. They just held off sending you the unfriendly computer message. Your following month's bill comes with a larger interest payment stuck to it. Neat trick!

Here's another danger: When your credit limit is raised—and they always do it just as you reach your previous limit, don't they?—you feel like they gave you an A+ on a test. You are proud that you are a valued customer, and you feel an increased sense of pride (and wealth). Out you go to shop!

This sales technique, coupled with obsessive spending, creates higher debt levels. If you can't afford to pay off now what you owe, what are you doing adding even more debt?

Credit card companies solicit insurance, securities, CDs and other financial products through their monthly statements. Never buy financial products from a credit card offer. You have no idea what quality you are buying and, even if you call the toll free number for more information, you won't know the right questions to ask.

Before shopping for a lower interest rate card, dial for dollars. Call your current issuer and request a reduction in the monthly interest rate (while you're at it, ask it to waive the annual fee.) Tell the issuer that you would like to stay but will not overpay for its friendship. Compare its reduced rate with other low interest cards on today's market.

Before transferring debt from one card to another, ask about extra charges or fees levied on the new balance. Some companies charge transfer fees or other hidden costs. Be careful when using check look-alikes that card companies send. They are loans with instant costs. Negotiate a waiver of the fees before your new card is issued. This industry is competitive, and a new lender may waive your charge to get new business.

Don't collect credit cards. Each open line of credit is reported on your credit report. If you look like you could, at any moment, charge enough to retire in style, you may tarnish your chances for a more important loan you are seeking. When switching credit companies, close out your old account and request they report its demise to their reporting agencies. That way, it won't count as open available credit on your record.

Buying credit card protection: the $15 phone call

Some credit card companies will happily sell you credit card loss protection against theft for as little as $15 a year. The company (after notice from you) will contact every company with which you do business, so you will not be liable for any fraudulent use. How does it know where you shop and how many cards you own? You send a list for its files.

This is a fear solicitation. You are only liable for $50 on most cards (if at all), even if you never notify the issuer. Maintain a complete list of cards and phone numbers. If your wallet or purse is stolen, call the companies yourself (they have toll free telephone numbers). Use the $15 for your own benefit. Complete the **Credit Card Register Worksheet** in the Appendix.

Out of financial order

The following danger signals of credit card debt must be addressed immediately:

- You don't know how much credit card debt you owe, and you are afraid to add it up.
- You hide credit card statements from your spouse.
- You juggle the monthly budget to keep up with incoming bills.
- You have reached maximum credit limits on your credit cards.
- You are frequently late paying some or all of your monthly bills.
- You have borrowed money to pay off an overdue debt or have consolidated loans.
- You are applying for additional credit cards to increase your borrowing power.
- You have little or no emergency fund or "rainy day" money.
- You are drawing from savings to pay regular bills.
- Creditors are sending overdue notices.
- You postdate checks so they won't bounce.
- You hurry to the bank on payday to cover potential overdrafts.
- Life without credit cards seems unthinkable. You believe life without credit is *unspeakable*.

If any of the preceding describe your present financial health, you are a prime candidate for the following prescription:

Pay down your consumer debt slowly but surely. Target the card with the highest interest rate first and pay only the minimums on the remaining cards. The size of the balances does not matter. It is the cost for the borrowed money (the interest rate) that really counts. Use the **Credit Card Management Strategy Worksheet** in the Appendix.

Total up your budget and subtract all monthly take-home income excluding overtime and bonuses unless you *know* those dollars will be dependable. The remaining funds are "fritter money," leftover dollars slipping through your fingers. Recapture their value by dividing by two the extra dollars from the budget and putting half into a savings vehicle and the other half directly toward the card with the highest interest rate.

Do not get so zealous with paying off debt that you forget to build your emergency fund. If you should find yourself short of cash, you will be borrowing again. Dig yourself out slowly but systematically.

When you have paid off the highest APR (annual percentage rate) credit card, tackle the next highest card and continue to pay only monthly minimums on the remaining cards. Defer *all* major purchases until your consumer debt is under control.

Hey guys, let's play *my* game

If you intend to use other people's money religiously, look for credit cards with no annual fee, even if the APR is 30 percent. What do you care? You will be paying off the card every month, playing by your set of rules with their money.

If, however, you are in the habit of overbuying and paying monthly bills on credit, look for the lowest interest rate you can find, then compare annual fees.

How many credit cards should you have? That depends on your buying habits and self discipline. Two major credit cards are usually sufficient. If you own a business, it should have its own set of credit cards to keep business and personal expenses separate.

The more debt you have, the fewer cards you should own. Credit can become obsessive. If you do not have a candy bar lying around, it becomes more difficult to add those extra pounds. The same is true for credit cards.

Whose big brother is watching?

Many consumers require a service they may not realize they need. Every year thousands of upright financially fit consumers are turned down for credit or are otherwise damaged by incorrect, misleading, and downright erroneous credit data. Have you checked your credit history lately?

Since paying your bills on time is no guarantee against reporting errors due to sloppiness or mistaken identity, it is vital to periodically investigate your credit history. Check who has been inquiring about you, if credit cards were issued in your name without your permission or were never received in the mail, and for any entries that do not belong in your credit record.

For 30 days after being rejected for credit, you can request a copy of your records at no charge from the credit company that issued the notice. Every year, for a nominal fee, you can request a current picture of your credit history. If you find errors or omissions, contact the agency in writing and request proper adjustments. Also ask for a copy of the new, amended report.

Check your credit history on a regular basis. Some credit reporting agencies are notorious for inaccurate reporting and record keeping. The most popular credit reporting agencies are Experion, TransUnion Credit Information and CBI/Equifax. Check your telephone directory for local listings.

Because credit, lending and other financial institutions may know more about your personal financial affairs than you do, it is vital to schedule an annual credit check up to correct inaccurate information hazardous to your financial health.

The Fair Credit Reporting Act provides consumers with some protection regarding the information contained in their credit bureau files. The Act is intended to ensure consumer credit rights and guard against errors made by credit grantors and credit bureaus.

If you are plagued by a poor credit history, you can include in your file a 100-word statement that attempts to put it in context. The death of a family member, loss of a job, serious medical bills, a financially devastating divorce or other one time maladies can explain the bad marks in your record.

The most effective remedy for poor credit is to tighten your financial belt and pay off old bills—*late* pays are more favorable than *no* pays. Then begin charging small items on a regular basis—and pay them off fully each month. This will begin your new credit history of disciplined spending that will, in time, offset most of the negative impact of your earlier one.

A credit card checklist

Shop for the lowest cost dollars. Credit cards are individual agreements with lenders and can vary a great deal, even though the "brand name" (MasterCard or Visa) remains the same. You must comparison shop for money. Here are questions to ask:

1. What is the annual fee? Can it go up in the near future?
2. What is the annual percentage rate? Is it fixed or variable? How is the monthly interest calculated? How long will it remain fixed at that rate?
3. What is the grace period before interest is charged? (Be careful: Some low interest cards allow no grace time!)
4. Is there a charge for late payments? How much?
5. Are there transaction fees for purchases, transfers from other credit cards or cash advances? How much?
6. What is the annual percentage rate for cash advances? Or transfers? Is it higher than that for purchases?
7. Is the minimum monthly payment lower than last month's interest charge?
8. Does interest start immediately after you receive a cash advance?
9. Is there a user fee for each cash advance?
10. What is the penalty for over-the-limit purchases?
11. Are there any agreements in the fine print? (You may, for instance, be promising to borrow a certain amount or to make some other hidden purchase.)
12. Have you read everything on the application?
13. Did you understand every word you read?
14. Can you afford another credit card now?
15. Will you save interest (not just lower your payments) by switching existing debt to a new credit card?
16. Does your budget show enough income to pay for all new purchases?
17. How much credit do you need?
18. What credit limit can you afford?
19. How will this new financial obligation affect your existing loans?

20. Will this new card encourage you to spend more than you can afford?
21. Do you realize this represents an emergency and convenience option and not a method of living <u>above</u> your means?

Once plain vanilla, credit cards now come in flavors. You can get credit cards that earn free airline tickets or rebates toward cars or trucks, refund cash back at the end of the year, deposit money into an insurance annuity, gain coupons toward toys, shoes and other retail items, even pay for tax return preparation.

Consumers are biting. They charge groceries, fast food lunches, dry cleaning and movies. Do these "something-for-nothing" offers make sense? If so, which cards provide the best deals?

The more you charge the faster you earn your award. Be sure the deals are better than you can negotiate for yourself. Airline cards, for instance, may require you to use points within a certain period of time.

If you pay off your card each month, the only real cost to you is the annual fee (unless a creative marketer adds some extra charge you must watch for). Compare the annual fee charge to the value of the rebate or reward you will earn.

You must be very disciplined or you can build a mountain of debt in no time.

Be sure you will use the product you are trying to earn. Buying three items to get the fourth free (when you really only need one or two) spends money foolishly. Airlines often have price wars, so you may find an even better deal, considering the cost of the credit card fees or interest charges.

Cash-back credit cards and phone card offers must also be evaluated. Don't let greed blind you to charges that make such a card more expensive than the one you carry now.

Debt consolidation: Con?

Are you receiving letters from friendly credit card companies or finance corporations offering you the chance to trade those other credit card balances for smaller monthly payments? The first three letters in "consolidation" are "C-O-N," and most offers to refinance debt to reduce your monthly payments should be ignored. Finance companies charge horrendous interest rates and lengthen the time for payoff so the monthly minimum payment looks smaller than what you are paying now.

It's not the size of your monthly payment that matters, but the price per dollar of borrowed money. Eight-percent loans are cheaper than 10-percent debt, even though the latter may offer a cheaper monthly payment. The company has cleverly increased the time period until the debt is totally paid off. Debt consolidation helps **only** if the new compound annual interest rate is lower than what you are currently paying and you have reason to believe the new card's rate will remain lower in the foreseeable future. Some loans or cards offer an initial introductory rate, then raise it over time. Credit cards are usually issued on fluctuating adjustable interest rate rules, and as general interest rates rise, so do they.

There is an easy formula to reveal whether you will benefit from refinancing your consumer debt. If the annual percentage rate (compounded monthly) is less than what you now pay, you have found a lower cost for borrowed money (at least for now).

When shopping for a lower cost credit card to shift existing debt, look for lower interest rates, not lower payments.

Don't grab a line of credit or home equity loan solely because the lender tells you it can be written off your taxes. You may pay more total interest because these loans are usually written for longer time periods. It does not make good common sense to spend an extra dollar to save 28 cents.

Since a home equity loan is really a second mortgage, the payments could stretch for 10 or 15 years, exchanging short term debt for a more dangerous long term loan.

Each time you sign your name and commit future dollars you have not yet earned, you destroy a little more of your financial future. Control debt or it will control you and your financial future.

A credit card can become a valuable tool, like a hammer to a carpenter. With it you can rent a car, show dependability for future car and home purchases. Keep it handy for convenience and emergency use. But if you start nailing down everything in sight with tomorrow's income, you will learn some hard lessons.

Credit isn't a birthright. It's a privilege you must protect. Every credit card in America should have the following label printed on it: "Warning! Overuse can be hazardous to your wealth!"

Chapter 7

Insurance: cover your ass-ets

Of all the insurance listed below, which policy do you think you would most likely need?

1. Life insurance.
2. Major medical or hospital expense insurance.
3. Homeowner insurance.
4. Auto insurance.
5. Credit life or mortgage debt protection.
6. Disability income.

Surveys state: disability. If you are under 65, the likelihood of your being disabled for 13 weeks or longer is greater than dying, losing your home by fire, suffering a catastrophic medical loss, having a major auto accident or needing home mortgage insurance to pay off the debt.

Disability income was probably not your answer. Why? Because no one teaches consumers how to assess risk, how to purchase the correct kinds and amounts of insurance you do need and what kinds of insurance you don't need (or don't need as much of).

Spreading the risk

There are rules for managing risk and choosing the best values for your insurance dollars. Since risk is everywhere, you can respond in several ways.

First, you can *avoid* risk. Most people resist any temptation to free fall from an airplane, but it is nearly impossible to avoid traveling in a car. Some risks can be easily avoided. Others cannot.

Second, you can *reduce* risk. Everyone has been through some "close calls." You probably made an immediate resolution to be more careful. This is risk reduction, as is keeping equipment in good repair, eliminating cigarettes from your lives, installing smoke detectors and security systems, wearing auto safety belts and driving defensively.

Third, you can *retain* risk. This means to actually keep the risk; in order words, to insure yourself. That may sound inadvisable since you thought you were buying insurance precisely to protect yourself from risk. But that low $50 deductible on your auto or homeowner policy is costing you money that could be working overtime for you.

Through the use of higher deductibles, you can invest those extra dollars until you need the money. Your emergency fund is designed to support these minor losses. Risk retention, however, is not a total solution.

Finally, you can transfer the loss through insurance. Though it is easy to recover from a $250 deductible, you cannot recover easily from catastrophe. The loss of your home, a tragic medical disaster, a million dollar suit by a neighbor or someone injured by your auto can destroy your financial life.

Examine your auto policy, checking the liability coverage you have. Compare that amount with the actual reimbursement if your car is damaged. You will find that a lot more liability can be bought for less money than it would take to replace or repair your car. In your homeowner policy, liability also costs significantly less than property damage coverage.

Where is it hurting?

Insure yourself first against those losses from which you could not recover—death, catastrophic medical costs, total disability and liability. You can recover from a fire in your home, even the total loss of your home. It would not be easy, but since you are still healthy and working, it could be done. How could you ever recover from a $1 million personal injury suit against you and your family's assets and future earnings?

Next, you should insure yourself against those losses that would cause you to borrow heavily against your financial future. A total loss of your dwelling and auto would adversely affect your financial goals over the short term.

The areas you should not protect through insurance are the small but pesky claims—a ding on your auto is not catastrophic (unless it is a Lamborghini), and if there is not enough in your emergency fund for the repair bills, you can usually find someone who loves you enough to bankroll you.

Everybody sues somebody sometime

Clients frequently ask how much insurance is enough. My response is usually to ask them what kind of accident they are planning to have. I can only tell them what amounts most claims are settled for. The more affluent you are, the more the "deep pockets" theory applies. Plan on being sued for more rather than less.

Our society is lawsuit happy. What is the monetary worth of an arm, a leg or an eye? Whatever the lawyer in a courtroom can convince a jury its worth. Juries are swayed by a victim wheeled into a courtroom or a small child who has lost his or her sight.

Juries believe they are giving away someone else's money and striking a blow for the underdog, the little guy. They won't know that you are also a little guy, so little that you, unfortunately, have only a $100,000 liability insurance policy.

Most of you probably believe that the primary purpose of your homeowner and auto insurance is to protect your home and cars from damage. If you have ever been sued, however, you know property damage is subordinated (secondary) to liability exposure.

A jury may award a large settlement based on the future earnings of a defendant. A young medical, law or business student looks like an attractive future bankroll. The more assets you have now or will have in the future, the more likely someone will want to share your goodies.

Parents may think that once a child has reached the age of majority (from 18 to 21, depending on the state) their own assets can no longer be touched. If your child is still in any way dependent on you, you may be held at least partially responsible.

Therefore, the greatest (and cheapest) benefit a homeowner or auto policy carries is liability protection against the other guy.

Those fair and friendly insurance contracts

You wouldn't buy a typewriter with half the keys, or a set of "pre-punctured" tires. But many people pay exorbitant insurance premiums while not protecting themselves from far more critical (and more likely) occurrences.

Insurance companies are well staffed with two categories of personnel: agents and lawyers. Both are paid by and owe their loyalty to the company that hands out their weekly paychecks.

You cannot rely on what agents tell you. The words in your contract, not the promises passionately made over your kitchen table, are what you have bought.

Some agents grossly and knowingly misrepresent their product. Others simply don't know enough about the coverage they're selling. In either case, you must know enough to be able to ferret out critical protection and exclusion clauses.

Getting past the salespitch

Getting the greatest value for your insurance dollar demands that you rid yourself of certain myths and fallacies.

Fallacy: Insurance companies' primary interest is your well being, even at the risk of their own.

Fact: Insurance companies are profit making corporations with owners and stockholders who expect large bottom line earnings. They are not charitable organizations dedicated to the consumer.

Fallacy: All companies are created equal and charge relatively similar premiums.

Fact: Even some insurance agents believe this, though it is completely bogus.

Fallacy: Only well known companies are solvent and pay out claims.

Fact: Big is not necessarily better. It probably is not cheaper either. Does a TV ad really say anything important about a company's claims history, its value per consumer dollar or even its real reputation? Insurance companies pay their ad agencies big bucks for images that create a sense of stability, friendliness, good value and even sexual attractiveness to induce you to buy.

Do not be coerced into paying more for a "professional." If I needed a heart transplant, "professional" would mean everything to me. But shopping for insurance, I only want a solvent company with rock bottom prices.

Fallacy: The larger the premium, the better the product.

Fact: In other words, the more you pay, the more you presumably get, right?

Wrong. Unfortunately, price is no protection from mediocre products, many of which are overpriced because of the higher commission that must be built in to induce salespeople to sell inferior products to the public.

For a true comparison, call smaller companies rated high in consumer publications. You will find significant differences between companies and recapture some savings for your other financial goals. Consider it your moral imperative to support less greedy companies whose products are of top quality and more reasonably priced.

Fallacy: You should only work with one agent for all your insurance needs.

Fact: Do you only see one doctor for all your body parts? Shop at one store for every item you buy? Always eat at one restaurant? Companies and their agents spend a lot of advertising dollars to foster customer loyalty, knowing that if the price on one product must remain competitive, they can make up the difference on others.

Fallacy: "Updating" improves your insurance program.

Fact: Every three to five years the industry develops another "new and improved" product and unleashes it on the public via agents who will gain new commissions.

Overselling and churning policies is a popular pastime for some insurance agents. If you need new coverage that often, your insurance agent is not doing effective long term planning with you. In some cases, you should probably be *decreasing* your insurance coverage as you and your property get older, not buying more.

When it rains, it can pour

Homeowner insurance is relatively easy to understand and compare. Examine your latest declaration page (which is only the comfort sheet, not the real contract) for the following:

1. The limit of liability coverage.
2. The basic form of the policy.
3. The amount of coverage on the dwelling and other structures.
4. Replacement (new construction) or depreciation (fair market value) coverage on the dwelling and separate buildings.
5. Inflation guard endorsement on all buildings.

6. Personal property damage—including the overall limit, whether coverage is for replacement or actual cash value, and your scheduled property list for special belongings.
7. Sewer back up or other perks you need.
8. Total premium per year.
9. The loss deductible.

Don't risk a lot for a little

Liability coverage is the cheapest and most vital insurance coverage you can buy. Liability insurance protects you if you are held responsible for another party's loss or injuries. Many agents are now recommending a base policy of $300,000 and an umbrella policy of $1 million or more extra coverage—$100,000 is not enough coverage. Attorney fees and medical bills can add up quickly.

You have an even greater liability risk if you own any of the following: a teenager, a pool, a pond or recreational lake, an old shed or dilapidated barn, vacant land or land in another state, swings or other playground equipment that can attract neighborhood children, any item in disrepair (an old fence, unfilled well or cistern, open ditch, an old tree), accessible electrical wiring, or a pet—dog, cat or horse. "Beware of..." and "No Trespassing" signs offer limited protection. By law, you must maintain your property in a safe condition for all strangers, even uninvited ones.

Go through your home and yard, looking for conditions that should be repaired, filled in or otherwise made safer.

If you own bare land or unoccupied dwellings, they are potentially more dangerous because they can attract children who use your property as a "clubhouse" or trespassers who use it as a meeting place or refuge. A boat either docked or stored on yours or other property is dangerous as well. One match or one cigarette in an old barn or under a boat canopy can trap an individual in a raging inferno.

Liability is limited to individual and non-commercial pursuits, not business or rental ventures. Don't expect your regular homeowner policy to cover you for a home occupation, special business or rental property. If you own storage facilities that you rent out, or real estate investment property, you need additional coverage.

The insurance company has a duty to defend you (unless the loss was intentional, excluded in the contract, or you made a material misrepresentation when applying for the coverage) up to your policy's limits.

No one wants a claim history on his or her record, which may increase insurance premium for three years or longer. So there is a temptation not to report relatively small mishaps or collisions you feel can be ironed out on an informal basis. ***Always report losses as soon as possible, whether or not you plan to collect from your company. If a loss claim is filed later and you have not reported the event, your company need not defend you.***

Umbrella liability policies have become popular because of astronomical court and jury settlements. An umbrella policy fits tightly above both your homeowner and auto policies and can be added for a relatively small annual premium, adding $1 million or more to your basic liability protection. Its deductible is whatever liability coverage you have on your basic policy.

An umbrella policy is a small price to pay for reassurance that you will not have to raise someone else's family or become a permanent meal ticket for a stranger. **Never risk a lot for a little.**

Professional liability

Personal liability policies generally do not cover business risks. Seek a professional liability policy which covers your particular career. A teacher is exposed to a different risk than a surgical nurse may encounter. The problem is the same, however: you may need extra coverage of a specific nature.

Compare several policies before purchasing from an agent. Request a specimen contract before you sign an application. Read the contract from cover to cover, marking all risks, limitations, and exclusions with a marker. Then discuss these concerns with the agent (or company if it is a group contract) and get your answers in writing.

Oh, give me a home

Homeowner policies come in several basic types: HO-1, HO-2, HO-3 and HO-5 for homeowners; HO-4 for apartment dwellers and other renters; HO-6 for condo owners.

HO-1 and HO-2 are broad forms of coverage. I refer to these as "call if it burns down to the ground" policies because they cover so few perils.

HO-3 provides all-risk coverage on your dwelling, better coverage on contents and transfers more risks to the insurance company.

HO-5 is the cream of the crop if you have an expensive or custom built home. Compare the increased benefits to the higher premiums charged.

HO-4 for apartment dwellers covers liability protection in case of injury to someone, as well as personal property contents coverage.

HO-6 is for condo owners. Since the outside property and common walkways are covered by the association's insurance, these contracts protect your liability exposure and personal contents from fire, theft and other perils to the middle of the exterior walls.

Covering home sweet home

The amount of coverage on your dwelling will need to be maintained at either 80 percent of the total cost of replacement (minus land and foundation) or 100 percent, depending on company policy.

Replacement cost has nothing to do with current resale value or tax basis figures. It means the cost of re-building (with new materials and today's construction labor costs) the dwelling as it stood before the calamity.

The disadvantage of using only the 80-percent is, say, that the replacement cost would be $100,000, the insurance company's maximum payment will be only $80,000, even if the house burns to the ground. If it will cost $100,000 to replace your home (at present construction costs, not market value), insure it for $100,000, not $80,000.

Replacement or fair market value?

Replacement coverage generally reconstructs your home to its general condition before the loss. Actual cash value reflects only the fair market value, and may be much less. You do not want fair market value unless there is such a large differential between the premiums for replacement and costs for market value coverage that guaranteed replacement is not affordable.

Check your declaration sheet to be sure you have paid for replacement cost coverage for dwellings as well as for personal property. Even if you have an inflation rider that increases the dwelling amount on an annual basis, you could still be underinsured because the original dwelling figure was too low.

Century old homes generally cannot be insured for replacement value because of the astronomical cost of redoing them in the grand manner of the past.

Many folks think they have replacement coverage on their home when, in fact, they have depreciated or fair market value. Your policy may include a *guaranteed replacement clause*, but you won't qualify unless the dwelling figure is high enough and unless the actual contract language inside the policy states there is no limit to what you can collect.

Many insurers state "replacement value" on the policy's cover sheet but limit its effectiveness in the contract's fine print. It's not what they say but what you have signed that matters. The best policies have no dwelling amount figure and state "guaranteed replacement," no matter what the final cost to rebuild.

Inflation guard endorsement

Inflation endorsement coverage is an optional rider that makes good sense. It allows the dwelling coverage (and premium) to creep up yearly to match increased construction costs in your area.

If it is not automatically covered through a rider, you might be tempted to forget to increase your premium every few years.

Many contracts state if you abandon your dwelling for more than thirty (30) days, it is no longer covered. If you are a snowbird, care for or own the home of a parent in a nursing home, or travel extensively, be sure your agent provides you with a written letter stating the dwelling will remain covered, though your home may be vacant for longer periods of time than your contract allows.

If you have turned a dwelling into a rental property, the insurance company must know immediately. This is an increased insurance risk to them, and your contract probably excludes such use of your property (business). You will need rental coverage to be insured in this circumstance.

Personal property coverage

Personal property coverage ranges between 75 percent and 100 percent of the amount on your dwelling, depending on the company. Check for replacement coverage. If the 10-year-old TV set is stolen, a check for depreciated value from the insurance company for $25 will not go far. A five-year-old couch will likely bring only a few dollars from an insurance adjuster.

If you do not see replacement coverage on your declarations page, contact your agent and get it in writing. It is important to understand in advance what you are not covered for so that any gaps can be corrected before your policy is underwritten.

No insurance company will take additional risks on unique or special items without a corresponding increase in premium. Your contract will spell out the limitations on such categories as jewelry, money, securities, collections, statues and fine arts.

If you wish to add special items, you must request a *scheduled property endorsement*, then list each item and its appraised value. Discuss with your agent what constitutes scheduled property. Have these items individually appraised by a reputable company at today's replacement values, send a copy of the appraisal to your company, and keep the original for your records.

Many special items will be covered only for fire and theft, so also request breakage and mysterious disappearance coverage. This costs a little more but is well worth the extra premium.

Videos or photographs of your possessions should be recorded annually and stored elsewhere. Be sure each special item is listed on the policy when you receive it, and reappraised every few years. Inflation can outdate appraised values in no time.

If you own collections, list numbers, editions or serial numbers along with your appraisal. An artistic piece you value highly may not be as appreciated by an insurance adjuster lacking receipts or other supporting documents. Keep receipts for large items.

After a loss it is virtually impossible to remember everything. A current inventory also adds credibility when you want to collect.

Important deeds, security certificates, wills and insurance papers should be copied and stored in a fireproof box in your home. This box may be kept near an exit to grab if there is time during a fire or other disaster. Store copies of valuable papers in a safe deposit box or at someone else's home.

The insurance industry has backed out of the flood business because it was too costly. But your agent may be able to direct you regarding national flood coverage: where to find it and who is eligible to purchase the protection.

The best water protection you can buy on an ordinary policy is sewer backup. It is cheap, so probably worth the money.

Medical payments

Purchase enough coverage so that anyone falling on your lawn sprinkler can receive emergency room care, some x-rays, and a follow-up medical check-up.

This inexpensive coverage allows the insurance agent to write out a check to the injured party without the hassle of an investigation, etc.

Your premium

When comparing total costs, get an apples-to-apples comparison from each company so you can compare premiums for the **same** coverage. Some agents compete for your business by changing or cutting types of coverage so they can show you a lower premium than what you are currently paying. If you don't know what you currently have, you have no way of knowing whether the cost comparison is a fair quote.

Ignore gimmicks. You are not impressed with a 2-for-1 exclusive this week. All you want to know is the quality of the coverage and the bottom line cost.

Deductibles

By raising deductibles to $250, $500 or higher, you can reduce your premium. When you have a loss, dip into your emergency fund for the amount of the deductible. It is more important, over the long term, to be adequately insured in catastrophic areas.

Insure yourself properly against the most dangerous risks first. Retain those small and pesky outlays for property damage.

Working at home

With more downsizing and family pressures for greater income while the children are growing up, many folks perform business tasks in their home, providing services such as baby-sitting or other child care, or work full time in their home offices.

If you have a home occupation, particularly one that draws business customers to your premises, you should ask your agent about an incidental business rider to cover this specific peril.

Some businesses can be readily covered by liability coverage. Even small business such as cake decorating and sewing or alterations run the risk of a customer falling down steps, slipping on the ice, or otherwise injuring themselves and suing.

Some policies will pay for awards if you are found guilty, but offer no duty to defend in case you are accused in a liability or personal injury case while performing certain business occupations. A part time monthly income may not be worth the potential for losing your assets in a lawsuit.

Your only protection against "going naked" is reading the contract carefully and getting **written** assurances from your agent regarding what you are covered for *and* what risk you are uninsured for.

Covering your home office

Don't assume any home office equipment is covered, especially computers and other high tech instruments. Request riders which will cover the equipment and your loss of income if a disaster shuts down your business for a period of time. Backup all business records, clients lists, and computer data bases and maintain these tapes/ files in another location. When disaster strikes, the primary focus is to get you back in business again as fast as possible.

Auto insurance

The following checklist of auto insurance do's and don'ts should give you a sense of *déjà vu* from the last section:

1. Buy the highest liability you can afford.
2. Raise those deductibles.
3. Check out smaller companies. They may be cheaper, yet still carry quality products.
4. Check claim satisfaction ratings through consumer publications.
5. Consider dropping comprehensive and collision when the car is 6 years old (unless it is a Rolls Royce); keep liability on **all** cars—even those you no longer drive or store in the winter months.
6. Carry medical payments coverage for others and sleep better.
7. Choose perks such as rental car coverage or towing.
8. Add an umbrella policy to your ordinary liability limits.

If you are a small business owner, own rental property, or use a company car for business (and personal) purposes, you have special risks. If the car is in your name, used for both business and personal reasons (be honest), you need 24-hour coverage for either kind of accident coverage: business and personal.

Many business owners have serious gaps in their liability protection because they have purchased a personal auto policy which excludes business or other usage.

If any of your employees use your car to perform outside tasks for you (banking, mail delivery, dry cleaning pick-up, etc.), you are liable in case of an accident. To avoid this, insure employees as an additional covered insured on your business policy or business rider endorsement.

If you drive a company car, get a copy of the company's insurance policy and review the amount of liability in case of bodily injury as well as all exclusions (the fine print). These types of coverage may be purchased on the friend-of-a-friend-of-the-company-president basis and have serious gaps in coverage.

Many parents also take auto insurance risks they do not understand when their teenagers drive. Of course, you want coverage for everyone in the family and **would never let an agent talk you into waiving the rights of your Rambo to drive**

family vehicles in order to get a better rate on the family car insurance premiums.

In addition, check the insurance privileges your teenage drivers are covered for. They must appear as **named insureds,** not just drivers of your cars. This is very important, as the covered perils are different for each category of driver. If, for example, your teenager allows a friend to drive and an accident occurs, generally only "named insureds" are covered when turning over the car to someone else with permission.

Check your policy for the following: names of everyone allowed to drive, number of miles your vehicles are assumed to be driven per year, location of all autos, boats, etc., and other information detailed on your cover (comfort) sheet.

If you discover any inaccurate information, call your agent immediately and provide the correct data. Request that a letter on his or her letterhead be sent to you confirming the phone conversation and your agent's response whether or not you are covered.

An auto insurance agent may omit an increased risk in reporting your information to the company because the coverage may be rejected and he or she will lose the commission.

If you replace an older vehicle with a new one, you are generally covered for the same risks of the previous car. However, if you add a new auto to your stable, you must contact your agent immediately, preferably before you drive it out of the showroom.

Leased car types of coverage are new and may differ from ordinary auto types of coverage. Read the exclusions and limitations in your contract.

Rental car insurance adds a neat profit to the rental company's profit margin and may not be necessary. You may be covered for rental occasions with your personal auto insurance. But there may be items your insurance will not cover, for example, loss of use of the rental company's income while the damaged car is being repaired. What can I say? Sit down, brew a strong cup of coffee and read the contract before placing all your worldly possessions at risk without your knowledge.

Place both homeowner and auto policies with the same company, if possible. This increases your protection in case you have an accident on your homeowner property with your car.

If an accident occurs on your property with your auto, separate insurance companies may argue about who should defend you. If your homeowner, auto and personal liability umbrella are with one company, there is no question regarding who should stand behind you.

This also buys a little extra goodwill if you become more accident prone with your car. An agent may consider retaining your auto coverage if he or she is afraid that dropping you will cost your homeowner business. Homeowner insurance is relatively cheap to insurance companies; auto insurance poses a far bigger risk to their profit margins.

Your teenager is an accident waiting to happen. Your need for heavy liability protection will never be greater than during your child's adolescent years. If you would balk at handing over a credit card to your 16-year-old, perhaps you may want to postpone allowing him or her a permanent driver's license. All the damage kids can do with a credit card is overcharge. With a mobile weapon, they could hurt others, damage themselves, and expose your personal assets to financial ruin.

Some policies exclude coverage when the driver has been drinking or using drugs. Check your contract and have an adult talk with your teenager. If you feel you are wasting your breath having this parent to almost-adult discussion, get a grip and get the keys to your car back!

Driving abroad

Before you sit behind the wheel in a foreign land, check your policy to see what types of coverage you can depend on when you leave our borders.

In some countries an auto accident is punishable by a jail sentence. Or you may cool your heels in a foreign jail, waiting for your case to be tried. Rights we take for granted as Americans are not so generously dispensed in some foreign lands. *Cuidado*! (That's Spanish for "be careful.")

Health insurance

Health insurance follows the same risk management principles already discussed. The main elements in any policy are:

1. Maximum lifetime payment (how much in your lifetime the company will pay, regardless of how high your medical bills climb).
2. Coinsurance provision (the percentage of the bill you pay).
3. Stop-loss limit (the amount at which the company starts paying 100 percent of all eligible covered expenses).
4. Eligible covered expenses.
5. Excluded from coverage.
6. The deductible.

With so many health coverage types available, keeping up is challenging. Look first at what the healthcare supermarket has to offer.

Fee for service traditional plans are disappearing. It pays 80%; 100% of eligible covered expenses after the annual single or family deductible, then 100% after a higher dollar amount spent per year.

You choose the physicians, you shop the healthcare market, and the insurance company picks up the remainder of the cost, negotiating with the physician regarding the bills.

A Preferred Provider Organization (PPO) has a specific network of participating physicians. PPOs don't require patients to become eligible through a gatekeeper system in order to see a specialist.

Winning the Money Game

When choosing a PPO over other types of plans, you are paying for self-referral ability. Patients can generally go directly to a network specialist without dealing with a general physician who might refuse to grant a referral to a specialist.

If you use outside providers, the insurance company pays less of the cost. But you still have physician choice regarding network physicians or outside doctors.

A Health Maintenance Organization (HMO) often mandates you stay within its own network or it may pay little or nothing for the health care expenses. It must refer you outside of its own network for such costs to be picked up by the HMO.

You are usually circulated within the HMO group or told you need to live with your symptoms. In essence, HMOs cut deals with doctors and hospital to further hold down fees in return for treating large numbers of HMO members.

HMOs can be beneficial if you want first-dollar coverage and your employer will fund coverage, or you are willing to pay the additional premium. One caution: HMOs usually have staff doctors that you must use. Your personal doctors may not be included.

Nearly 80% of American physicians now contract with at least one managed care organization, offering discounts as great as 50% from previous fees. HMO members get lower cost health care as long as they patronize participating doctors and hospitals.

Many plans now offer point of service arrangement, hybrids between an HMO and a traditional health coverage. With a point of service arrangement, an employee can stay in the network and pay, say, a $10 fee to see a doctor on the list.

However, that patient can see an outside physician for a deductible and a copayment.

Think in terms of catastrophic loss. Find the highest maximum lifetime benefit. A medical tragedy could wipe out your family's savings. You may have little choice under an employer's plan, but opt for the highest benefits, before looking at deductibles.

Coinsurance percentages vary. The less you pay out of pocket, the greater the premium cost. If your employer is funding the plan, you may care little about premiums. If you have an individual policy or are paying part of the premium, keep the premium down by choosing at least a 20-percent provision.

A stop-loss limit is the total out-of-pocket limit you will pay for eligible expenses within a certain period, usually a year, before the insurer will pay 100 percent of the additional eligible expenses. That should be reasonable, depending on your emergency fund and short term savings. The lower the stop-loss breakpoint, the higher the premiums.

This deductible should be $250 or greater if you have other methods of covering small medical emergencies and expenses. Some two-income families have two-employer plans that can overlap to fill in gaps in one spouse's plan.

Pay attention to the definition of the specified types of coverage. "Medically necessary" is a broad term which could later restrict treatment you believe is needed while the insurance company disagrees. Stay away from mail order or TV insurance offers. The insurance is pricey and generally contains limited benefits.

Don't purchase policies without medical underwriting (a policy for which anyone can sign up, no matter his or her health problems). Such contracts attract very sick customers who are uninsurable and cannot get coverage anywhere else. Therefore, benefits are either costly or limited, or both.

Avoid insurance that comes with a period of free coverage, other gimmicks or offers of discounted sales. A good product doesn't get marked down.

If you are self-employed, request quotes for several deductibles and compare premiums and benefits. If you have young children or an accident prone family member, the lower deductible may be more attractive. Add up last year's medical bills and see which options benefit you more.

When considering maternity, dental or supplemental accident benefits, compare the additional premium for each benefit to the times you predict you will be able to benefit. For example, the cost of maternity benefits, in vitro or fertility procedures should be compared to the number of times you expect to use them.

Dental coverage may not cover preventive or annual visits, braces or cosmetic surgery deemed "medically unnecessary." Supplemental accident riders (which pay first dollars for emergency accidents) may be cost effective if you have any accident prone children. Change your benefits as time and your family's personal and medical needs change.

Don't automatically opt for the cheaper premium before analyzing the treatment benefits and choice of doctors. You may want to pay higher premiums to get doctors you choose. Managed care policies may restrict choices of treatment or amount of testing in the future.

No free lunch

You can't purchase a kidney at 50 percent off or a double hip replacement for a $15 co-payment. Don't scrimp on your health plan. **Unfortunately, no matter what the advertisements claim, the bottom line in health care is its bottom line.**

Use the following checklist to stimulate questions of the company's enrollment department or sales agent before signing up:

1. Is the plan accredited? Has it been through a review process and by whom?
2. What services are covered? Which are not? Which emergency treatments are excluded? Ask for specific examples of eligible and excluded services.
3. How many participants are enrolled?
4. How many have signed up in the last year? Several large health insurance companies' profits are suffering because they grew so fast, they cannot handle the onslaught of new enrollees.
5. How many members left in the past year?
6. How many physicians have left the plan in the same time period?
7. Who are the plan's doctors? Are they all board certified in their specialty practice? How many are taking new patients? How many are not?

8. How much flexibility is there in choosing a doctor? Are you assigned to a physician or can you choose?
9. How are doctors in the plan paid? Are there bonus incentives? Does the insurer discourage doctors from referring patients to specialists?
10. Does the plan have a "gag" clause? Some plans don't like their physicians to discuss treatment options with patients (and the associated costs), although such "gag" rules are clearly outlawed in many states and not in the interest of patient care.
11. Are there hidden arbitration clauses in plan documents?
12. What hospitals are in the plan? What services must be authorized in advance?
13. What is the level of preventive care?
14. How comprehensive is the drug program? Must you use only generic substitutes? What prescription drugs are not covered?
15. What is the complaint procedure when coverage is denied?
16. Do you need permission from a gatekeeper to see a doctor?
17. Do you need to be certified before seeing a provider?
18. What is the procedure regarding medical emergencies? How does the plan define "emergency?"
19. How are high risk patients handled? Is acute rehabilitation care discouraged?
20. How are chronic ailments handled? Are there special services regarding ongoing medical services?
21. How long does it take to get an appointment? Are follow-ups allowed after most procedures?
22. Will the plan cover you when traveling? What if you move out of state?
23. What are the registration requirements? Does family coverage include children in college, step-, foster, or previous marriage non-custodial children?
24. Can patients be terminated from the plan? If so, how and for what reasons?
25. Does the plan receive feedback from its customers? Is the input meaningful?
26. How does the plan treat new enrollees with pre-existing conditions?

Do you have a record?

Whenever you apply for individual life, health or disability insurance, a brief summary of the medical information you agree to provide to the insurer can be sent to the Medical Information Bureau. This coded record indicates key risk factors like health-related conditions and hazardous sports activities that other insurance companies can access, review and confirm.

The companies claim the data are necessary to prevent fraud if you again apply for such insurance in the future. But a misdiagnosis or negative information gathered by one insurer can prevent you from future coverage somewhere else.

Insurance: cover your ass-ets

Insurers base their decisions on many sources, relying most heavily on the detailed information provided by applicants themselves., So it is important for you to know that the facts you provide are recorded correctly.

Even your parents' ailments may count against you. Many insurers will consider you a greater risk if one of your parents died before a certain age, or if they are still alive and have certain medical conditions such as diabetes, high blood pressure, stroke or heart disease.

You can access your records by making a written request to the Medical Information Bureau and authorizing it to release to you all medical information contained in its files. Contact: Medical Information Bureau, P.O. Box 105, Essex Station, Boston, Massachusetts 02112. If you discover inaccurate data, contact the Bureau immediately.

Disability income protection

Protecting future income is the most commonly overlooked risk. If you fell off your roof next weekend, who would work for you and bring home the family paycheck? If you were seriously injured in an auto accident tonight, who would feed your family until you went back to work? If you never worked again, how would you fare?

It's sad to say, but total disability may be a greater financial disaster to your family than your death.

A scorpion needed to cross a deep creek. She presented herself to a frog sunning on the bank and offered to pay him handsomely to carry her across the creek on his back. The frog justifiably refused this dangerous proposition, reminding the scorpion that it was basic to her character to kill frogs.

The scorpion rationally explained to the frog that it was in her own best interest to allow the frog to live because the scorpion would also drown if she attacked the frog in the water. After some thought, the frog agreed to the expedition.

As the strange looking twosome approached midstream, the scorpion violently stung the frog. The frog, realizing that he would soon be history, was outraged. He screamed at the scorpion: "Knowing full well that you are about to drown, too, why have you done this tragic deed?" The scorpion, lowering her eyes, answered, "I am not evil, nor am I stupid. But above all, it is my basic nature to sting and kill frogs."

Disability products vary so in quality that some are worthless as major disability coverage. Disability insurance is also so confusing that it rarely takes up much space in insurance money books. Like the scorpion, as long as the free enterprise system prevails, it will be the basic nature of some companies to sell the lousiest product at the greatest profit.

The disability insurance industry is still rocking from the increased claims in the past five years. Some of its most prized customers, doctors and attorneys, packed up their briefcases, sold off their practices to hospitals or large law practices, and applied for disability.

The onslaught of new claims has changed the face (and watered down the contracts) of disability coverage forever.

Most workers assume their employment disability or worker's compensation will suffice. In fact, most Social Security claims are denied the first time, and group employer plans can be very restrictive, usually only cover short term conditions, and offer little real protection against long term employee disability.

At best, disability benefits from your employer replace only a portion of your prior income, usually no more than 60 percent. If the list of exclusions is long, or if your employer doesn't offer any long term disability benefits, you may need your own disability policy.

Under most large employer-sponsored group disability plans, employees do not have to provide evidence of insurability, and premiums are generally lower than for individual coverage.

Unless you are disabled under the plan, group coverage lasts until you terminate employment or the insurance company decides to terminate your employer. There are no guarantees, no real long term contracts. Group plans generally do not discriminate against employees with medical conditions although management may receive a better contract than the rank and file workers.

Disability policies can hide more traps than an 18-hole golf course. The specific wording is crucial to the quality of the contract because there are so many definitions of disability. When buying a product, request a specimen contract beforehand and compare it with others you are considering. Ignore the agent's sales pitch. The policy comes with a generous commission attached. So do your own homework.

Disability types of coverage divided into two major categories: short term (three or six months from the time the policy's benefits start) and long term (from six months on) coverage. Companies tend to offer better short term disability packages because they are less costly to the employer. Especially if you are young, you need a secure, long term disability program. Most people can handle a three-month or six-month period without income; few can handle the loss of all future income forever.

The crucial elements of long term disability coverage are:

1. The definition of total disability.
2. Noncancellable and guaranteed renewable clauses at a guaranteed premium until age 65.
3. Length of benefits and maximum monthly benefits.
4. Elimination period (the time before benefits start).
5. Social Security disability benefit integration, called the "offset."

There are a variety of ways the company can define "disability":

1. Your inability to perform one or more of the primary duties of your present occupation, called "primary occupation."
2. Your inability to perform all of the duties of your regular occupation, called "own occupation."
3. Your inability to perform all of the duties of any occupation for which you are suited by reason of training, education or experience, called "any occupation."
4. Your inability to perform any *gainful employment* (including broom-pushing, envelope-stuffing and dog-walking).

Numerous policies offer "own occupation" coverage for a period of two years, then change the disability definition to "any occupation" after that time. These are split definition policies and should be avoided if possible.

There is a world of difference between each of the preceding definitions. Those differences in contract terms will determine whether you actually qualify for benefits. Your definition and the insurance company's may be totally different.

The company may demand that you cannot engage in any other occupation while receiving disability benefits. Or it may require the continuous treatment of a physician, hampering a permanently disabled insured if continuing medical treatment is useless.

There may be limitations regarding recurrent disabilities or the length of time between disabilities that the company deems a recurrence of the same disability, disallowing benefits.

Generally, disability policies offer a waiver of premiums after 90 days of total disability, with a refund of the premiums during the period. Policyholders also have a grace period in which the policy cannot be canceled for lack of premium.

An accident supplement (for emergency care) may be added. This generally pays first dollars for an emergency trip to the hospital.

An accidental death and dismemberment option pays a lump sum in such an accident. But some contracts contain a restrictive clause of "accidental means" defined as an injury which is not only unintentional but unforeseen. Falling off your roof on Saturday repairing shingles, you will have a difficult time attempting to prove you appeared "up on the chimney" like St. Nick, hammer in hand, by accidental means.

There's always another agent

If you are a fire walker or a weekend crop duster pilot, you may be limited in the kind of disability coverage you can find. But if you have a less hazardous occupation, you should opt for the most liberal definition of disability you can buy. If you are told you cannot qualify for a better plan, check with other companies. Companies have different standards—you may be able to qualify for a better contract with someone else.

The contract should state that it is noncancellable *and* guaranteed renewable at a guaranteed premium. This means that the company cannot cancel your contract in the future unless you change to a more hazardous occupation and can't raise your premium. If your policy is merely guaranteed renewable *or* noncancellable, it means the company has the right to raise your premiums as a class as high as its little profiteering hearts may choose.

Renewable or optionally renewable are terms that speak for themselves. You have a gun with no bullets. All the options for the policy renewal or premium increases are at the discretion of the insurance company.

The length of time for benefits is next in importance. Lifetime benefits for accident and sickness are best, followed by benefits to age 65. Benefits for five years or less will be of little help if facing a total disability for the next 30 or 40 years.

An inflation clause or guaranteed option to purchase additional future monthly income benefits is an obvious advantage, because cost-of-living increases will be necessary as inflation outpaces your monthly fixed income check.

The elimination time will determine when, after a loss, you begin collecting the monthly income checks. Use the same strategy that works for homeowner and auto coverage. A longer elimination period (90 to 180 days) will decrease your premium significantly.

Lengthen the elimination period in favor of a larger monthly benefit or longer benefit period. Income from vacation pay, sick pay, worker's compensation, severance pay, short term disability employment benefits or your IRA funds can provide income until your disability benefits kick in.

You can add a Social Security integration rider, which, if you qualify for disability under the terms and conditions of Social Security (good luck!), will reduce your regular disability income check by the amount the government provides you. If you do not qualify for Social Security, the insurance company pays you the originally promised amount. By agreeing to seek Social Security if you are disabled, you will decrease your policy premium further. This is the "offset" and may reduce the disability payment from the insurance company. Offsets are imposed not only for Social Security payments but also for some worker's compensation programs and group disability employer plans.

If your employer pays your disability premium, your benefits are generally taxable to you. If you pay your own premiums, the payments are tax free.

Worker's compensation may be integrated and expected to cover occupational injuries. Your private insurance may be a secondary carrier. Watch for such limitations. Changing to a more hazardous occupation without notifying your insurance company may void contracts.

There are fewer disability insurers than a few years ago. Some also underwrite the same product for other companies who put their brand name on the product.

If a company wants to jettison you, it has a variety of methods. It can raise the premiums on its customer list in the class or area where the risk exposure is the greatest. It can send everyone home, staying it will not produce such a product any longer.

They can sell off your block of business to another company, perhaps at a discount, who now has final responsibility for your future benefits. If that company becomes insolvent or is insolvent at the time of the re-assumption (does that sound like a corporate plan of escape to you?), your contract is void.

Choose a company which majors in disability, instead of a multi-line insurance company who also offers this product.

Spend time at your library researching company solvency and policy options. Consumer publications spell those out.

Long term care or nursing home hype?

These policies often have so many limitations, the fine print spelling them out takes up more space than the bold print explaining what they cover. And they can be so misleading that it's difficult to give you all the ammunition you need to protect yourself from the many inferior products marketed today.

To make matters worse, older people are often bombarded with sales literature or hounded by high pressure sales reps who use fear as a closing tool. Grown children whose older parents may be vulnerable to such tactics should be aware and intervene as necessary.

Policies have also become more standardized. You can purchase "qualified" contracts which require stricter standards for qualifying for benefits, but you can deduct the insurance premiums on your tax return.

Or you can opt for "non-qualified" contracts which offer more lenient benefit qualifications, yet provide no tax write off of premiums.

If the policy requires prior hospitalization before entering a nursing facility, pass it up. Policies should not restrict certain conditions or diagnosed diseases—such as Alzheimer's disease or certain types of cancer. A policy should protect you no matter what type of disease you contract.

How many days of nursing care are allowed? The best contracts allow up to four years of nursing home care and lengthy levels of step-down care.

A cheap policy may very well mean an inferior one. Call local nursing home facilities for their daily rates, and purchase enough daily coverage to protect you from inflation. Currently, $130 to $150 per day is the average cost in most areas of the country.

Consider forgoing a short elimination period (the length of time before the policy benefits kick in) for a larger daily amount of coverage. Increasing benefits in one area may subtract coverage from more critical areas in another part of the contract.

Is the policy noncancellable and guaranteed renewable? The words "guaranteed renewable" by themselves are not enough. Some contracts state they are "guaranteed noncancellable," but then outline the conditions under which the company can choose to "non-renew" the policy in the following paragraphs.

When filling out your application for coverage, be sure all medical questions are answered completely and honestly. Some companies use "misinformation from insured" as a basis for rejecting future claims. Read the medical application after the agent has completed it and before you sign it. Insist that the agent add any pertinent information, whether he or she thinks it's "important" or not. The agent will always get his or her commission even if you never receive any benefits.

Research the reputation of the company issuing the policy in the library. But remember that most rating agencies are paid by the insurers for their ratings and may not want to bite the hand which feeds them generously year after year.

Long term care policies are more inclusive than they used to be. The younger you are, the lower the premiums (because the longer the company has to work your money for its own vested benefit).

Some points to look for in a long term care or nursing home policy:
1. Does it require a hospital stay before you can collect benefits?
2. Does it exclude certain physical or neurological conditions like Alzheimer's?
3. What is the daily benefit? Can you buy an inflation rider? How does the rider calculate increases in benefits? From the initial year or from the previous year of the policy?
4. What are the conditions for receiving home care? What are the daily living activities that must be met to receive home coverage? How many are needed for benefits to start?
5. What is the elimination period? How much lower is the premium for a longer elimination period?
6. Does the policy allow admission at any level: skilled, intermediate or custodial care?
7. Are the benefits the same at any level of admissions?
8. Will the coverage be underwritten at date of issue or at the date of a claim? A company may not actually provide coverage until you make a claim.
9. Does this policy waive premiums after a period of benefits?

No one can assess the future costs of long term medical care, and a company that finds a product is not profitable could simply decide to drop it. If you develop medical problems in the meantime, you may not be able to purchase coverage from another carrier. **Read every word in the entire contract and be sure you clearly understand before you sign. Do not be misled by "agent translations."**

Compare policies from several companies. Request a specimen contract so you can read it over carefully and see exactly what you're buying. If one is not available, scrutinize your policy as soon as it arrives. You will have a short period to return it and receive back your full premium if it is not what you want.

If you do decide to return the policy, be prepared to hold your ground against the agent's most urgent ministrations. He or she has already received a commission and won't want you to change your mind.

Never respond to fear sales tactics or believe that a specific policy is the only contract available to you because of your current health. Do not be pressured into signing by an aggressive sales pitch. If it is a quality product, it will still be available tomorrow, next week or next month. Avoid the sizzle and buy only the steak.

Nonprofits and volunteering: sometimes nice guys finish last

When you volunteer, you can sometimes open yourself up to liability. If the starting pitcher on the youth softball team you coach falls on a piece of glass and is injured, both you and your group could wind up in court.

If the treasurer of your local charitable organization leaves with some of the funds, you could be accused of negligence in handling public money.

A loss in court could mean damages out of your pocket. But defense costs could total several times the ultimate settlement award.

A nonprofit group should purchase insurance coverage to protect itself, its employees, directors, officers and volunteers. Don't expect a general liability policy to automatically cover these perils. The contract should state all types of coverage and exclusions. Request a specimen contract before you buy and inspect the "exclusions" and "limitations" clauses. The more catastrophic the potential risk of suit to you, the more likely the insurance company may want out if it can find loopholes.

The company should have a duty to pay defense costs even if you are later found guilty. Retroactive coverage is also a plus, while hard to find. Check if the policy can pay out for a loss without your permission. If payment is made in spite of your innocence, your reputation may suffer.

The policy should be underwritten at the time you are issued the coverage, not later when the claim has been made. In other words, the company should advance funds for attorney fees and legal costs instead of reimbursing them later.

Your homeowner policy may also have provisions for some liability protection. If so, who is the primary protector and who reverts to a secondary standby position?

Insurance coverage generally will not protect you from malicious acts. Check your auto policy for any overlaps in coverage if your car is involved in an accident during volunteer activities or if you drive the group's vehicle. You may not be covered if you are reimbursed for such travel and transportation costs.

Life or death insurance?

As you already have discovered, I prefer to call this "death" insurance, a more accurate description of what it does. Who needs it? Your dependent beneficiaries. The most common reasons are to provide a dependable income for your family, to pay off debts, to protect a business from insolvency and to pay funeral expenses, a bank mortgage and other postmortem expenses.

Who gets solicited for life insurance? Everyone, regardless of real need. It is sold to pay federal estate taxes far into the future, for burial benefits when you have other assets that could be liquidated, to singles who don't need insurance, to investors who believe that anything tax deferred must be good, and to clients investing for college and retirement.

When you are young, a serious concern is **dying too soon**, leaving a family and spouse behind with little economic means of support. At retirement, however, your concern should turn toward **living too long**. Your need for death insurance at that age should be minimal, if any.

The good, the bad and the much too expensive

Most of you are probably aware of the perennial argument: Which is better—cash value life insurance or term death insurance?

Consumers have become increasingly aware that cash value insurance (marketed as whole life, ordinary life, single premium, limited pay, single pay, universal life, flexible premium-adjustable benefit, variable life and variable universal life, among other names) offers higher commissions to insurance agents than term insurance.

Therefore, many informed consumers have decreased their insurance costs by buying term coverage (which offers a death benefit only) and investing their assets elsewhere. Most agents, meanwhile, tout the savings and investment virtues of the higher priced—and much higher commissioned—cash value products.

Whether to purchase cash value or term insurance is the third question to ask. The first should be: How much death insurance do you need? The second question: What kind can you afford?

Most families don't look at their future earning power in the right light—as a paycheck that will only continue if the breadwinners remain alive and working. Families whose bread-winning fathers or mothers have died think of little else.

A home isn't the only dream you have promised your family. There are basic necessities such as food, clothing, shelter, utilities, a college education and the retirement you and your spouse look forward to. All of these cost dollars, dollars you expect to earn in the future. But if you are cut out of the picture, where will that kind of money come from?

When a young couple with a child or two (or more) has a $25,000 or $50,000 death insurance policy, if the breadwinner died tomorrow, the family would be broke within two or three years...at most. The mortgage would have to be paid off. The credit card companies would want their money. The car finance company would demand full payment. Doctor and hospital bills for a last illness would blossom. Not even the funeral director would wait around for a check ($6,000 in today's dollars).

Unless you leave behind the blueprints to Fort Knox, your family gets the pittance left over, even though you thought you were leaving everything to them.

I am disgusted with insurance agents who underinsure young families with children and a home because their companies motivate agents to sell smaller death benefits with higher built-in premiums and commissions. Those agents and companies make a conscious decision to deliver a smaller check to the grieving family, a check that may only be a fraction of what it needs to survive. It's a practice that should be illegal. In fact, it's commonplace.

I would rather see you insure your home for one third of its value and buy enough death insurance in case you die. At least if your home burns down, you will be there to help rebuild it. But you can't come back and correct the mistake of buying too little death insurance.

I'm worth that much?

So how much death insurance do you need? Agents seem to have ready answers. I am amazed that some of them can so easily pull a nice round number out of the air and, like the Wizard of Oz, make an instant recommendation for the amount of death benefit that will take care of your family. I am even more astonished at agents who leave the entire decision up to you, simply asking how much premium you want to pay.

Look at your homeowner and auto policies. Do you see any nice round numbers? No. The amounts you see are exactly what will be needed in case of loss. Death insurance works the same way. There is a precise amount that, if you died tomorrow, could be invested at a certain rate of return (after taxes and inflation) to pay off your debts, replace your present income and keep your family going.

But arriving at that figure requires several pages of data, including a financial statement of your assets and liabilities, the ages of your children, the earning power of your spouse, whether you desire to fund some college for your children, your pension survivor benefits and whether you want to fund your spouse's support after the children leave home.

A thorough insurance analysis should also include the value of any Social Security survivor and dependent benefits (although they may not be dependable in the future), the amount of term insurance you have at work (though group term is no substitute for an individual guaranteed insurance contract), the savings you have built up and whether you want your family to be able to keep its home.

The result of all this analysis is that most young families need between $350,000 and $500,000 of death insurance to provide sufficient payments when their children are young. How do those figures stack up against the amount you have?

This is why the question of which kind of insurance is best—cash value or term—is a moot point for most of you. There is simply no way an average family can afford enough cash value insurance. That leaves term insurance as the only option.

What is term insurance?

Term insurance isn't designed to make you rich or provide you with any retirement benefits. If you don't die, you get nothing back. Just like your homeowner and auto insurance—if you don't have a loss, you get nothing back.

When you purchase death insurance, are you protecting your liabilities or your assets? If you won the lottery, how much death insurance would you feel you needed? Probably none. You are protecting your liabilities because you don't have the assets yet. You are protecting yourself as a money making machine for your family during those years when your paycheck is vital.

When your child is two, you need income to support him or her for at least 16 more years. When he or she is 12, you only need to provide support for six more years. If you intend to fund a college education, you need a certain amount of insurance only until the child graduates.

So as you grow older, your liabilities tend to decrease. In the meantime, you are supposed to do everything you were taught in this book to become mercenary and develop your own assets that will protect you in your old age. **You simply can't live and die in a cost efficient manner at the same time with one contract.**

Term insurance is criticized because as you get older it gets increasingly expensive, to the point where you can't afford the coverage. But as you get older, you should have fewer liabilities to protect. So you should be decreasing your death insurance to match those liabilities and socking everything else you can into your own pocketbook. As you decrease your amount of coverage, you will reduce the premiums payable, and it will remain affordable.

Term insurance isn't advertised by the insurance industry as a whole. Agents don't want to sell it to you. If *I* ask an agent why, the answer will be that he or she can't make a living on term commissions only. If *you* ask an agent, you will hear other reasons:

"Term insurance won't protect you permanently. Do you want to give up your insurance at age 65 because you can't afford it anymore?"

"You can't borrow from term insurance and get a cheap loan when you need the money."

"You really don't have the discipline to pay yourself first, and this will be a simple method of accomplishing that objective."

"When you die you need money to pay all those estate taxes. Maybe you can't get it after retirement age."

Let's examine each objection in a little more detail and see how well these arguments hold up.

One for the price of two

When you die, a term insurance policy pays you whatever death benefit you've purchased. But so does a cash value policy—a $100,000 policy pays $100,000 when you die, no matter how much extra money you will have accumulated in your savings. Who gets the rest of your savings? Right! The insurance company.

You originally bought two things with your cash value policy—an insurance policy in case you died and a savings plan if you lived. But it seems like you only got one—the death benefit.

Why? Because that's the way it works. If you live to be 99 and have $49,000 in the savings portion of your life insurance, you will still only get $50,000 if you died. The insurance company would get to keep the $49,000 that was once your savings.

Something seems wacky here. If I purchased a three-piece suit (coat, skirt and vest), I am paying something for each piece, even though the outfit is sold for one price. After the outfit is altered, I expect to receive all three pieces back. (Wouldn't you?) What if the sales clerk asked me which part of the outfit I wanted—skirt, coat or vest? I paid for all three, and I want all three.

When you buy two things, you had better get two things, or your money is not working effectively. And although you are paying for two things in a cash value policy, you only get one. This "bundling" concept is the basic problem of cash value insurance.

If you are never going to put away any extra money, and you don't die, perhaps you are better off with the small savings you will have at retirement from a cash value policy. But because of the time value of money and inflation erosion on future savings, you may not be very much better off.

Personally, I don't need (or want to pay for) a large insurance company looking after my money and working it for 40 years or more for itself before I get my hands on it. Insurance companies, as a whole, have assets in the *trillions*. What are your assets? Can you afford that kind of expensive money management? And what if the insurance company dies before you get to withdraw that savings?

I can't afford to die

The argument that a retiree may have to give up his or her insurance coverage because term insurance gets too expensive is persuasive. At a time when money will be at a premium, how can you afford to pay more for insurance?

But because you only receive one benefit or the other, if you take away your savings, your insurance coverage disappears. If you withdraw your savings from your policy for a retirement monthly income, either in one lump sum or in monthly installments for the rest of your life, you give up your death benefit.

So if you want to use your cash surrender value as a retirement savings plan, you will have no insurance coverage after retirement, even if you buy the expensive cash value policy.

So, what is the agent's point? The enormous commission he will generate if he can divert your attention toward one benefit or the other instead of looking at the whole policy picture.

Of course, there is a solution to the above problem, one your agent will happily point out: You can borrow the money out of your policy. You don't even (supposedly) have to pay back an insurance loan. Or even the interest on it. But you will. The insurance company will just keep taking payments of interest out of your cash savings until it is all gone. You know what happens then—your insurance policy self-destructs.

Otherwise astute people have bought this ideology without thinking it clearly through. It would take a bank very creative marketing to convince people to put money into a savings account and then, when they wanted it back, force them to take out a loan against their savings instead.

(Of course, that is what collateralizing a CD for a bank car loan means. And folks will do that too because their thinking machines are asleep at the time.)

Cash value is cheaper than term when you reach a certain age. Why? Because you pay so much more in the beginning (when you are young) so you can pay less when you are very old (after age 65). So how does the company make out? When you pay your premium into a cash value policy, the company immediately purchases a term insurance policy on your life, then invests the rest of the money.

If term insurance is good enough for it to buy for you, why isn't it good enough for you to purchase for yourself?

When you cancel your insurance at retirement because you want the savings, do you get a rebate for all those earlier years you overpaid? No. Does the insurance company get a giant profit for all those years it worked your money instead of you? You bet. That's how they can afford to pay out all those hefty agent commissions over the years. And still post fat profits.

Since death insurance is designed to cover your liabilities and replace your income, what are you doing with any insurance after retirement? Where is the income you are supposed to be replacing? Where are the liabilities you had when you were younger? Your insurance liabilities tend to go down because you have less time to have to replace income and less responsibility as you get older. **Death insurance for most readers should be a temporary solution to a temporary problem—dying too soon.**

Tax free insurance dividends

Insurance dividends are not real dividends in the sense we know, like distributions from IBM, AT&T, Microsoft, and other companies that share profits with their stockholders. Insurance dividends are actually a **return of surplus premium overcharges** that collect interest for the insurance company all year long, then are handed back to you. Folks love getting something back, and they believe this is money the company has earned for them.

These "dividends" are tax free because they are a return of the policy owner's money. Only the "dividends" kept in your account year after year that compound annually are taxed.

I would rather pay less up front in premiums, and work the remainder of that money for my own benefit. Taxpayers hate to give the IRS an interest free loan by paying more taxes than they need to. Why give the insurance industry the same deal?

Another fixed retirement check

As you approach retirement time, you may be advised to choose a monthly income option either for your single life or based on your life and that of a beneficiary. This is usually not in your best interest, and the insurance agent may receive a commission for convincing you to annuitize. Here's why:

By signing up for the monthly retirement income, you give up all rights to your cash value forever. The company only owes you a monthly check, while they can safely work your money without fear you will surrender your contract.

In addition, you also lose your death benefit. No insurance and another monthly fixed income check but no lump sum if needed: insurance company ahead by 2 points, consumer 0.

We're here to help you save

The one argument that stands up in favor of cash value is that if the company doesn't force you to save, you probably won't save anything. With Americans saving 4 percent annually, this is a valid point. If you are planning to purchase term insurance and fritter away the rest of your money, you should under-insure your family, purchase the higher priced insurance and hope you don't die.

Why the stuff at work is cheap

Group insurance purchased at work may appear cheaper. But the benefits are temporary and should not be confused with or used as a substitute for a guaranteed individual contract that can't be taken away or terminated at any time.

Group insurance companies can walk away from their customers without warning because there is no real contract guarantee between your employer and the insurance company. The company could become insolvent, you could be terminated or otherwise leave your present job, and you will buy coverage with no premium guarantees as the work force grows older.

Considering the uncertain employee benefit environment, save precious employer perks and flexible spending dollars for more important types of coverage such as health, dental and disability insurance. Term insurance is cheap even when purchased outside the workplace. If you are not insurable, however, group coverage may be the only insurance you can purchase because it generally requires no medical underwriting.

Good and bad terms

Before converting your insurance to term coverage, you need additional information about the three basic kinds of term insurance: 1) annual renewable or yearly increasing premium term; 2) level term; and 3) decreasing term (also known as credit life or mortgage insurance).

Annual renewable term insurance has a level death benefit, but the annual premium increases each and every year. You are charged for one year's mortality at a time.

This type of term may not be able to be decreased over time, and its cost will eventually outpace a family budget, especially after you hit 40. It is, therefore, most appropriate when coverage is needed for a short time, such as two or three years. If you are contemplating taking out a large short term loan for a business or other purpose, for example, this type of coverage is the most cost effective way to protect your family from the extra debt in case of your death.

Level premium term insurance has a level benefit and a level premium for a stated period of time. It can be purchased for periods of 5, 10, 15 or even 20 years without an increase in premium. Good term policies can be renewed automatically until the age of 90 or 100. You will never have to take a physical again.

If you have a young family, buy a policy with the longest time period before any premium increase. If your children are older and your future need for death insurance is rapidly decreasing, the shorter time periods may be your best buy.

Review the agent's illustrations that come with the policy to be sure the premium is guaranteed for the full time period. Some companies sell insurance with projected or assumed premiums but don't guarantee them, hoping they will not have to raise those rates in the future. You want rates that are guaranteed to remain level for the entire term period.

Also be sure the contract guarantees you will not have to show evidence of insurability to qualify for the next term period if you need insurance after the initial period is over.

Some companies offer initially cheap term but insist you pass a physical exam to re-qualify after the initial time period (called re-entry). Buy a policy that guarantees you can renew without re-qualifying.

Waiver of premium is usually available. The insurance company promises to pick up the policy's term insurance costs if you become disabled. But the definition is broader than terms in a high quality disability policy. If you are young, the waiver premium should be considered as it is inexpensive enough to purchase, considering the devastation of future income and the length of time you may be disabled without the ability to work.

Paying more for less

Decreasing term (also commonly known as credit life or mortgage insurance) is heavily promoted by banks to new homeowners. This is the most costly form of term insurance and the poorest buy.

The death benefit in this type of policy decreases as your mortgage does...but the **premium stays the same.** So the most cost effective time to die if you own this type of insurance is near the beginning of the insurance policy. Near the end of the term, you are paying the same rates as in the beginning, but you are getting very little coverage for your money.

I have occasionally found the mortgage insurance premium wrapped into the monthly mortgage payment, which could mean you're paying interest on your insurance premium. This is illegal. To be sure you're not getting shafted in this manner, contact your bank and ask them to isolate each charge built into your monthly mortgage payment.

There is a more serious drawback to decreasing term: The lender is often the beneficiary of your mortgage insurance policy, not your family.

Your family will never see one penny of that death benefit. If anything should happen to you, the institution will keep the death benefit, even if there are not enough other assets to keep your family fed and clothed.

Lenders may demand that you have death insurance sufficient to cover the amount of the mortgage loan, but they cannot demand you buy it from them. When buying a new home, add a rider (an additional amount of insurance coverage) to your existing term policy. Gracefully decline your lender's invitation to further profit from you.

What a clever marketing device! Lenders have discovered a method to cover their risk in case of your death through an insurance policy on your life with you paying the monthly premiums out of your pocket, and with them as the beneficiary.

You probably would like to have your home paid off after your demise, but shouldn't your spouse have the option of making that decision if there are greater expenses or larger family needs than the death benefit you left behind?

If this kind of risk management is attractive to you, please drop me a line. I would be happy to assist you in purchasing—and letting you pay premiums on—a $50,000 life insurance policy with myself as the beneficiary.

Forget bells and whistles

The following extras raise the premium cost, yet provide minimum benefits:

Accidental death coverage. In order to qualify for the extra death benefit, you need to have died of a direct and independent accidental bodily injury as experienced by an exterior wound, excluding any and all medical complications. A lottery ticket is a better bet.

Children's term insurance rider. Children have no debts, therefore, no need for insurance. Child riders often attach a guaranteed feature that allow children to qualify for five times their original death benefit at adulthood without a physical. This may be a piece of mind purchase, not a financial issue.

Living needs rider. This provides a partial death benefit early for living expenses, medical bills, or other costs associated with a terminal illness before the death of an insured. Sold as a no-cost item, there may be later costs for the actuarial risk to the company for paying funds early. Primarily a marketing tool to generate a policy commission.

Convertibility clause. A mechanism to switch to whole life in the future without a physical. But I ask you, why would you want to buy the expensive stuff at all?

Whole life with a term rider. If, according to these agents, term is fine as a rider, why isn't it even better as the entire death benefit? This slapstick is an attempt to lower the premium within striking distance of your pocketbook.

Insurable interests

This is a legal requirement. A financial loss must exist before a life insurance contract can be legally issued.

From the legal standard every individual is considered to have an insurable interest in his or her own life. (Every person is presumed to have more to gain by living than by dying.) Thus, the individual may generally name anyone he or she wish as the beneficiary.

However, when the analysis supposes that the beneficiary has more to gain from the proposed insured's demise than from his or her prolonged life, the beneficiary's standing may be in jeopardy.

When a parent insures an adult child or domestic partners insure each other, and no clear financial link exists between the two relationships, contact the insurance company for assurance in writing that any beneficiary designations will be honored in case of death.

I can't die for two years?

The incontestability clause states that if an insured makes a **material misrepresentation** on the insurance application, then dies in the first two (2) years from the original policy issue date, the company can refuse to pay the full death benefit. Any material misstatements are also considered fraud, another reason for nonpayment of the death proceeds.

Fibs, sins of omission, or "little white lies" have no place in this arena. The stakes are too great for the financial health of your family.

Where's the death benefit?

Today's insurance companies realize that when you receive death proceeds by mail, you may find another financial home for the funds before their agent can approach you to purchase another insurance product.

So you will likely receive, instead of a death benefit check, an insurance account with check writing privileges, to slow you down enough for the incumbent agent to make an appointment with you after the funeral.

Even if you liquidate all funds from the account, they have worked your money in their interest until you redeem the account.

No one said these people weren't clever. Imagine what could be achieved if they would put these brilliant minds to work in the interest of the customer!

Designer life insurance

If you think buying a home is an emotionally charged experience, wait until you attend an agent's life insurance presentation. Like a revivalist meeting, promises don't come cheap. But pages of illustrations will attempt to convince you the price is well worth the future savings for college or retirement.

You never see ads with future projections for a mutual fund. That's illegal, and your government forbids such deceptive sales practices, even on late night TV. But across America such insurance pitches are commonplace in homes, insurance offices and at businesses.

Agents promise gazillions of dollars and come prepared with their crystal balls: "dream sheets," creative and misleading projections of future death benefits and cash value accumulation accounts. The company disavows any such figures (does it know its agents better than the consumer?) and shows the guaranteed column, the only promise the company intends to back up. But these numbers may be buried under the agent's elbow, at the bottom on the last page or torn off before the appointment.

These contracts are sold under numerous names: universal life, adjustable-premium, flexible-benefits life, variable whole life, interest-sensitive whole life, graded premium whole life, and variable universal life. The common link between these labels is that the insurance policy includes an internal cash value savings element, and the illustrations you are sold during the agent's presentation won't predict the future any better than your goldfish can.

When the projections don't transpire, the internal costs increase faster than your cash value. Policies can eventually self-destruct, leaving the insured (and beneficiary) no coverage unless huge premiums are paid to keep pace with the constantly rising internal charges.

By this time, your agent may be sunning him- or herself in the Boca Raton sun, out of reach.

Variable whole life or variable universal life is internally funded by the invest experience of the insurance sub-account(s) you choose as your investment vehicle(s).

Do you want your family's death benefit riding on the whims of the stock market, the international market, or the junk bond arena? Risk management means you throw the risk to the insurance company for a stated premium and let it figure out how to make the profits to underwrite your future death benefit.

When buying death insurance, consider your *need,* not your *greed.* Only by deception do designer policies look better than term insurance and a high quality mutual fund (even if it is taxable) by your side.

The insurance industry is basically exempt from federal regulation, and some state insurance departments would rather switch sides than fight.

Whether it's a vanishing premium contract that doesn't vanish when promised, variable life funded by the investment experience of an internal separate insurance account the agent may illegally call a mutual fund, or any whole life policy founded on future performance, all you have in your hand is thin air. The policies are so complicated you need an insurance degree just to understand them.

Because today's cash value policy predictions may be a mirage, you need pricing you can depend on. Purchase term insurance and start a real investment you don't have to give up to get the death benefit, you don't have to borrow to use, you know how much coverage you have, and how much premium you will owe next year. How much do you really want to pay to die? Don't fund a larger home, a bigger college fund and a more luxurious retirement for your agent than you do for yourself.

The winning death insurance strategy

Purchase a term insurance policy whose benefit can be reduced at any time, and re-examine your financial position every three to five years. As your mortgage decreases, your assets increase and your children get closer to going on their own, reduce the face amount (death benefit) accordingly. Then use that reduction in premium to increase your assets even more. Every time you reduce your death benefit, add the premium difference to your present investments. You will gradually transfer money spent on dying too soon to the impending problems of living too long. Eventually, you should need little or no death insurance.

Insurance companies base premiums on data from large random samples. Seek the lowest risk group for your specific situation. If you are a nonsmoker, consider only a preferred or nonsmoker (not standard) death insurance policy and find a company that penalizes smokers by charging them much more.

On the other hand, if you are a poor risk, choose companies that tend to lump together good and bad risks. That way another policy owner is paying part of your real premium. Group insurance is a good example. Rates are based on the average age, occupation and health of any group. Individuals may pay the same premium but separately offer various risks to the insurance company. If your health is poor and you can get into a relatively healthy group, your cost will be absorbed by the other members of the group.

"Churning," or "rolling over current coverage into new policies," is a deceptive insurance agent practice to induce you to cancel your current coverage and purchase a new policy. Though illegal, it is a popular technique for generating new commissions. Agents may promise you more insurance for the same price, maybe even for free. A thinking person should question the veracity of this offer. In return for more coverage, your current policies may be "doctored" internally. Only later may the deception be found out when your previous policies self-destruct or generate fewer benefits than you originally bought.

Don't expect to successfully complain later. You voluntarily signed the papers. In the thousands of contracts I have examined over the years, I have never seen the terms "fair" and "friendly." All insurance contracts are created by attorneys, and these counselors are paid by the insurance company offering the product.

Before buying any life insurance (or any other insurance, for that matter), request that the agent sign the following declaration:

An insurance agent's personal contract with a client

The advice I have given you during the time we have spent together has been totally objective and in no way based on any self interest or monetary gain as a result of your purchase of my product. I have thoroughly explained all available options that may accomplish your objectives, regardless of the difference in commissions I may receive on various products.

*All advantages and disadvantages of any product have been presented. I have also provided a full disclosure of any and all hidden costs or internal charges involved in each product, **including explaining in full the guarantees backed by the company**. My recommendations are based on the most cost effective method of accomplishing your financial goals. All information provided is the result of my expertise in each area. All recommended solutions are based on your unique financial, personal and risk tolerance objectives. I offer you the relative assurance that these solutions will withstand the test of time.*

I have acted first and foremost in your best interest and in a manner consistent with the highest standards of honesty, integrity and ethics.

_____

Agent

If an agent is truly ethical, he or she will sign the statement. If you later find out that you were not advised of material facts that would have caused you not to purchase the product, then you can hold him or her to the written word...in a court of law, if necessary.

If an agent balks at writing down the verbal promises he or she had made, show him or her to the door.

Trusting them with your money

Fixed insurance annuities sound attractive because they offer guarantees of safety and tax deferral. Today's variable annuities are created to look like mutual funds with an insurance wrapper (to the unsuspecting eye) offering tax deferred benefits, which makes them sell even better.

Banks are even getting into the annuity game and are using private customer records to solicit sales and net themselves 7% or better. They are definitely a good deal for the agent or the lender. But how good are they for you?

The insurance industry suffers from the same symptoms of greed and mismanagement that banks exhibited in the 1980s. Some have even become TV stars on investigative programs. They may hold devalued real estate or lots of junk bonds inside their investment portfolios.

Unless you have been on vacation in the Australian Outback, you know that some insurance companies have been closing their doors and locking up (what's left of) policy owners' funds while state agencies sort out their options. In the meantime—sometimes for years—their policyholders don't eat as well as they previously did.

An insurance annuity is essentially an IOU with the company. You agree to loan them your money and they agree to pay you income later after retirement age.

When you want to leave, there are large penalties for early withdrawal (which is really the agent's original commission) called surrender charges. They can amount to as much as 15% in the first few years. In addition, there is a 10% tax penalty on early withdrawals if you are not 59½ or older.

Insurance annuities, fixed or variable, are one of the most inflexible and restrictive investments you can purchase, even if the company remains in business. I would rather invest my money where it can be diversified, where I can monitor it on a daily basis, choose more than one company to invest with (how many dollars do you want resting on the financial solvency of one private corporation?) and have access to it at a moment's notice, without surrender charges, early withdrawal penalties, penalties for withdrawal before age 59½ or lapses of time before my money arrives at my doorstep. After all, it is my money, isn't it?

The solvency issue should be of great concern. A company with a decent rating today may deteriorate tomorrow. You probably will not know it is failing in time to retrieve your savings, and if you have prior notice of a potential shutdown, will you be willing to pay all those withdrawal fees and surrender charges plus another 10-percent penalty for early withdrawal before age 59½? Why anyone would accept all these restrictions on their own money for the privilege of **temporary** tax deferral is a tribute to an insurance agent's presentation motivated by large annuity commissions.

The agent gets a whopping commission for a successful sale. You have little visibility regarding how your principal is invested. You get the risk if the investment later goes south. Sound fair?

If the insurance company drops dead, your agent will trot across the street, sign with another company and start peddling new products for new commissions.

As the owner of a fixed annuity, where will you go? Don't take big risks for dubious guarantees and temporary tax avoidance in the face of three financial truths: diversify, diversify, diversify.

Don't let greed cloud your common sense investing.

Flavor of the month

Today, you can find every flavor of the rainbow, often managed by big name investment companies, through variable annuities. A hot insurance investment product, variable annuities are often sold as tax deferred mutual funds.

In truth, they are the same annuity insurance "duck" donning a new set of feathers. An insurance annuity, variable or fixed, is still a highly commissioned, inflexible, restrictive product with large internal expenses, horrendous surrender charges, hefty withdrawal penalties, and a poor substitute for its big brother, a tax efficient mutual fund.

Large commissions, expense and other internal charges take their toll on the returns of the product—**which is a separate insurance company account, not the popular mutual fund you may believe you are buying.** It may take 20 years for this laggard to catch up with a similar mutual fund, even with the tax deferral advantage.

Purchasing name brand chicken and burgers may guarantee quality products, but these "clones" can act quite differently than their mutual fund counterparts. They may have small asset bases that are harder to diversify prudently. They may be managed by a nobody inside the popular fund company instead of the superstar you have seen on TV. They carry all the major disadvantages inherent in annuity products.

Instead, consider mutual funds for your investment dollars, even if you have to pay the taxman on an annual basis. Unless you intend to maintain this kind of annuity for 20 years or more (and who wants to wrap up savings for that long in today's uncertain investing environment?), the advantages of high quality mutual funds can outweigh these twists on an old theme.

Insurance annuities tax all profits as ordinary income at the owner's **highest marginal tax rate**. When the new tax law lowered the capital gains rates on long term investments like stocks and mutual funds to 20% (after an 18-month holding period), the insurance industry nearly had a stroke!

Why purchase a product which turns every dollar of profit into the highest tax rates allowed by law. If you surrender the contract during your lifetime, you pay immediate taxes on all earnings above the original investment.

If, instead, you hold the contract until you die, you die, your heirs must immediately pay the taxes as well. The more money you accumulate inside the product, the more taxes you are building for a future date.

You can't talk about variable annuities without discussing their fees, fees, and more fees that you cannot see (and which few agents disclose), rendering them mediocre runners against mutual funds, even if the mutual funds are taxed on an annual basis.

The internal mortality charges (you are buying insurance inside the contract) plus the administration costs and expense charges (no, not the $35 per year contract fee you can see) slows them down considerably.

Why are annuity products so popular today? **Because they are sold, not bought.**

Pitched by insurance agents who earn huge commission rates and annual trailing commissions as well, year after year after year. If the insurance company doesn't continue to pay the agent on an annual basis to keep you in their contract, the agent may find you a "new and improved annuity," perform a 1035 exchange (tax deferred switch), and collect a brand new double digit commission.

Don't expect full support from the media industry regarding the truth behind the variable annuity versus mutual fund debate. Many publishing companies receive large checks from insurance advertisers for full page advertisements, then designate staff writers to write positive features to please their ad customers.

If you were a magazine editor, how would you handle this issue?

Insurance you can do without

Failing to protect yourself and your family against serious financial loss is a huge mistake. Still, you can be over-insured, while benefits from some types of coverage are limited, overlapping, and downright wasted premium money.

If you currently own the following insurance policies, read your contract and cancel those policies that cost you more in opportunity cost than the benefits they offer.

1. cancer insurance.
2. life insurance for children.
3. credit card insurance.
4. accidental death protection.
5. accident insurance.
6. flight insurance.
7. trip cancellation policies.
8. hospital indemnity policies which pay you money instead of for services.
9. extended warrantee service contracts.
10. wedding insurance.
11. rain insurance for major events.
12. mortgage payment insurance if you are unemployed.
13. comprehensive/collision damage on old cars.
14. credit life insurance on purchases or loans.
15. disability insurance sold on credit cards or loans.
16. Low deductibles on auto or homeowner policies.
17. Lost credit card insurance against fraud.

Checking out your insurer's health

Insurance companies were once above reproach regarding solvency. But there may be more troubles ahead for this industry, which has undergone insolvencies that have left some folks without access to their funds for long periods, sometimes even without death benefits.

To find out how good an insurance company is, check with an industry rating service. Don't rely on one rating service only. **Most rating companies are paid by the insurance companies themselves**. So a rating company may grade everyone generously. An "A+" from one rating service may be a lower grade than an "A" from another agency. Favor companies with a top solvency rating from at least three rating services.

When presented with a well heeled insurance pitch, ask for the following: the safety rating from A.M. Best, Standard & Poor, Moody's, Duff and Phelps and Weiss Research. The first four are paid for their ratings by the industry itself; Weiss Research is paid by the public. (Remember: That lifetime guarantee promised by an insurance contract relies only on the lifetime of the company.)

Never purchase a contract because the agent states your policy is guaranteed by a state agency. Most of these are not funded (they have no money to repay you now). It may still take years before you receive any of your funds. And state guarantees only kick in when the company goes bankrupt, not when it closes its doors under rehabilitation procedures. The state guarantee promises are comforting, but their ability to respond by returning your investment funds is suspect.

As your agent tools up in his or her fine new Mercedes, ask yourself, "Do I really want to deal with a successful salesperson?" Strange question? Think about it. If they are successful, they are making a lot of commissions. Who is paying their high commissions? The insurance companies they work for. Where are they getting the money to pay those fat commissions? From you.

Low cost protection is still available. But don't expect an agent to voluntarily cut his or her own income when you are so willing to accept less.

While insurance is something no one likes to think about, there are certain risks that are crucial to protect yourself against—and others that could be a big waste of money. Arm yourself with as much knowledge as possible before committing your hard earned dollars.

Chapter 8

Will the real financial planners please stand up?

The financial markets—insurance companies, brokers, bankers and the like—will produce anything they think they can convince you to buy, no matter how risky, how inferior or illogical, with the sure knowledge that you will buy the sales presentation. Effective advertising and marketing blitzes use greed and fear tactics to push your hot buttons, trip your greed triggers and reduce your sales resistance.

With friends like these

If your insurance agent is driving a better car than you can afford, your banker is wearing better clothing and purchasing a more expensive house than you, or your investment advisor is taking more exclusive vacations and sending their children to private school while you are struggling to keep yours in a public university, you are paying them too much.

In order to get ahead in the money game, it is essential for you to know how to play well. You'll learn most of the basics in this book, but I urge you to read, investigate, explore, study, examine and demand as much information as you need to make the best bottom line decision. No matter what happens to your investment capital, the salesperson always receives his or her commission up front. You alone will either enjoy future benefits or suffer investment losses.

Sales pitches that work

There are numerous sales approaches commonly employed to elicit action on the part of a client and a commission check for a salesperson.

1. The expert from afar

It has been said that a prophet is never recognized in his or her own time. Likewise, a financial guru may not be recognized in his or her own neighborhood. By the illusion of distance, however, an otherwise overlooked soothsayer may become more credible. The popularity of investment newsletters from various favorable climates of the country has created a positive net worth for numerous financial advisors and investment counselors who might otherwise not have had the opportunity to send so much advice to so many grateful small investors waiting so faithfully by their mailboxes.

The critical element of such promotions is to publish a fancy, glossy brochure. By filling sentences with words like "safe," "high yields," "simple," "convenient," "ultra-safe," "grow rich," "cautious," "recession proof," "urgent," and "low risk," they can appeal to a broad base of uninitiated investors, who feel only a fool or a speculator would go it alone when for just a few dollars they could make millions safely, without leaving the recliner.

The similarity between these and a carnival barker's spiel about the incredible shrinking man is striking, but these ads must work or intelligent marketers would not use them.

2. The credibility builder

This next approach is harder to spot. If you listen carefully, you may hear one or more of the following phrases designed to reel you in:

1. "If I had lied to my clients, I wouldn't have any."
2. "Here is a list of satisfied clients."
3. "This is exactly what your deceased spouse would have wanted you to do with the insurance money."
4. "You must buy this! I wouldn't forgive myself if I left here and something happened to you and you weren't covered."
5. "We have five jillion dollars under management."
6. "Our company is older, therefore, solid and more reliable."
7. "That's right, we do it all. We have the best of everything."
8. "I'm really a financial planner."
9. "You've got to trust me on this one."

3. The strategist

Then there are the schmoozers who could sell time-shares in the Bermuda Triangle. They are good. They are very good. They work primarily on emotional appeals and finding your "hot button." The following represents just a portion of their repertoire:

1. "Safe as money in the bank." (Appropriate question to ask: "In which country?")
2. "Fifteen percent! Guaranteed! Honest!"
3. "First, tell me what you want so that I can tell you we have it."
4. "You want income? You'll have income coming out of your ears."
5. "This is really hot now."
6. "This nursing home policy covers it all."

7. "You better buy it now before it goes even higher."
8. "Don't worry, I can get you insured for anything."
9. "This is how the rich make their money."
10. "I would sell this to my mother." (Probably true.)

4. Selling the greed motive

These are easy to spot unless you are deceived into chasing high yields and exorbitant returns without understanding that these come only at increased risk:

1. "We'll pay you 10 percent on your money [really on what's left after we carve out our share]."
2. "Need short term money storage at higher yield? This is it, and perfectly safe."
3. "Look how rich you'll be!"
4. "Of course, it's not cheap. You get what you pay for."
5. "This is perfect for you."
6. "This is a lot better than what I sold you last year."

5. The objection-overcomer

You may want to take your time to research investment alternatives, but the good salesperson knows that if he or she can't sell on the closing call, there is a good chance that the sale will never be made. There are only so many arguments against purchasing any product or service, and the objection-overcomer has a rebuttal for them all:

1. "Take my word for it, your accountant will love this."
2. "I thought you were the decision-maker in your family, Mr. Prospect."
3. "Why compare? You'll only waste time and buy this anyway."
4. "Read the prospectus first? You won't understand it. Just listen to me."
5. "Pay no attention to this complicated contract. I'll tell you everything important in it."
6. "Don't bother to shop around. No one else would insure you."
7. "Your attorney doesn't understand complex investments." (That could be true. Even professionals buy the sizzle instead of the steak.)

6. The tax expert

These magic phrases—"tax deductible, tax deferred, and tax free"—have produced sales to customers who didn't care whether their investments were in pygmy bonds, goldfish breeding or basket weaving...just as long as Uncle Sam didn't get their money.

Tax-advantaged products are often marketed to disguise otherwise inferior investment products. Beware the salesperson who touts these above all other benefits:

1. "This will sure fool the tax man."
2. "The tax man cometh, and leaveth empty handed."
3. "This tax shelter is so shrewd that even the government doesn't know about it."

7. The closer

Since sales are mainly created by aggressive and assertive efforts, a good salesperson understands that pressure and intimidation may work even if nothing else has. Defend yourself against the "hard sell," even if it means doing some intimidating yourself.

1. "I really must know today."
2. "The price is going up tomorrow."
3. "I can't come back."
4. "Why don't we just wrap this up tonight?"
5. "If I knock down the price right now, will you take it?"
6. "If you give this up, you'll be making a terrible mistake."
7. "Even if you sign tonight, you can always cancel it later. It's just an offer to purchase."

All of the preceding are direct quotes. I am sure you could add even more creative (or more abhorrent) examples to the list. These are perhaps the most dangerous sales pitches of all:

1. "I can't think of a single thing wrong with this investment."
2. "Just sign here. I'll finish this application at the office."
3. "Don't tell the company I am doing you this favor."
4. "You'll never regret this."
5. "This is safe."
6. "This is guaranteed."
7. "Trust me."
8. "This is so complicated, you'll never understand it."
9. "We are the experts."
10. "We're so big, we have to be good."
11. "You know us [from the advertising]."
12. "You have better things to do with your time—let us watch your money."
13. "Our reputation is spotless."
14. "You can't get out now. You'll lose too much money."

The thrusts of selling financial products depends upon greed and fear. Many in the financial services industry spend more time in seminars learning to close a sale than learning to utilize their investment products properly and appropriately. Sales pitches work because they appeal to basic instincts. Naiveté, gullibility, greed, laziness and fear can leave you caught in a psychological trap or lead you down a path of illogical thinking.

Money may calm the nerves but it also attracts the vultures. Beware of those calling themselves financial advisors, investment counselors or other fancy business card titles. If these money "experts" were so good, they would be buying securities, not selling you advice and products.

In this chapter you will learn how to separate your financial friends from the "other guys."

Anyone reading this book could call themselves a financial planner. There is little regulation on the industry and few methods of policing activities and separating the "advisors" from the real "advisors."

In many states, a salesperson could flip hamburgers on Monday, then hang up a "financial planner" sign on a rented office on Tuesday.

Yet, financial planning is not selling products and pitching dramatic sales presentations. It's not dubious promises of safety, high returns, tax relief and "guarantees." Financial planning is the process of educating clients, teaching fundamental skills to put consumers in charge of their own financial futures.

If you are being shown shiny brochures of financial products as a substitute for real financial planning, you are working with a product vendor, not a real financial planner. Real financial planners come with *real* credentials and help you solve *real* financial dilemmas and challenges.

Money magazines

Everyone wants to be your investment advisor. Monthly consumer magazines, newsletters and other kindly strangers want you to become rich. For just a small monthly fee, you can benefit from their experience—so they say. Next time you pick up one of these publications (don't buy it, just pick it up) notice the actual credentials the advisors possess. Chances are, they have none!

Would you let a stranger who had never attended medical school perform heart surgery on your precious ticking machine? Then why would you follow like a rock band groupie hoards of wizards with no real education in their field? Media journalists and freelancers, not expert money managers, write investment articles. Three months ago they may have written for a wine-and-dine magazine, a clothing fashion rag or a special interest lobby group to bring back the passenger pigeon.

If these publications are the experts, why do they suggest different investments, differing strategies and their own brands of money management advice? And if they are so adept, why are they firmly entrenched in the business of publishing?

How do such publications make profit margins? Not by investing in the companies they lure you to. They sell full page, full colored advertisements paid by the companies they discuss in their (unbiased?) articles. They also gain revenue from your subscription fees.

Look at their front page teasers:

> "Turn $10,000 into $20,000 in five years."
>
> "The top 15 mutual funds right inside!"
>
> "Put convenience into your life—use us instead of your brain!"
>
> "Retire at age 35 and live long enough to tell about it in next year's issue."

Save your money on those publications and newsletters that major in tomorrow's investment winners, and purchase only the ones with solid, fundamental basic money management advice.

Meet the public's financial advisors

Numerous surveys have been conducted to determine where consumers solicit investment and money management advice. The response percentages differ, but the same professions invariably make the list as credible money experts—even though, for the most part, their specialties are totally unrelated to investing and money management. Here are the groups that most people traditionally go to for investment and money advice:

Doctors. All too many people believe that physicians are great investment pickers (and that they are becoming even richer by overcharging patients, whose money they immediately wire to their brokers to make even more money). The truth is that many doctors take little time to actively manage their own financial lives.

Medical school never did, and hopefully never will, offer courses on financial planning or investment strategies and techniques. I, for one, heartily endorse the tradition that the entire curricula of pre-med, medical school, residency and specializing continue to concentrate 100 percent on my body parts (and how to repair them) rather than on a significant number of courses dealing with modern portfolio management analysis.

Lawyers. Let me state emphatically and conclusively that some of the most admired professionals I interact with in my practice are lawyers. Additionally, I know how cheaply you attorneys can sue when offended. Thirdly, I had nothing to do with any lawyer jokes ever perpetuated and don't even pass those jokes on to others when they are really funny. (Like the one when the lawyers were out playing golf and...)

Attorneys are, by nature (and seven expensive years of college tuition) profound individuals who spend a lot of time prefacing every response with, "Although I am not qualified to speak directly on this issue, in the case of ..." I know this because I raised one.

It's easy to understand why consumers would believe that attorneys can think and talk their way in, out and around anything, even bad investments. If you were a salesperson, would you sell F. Lee Bailey something that could possibly head south?

Some attorneys, after wrestling an opposing side into a large settlement or extracting a favorable verdict, may feel they also owe some responsibility to a client for directing any recently awarded tangible assets. Some clients foster this dependency by showing concern (fear, terror, paralysis) at the thought of taking so much money home in a paper sack and being responsible for its prudent management.

In the world of business, there is a term called "reciprocity," better known to us common folks as "You scratch my back, and I'll scratch yours." So if an attorney recommends a certain individual to assist you in making your investment decisions, gratefully decline any such offer and actively conduct your own interviews and research to find competent financial advisors.

Bankers. In case you mistakenly believe you will escape selling pressures and uninvited advances when depositing your money into a lending institution, you have missed the wildest ride savings and loans have taken since the Depression and the recent bank investment specialist phenomenon.

Bank deposit insurance (FDIC), plus fear of investment losses, keep money in banks. With today's mediocre CD and savings account rates, many banking customers are voting with their feet and pocketbooks.

Lenders are as desperate for your deposit and investment dollars as any other financial product vendor. The only reason they don't greet you on your front porch at 6 a.m. is their image. How would it look for your neighborhood lender to stand in line behind the insurance agent waiting to see you, tongue out, panting in anticipation and anxiety? Do you think your neighbors would feel comfortable leaving their hard earned cash in such a bank?

No, your lender has to be content to wait around the branch office and nervously pace through the corridors in hopes of spotting you on your way to the teller window. He or she may spontaneously engage in idle conversation about the weather, your soon-to-mature CDs, your health, his special on interest rates, how clever your poodle looks in ribbons, the bank's latest hot investment, when the two of you should do lunch (and sign some papers).

Accountants. The ability to read and understand year-end corporate financial statements, sort out all the important plus-and-minus figures, and spew out meaningful conclusions has always amazed and impressed me.

I have worked with a number of accountants over the years. Some are brilliant. Then there are some who call me annually to ask why I suggested that their clients purchase a nondeductible IRA. (These live by a simple oath: If you can't deduct it, you don't want it.) We expect accountants to be knowledgeable enough to deal expertly with all financial aspects in addition to understanding basic accounting procedures.

A perfectly admirable tax maneuver may turn into a future disaster if tax planning is not viewed by the light of more important issues: the length of time for your investing policy and your choice of the finest investments available.

Planning primarily for tax reduction may destroy your primary goals and the real focus of your investment planning.

Beware of "tax advisors" who solicit you with annuities or other investment products when they do your annual tax returns. For the most part, they are sales vendors using a more credible profession to camouflage their motives. "Tax advisor" is as misused a label as "financial planner."

Consider your accountant as a vital part of your financial team and as a reserve against IRS onslaughts, not your ear on the investment world.

Real estate agents. The real estate industry makes money only when you purchase property and buildings.

Can you think of any reason that a realtor would advise you against buying your dream house? Neither can I. So don't expect the traditional realtor or real estate agent to distract you with other investment options such as CDs, insurance products or mutual funds.

Stockbrokers. Today's stockbroker (more properly called a registered representative) has a greater variety of investment options for your pocketbook. In fact, you name it and he or she probably has (or can get) it. An accurate slogan for most brokerages might be: "If you want it, we'll hunt it down, create it, develop it, strip it, dissect it, introduce it, disguise it or imagine it."

The stockbroker's primary job is to generate $350,000 of gross brokerage commissions or next year she or he won't be dialing for dollars with the same company.

Your parents. It's easy to assess the quality of financial advice you receive from your parents without even broaching the subject of money. If they seem financially well endowed—they're able to travel often, have a comfortable retirement lifestyle and maintain a well diversified portfolio of CDs, money market funds, mutual funds, quality stocks or bonds, and even a piece or two of investment property—listen to whatever they say. They understand how money works.

If, however, there are constant squabbles about paying bills, worries that they will live long enough to outlive their assets and concerns about health care costs, take their advice with the proverbial grain of salt. If they receive most of their monthly income from fixed-income vehicles such as Social Security, pension annuities, bank interest and monthly insurance checks, their boat has sailed without them. The power of time has vanished, and their dreams and goals have turned to fear.

If you follow the path of these traditions, you cannot expect any more comfortable financial future. Seniors primarily purchased three so-called investments: 1) they bought a home; 2) they loaned their savings to banks at lower-than-inflation rates; and 3) they loaned the remainder of their savings to insurance companies, who paid them even lower rates of return and had the use of their money for decades. How well have these institutions served today's retirees? I rest my case.

Insurance agents: Suppose you are planning to invest $10,000 into an investment, and I presented you with a computer-generated printout showing what your account would be worth in 20 years. Ridiculous? Yet that's exactly how death insurance is sold today.

The most effective weapon in an insurance agent's arsenal is the infamous illustration or policy ledger sheet. It supposedly predicts how an insurance policy's cash values and death benefit will grow over time. These "dream sheets" are far from the truth, and nothing obligates the insurer to deliver on these projections, while almost nothing inhibits the imagination of the agent creating these hypothetical future returns.

Deceptive selling, churning (inducing the replacement of an old policy to receive commissions) and misleading sales literature proliferate in the industry today. Actual contracts often vary from the verbal promises, and with today's declining interest rates, some life insurance policies are currently self-destructing without their owner's knowledge.

Reread my insurance chapter before doing battle against a hungry agent facing the financial challenges of a new car, vacation funding, house payments and retirement savings. Faced with a choice between your welfare and their own pocketbook, you already know the rest of the story.

Pappa Government: Don't depend on the government grasping the reins for long range financial directives. With a reelection facing every official, the last thing a politician worth reelecting would advise you to do right now is to stop your consuming, to stop spending and to increase your savings habits. Furrowed political foreheads have *spend, spend, spend* written all over them.

Which politician wants to freely discuss the future of Social Security and who must tighten his or her financial belt so that others can receive benefits?

Someone has to keep this hamster wheel of currency revolving through the economy. So it might as well be you, the average consumer. Call it default planning or short term political expediency, sporadic sanity and spontaneous spurts of thinking are all we can look toward. If your budget were in the red as consistently as the national balance sheet, you would have been forced to declare bankruptcy long ago!

Who's minding your money?

Registered Investment Advisor is a term with little true meaning. It merely signifies that the person (or his or her firm) has registered in Washington, D.C., with the Securities and Exchange Commission (SEC) as an investment advisor. In other words, you pay your money, you sign up and you can use the label.

This title does not connote the completion of any course work or the passing of any exams in the financial planning field.

If you find that you have been damaged by someone using this title, you can complain to the SEC. But it is very difficult to prove deception or fraud, especially when the hand of greed (yours) signed the application 23 times, acknowledging you had read the prospectus with the word "risk" printed in bold type in 147 places.

There are several trade industry organizations who police their own members and require certain standards of practice. Most cannot levy penalties such as prison, but they can isolate the "bad apples" by censuring certain members from doing business with the rest of the industry.

One such group is the National Association of Securities Dealers (NASD). It can also handle your customer complaints regarding one of its members, and has the power to investigate alleged consumer violations of fraud or deceptive practices. It regulates brokerages, their employees and sales forces.

Brokerages are ordered by both the SEC and the NASD to adhere to compliance standards as agreed to by the industry. You can also complain to the SEC directly on any matter of economic loss or some alleged deception under the general securities category. But don't bother complaining to them because you can only understand the title page of your investment prospectus.

Prospectuses are regulated by the SEC and followed through by the NASD, and it would take more than an act of Congress to convince either group to change them into simple language that anyone could read and understand. Just keep struggling through those prospectuses. Someone, somewhere, must know what they mean.

You can call the NASD to check on a financial advisor's background and any past violations.

On top of these layers of regulation, there may be state security departments. They are usually very busy because they are all located in urban districts where there are few good parking spots. So employees spend much of their working hours running to the parking meters with change. Use them only for backup; they are very tired.

Since states enact their own securities laws for sales occurring within their boundaries, some have more rigorous rules than others. Some states require competency or state registration testing for financial advisors. Some just want to know if the advisors are still breathing and can sign registration slips. And some leave you and your advisor alone, believing you don't want to be disturbed at a crucial point in the sales presentation.

Alphabet soup

A *Certified Financial Planner* (CFP) has taken courses and completed exams in six major areas: risk management, comprehensive planning, tax planning, asset allocation, retirement planning and estate planning. After progressing through these courses, the candidate must generally pass a two-day comprehensive examination before he or she can use the credentials and the title.

This curriculum is taught and administered by the College for Financial Planning in Denver, Colorado. The public can check on a financial planner's credentials from an active list of those still in good standing and of those whose standing has gone into the toilet.

The International Board of Standards and Practices for Certified Financial Planners (IBCFP), in Denver, regulates all the Certified Financial Planners, who now have to pay annual dues. The IBCFP expects its members to adhere to a code of ethics and disclosure practices. It regulates its members and can exclude any wrongdoers from its membership and publicize their name with a nasty article in every paper they subscribe to.

The *Chartered Financial Analyst* (CFA) concentrates on portfolio management and securities selection analysis. The certification is awarded by the Institute of Chartered Financial Analysts in Charlottesville, Virginia for passing exams in economics, financial accounting, portfolio management, securities analysis, and standards of conduct.

The *Certified Employee Benefits Specialist* (CEBS) designation is offered jointly by the International Foundation of Employee Benefit Plans and the Wharton School, University of Pennsylvania. It normally takes five years to complete and covers the comprehensive format of employee benefits, often leading to a separate career as a benefit specialist in the public or private sectors. Ten courses and their examinations must be successfully completed.

The *Accredited Personal Financial Specialist* (APFS) mandates that candidates hold a Certified Public Accounting (CPA) degree and spend 250 hours annually in personal financial planning for three years preceding the compulsory six-hour exam. The supporting organization is the American Institute of Certified Public Accountants (AICPA), New York City.

The National Association of Personal Financial Advisors (NAPFA) has recently adopted tougher membership standards. The parent organization, located in Grove, Illinois, now requires that a member be primarily engaged in comprehensive financial planning, have a bachelor's degree and additional credits in specific course areas and offer advice on a fee-only basis.

A *Chartered Life Underwriter* (CLU) is the designation for an insurance agent who has completed six subjects and passed various insurance specialties exams. Don't confuse insurance agents with financial planners. Conferred by The American College in Bryn Mawr, Pennsylvania, insurance agents who have earned this designation know everything about how an insurance product might creatively fit into your financial life, while planners concentrate on the planning process, which should always come before any product.

The title of *Chartered Financial Consultant* (ChFC) can be earned by passing the CLU courses and then progressing through four more successful exams in related financial planning areas. Although not as well known as the CFP, this mark is considered a financial planning credential. Be careful: With such a heavy insurance background, a ChFC may not look at your financial life from a total planning perspective; there are far more solutions to financial challenges than insurance products.

Certified Fund Specialist (CFS) is the designation awarded by the Institute of Certified Fund Specialists, La Jolla, California, after completion of study and a national examination regarding mutual funds. This rigorous course separates the generalists from those who have chosen to gain greater expertise in the mutual fund arena. They must upgrade their knowledge annually as well.

Today's mutual funds are more integral to the average client's portfolio than ever before. Merely passing an examination to sell them does not provide enough training, given the popularity and number of options to choose from. If possible, find someone who has added this in-depth educational area to his or her résumé.

Continuing Education Credits (CEUs) are ongoing annual units of additional education course work required to keep some certifications, and recommended by all industry trade organizations. Maintaining the most current information in such changing areas as investments and tax law brings greater expertise to you, the consumer. You should request a recent list of CEUs from any financial planner you interview.

Registered Financial Planner (RFP) is offered by a trade organization in Ohio whose only membership requirement is the paying of dues. There are no educational credential requirements, so this mark should not be looked on as anything more than membership within an industry group.

The International Association of Financial Planning (IAFP) is another trade organization, in Atlanta, Georgia, whose membership consists of financial planners, accountants, insurance agents and companies that create and distribute financial products. Membership is open on an annual dues basis.

I urge you to request and examine the credentials of anyone you may consider assisting you in making investments or planning your financial future. We are talking here about an issue as important as brain surgery—your money. If you were diagnosed with a brain tumor that demanded immediate surgery, would you search for a doctor with specialized credentials and a résumé a mile long or for someone without an M.D. who volunteered to operate on you because he or she had a lot of experience around the operating room?

What's this about *paying* planners?

Planners may charge by the hour, by the project or by a combination of fees and commissions from investment products they may recommend. More important than the method by which they are paid, is the quality of their advice and your involvement in all aspects of the financial "plan."

You can receive all the free advice in the world with one call to any financial supermarket, insurance company or lending institution, all of whom have vested interests in where you will put your money. When you buy something for a song, watch out for the accompaniment.

You need to know the whole truth about your money, not what is popular or profitable to someone else. In order to receive objective and unbiased money management information, you may want to pay for it on the same basis that you pay for the services of other professionals.

Looking beyond the résumé

The more credentials an investment professional may possess, the more facts and knowledge in a given area he or she has at his or her disposal to assist you with your financial goals and objectives. But I have known some highly educated individuals who could not think their way out of a paper bag. So memorizing facts and regurgitating them at exam times will not guarantee an ability to organize and analyze your problems or skillfully assemble the various sectors of your financial life into a tight fitting plan, custom designed for you. Even with impressive credentials, there is no guarantee of clinical competence.

Real financial planners do not promote investment products at the first meeting and do not hype you with marketing gimmicks like "tax free," "tax deferred" and "tax deductible." They don't present you with programs that disguise the basic investment vehicles.

A real financial planner cares personally about your welfare, not just where the rubber hits the road (the pen hits the check). If any money advisor seems more intent on showing you product solutions to your problems than assembling the various pieces of your financial life, find one who cares more about your financial health than about his or her fees or commissions.

Put prospective planners to the test

One way to find the best financial planner for you is to interview several. In addition to looking for intangible signs (a "gut" feeling that you're dealing with someone who'd sell you oceanfront property in Arizona), look for positive responses to these questions:

- Does the planner put you in charge?
- Does he or she reveal the inherent disadvantages in all financial products?
- Does the advisor disclose all fees and charges (even the hidden ones)?
- Does he or she encourage you to read and discuss all documents or prospectuses?
- Does this individual volunteer specimen contracts to look over at your leisure?
- Are you gaining helpful information instead of hearing just a sales pitch?
- Is the advice appropriate for your total financial picture?
- Does the planner recommend products other than proprietary ones (ones that only their company sells)?
- Do you feel comfortable with this person?

There are several major areas that a planner should investigate and analyze, whether you are paying a fee or not:

Will the real financial planners please stand up?

1. Risk management: auto, liability, health, disability, homeowner's and death insurance considerations.
2. Current status: your cash flow (expenditures) and your statement of financial position (assets, liabilities and net worth).
3. Short term and long term goals, including college and/or retirement.
4. Current tax status and general tax planning.
5. Asset allocation: your portfolio mix and appropriate investment options, including estimates of Social Security and pension retirement benefits.
6. Estate planning: wills, powers of attorney, trusts, ownership titles and beneficiaries on assets.

Real financial planners come in all shapes, sizes and educational backgrounds. But they present similar themes and are committed to fiscal fitness and high ethical standards.

A good financial planner won't let you:

1. Borrow more credit card debt than you can really afford.
2. Avoid putting money into an emergency fund, even though it is only a few dollars each month.
3. Buy a house with more than a 15-year or 20-year mortgage.
4. Buy a car for longer than 36 months.
5. Forget that either you work your money or someone else gladly will.
6. Buy into the philosophy of living today and forgetting tomorrow.
7. Forget that the government cannot prepare for your retirement; that responsibility is primarily up to you.
8. Believe that a nondeductible IRA isn't worth the extra trouble.
9. Throw some money at your goals, cross your fingers and hope for a happy financial return.
10. Depend on winning the lottery to solve future financial challenges.
11. Forget that "time is money." (The time value of money concept is top priority for others who want to work your money for their benefit.)
12. Ignore the reality that inflation is the deadliest, long term money killer.
13. Convince yourself that you can spend more than you make.
14. Wait another year to take action and put yourself in charge of your own financial destiny.
15. Deceive yourself into believing things will automatically get better.
16. Believe in the words "safe" and "guaranteed."
17. Believe in a perfect investment.
18. Take action on financial matters until you've examined all options.
19. Do business with anyone before reading and understanding the written contracts and the fine print.

20. Accomplish the above alone. (He or she is willing to assist your research but wants you to remain in charge of your basic financial decisions.)
21. Forget that on the road to financial success, where you are now is not nearly as important as on which road you are traveling.

Chapter 9

Home is where your money pit is

There are few subjects that evoke as much emotion and patriotic defense as the concept of owning a home, the cornerstone of the American dream. Home ownership has come to symbolize an American birthright and invariably represents the largest single purchase most of us will ever make.

Let me tell you a story:

There once lived a fox whose fur was full and luxurious, most notably on his fine russet tail. He was secretly admired by all of the other wildlife, especially for his tail. Over time, the fox became vain and self-impressed.

One day, while preening along a riverbank, he lost his footing and slipped down the bank, barely missing a large muskrat trap set by a hunter. Only his tail was caught. He sighed, greatly relieved that he had not been mortally wounded.

But as nightfall approached, the weather grew cold and the fox, still shackled by his trapped tail, began to worry about freeing himself. Try as he might, he could not get his tail out of the trap's gripping claws. The river grew colder, ice formed on its surface, and the fox's beautiful tail was frozen into the river.

The fox examined his options, lamenting that to save his life, he would have to lose his beautiful tail. A sad but determined survivor of nature, he broke off the frozen tail and fled back to his forest home.

When the other forest creatures saw his injury, they were at first bewildered. Since the fox had said nothing, they whispered among themselves until a rabbit finally asked the fox what happened. Embittered by his loss, the fox spoke up defensively.

"Nonsense!" he exclaimed. "This new look is my own invention, and a clever one too. It will be cooler in the summer, cleaner and lighter to carry around with me and will allow me to run faster. Mark my words—it will soon be the fashion in the forests around us."

As the animals circled the fox, little by little they began to appreciate the improvements the fox described. Eventually, all the creatures of the forest cut off their tails so they, too, could benefit in the obvious ways the fox had.

The moral of this story: Whether you are purchasing a home, a melon at your grocery store or a used car, the sale may depend on the quality of the sales pitch, not on what the product or item is worth in real benefits.

Real estate reality

Say good-bye to the notion that houses always beat inflation, that they are risk free investments and that they should be the first investment on your list.

Whether you should own a home or rent an attractive appliance carton for the next 20 years is not the issue. You should not believe the bunk you have been fed by the foxes of the world. Buying your personal residence is *not* the wisest investment you will ever make. Buying a home is a lifestyle decision.

Seize the day!

When is the best time to buy a new home? Just ask a real estate agent, broker or lending institution: *right now*. This very minute. Don't even wait until after breakfast. If interest rates are low, buy before they go *up*. If rates are soaring, buy now before they go *higher*. Can't afford a reasonable down payment? Don't worry. That's what creative financing, PMI, and government subsidies are *for*.

Don't know how long you will stay in an area? Buy that house now and when you move you can take your profits or rent it out and have a monthly income. Can't afford the monthly payments? No problem. Just spread them out over 30 years, giving you *lower* payments that can *easily* be squeezed into that already sagging monthly budget.

Thinking about renting for a while first? Good heavens, you don't get anything *back* when you rent. Look at all of the equity that you could be building up in a home instead of making a landlord rich.

Meet the foxes

The real estate industry makes its money by selling real estate and real estate *only*.

When money comes in one revolving bank door, it must be loaned back out. What can the average American do with loaned money? Why, he or she can buy real estate. So the lender finds its market by perpetuating the virtues of home ownership.

The federal government must find ways of keeping the country expanding and workers employed. The nation's economic health is tied to new and existing housing sales and housing starts. So Uncle Sam also has a vested interest in encouraging you to purchase the American dream.

The building industry turns its product over to the real estate industry, which feeds the banking industry, which turns to the government for guaranteed backing (which the government gets from us).

This cadre benefits even if you purchase too much house for your pocketbook. If lending institutions get stung by bad loans or mismanagement, they will be bailed out by the government, who subsequently taxes us. This keeps the economy flowing.

The government favors the building, real estate and banking industries through clever gambits it plays with the taxpayer, offering tax tidbits to lure homeowners into debt.

Homeowners can have mortgage interest tax deductions, tax-deferred capital gain profits, VA and FHA low down payment programs, GNMA and FNMA guarantees which encourage lenders to loan, guaranteed investor securities via packaged home mortgages, federal home loan programs, investor bond issues, first-time home buyer incentives, rehabilitation low-cost loans, low-cost housing landlord subsidies, senior citizen housing developments, tax deductible home equity loans and plump $250,000 per person tax-free gains every two (2) years even if we purchase a less expensive home.

And this is only *part* of the home industry's agenda designed to keep its bottom lines healthy.

Can you think of a reason why any of the above groups would advise you *not* to buy your dream house? Certainly none that would benefit *them*.

More news from home

The above merchants offer an attractive spiel. With a home, they promise, you can have status, an inflation hedge, tax write-offs, a sound, low risk investment, increased home value through improvements, marketability, the pride of ownership, greater privacy and a proper environment to raise a family. After all, this is the American way.

But compare real estate to a bank CD as an alternative investment. Can you sell your home as fast as you can cash in a CD? Does a personal residence generate monthly or quarterly income? Can you purchase a home as cheaply as a CD? Since most advisors recommend that only one third of your total portfolio contain real estate, do you have an additional 200% in other investments? Or are you over-invested in "home sweet home?"

What about liquidity? Will you be able to retrieve every dollar you sink into your home at sale time? The cost of buying and selling, as well as improvements and maintenance over time, must be subtracted from your eventual profits. If you rent, these expenses are the responsibility of the owner, and you are free to move when you want. The most you can lose is your security deposit.

The costs of borrowed money over the life of the mortgage are not even whispered in hallowed mortgage departments. Have you seen how much of your livelihood you will sacrifice for that $100,000 mortgage? On a conventional 20-year loan, you will fork over *twice* the amount you borrowed. Over 30 years, you will hand out nearly *three times* the original debt. A home would have to double in price every 20 years just to keep even *on that point alone*. For a 30-year loan, you would have to net three times the price you paid. The average home is not appreciating anywhere near that fast.

Examine the low risk investment concept. Does real estate always go up? Some homeowners have suffered major losses by buying at the top of their regional property market. Home equity they were depending on for financial freedom disappeared.

Even if a home appreciates over time, have you considered the expenses of insurance, real estate taxes, assessments, buying and selling costs, improvements and maintenance?

Inflation increases housing prices more than any other element. When inflation is performing wonders on the value of your real estate, it also increases basic costs of living. If inflation increases your home's market value 6 percent a year while living costs escalate at the same rate, you have made no real gains. If inflation moves even higher and your home does not keep pace, you are actually losing ground—your home is really *depreciating* over time, due solely to the decreasing value of money.

Your home is the *largest* investment you will make but generally it won't be one of the top 10 *best* investments you'll ever purchase. It may even rank as the *lousiest*.

I have to live somewhere, don't I?

Some buyers have bought homes at the expense of their emergency funds, their IRA contributions, company pension plans, even their college savings. The family homestead is often the largest asset folks own (along with the lender).

Before you become totally convinced that I am anti-American and don't support private home ownership for individuals, let me explain. If you can afford a Rolls Royce, by all means buy one. If you can spring for a yacht or a mink coat, then reward yourself or your loved ones. If you can afford a home, you should have one to raise your family in.

But to buy the most expensive home you can squeeze into your budget with the conviction that you are pursuing a sophisticated investment and tax strategy is sheer folly.

Whose manure is it, anyway?

There was once a small bird who waited too long to migrate south. When it finally took off, it flew beak first into an ice storm. Nearly frozen to death, it fell from the skies and into a barnyard. As it lay in the pasture, its heart barely beating, a cow passed by and deposited a coating of manure on top of it. This was a final cruel act, it seemed, given the little bird's already poor luck.

But the manure generated heat—warmth that acted like a blanket for the little creature. As the bird was warmed, its heart pumped more blood, the temperature rose throughout its body and it began to recover. It was so happy to be alive it started to sing.

At which point a cat heard the commotion, found the bird and ate it.

The moral: Not everyone who dumps manure on you is your enemy, and not everyone who pulls you out is your friend.

You must learn to separate your real friends from those whose *self*-interest is much stronger than any commitment to work in *your* best interest.

Do you remember the day you closed on your first home? You sat in the lending institution and signed away the next 20 or 30 years of your life as paper after paper was pushed in front of you. How many of those documents did you take the time to read through carefully? Probably none. There was no need. After all, you were deep inside the large and impressive protection of the institution where they kept the "Big Money," with all those professionals helping you, with the real estate agent and your banker cheering you toward the goal line.

Why, this was an everyday, mundane occurrence. There was no need for you to hold up everything at this critical point to read through all those documents you wouldn't have understood anyhow. Why bother to have a lawyer look anything over? *Their* lawyers already had and *they* weren't complaining. Just sign, sign, sign.

Here was the sales and intimidation process at its finest. With so many professionals already "protecting" your interests, it seemed impudent and downright rude to actually ask someone what you were signing and to translate all the words you didn't understand. After all, there were other customers waiting their turns. Maybe you even felt the bank was doing you a *favor* by giving you the money you had so anxiously waited for. If they had this much confidence in you, how could you question their motives?

With hearts pounding, eyes glazed and mouths closed, Americans transact the most expensive purchase of their financial lives in the worst possible emotional condition for clear thinking and evaluation. Perhaps you survived without adverse effect; some home buyers do not.

Let's assume we know an older couple who purchased a home 20 years ago for $25,000 and have just sold it for $75,000. Ignore for the moment the costs of the mortgage, improvements, maintenance, taxes, insurance, closing costs, points and real estate commissions. Also ignore the opportunity costs—where else their money could have been earning for them during that 20-year period. The home never needed painting, nothing ever broke, the tax assessor ignored them, and the bank gave them the mortgage money free.

How much profit did they make? The simple answer is 200 percent over 20 years, and that is what you are encouraged to believe.

Winning the Money Game

But it took 20 years to triple your money. With a compound interest calculator we can calculate that they actually earned 5.647 percent per year on their initial $25,000 investment, approximately the same rate of return as a bank CD. Instead of getting the 8 percent to 9 percent per year they could have earned from a variety of investments—with no extra fees, no hassle, no maintenance, no leaking roof, freedom from weekend lawn chores, liquidity and instant marketability—our couple opted to invest at 5.647 percent...before capital gains taxes.

That's a lot higher return than it should be. Why? Because we specifically exempted all other costs associated with owning a home from those calculations. So let's ask our couple to rejoin the real world and look at what their home really cost them over that 20-year period.

First of all, our couple didn't have $25,000 to invest. They made a 10 percent down payment ($2,500) and borrowed the rest ($22,500) on a 20-year mortgage on which they were charged 9-percent interest.

When they bought the house, they had to pay a 7-percent real estate commission ($1,750) hidden in the price of the house and $2,000 for closing costs and points on their mortgage. The mortgage they signed called for monthly payments of $202.44...for 20 years—$48,585.

While they owned the house, they had to pay property taxes ($600 a year), insurance ($200 a year) and keep the house in reasonable shape ($500 a year). This all cost them $26,000 more over those 20 years.

Finally, when they sold the house for $75,000, they had to pay another 7-percent real estate commission on the proceeds (7 percent of $75,000 = $5,250). There were probably some additional closing costs. But we have left them out of our calculations.

So, including the down payment, insurance, property taxes, minimal maintenance, closing costs and real estate commissions, and the cost of the mortgage money, this couple paid out a total of $86,085 over 20 years. And they walked away from the home sale with $75,000.

Conclusion: They paid out $11,085 more than they sold the house for!

Wait a minute. Real estate is supposed to be a great investment. Aha, I left out tax deduction!

First of all, we were, as I said, kind. We left inflation completely out of the picture, figuring that insurance cost the same when the house was worth $25,000 as when it was worth $75,000, for example. Ditto with property taxes. And we only included minimal maintenance. Over 20 years, you would have to add *some*thing for major repairs, additions, exterior painting, repairing major structural damage or landscaping and improvements that are not salable but improve living quality and comfort. Add in *any* additional outflow of money, including the inflation on insurance, property taxes, etc., and this calculation looks even worse!

Ah, but what *about* home mortgage interest tax write-offs? Let's say that every penny paid out—all $86,085—was fully deductible. And our couple was in the 50% marginal tax bracket.

The result would be tax savings of one half the total amount spent, or ½ x $86,085 = $43,043. Therefore, if our couple sold the house for $75,000, but only spent

$43,043 after taking tax savings into account, they made a net profit of $31,957, or 4.2% compounded over their 20 years of home ownership.

Feeling better?

Not so fast. I have given our mythical couple every benefit, understating expenses, ignoring inflation, offering hefty tax breaks the IRS would cringe at. Agreed? And the result was a $31,957 profit, right?

Instead, assume that our couple rented for the entire 20 years and invested the money they would have put into a house into a variety of vehicles on which they earned 8 percent a year, a modest return (especially considering recent mutual fund and stock market performance numbers). Assume that they could have rented a nice place for $202.44/month—exactly equal to their mortgage payment—not an outrageous assumption when houses were selling for $25,000!

Instead of turning over a $2,500 down payment and $3,750 in closing costs, commissions and points at the very beginning, they took this $6,250 and invested it for 20 years, reinvesting all of the interest earned along the way.

Once a year (at the beginning of the year) for 20 years they took the $1,300 they would have spent on taxes, insurance and maintenance and invested that as well. At the end of the 20-year period, they added the $5,250 they would have paid for real estate commissions to their investment portfolio, though there was no time to earn any interest on those funds!

Meanwhile, their investments returned 8 percent to 9 percent per year and didn't need painting, landscaping or gutter cleaning. What's more, those alternative investments would have been liquid.

By renting and investing the funds ordinarily used to pay those extras that come with home ownership, they would have accumulated $98,631 at the end of 20 years—more than three times as much as they made from owning a house. And that includes our overly generous tax savings figures. By renting, instead of owning, including the loss of $11,085 after the sale, the difference in their pockets would have been $109,716.

I am not suggesting that you rent forever or live in the streets. I want you to understand the absurdity of attempting to pass off the American dream as the wisest investment you can make. Sadly, most people never do the math and don't discover how they have been duped. They continue to buy again and again, each time a bigger home with an accompanying bigger mortgage, right up to the day they retire. Then they wonder where all their money went!

Singing the money pit blues

There is one clear lesson from all of this: If you *do* decide to buy a house, buy the one you *need and can afford,* not the grandest one your banker wants you to fund. *And invest the rest of your money somewhere else.*

You only have so many dollars in your lifetime to make work for you. Mortgage payments are made with after-tax dollars, right out of your take-home paycheck. They never have a chance to work for *you*. If you purchase an $80,000 mortgage and pay the lender a total of $160,000 for it, you have already spent $160,000 of the total you will earn in your lifetime. Since the median yearly take-home pay for today's adult worker is $35,000, you only have, on average, $1.4 million over your working lifetime available for all financial goals. And you've already spent 11.4 percent of it on your house. Other housing costs outlined earlier will sap up many more of those original dollars.

Cheating the taxman!

Even if you are convinced that your home loses a blue ribbon as an investment vehicle, you may feel you have a viable tax shelter, just like the rich, to thwart the taxman. Before you compliment yourself for practically stealing money with the tacit approval of the IRS, let's examine your home as a tax shelter.

Assume you buy a home for $62,500, using a 20-percent down payment ($12,500). You borrow the remaining $50,000 at a 8-percent fixed interest rate for 20 years. Your payments on this mortgage will be approximately $418 a month for 20 years. We'll also assume, for the moment, that you are in the 15-percent marginal tax bracket, so that little of the interest is deductible unless you can add a lot more itemized deductions to Schedule A. Assuming that you found enough deductions to use Schedule A, here's a breakdown of the first and last years of the mortgage:

Year	Effective APR	Payment per Year	Interest	Principal
1	78.9%	$5,019	$3,962	$1,057
20	4.2%	$5,019	$211	$4,808

The first year, $3,962 goes toward interest and $1,057 toward principal (or home equity). So you have a whopping $3,962 in qualified residential interest to deduct off Schedule A of your 1040 tax form. A 15-percent tax bracket means that each dollar in deductions is worth 15 cents (15 percent of a dollar) in actual tax savings. That means you have saved $594 in income taxes. Sounds great, right? You sure showed old Uncle Sam.

But you *paid* $3,962 in interest to get that $594 in tax relief. There is an extra $3,368 still left. That is money you paid out of your pocket and wasted on interest. For some reason, people think this part disappears. It doesn't, and it is "money out the window" unless the appreciation of the home makes up for it.

In a 28-percent tax bracket, the interest paid gives you $1,109 in actual tax savings, but $2,853 of *that* interest payment is money down the drain. Yes, you get to deduct *all* the interest, but you only get 28 percent back on your tax return. The other 72 percent of interest is "lost." Though residential interest is 100-percent deductible, that concept is misleading because a tax deduction is not the same as a tax credit. You only get to deduct part of the interest—a 15-percent or 28-percent tax write-off. It sure sounded better the other way.

Does it make sense to borrow a dollar of debt so you can deduct 28 cents of it off your taxes? The other 72 cents goes to the bank with no benefit to you.

If you have done your own taxes lately, you will notice that Schedule A is getting skinnier each year. The only significant benefits remaining are residential real estate interest and real estate property taxes.

Did you take the Schedule A total this year or just the standard deduction? If you spent more than the standard deduction in itemized deductions, you deducted your write-offs from Schedule A. But, instead, you had to forgo the standard deduction that any renter could deduct.....without spending a dime in mortgage interest. In other words, you had to give up the "freebie" money Congress offered you in order to qualify for the deductions (write-offs) on Schedule A.

How valuable was your home interest when it cost you the free standard deduction to get onto Schedule A? Unless you own a mammoth mortgage or had enormous debt levels or catastrophic medical expenses, you may have taken the standard deduction, after turning somersaults for a few hours trying to come up with more deductions. If you itemized, you lost the standard deduction, so your home interest *cost* you that money. If you gave up and finally took the standard deduction, you lost *all* of the value of your home interest—the whole 100 percent, not just the 85 percent (in the 15% tax bracket) or 72 percent (in the 28% tax bracket) from the tax calculations.

For those of you with monthly mortgage payments that rival the national debt—how have you won? That high mortgage debt is going to cost you dearly over time. An $800 monthly mortgage payment over 20 years amounts to $192,000 of your take-home dollars. Can you really afford to devote that much to one financial goal when you have college, living expenses and retirement still to come?

Over the years, more and more of each payment is applied to principal and less and less goes toward interest. Therefore, you have less and less each year to use as an itemized deduction. However, as the years unfold, you are probably getting *more* successful and earning *more* money. You may have moved up to the 28-percent or, because more of your monthly payments are now principal, an even higher marginal tax bracket. *But as you pay off your mortgage, you have less interest to claim than when you were in a lower tax bracket.*

If a tax shelter was attractive to you when you were in the 15-percent or 28-percent tax bracket, it should be even more vital when you move up the tax ladder. Instead, you are moving in the opposite direction. You created a dilly of a tax loss when you were in a lower tax bracket. Now when you *need* greater tax relief, you have less and less interest to deduct! In other words, you created a tax shelter when you needed it *least*. You didn't cheat Uncle Sam after all; you have literally *helped the IRS*, bless your heart.

I'll just churn that old house

Maybe you figure to beat this losing game by buying and selling homes more frequently, every five or 10 years. That way you are always deeply in debt, purchasing a more expensive house each time.

If you ever looked at a loan spread sheet and saw the actual percentage of money credited toward principal during the first few years, you would be in danger of cardiac arrest. As we saw earlier, the actual percentage of interest to principal in the first year of a 20-year loan is 78.9 percent! And you thought you got your loan for 7 percent or 8 percent. A loan shark might give you a better deal in the first few years of a mortgage.

Now do you understand why the lender gave you the original mortgage money? It wasn't a favor, after all.

The glory days of the 1970s and 1980s are gone, and so is the surging demand that inflated housing prices. Implement winning money game strategies to protect *all* your total future goals when you buy, improve or sell a home.

The Greater Fool theory states that even though you purchased an overpriced commodity, there is a greater fool out there somewhere who will buy it from you at a profit.

You may not be able to find a fool greater than the one whose shoes *you* are wearing.

What about pride of ownership?

That's one thing that you can't itemize in a column of numbers. But that intrinsic lifestyle value comes with an awfully large price tag. Buy the home you *need*, not the biggest and best that your mortgage lender or piggy banker qualifies you for. Then *invest the rest of your precious dollars somewhere else.*

How much home can you afford?

How much should you spend on a home so that you can give your family a nice place to live in a safe neighborhood with good schools?

Look at the take-home pay figure on your budget, multiply it by 22 percent, and subtract expected costs for real estate taxes, PMI, and homeowner insurance. That answer is the monthly mortgage payment you can afford without sacrificing other financial objectives. A 15- or 20-year loan is the longest sensible loan period. Only serious criminals should get 30-year sentences.

Determine the type of loan that's best for you—fixed rate or adjustable. Adjustable rates have an attractive low initial rate but can increase substantially if you remain in your home for many years. In general, the longer you intend to live in your new home, the more important a fixed payment may become.

Have your lender print out the highest interest rate scenario that your contract can charge, so you can see the effects that rising interest rates might have on your family's bottom line. Ask about the cap (maximum payment) that the adjustable rate mortgage (ARM) can climb to over the life of your mortgage.

That ARM may ultimately cost you an arm (**and a leg**) if future payments increase after a number of years. Generally speaking, it's best to get a fixed interest mortgage.

To win the money game you must divest yourself of as much risk as possible. ARMs are created so that the customer, not the lender, becomes responsible for the risk of future rising interest rates. Since time is the biggest risk of all on your money, forfeit this risk to your lender and opt for a fixed interest rate.

When shopping for your piece of Mother Earth, it is vital to pre-qualify for borrowed money. Walking into must-sell situations (due to bankruptcy, divorce, relocation, death, etc.), you will have additional leverage if the owner knows you are someone who can take the house off his or her hands quickly, without the time and uncertainty involved in the mortgage approval process.

But before shopping, prepare to defend your pocketbook against lenders and real estate agents which may encourage you to purchase "too much house." Whatever their arguments, you must stoically resist, insisting that you have only "X" dollars per month to spend for your mortgage, taxes and insurance (based on your 22-percent budget figure).

Then, keep in mind the three major rules of purchasing real estate: 1) location; 2) location; and 3) location. Look for one of the least expensive homes in the best neighborhood you can afford.

Playing hard to get

You are no more expected to pay the list price for a house than you are to pay the sticker price for a new car. Don't be afraid to put in a low bid. Do you care if you hurt the owner's feelings?

The most expensive financial blunder you can be talked into by mortgage lenders and the real estate industry is purchasing too much home.

When these institutions assure you that your dream house is affordable and you "owe it to yourself," remind yourself who will pay each monthly mortgage payment and of the other goals you may be sacrificing by tackling a treacherous pile of debt.

Checkbook clutched in hand, the average home buyer sets out to negotiate the largest purchase of his or her life with as many effective tools and defenses as David carried on his way to meet Goliath...minus the slingshot.

Bewitched, bothered and bewildered

Purchasing a home is a highly charged and emotional experience milked for all it's worth by each group that will benefit from it. The average couple approaches this journey without suspicion and in a backwards manner.

They search for a home with an agent, whose commission is paid by the *seller*. They qualify with a lending institution whose mission is to loan out money...for a profit. And they often fall in love with the most expensive home they are shown (which benefits all of the above except the buyer).

Only then do they feverishly attempt to figure out how to pay for it.

A smart seller will host an open house that bears a striking resemblance to a major revivalist tent show, with fresh flowers in every room, no sign of children and their respective messes (they are usually sent to the neighbors' to demolish *their* home for a few hours) and brownies baking in the oven. No human can resist this much temptation. And the agent is encouraging your euphoria.

You know the feeling—you are being reeled in like a fish and don't know how to break the line. If you're ready to purchase a home and sign your life away on the bottom line for the next 20 or even 30 years, you need an approach to insulate you from these common sales tactics.

The appropriate place to start purchasing a home is at your kitchen table, with the family budget in hand. Look at the budget formula I proposed. You were advised to keep your mortgage payments plus real estate taxes and homeowner insurance under 22 percent (22%) of your monthly take-home pay.

Now proceed with caution.

"Why do you want so little?"

Visit your favorite lending institution, preferably with a 20-percent down payment in hand, and pre-qualify for a loan on a 15-year or 20-year mortgage only (*not* on its 30-year indentured servant plan) with affordable monthly payments, using your budget as a guide. The lender will likely assure you that because of your splendid credit record and secure employment, you could have a *much* bigger pile of money to take home with you. Just *ask*.

At this point you must clear your head. In addition to your new home, you also need an emergency fund, a college fund, food, furniture, cars, clothes, and the money to fund a comfortable retirement. Your lender, on the other hand, *wants you to buy the biggest house you can qualify for*. He or she is *not* thinking about your emergency fund, college for your kids or your retirement.

If you stick to your budget guns, this may not be a fun session for your lender. You may notice a series of scowls across his or her forehead when they can't talk you into a bigger pot of gold. Don't let that bother you. The lender will recover within the hour—as soon as a more willing (and pliable) buyer walks through the door.

Two major points should be added. If your lending institution attempts to make you feel like pond scum for asking about points, rate caps, maximum rates and what those rates will be based on, you are in the wrong institution. These terms (and their explanations!) can be so confusing that you must make sure you fully understand all of your options. Have the loan officer run several options on paper for your examination. And you will want to talk to more than one lender.

If you are planning to live in a home for only a few years, you should reconsider whether you should even be buying a house. There will be too little time to develop any equity and recover your initial purchasing costs before trying to resell it, pay the reselling costs and, in addition, attempt to reap some kind of profit on the sale.

Do not feel that any institution that asks you to sit down is doing you the favor of your life. Lenders loan money only when they can make a profit on you. You should remain in control. Lenders should compete for your business. Take your time. Each dollar you spend in this area will take more than a dollar away from another goal, so guard your pocket.

How to sound like a broken record

When you are fully qualified for the loan, it's time to go house hunting.

As you prepare to confront the first real estate agent, practice your "broken record" strategy. You should be familiar with this tactic—it's the technique you have successfully used on your children since they were toddlers. No matter what the sales agent says or does, your answer must always be the same: "I have only 'X' dollars per month to spend for a mortgage, insurance and taxes and only 'X' dollars for a down payment, so I can't afford a house that costs more than 'X' dollars."

Just keep remembering how much it cost you the last time your kids won. That should bolster your resistance.

Bargain hunting

You have to negotiate for everything in life. So get good at it.

Since you are attempting to make this purchase look as much as possible like an investment, there are several strategies for finding undervalued property. First, look at the general neighborhood around a home you have spotted. Neighborhoods improve and appreciate, hit their peak, then depreciate. How can you tell which kind of neighborhood you are visiting?

One good clue is the number of children you see and the kinds of toys they are playing with. If a group of neighborhood youngsters playing by the curb looks a lot like the weekly meeting of the local Hell's Angels chapter, you should immediately return to the car and search elsewhere.

Once you've found a home that your family likes, walk around the neighborhood *without* the real estate agent at your elbow. Neighbors can fill you in about the neighborhood in general and your potential new home in particular. A neighbor may remember the family rowing out in front of the home after the last big storm. People may not be vocal about things they are pleased with, but they will be more than happy to share their misery with you—and every other piece of local dirt and gossip.

You should contact county or city planning agencies to inquire about existing or proposed roads and other facilities. The day after you move in is not the best time to find out you have bought a house near the proposed toxic waste site.

Buy the cheapest home in the best neighborhood. The bigger and more lavish houses on each side of yours will appreciate yours just by association. Don't expect any other kind of association with your new neighbors, as they will be mad as heck that your house is there at all, because it is depreciating their properties.

If you put up new siding and give your new home a general face lift and landscape makeover, using sweat equity (physical labor), you should improve your chances of being invited to the next July 4th neighborhood barbecue, and you will definitely improve your chances of making a profit when reselling.

Playing Sherlock "Homes"

Though the seller may be required by law to disclose a host of potential problems—even if doing so may change your mind—proving you were deceived after the fact may be difficult. You must be a scrutinizing buyer.

Wet basements, for example, are a common problem. Visiting homes only during thunderstorms or during the spring rainy season will allow you to ferret out those leaks easily. (Snorkeling equipment on the first floor is another clue.)

Tiny piles of sawdust in corners may indicate termites or other "unfriendlies"— not the harmless result of the toddler bringing in sand from the backyard, as the seller may have suggested.

Always check the basic structure, the foundation and the roof. Ceiling jackposts in every room are not a good sign.

Improper wiring can be creatively hidden by hanging Chinese lanterns or Christmas tree bulbs from loose wires. All Christmas tree decorations should be down by June, no matter how sincere the seller's excuses seem.

You should make any purchase agreement contingent upon an independent appraisal and construction inspection by a firm of your choice. An independent inspection is worth the extra dollars when you are contemplating the single largest purchase of your life.

Home inspections, property surveys, certified termite and other pest inspections, earthquake crack checks in certain geographical climates and a real estate attorney who can skew a purchasing contract in your interest, are allies you cannot afford to bypass. Home buyers tend to forget that everyone else—seller, real estate agent and lender—has a vested interest in moving property. But you will have to live with any problems for a long time.

'Tis the season to house hunt

The season you choose to house hunt is more important than you think. The more competitors for each home there are, the more likely the buyer will insist on top dollar for a property. Most buyers house hunt in the spring and summer, when there is built-in competition. The simple rules of supply and demand work in those seasons. The more buyers for a home, the better for the seller and the poorer the negotiating position of the potential buyer.

The best time to buy may be winter. A certain percentage of homeowners are always in transit from one area to the next. A job transfer, change in financial status, unemployment, family death, or change in health may force a seller to move quickly in an off-season.

Winter is also a good time to look for distress sales. You won't have to stand in line in 20-degrees-below-zero weather to wait for a hungry seller to let you in.

The length of time a home has been on the market will also expose a potential bargain. If your real estate agent is not cooperative when you request to see all listings that have been on the market for a year or more, you may be able to spot these gems by yourself. Look for rusty "For Sale" signs, cobwebs over the front door and a welcome that makes you wonder if you have just won the lottery.

The longer a home has been listed, the more negotiable the price becomes. Don't be afraid to bid well below the asking price. A seller will not advertise they are desperate to move. But if you are a good poker player, you should be able to assess a seller's situation and ferret out the truly desperate homeowner.

For best results, deal with more than one agent. Don't be coerced into a bidding war with another buyer. There is always another deal around the corner. This is a decision that will affect you for many years. Buy with your head, not your heart.

Slip-sliding away

I am frequently asked about bank foreclosures and sheriff sales. These can be bargains but can also trap an unwary buyer into an unwanted purchase. There may be no opportunity to inspect the home or view the interior of a property on the auction block, and any purchase is considered final.

If you later discover the home is sliding down the scenic hillside it was constructed on, is located under an airline flyway or is slowly sinking because of an underground river or quicksand, it will be impossible to unload it onto another unsuspecting buyer. You will be forced to disclose the negative facts that were unknown to you when you purchased. In general, these types of sales should not be attempted by the novice.

Making an offer they can't refuse

Once you have found your new home, you will have to make an offer. One friendly reminder: do you remember the last time you made a first offer on a car, a boat, a stereo or piece of furniture, and the seller grabbed it like he had been told beforehand what was behind door number three? I'll bet you still remember the empty feeling in the pit of your stomach that told you in no uncertain terms you had offered too much.

Bidding and counter-bidding are part of the Money Game. Do not be afraid to offer less than the agent told you the seller would accept. The owner wants the most he can get for his home. The agent is working for the seller and for his or her commission, which is a decent percentage of the final sale price. You are virtually on your own when it comes to friends along the final stretch—you can always go up; you can never come down. This is no time to worry about your image. It is far better to haggle like an Armenian rug merchant than to get the seller and agent to like you—by paying them more. Buyers' agents can be hired to protect your interests.

All conditions and costs in purchasing real estate are negotiable. Don't be led into paying for extras because you are told that "the buyer always shoulders that charge."

Do you really care if you all part friends...but you get shafted?

Not more insurance?!

A title guarantee, as it is called in the real estate business, is not really what it seems. Title insurance is a backup insurance policy which pays the lender in case your new property comes with hidden title defects, for example, a claim from the past.

Even though a title search is made before your property transfers from the previous owner, title defects can be overlooked. Therefore, the **lender** will probably require you purchase an insurance policy with your money naming them as the beneficiary.

If your property title is ever disputed and a previous ownership claim is upheld in court, you will downsize into an attractive appliance carton with your family. But the lender will have the insurance proceeds instead of your monthly mortgage payments in the future.

Since lenders usually insist that you pay for an insurance policy (an ALTA policy) in case a claim against your rightful ownership should be upheld, it makes sense for you to purchase an **owner's** title policy to protect your financial interest in the same manner. Title insurance **does not guarantee** a clear title to you: it merely guarantees that if your home is taken from you due to a previous claim that is upheld in court, and you must vacate your property, you will receive the insurance proceeds for the mortgage loan amount you borrowed.

My lawyer is bigger than yours

You should engage a good real estate attorney from the beginning. The contracts you will eventually sign have been written by lawyers who were not paid by you. You'd better have someone on your side.

If an agent or lender attempts to talk you out of consulting with legal counsel, ask yourself why he or she doesn't want you to have a lawyer. Lawyers are also known as "deal killers," which certainly makes them sound like the kind of pros I want to go into battle with.

If possible, try to time your transaction to coincide with low interest rates—1 percent would be ideal, but I doubt you can outwait the market that long.

Make your purchase agreement subject to every condition you can think of: financing, locking in a specified interest rate, a completion date if the home is newly built, required dates of occupancy, health permits if necessary, survey date, FHA or

VA requirements, the absence of any encumbrances or liens on the property, and the adjustment of taxes, water and other prorated bills that may become issues later.

If you are selling one home and buying another, never, never, never allow the new buyer to move into your old home before the transaction has closed and the deed transferred. Until the purchasing deal is completed, you are still the legal owner. If the buyer finds a problem with the home, changes his or her mind or has other problems, the deal may collapse. If the buyer's lawyer has been aggressive enough to add escape clauses to the purchasing contract, the buyer may walk away before the transaction has been completed without owing you one thin dime. If the home burns down or a liability problem arises, you are still responsible.

If you are forced to allow a buyer to rent for a brief period of time, perhaps because his or her house has sold and their furniture is out in the street, there may be a temporary solution. If your lawyer has added a rental clause of $800, $1,000 or $1,500 per month—not a "small stipend" by anyone's standards—the buyer will be motivated to help you, the bank and his or her wallet by completing the deal as soon as possible.

If you follow the rules outlined in this book, you will make the best possible decisions and, therefore, the best possible deal.

Home equity loans

An equity line of credit (ELOC) is generally easy to secure, tax deductible as an itemized mortgage expense, and a **big, big problem** if you lose your job, fall off the roof and can't work or otherwise fall on hard financial times.

The contracts often have impaired risk clauses that allow the lender (or the new lender who just bought your loan) to demand full payment without recourse if she or he believes (or can construe) that you have become a deteriorated financial risk. The agreement can become a demand note with all principal and interest due promptly. Without notice or protest, or due process of law.

This clever tax strategy, which some "experts" are quick to recommend, could be the undoing of your property because you are collateralizing it in return for money at a time of distress. Three strikes (three payments missed) and you are out (of your home and into a court foreclosure mode). You may be putting your home on the auction block.

Consumers often secure one "just in case." But in such an emergency you would be putting your home in danger. If you become financially troubled, you cannot activate it! That would jeopardize the roof over your head! Paying off other debt with your home as collateral is not smart! I would rather you borrowed unsecured credit card debt at 18% per year than to risk your family's homestead!

What about refinancing?

Refinancing in today's interest rate environment may lower your monthly mortgage payments and total mortgage interest. But hunting for mortgage money in this lending arena takes more questions than just asking about the interest rate. You must gather the following information from several local lenders to make a competent decision:

- The current interest rate.
- The points required to lock in that interest rate.
- Closing costs.
- Additional (hidden) fees and expenses.

Get a written estimate of the closing costs as well as a promise of a 60-day lock-in rate. Mortgage money moves quickly, and you will want the rate you were promised when you finally sign that refinancing application and are locked into an agreement. Do not be sold on any gimmicks. Don't go for a low mortgage rate with higher points or be lulled into a lower than market rate adjustable mortgage that will move up sharply later. Let the lender take the risk of rising interest rates. Now is the time to lock in a low fixed rate.

Don't opt for a balloon mortgage (one that has to be re-financed in a number of years). This temporary solution just postpones the inevitable same re-financing problem to the future.

Comparing one mortgage to another is easier if you understand how points affect the ultimate interest rate. The points must be converted to a comparable amount of interest since they will most likely be rolled over into the new mortgage amount, which means you will borrow both the money for the mortgage and the extra amount for points.

You may have learned that one point equals 1 percent of the total mortgage. Forget that banker talk for now. To compare a mortgage for twenty (20) years or less, translate each point into 1/8 percent of additional interest.

For example, compare the following deals: 8.5 percent interest and zero points vs. 8.25 percent interest plus two points. First, convert the points to equivalent interest by multiplying 2 x 1/8. Then add that .25 percent to the stated interest rate (8.25 percent), which equals 8.5 percent. So the offers produce identical monthly payments.

Whether you pay the points from your savings or roll them over into your refinanced loan, the math is the same. Even though you don't borrow the point money—and, therefore, don't actually pay any interest on borrowing it—you are losing the use of those funds for 15 to 20 years. That means there is an opportunity cost to you, whether you pay the points out of your pocket or borrow them and pay interest.

When you have found the best combinations of interest rates and points, look for the cheapest closing costs and smallest extra fees. In addition, try to negotiate the ability to pay real estate taxes without an escrow account. This will enable you to work your own money in an interest bearing account until tax time (every quarter or semiannually). Don't trade for this by increasing the cost of the money you're borrowing. However, all other things being equal, this additional benefit will enable you to keep more dollars in your pocketbook and working for you longer.

Does it matter if your mortgage is sold? Check your loan agreement to be sure that if your loan is sold, full payment cannot be demanded earlier than stated and that the promised interest rate can't be changed.

When should you refinance? In general, consider refinancing when the current interest rate is 2 percent lower than what you are paying, **and** when you can recover the cost of the points and closing costs through lower payments over the length of time you intend to stay in your home.

For example, if you can save $50 per month on mortgage payments by refinancing, but you have added $2,500 to the mortgage balance payoff by the costs involved in refinancing, divide the $2,500 cost by the $50 per month savings. If you intend to stay in your home for more than 4 years ($2,500 divided by $50 a month = 50 monthly payments or 4.16 years), then refinancing makes good economic sense. If you have an adjustable mortgage today, consider refinancing to a fixed mortgage while rates are low on fixed mortgage money.

One final thought: If you refinance, you will probably stay in your current home for several years. It may make more sense to purchase a new home. If your income is secure, there are some great distress sales sitting on real estate ledgers across the country.

Games people play

In their haste to generate client turnover and boost sales commissions, some real estate agents may play games designed to get the sale off the ground in the same manner your kids get you to do what benefits them most. Here are some common traps you should be wary of and the red flags that should make you skeptical:

1. If an agent can get you in the home of your dreams without showing you 49 others, this saves time, gas money and gray hair for him or her. To bring the sale closer, the agent may show you three or four bad houses, then a decent one. Though the last home may not be what you really want, it may look wonderful compared to what you have been shown. By making a list of features you desire and the quality you expect beforehand, you can remain objective as the "For Sale" signs begin to blur together.

2. If the agent attempts to create a sense of urgency that the house may be sold out from under you at any minute, realize that if this happens there will be other desirable homes, perhaps even at a lower price. There is more than one home waiting for a particular buyer. So don't offer more to close the sale, and don't let any agent (or a team of agents) force you into making an offer before you are ready.

3. As recommended earlier in this chapter, selling your home should rank second only to a religious experience. Fresh flowers, brownies baking in the oven, your children next door ruining the neighbor's house for a change, will make your home more salable.

   That same decorator instinct could be used against you as a buyer. While there is nothing wrong with making a potential buyer feel comfortable and cozy, such a strategy could cover up a problem you don't want to miss. Behind every great smelling kitchen, there is the opportunity to bargain well. Remember when you move in, the previous cook moves out.

4. If an agent attempts to get a price range from you regarding a certain home you are interested in, play your cards close to your vest. Remember the agent is the seller's new friend, not yours. Never ask the agent for advice or a suggested offer. The more you pay, the more the agent's commission. This is akin to asking a life insurance salesperson how large a policy you should buy.

5. Promises regarding influential factors that may nix a sale for you should be checked out. An agent may tell you that a new school will be built close to you, that transportation is closer than really exists and that the neighborhood is high quality. Check all pertinent data out with disinterested persons.

6. Be wary of "handyman" specials. Some houses need cosmetic facelifts, while others may need intensive care units of their own. Be sure you understand how "handy" you must really be to make your new home livable.

Escaping PMI

Private Mortgage Insurance (PMI) protects the bank in case you default on the mortgage loan. It is required when the starting equity in your home is generally less than 20% or if you have blemishes on your credit report. The cost of PMI is $250 to $560 or more annually for every $100,000 borrowed on a mortgage.

Many homeowners are paying costly PMI fees unnecessarily. This is most likely if:

1. you live in an area where property values have recently risen;
2. you have never calculated when you will be able to stop paying PMI;
3. or you are prepaying regularly on your mortgage.

Unfortunately, lenders don't tell you when you are eligible to discontinue PMI.

Calculate your equity by figuring out your mortgage balance. Get this figure from your lender. Then subtract that number from today's value of your home, based on recent sales of similar homes in your neighborhood. Or ask a Realtor to give you an estimate. If the answer (your equity) exceeds 20 percent (20%) of the present-day value, you should no longer have to pay PMI.

When this is so, contact the lender in writing. Demand to have PMI eliminated. This is your right, though the lender may require you to submit a paid professional current appraisal on the property before eliminating the private mortgage insurance from your monthly mortgage payment.

Parents as bankers

Occasionally grown children expect their parents to play piggy banker. They may have a poor credit history or insufficient income to qualify for the home they want to purchase. Parents, thinking they are doing their kids a favor, may ultimately risk their own financial solvency by tying up a large part of their retirement nest egg.

They may even harm their children by bankrolling a project with no firm foundation, throwing them a financial curve because their children naively incurred debt they could not afford to maintain.

There are major drawbacks. If your child runs into financial trouble (illness, the loss of one family income, a messy divorce, death of a spouse, or a lawsuit), your money may be in jeopardy, at least temporarily.

Would you be willing to foreclose on the mortgage to retrieve your collateral? Do you have enough money for your own retirement needs well into the future, without the monthly income or principal you would loan them? Are you overinvesting in one project at the expense of diversification?

If their financial condition worsens, are you willing to foot the monthly mortgage payments until they can get back on their financial feet?

Can you afford to be this generous with all of your children? If not, how do you intend to justify such a "gift" to one child?

If you do go ahead with such a loan, collateralize (secure) the house you purchase for them so you have financial control should they default on payments to you.

Your children will want the mortgage interest deduction. So any contract must be drafted to give them legal control of the real estate. This leaves you in a secondary credit position.

Are you helping your children or feeding their instant gratification? Should you fund this potential financial fiasco, or is it time to give them their own copy of **Winning The Money Game** so they can become fiscally fit, then purchase their own home in time upon a firm financial foundation?

Nightmare on *ARM* street

If you have an adjustable rate mortgage (ARM), you may be tempted to accept the bank's periodic recalculations as interest rates change and, therefore, your monthly payments adjust over time. Don't. Audits of lenders around the country reveal that an alarming number of these loans are readjusted incorrectly.

For those who don't want to deal with the math (or the hassle of monitoring your institution's accuracy), there are service companies that will review your payment history and protect you from overcharges from now on. They can calculate your payments as well as the outstanding balance on the loan.

The most common mistake involves the indexes used. There are several bellwether standards on which the bank's profit margin is based. For example, the 90-day Treasury bill rate plus a spread for the bank, or the average rate on two-year Treasury notes plus a margin of profit built on top for the lender, are common bellwether indices.

Banks sometimes use the wrong index or the right index but the wrong date. There is also the potential for human error during any of the numerous coding procedures. Incorrect rounding of figures is also a problem.

Mistakes can occur in mortgages sold to other servicing companies or with loans originating at one institution that are sold to another service lender due to bank insolvency or other reasons. Other red flags to watch for are a rider or handwritten change in the note, the use of an unusual index that processors may be unfamiliar with or frequent changes from one mortgage service to another. Even loans written in the early 1980s should be examined.

Small miscalculations can add up over the length of a 15-, 20- or 30-year period. Though no hard evidence exists that lenders are intentionally erring, you are the loser when this happens.

If you discover the bank has undercharged itself, the law favors the borrower unless you feel morally obliged to refund the difference you underpaid. Banks must refund overcharges, once they are proven.

For more information regarding companies that will determine whether you are paying more than your fair payment, check your metropolitan telephone book or contact the Better Business Bureau in your area.

Managing your money pit

The following is a good checklist when hiring agents or contractors to repair roofs, put in new windows, remodel, repair wet basements, landscape, or provide other services.

1. *Get two or three estimates* before deciding on a specific company or agent. Do not be pressured into signing through fear or greed. Special sales, one time deals or last chance offers should make you skeptical.

2. If you have sufficient cash, *think twice about financing* the work. A company might lead you to believe it is cheaper to finance than to spend your savings. But it might not be giving you totally objective advice—some companies make extra money from finance companies if they can convince you to finance. It is usually a better idea to pay cash than to borrow.

3. *If you do finance the project,* you might have two contracts rolled up into one: 1) an agreement to complete the work by the contractor; and 2) a separate agreement for payment with a lending institution or finance company. If any contract price changes are made or the project is canceled, you must notify both parties, not just the contractor, to make adjustments or terminate your previous contract. When a contract is completed, you should also request a statement of payment in full on your account from the contractor and lending institution or financing company.

4. If a presentation is made at your home, *do not sign on the first appointment.* If a company is reputable and does quality work, it will not force you to sign a contract immediately. Take some time to think over the quote and compare it with others.

5. *If you are pressured into signing* a contract that you decide you do not want to honor, you generally have the right to void it within 72 hours. (This applies only to contracts signed in your home, not at the company's place of business.) It is far better, though, to take your time before you sign anything.

    Take a few days—or longer—to compare and research. It is much easier to protect your money while it is still safely inside your pocket than to retrieve it from someone else's.

6. When comparing contractor bids or do-it-yourself supply houses that sell materials to the public, be sure you are *comparing apples to apples.* Some firms whose prices beat the competition are lower because they purposely underestimate the amount of materials needed to complete the job.

    They can spot shoppers primarily interested in price, knowing that once the job is started they won't lose the customer, even if the buyer has to purchase more materials. If you have ever run out of tile, lumber or paint before completing your project, you were downright grateful to be able to match what you have already installed.

    You chalk up the mistake to somebody's error instead of the deception that closed the sale in the first place. Be certain everyone is on a level playing field when your bids come in.

7. *Get it in writing.* Get every promise, all specifications, dates of starting and completion and all monetary arrangements down on paper. This avoids any misunderstandings as to what the original terms of the contract were. You and your contractor should have a clear understanding so that everything can be included in the price estimate.

8. Read through *and understand every word* in the contract you are requested to sign. The fine print (look on the back, too) was important enough for the company's lawyers to include. It should be as important for you to understand.

9. Never let a contractor start work on your premises until you have seen the *worker's compensation certifications, a fidelity bond and a state license,* if ap-

plicable. This protects you in case of an accident so that you cannot be sued for injury to a worker on your property.
10. *Ask for references.* Competent contractors will be pleased to provide the names of satisfied customers. Call these people. Ask how they found your contractor, what work was done, and consider visiting the project if it is in your area. You can call a county association or the city or county building department to ask about the contractor's reputation.
11. *Pre-pay as little up-front money as possible.* Avoid paying the entire bill in full until the project is completed and you have personally inspected it or had the work inspected by someone else. Therefore, you will have financial leverage to bargain with if a project is not completed to your satisfaction.
12. *Do not allow workers to enter your home when you are absent.* Arrange a convenient time when you can be there. Keep your important papers, charge cards, Social Security checks and money out of sight while strangers are working on your property.
13. If your project is extensive, *call your county or city building code department* to see if a building permit has been issued to your contractor. Also, ask if there are any building practices that must be followed as you describe the work that will be done.
14. *If you are not satisfied* with the work as it progresses, contact the company's owner or manager immediately to discuss the problem. Do not allow work to continue without ironing out problems or misunderstandings. Workers on the site do not usually have the authority to change or alter any previous instructions. Have all changes or new agreements written either on the original contract or on a new contract signed and dated by both you and your contractor.
15. **Buyer beware**: A subcontractor who isn't paid by your remodeler could attach your home with a mechanic's lien, even though you paid your general contractor. You may not even know the attachment is on the records until you attempt to sell your property. To be sure all suppliers are paid by your general contractor, ask for the names of all suppliers and work crews who will be involved in your project beforehand and insist on copies of paid receipts before you pay in full at the completion of your project.
16. It may be wise to hold back about 10 percent of the total price until you are totally satisfied with the work. In that case you have leverage in the event of faulty materials, defective workmanship or unpaid bills that could come back to you later.

Your home as a tax shelter

When you sell your home (primary residence) at a profit, Uncle Sam expects you to share your wealth with him.

Therefore, it is vital to record and keep track of all improvements and eligible expenses that can add to the cost of your home. You will only be taxed on the difference between your original price plus improvements and the sale price minus selling expenses.

Improvements vs. maintenance

An *improvement* is a replacement or addition that increases market value, adds life to the property or creates new uses for it. It reduces gains because costs are added to the basis when the property is sold.

Any improvement must remain with the house in order to qualify as an addition to the tax basis. The deductions allowed are: 1) materials only, if the projects are do-it-yourself; 2) rental items and "outside help" wages; and 3) related costs (such as shrub removal, required surveys). It is also a good idea to take "before" and "after" pictures in case you have to substantiate your claim. By all means, save any and all receipts—even small items add up over the years.

Maintenance is a repair or replacement of items that provide proper functioning and prevent structure deterioration as a whole. These costs are not deductible.

Sometimes, the complete job is classified as an improvement, for example, the painting and wallpapering of a room being remodeled. Another example might be the restoration of neglected property needing a complete overhaul. The work done plus the materials are capital expenditures and the property cost basis is increased by the total of all work.

Assessments are considered improvements. Adjustments are done at closing time as provided by the Uniform Settlement Statement. In addition to improvements, you can add other expenses to the original price of your home, such as new streets, utility improvements and sanitary and storm sewers. Costs levied against affected properties are usually paid by the seller. Costs added to the tax basis of the property are assumed by the buyer. Interest charges may be tax deductible in the year paid, if the outstanding balance is paid over a number of years. A list of improvements in the **Appendix** will help you keep track of home expenses which reduce your potential housing profits when you sell.

Real property vs. personal property

Since maintenance and personal household items cannot be used to offset future taxes, you must know which expenses you can add in. Real property is connected to the land, such as the house or the garage. Everything else is personal property. On occasion, personal property can become real property if permanently attached (for example, built-in stereos and TVs). See the **Appendix** for a list.

Paying piggy bank off early

Once you realize you have bought your dream home on the indentured servant plan, hostaged by monthly mortgage payments for most of your working life, you may seek revenge by repaying the loan principal early, saving thousands of dollars in interest. At the beginning of a 30-year mortgage, your interest accounts for nearly 79 percent of your monthly payment. It will take 22.5 years before 50 percent of your payment is directed toward loan principal.

There are numerous clever methods of using additional monthly payments and adding your normal tax refund to the prepayment pot annually. Some companies will sell you computer software so you can design your own prepayment plan. Other companies sell programs to assist this goal. Avoid these and use your own ingenuity, because part of their profit is made by using your money until it is sent to your lender. Eliminate financial middlemen by paying extra principal directly.

This is, however, not always a smart move. Since major financial goals tend to occur in 10-year to 20-year intervals, perhaps you should, instead, invest those dollars in a college or retirement plan. The time value of money is awesome when dollars are allowed to accumulate early. The earlier you start saving, the more money you can accumulate or the fewer dollars you need to meet your goal.

You will not benefit if your home is paid off early but your college or retirement funds have suffered in the process. How will you fund tuition if those extra dollars went back to your banker? Back to piggy bank for another financial fix at an older age? After retirement, you need a comfortable roof over your head **and** a well fed feeling in your stomach.

Paying off that mortgage with retirement funds is also a common strategy to rid yourself of a monthly payment and guarantee that your home is paid for, no matter what!

However, the cost of living doesn't stop just because your monthly paycheck has, replaced by a smaller fixed monthly income payment instead.

Retirees often protest that if their home is paid for, at least they can keep it, if nothing else. **Not** if they can't pay the rising taxes. **Not** if they have to choose between health care, food, prescription costs and home maintenance expenses. A house is a virtual money pit. Home ownership expenses don't stop because the mortgage obligations have.

In addition, that lump sum mortgage balance will be working for your lender. Transferring gobs of money at this early point in your retirement phase to cash out a mortgage is a lot more dangerous than writing a fixed monthly mortgage check each month. Pay the mortgage balance down slowly because it is mostly principal, not interest.

Unless you have so much in retirement funds stashed away that you won't miss that money at the end of your retirement years, you cannot afford to pay off a mortgage at the expense of your limited nest egg.

You may believe you can borrow yourself through the college years. But debt won't fund your retirement.

Before prepaying that mortgage, determine whether you will have enough discretionary dollars for all your desired financial goals. Otherwise you will be back in the lender's line at college time or after retirement, with the money score at Banker 2, Consumer 0. You will have paid off one loan just in time to sign up for another.

Good financial planning demands common sense as well as a sharp pencil and a calculator.

Mortgages in reverse

For a generation of seniors whose biggest asset is their home equity, reverse mortgages may sound like the perfect solution. Borrowing against the value of their homes, owners can receive a fixed monthly check from a mortgage lender to supplement their fixed monthly incomes.

Later, after they have moved into nursing homes or died, their heirs can pay off the debt by selling the property.

High fees plus the reluctance of older folks to take on additional debt have limited this market to the most destitute of those attempting to avoid foreclosure.

For people without their back against the wall, this should be a last option.

First, realize that because life expectancy risk enters into this issue, the home will be "annuitized" at a price lower than what the homeowner would receive if they sold the house outright.

Secondly, the pretense of staying in your home when your rights are limited to a life estate, while giving up 20% of more of the fair market value for another fixed monthly income, only forestalls a financial problem.

A better proposition: sell the home outright, then use the lump sum funds for living needs while enjoying the freedom to rent with no strings.

There are variations on this theme which get even more sophisticated like selling the homestead and buying "up," mortgaging a more expensive roof over your head. Or creating a qualified personal residence trust. What will creative lenders come up with next to make a buck?

Deducting a home office

When Congress enacted the Taxpayers Relief Act of 1997, it provided greater relief for people who toil in basements and other rooms converted into home offices.

The home office deduction is now available even if a person's business is not the place where most business activities take place.

If a home office or portion of a home is used regularly and exclusively to conduct business, it can qualify for a deduction as the principal place of business.

Be sure your home office is a separate area used only for business purposes. For example, a television set used occasionally for entertainment may void a home office deduction.

A variety of expenses can be deducted such as electric bills, heating and air conditioning costs, phone expenses attributable to business only, equipment depreciation costs and depreciation of the portion of your home used as a home office.

A business owner may also deduct travel expenses for trips from the home office location if that is his or her primary place of business. Such trips may include picking up supplies, meeting clients, dropping off packages, and delivering finished work.

If you sell your home, special rules apply (and different tax rates) for the portion you have converted to your home office.

Contact your tax advisor before implementing this tax change, as a home office changes the character of your personal residence when you sell.

The $250,000 exclusion

Before 1997, if you waited until age 55 to sell your primary residence, you were able to deduct up to $125,000 ($250,000 per married couple) of capital gains profits from all your residences over the years.

But, under the new tax rules, no matter what your age, up to $500,00 of gain on a joint return ($250,000 on a single return) can be taken tax free on the sale of your primary residence. Even if you used the old $125,000 break in the past, you can still use this one.

Have you bought a house you can't afford? If you then purchase a less expensive home, or no home at all, you can still take a full deduction if you qualify under the rules.

The home must be your principal residence for two (2) of the prior five (5) years. If you have lived in the house for less than two (2) years, special rules apply. The tax break can be used over and over but, generally, only once in any two-year period.

When counting the two-year period, you can include the time that a spouse or a former spouse lived in the house without you under the terms of a separation or divorce agreement.

You can make a second home free, too. The multiple-use rule creates a sweet opportunity for taxpayers who have vacation homes.

Strategy: sell your primary home, take up to $500,00 of gain tax free. Then move into your vacation home. Two (2) years later, sell that home and cash in again on tax free capital gains profits from that sale.

The home must be your primary residence, and you must have lived in the house for at least two out of the last five years before the date of sale.

If you and your spouse file a joint return, you can avoid paying tax on profits up to $500,000. This option is open even if you or your spouse owned the property before you were married.

If you are single and have owned your residence for the required period of time, you can take the exclusion up to $250,000. If you are single and own your home with someone else (say a child or a companion), each owner who meets the above requirement tests can exclude up to $250,000 of his or her portion of the profits.

If your office is in your home or you rent part of your house, be aware that any profit due to depreciation claimed **won't** be tax free. Instead, it will be taxed at 25% above your adjusted cost basis when you sell.

Planning your final sale is vitally important. If you add a family member or friend to your property deed you may be gifting half of the real estate to them. Therefore, you may lose part of your exclusion when you decide to sell. This law is complex, so seek information from a tax advisor before implementing this tax strategy.

Since tax changes in Congress are common, this benefit could change. Expect politicians to keep this source of revenue on their discussion agenda well into the future. If the winds of tax change seem imminent, you may want to speed up a decision to sell if the other economics of the sale are also prudent and make good economic sense.

Money can't buy happiness. But it may allow you to be miserable in a much nicer neighborhood.

A home is an expensive lifestyle decision and one of the financial dreams you and your family plan for. Buy the home you can afford because that's how you want—**and can afford**—to live.

Chapter 10

Your child and money

Did you know that the best savers in America are three year olds? Imagine—from age four on, our children are taught it is more rewarding to spend than to save. The most creative excuse I heard came from a six year old. He told me he was robbing his piggy bank because he owed it to himself. Where do you think he learned that response?

High school and college students are graduating with impressive money making skills, yet lack a clue how to manage the small fortunes they will earn over their lifetimes. If they don't learn the basics of personal money management under your supervision while at home, they will be taught some tough lessons from the school of hard knocks.

You may earn the money in your home, but I'll bet that you don't spend the majority of it. That, many teenagers believe, is their job They pester their parents who dutifully sell another pint of blood to finance their children's newest spending habit and insatiable money eating appetite.

Your graduate will be among the slowest group of moving targets ever to be marketed by the financial industry who will tell the young adults to live for today. Sign here. Have it all now—sign some more. Can't afford it now? That's what credit is for. Sign, sign, sign.

Credit cards, new cars, homes, furniture, clothes, entertainment and vacations, even groceries—standards of consumption and lifestyles the kids never believed possible—will be theirs for the stroke of a pen.

Since they won't know how to tell their financial "friends" from the other guys, they may be artfully separated from their paychecks, their investment dollars, their cars, homes, and, in some cases, their future goals and dreams.

When your student arrives at college they will meet many new friends: Visa, Mastercard, and American Express. Since you won't be there to protect them from living life on the installment plan, teach them today how to save, invest, gift, and spend wisely.

14 mistakes your children will be tempted to make

1. Living now, paying later.
2. Procrastinating.
3. Paying themselves last.
4. Abusing OPM (other people's money).

5. Believing advertising.
6. Reading only the bold print.
7. Purchasing the sizzle instead of the steak.
8. Failing to plan.
9. Wanting too much too soon.
10. Using credit as a substitute for happiness.
11. Ignoring the time value of money.
12. Not understanding opportunity cost.
13. Ignoring inflation.
14. Failing to realize that time is their friend.

Opportunity knocks

Opportunity cost is one key to wise personal money management and efficient spending habits. If your child has $50 and spends it entirely on a movie and entertainment for friends, the opportunity cost is all the other things he or she could have done with that $50 now and the lost opportunities to use that same $50 in the future.

Opportunity cost is not a moral issue. It is an awareness that money decisions may be final, financial resources are limited, and priorities can be set before financial resources are allocated. Too many teenagers and their adult role models are living examples of the old saying: "Money talks, I'll not deny. I heard it one. It said 'good-bye'."

The ways to the means

Developing a simple budget is a must, even for young adults. Setting financial priorities will produce better spending and savings habits. If children are taught that some of every dollar earned (or gifted) should be saved, they will pay themselves first from an early age. Time will work with them and the magic of compound interest can do most of the work to reach their financial dreams.

A budget reveals a written record of their expenditures, which can be analyzed and improved. The ultimate goal—satisfaction from every dollar they earn, save and spend.

Their most important financial role model is you. Encourage teenagers to participate in family financial affairs. Hands-on experience is the best teacher.

Smart young consumers examine many things before handing over their money:

1. The price of the item.
2. The quality of the product.
3. How long the purchase will last.
4. How durable the product is.
5. How often the item will be used.

6. How necessary the purchase is.
7. The opportunity cost of buying this item.
8. Whether they can afford this item now.
9. What other associated costs may be involved (maintenance, insurance, or accessories).
10. Whether they need this item now.

Spending and saving mistakes

Does this describe your kids?
1. They see money primarily as a means to buy something now.
2. Money burns a hole in their pockets until spent.
3. They purchase many things but seldom derive long term pleasure from their purchases.
4. Saving is not important to them.
5. They spend more than they save.
6. Spending money makes them happy.
7. If they had $1,000, they would feel rich.
8. They can only save long enough to purchase small items.
9. They believe money has little future power.

Read the above list again and put yourself in your children's shoes. Does this sound like you as well? For many adults, this list reflects their own attitudes regarding the value of money.

Teach them that saving and spending are not conflicting goals. All saving really means is **not spending today so you can have more money to spend tomorrow.**

If your children have little respect for paper dollars, perhaps it's because they rarely see real greenbacks. Instead, they use "plastic" and small tear-out sheets with gray bunnies, yellow chickens or peaceful mountain scenes printed on them. Adults call them "checks."

Checks represent dollars and carry the same responsibility as real money. Teach children they can't spend money they don't have, and they don't write checks when they don't have dollars in their checking accounts. Opening a checking account is easy. Managing it properly is not.

Paying themselves first

Out of every paycheck or monetary gift your children receive, a portion should go into savings or investing. Like brushing their teeth while young, saving can become a habit over time. Your children can establish an emergency or rainy day fund early.

Without a financial backup of their own, they will borrow from their parents or from each other. This is the start of living ***above*** their means.

Overspending can become addictive. Not able to pay off excessive debt with their limited incomes, they become content to live life on the installment plan. They buy everything on the easy payment plan, with monthly interest on every payment.

Teach inflation and compound interest

Since inflation is the greatest money killer of long term financial goals, your children must learn how to conserve their purchasing power. Show them how compound interest can work for them. Don't confide to them yet, however, that they must become millionaires in order to remain middle class because of inflation's destruction of future purchasing power.

Show me the money: allowances

My children never received an allowance simply because they were born into our family. After all, I did all the work. First, I got pregnant, I got morning sickness, I got fat. Then I went into labor, a state of profound "discomfort." (Male obstetricians always use that term. If they told women how much pain was in store, we might find a way to allow our husbands to bear children.)

Then I devoted the next twenty-five years to raising and educating them.

Many parents believe it is important to have dress rehearsals for adult spending in the form of a regular allowance. They may negotiate incentive allowances for performing chores around the house. Be sure this strategy doesn't bite back. A child can quickly learn that he or she should be paid for everything, and self-interest might become the motive for pitching in.

A team family works together without thought of personal gain. If your teenager threatens to strike for a raise while your garbage fills up the kitchen, you have created a money monster.

If you give children their own money, don't punish them for poor behavior by withholding allowances or reneging on entertainment and activity funds. Supervised money management is your child's only financial training ground for the future.

Value lessons come automatically with use, or misuse, of money. When the allowance is spent and your children ask for additional funds, sympathize with their financial plight, but provide no disaster aid. When they receive their next allowance, encourage them to manage it better.

The teenage IRA

To start saving for retirement as a teenager is a great achievement. You can help your children do this. In the same manner as some employers match employee 401k contributions, you can motivate your teenager to start an IRA with part of his or her earned income, matching your child's contributions dollar for dollar.

For every dollar they add, say, to an IRA mutual fund, you put in a dollar of your own. You could even design a vesting schedule to promote a long term savings attitude (though this is merely rhetoric because IRAs are always 100-percent vested).

Since these dollars will most likely be tax deductible (they can write them off their tax return, as well as earn tax deferred compound interest until retirement time), your children get two tax benefits along with a powerful long term savings vehicle. The dollars you add will likely wind up in their pocketbook anyhow. And this activity starts a "pay yourself" plan, hopefully the first of many that they will initiate.

The dog ate my homework

Raising children has its events of significance. By the time they enter kindergarten, the pre-schooler no longer uses the cereal bowl as a hat substitute and the diapers are gone. No parent is immune to the ups and downs of teenage-dom, key years in which family structure may help ensure they metamorphose into adults you not only love, but may actually like.

Money in itself is not an end. It is a store of value that, when earned, inspires integrity and independence. Give your children the opportunity to learn and earn at the same time. As the old saying reminds us, "Give a fish to people feeds them today, but they are back the table tomorrow, hungry as ever. Teach them to fish and you will feed them for a lifetime."

Hazy, crazy, but definitely not lazy

Every summer they're back: those lazy, hazy, crazy days of summer. Family fun, however, costs more each season. Instead of contemplating a home equity loan just to fund summer entertainment, why not convince your kids to finance your next family outing on their allowance? With a little ingenuity, parents and grandparents can build lifetime memories without breaking the bank.

Family fun on the cheap

Visit the past and search the skies.
Museums of natural history and planetariums reveal secrets of the skies and wonder of our planet, often under one roof.

Follow a frog or hiss at a snake.
Each county has metropark areas offering nature trails, special educational programs, and activities. Some families are lucky enough to live in the country. The rest of us must import Mother Nature. Fly a kite, float a boat, or just count

windows in the cloud castles. Most are free. Call a park near you for its free newsletter.

Find a favorite fishing hole.
Grandparents often have more time, longer stories, and a larger lap to capture the imagination of youngsters. Memories from that first fish can last a lifetime. There are numerous parks, man-made lakes, and reservoirs where a special grandchild and can spend a lazy summer afternoon with a sack lunch and Grandpa or Grandma (no matter who baits the hook).

Talk to the animals.
When was your last trip to the zoo? A tropical rain forest, butterfly exhibit, polar bear area, baby seals, and a golden opportunity for teaching respect for life in many forms await your family. An inexpensive day long excursion for the entire family, you can pack a picnic lunch to snack on somewhere between the aardvark and the zebras.

Stop and smell the roses.
Arboretums, floral landscape gardens, and spacious public outdoor areas where kids can watch the seasons change often have lakes for meeting and feeding new friends. Don't forget to bring lots of dry breadcrumbs or stale bread for the ducks and geese.

Make someone's day.
Volunteering helps others and makes us feel good too. We make a living by what we earn in the marketplace. We make a life by what we give to others and leave behind.

Energize your mind.
In a flash, youngsters can visit the past, learn a new hobby, or experience their own "virtual reality" at the library. Many offer summer reading programs, story telling schedules, and reading contests to promote the power of knowledge.

Feed a feathered friend.
Pine cones dipped in melted Crisco then rolled in birdseed will make a hungry bird happy this winter. This is a great observation activity for a school snow day. Twist a wire around the cone as a hanger and store in the freezer until winter arrives.

Follow your family tree.
Teenagers love to trace their roots and map out their heritage. They can communicate with relatives inexpensively by mail and spend a summer improving family ties.

Create a collection.
Start a rock, leaf, shell, dried flower, postcard, stamp, arrowhead, painted stone, leaf, penny, badge, sticker, bird identification, or stamp collection. The list is endless. So are children's ideas. This hobby teaches organizing, analyzing, and **NEATNESS!**

Start Christmas in July.
Original hand-crafted treasurers are often the most loved gifts! Hand-painted tree ornaments, shirts, plaster molds, and other "originals" by budding artists keep hands busy and hearts in the right holiday spirit. They are also easy on the holiday pocketbook. Care enough to give the very best...YOU!

Sugar and spice and everything nice

Keep the important adolescent times in mind and your sanity in tact. I wouldn't trade the good times for anything. Nature invented selective amnesia to erase those "other times."

Chapter 11

Using your kids for a change

I raised a daughter and I raised *Rambo*—though we didn't receive any of Hollywood's royalties for our son. I am grateful that my children have grown into responsible adults and are contributing something to the world. They learned the meaning of that four letter word, w-o-r-k. They also know how to analyze, set and reach goals, and they care about others. A great deal of the credit for the close relationship I share with my children goes to them—they were patient with me.

The joys, the memories and the rainbows which you share with your kids are some of the most valuable times of your life. But along with these joys come great anxieties, responsibilities and financial burdens.

A couple planning a family today may spend more than $200,000 to raise one child to age 18 and another $150,000 to educate them in a public college or university. Children are financial disasters.

Kids eventually do leave and live (mostly) off their own paychecks. But, in the meantime, you may need to sell blood on a monthly basis to afford them. The annual dependent tax exemption is a cruel joke, considering the actual cost of raising children. Today's childbirth hospital bills should be a clue to what comes later, particularly when it comes to recent tax "reform."

Before 1986, children and tax relief were a better partnership. Called *income shifting* or *income splitting*, it was relatively easy to gift or otherwise transfer assets to your children so profits could be taxed at their lower tax rates, in some cases, transferred tax free. It was even legal to take back the principal after 10 years. Gift transfer and estate tax advantages were plentiful.

Tax reform changed all that.

Kids may still be less taxing

There are still avenues for reducing the financial drain caused by your kids. The Kiddie Tax is here. And gone is the child's ability to deduct an exemption off his or her income tax if the parent also claims the child.

But there are other options blessed by the IRS. If your child is already threatening to sue when you enforce bedtime rules, some of these may not be for you. (Though a brochure telling you the earliest age the French Foreign Legion will induct members may be helpful.)

Gifts to minors under age 14

The Kiddie Tax affects children under age 14. Gifts of property producing unearned income (dividends, interest, and capital gains) of up to $700 per year are generally tax free. In other words, if the child has no earned income (the kind that comes from *real* work), he or she can earn, each year, $700 in investment income tax free if you complete a tax return in his or her name.

The next $700 of profit per year is taxed at the child's marginal (top) rate, probably 15 percent (generally lower than the parents' rate). So, on the first $1,400 of unearned income, the total federal income tax per year will equal $105, a far cry from the $392 if taxed at the parents' 28-percent rate.

Gifts to minors age 14 or older

The Kiddie Tax disappears. The first $700 of profit (if no other earned income) is still not taxed, and any excess over the first $700 of unearned income is taxed at the child's lower rate, no matter how much profit is claimed. This saves 24.6 percent in federal taxes if parents are taxed at the 39.6-percent rate; 13 percent if parents are in the 28-percent tax bracket.

A gift to your child can qualify under the $10,000 gift tax exclusion, $20,000 if your spouse joins in your gifting mood. Currently, it is the business of the IRS if you give your children your assets (before or after you are deceased). So be careful you don't give more than the legal limits of generosity. A parent can gift $10,000 per year to each child (or to your favorite financial planner or author)—a total of $20,000 per couple per year without worry of a gift tax for giving away too much to loved ones (and none to your government).

There are disadvantages to every tax strategy. Not all parents want their children to own large piles of money while they are growing up. When you make a completed gift, you can't get it back. The money belongs to the child forever. You can become the custodian of your child's money, control where it is invested, and determine how it is spent for the minor's benefit until the child's age of *majority* (which might be a lot different from their age of *maturity*). But remember, legally, the money belongs to the child.

Gifts from grandparents are also eligible. If the kids play it right, they can clean up from all their relatives and friends—a $10,000 gift per victim per year.

The simplest type of gift is an outright one. Confer with your accountant (preferably over lunch so you can get free advice) about the reporting of cash and/or property gifts. Minors can report income either on their own tax return or their parents' Form 1040. Various types of income are reported differently.

Custodial gifts

The Uniform Gift to Minors Act (UGMA) and its expanded Uniform Transfer to Minors Act (UTMA) allow a minor to own money (or property) but retain the control and the investing decisions in the hands of an adult custodian. One custodian to each account, thank you. But the child could have many accounts, each with a different custodian.

They are easy to open and administer. College funds may accumulate faster than if the same funds were taxed at a parent's higher rate. An UGMA account restricts the types of securities that can be purchased, while an UTMA may hold nearly any type of investment property.

Depending on what your state will allow, more than cash or securities can be purchased. More sophisticated investments such as real property or the family business may also be transferred to your minor under a UTMA.

If the custodial parent dies before the child's age of majority, the legal age of adulthood (generally age 18 or 21 depending on your state's statute), the assets will be included in the parent's gross estate, though the child legally owns the money. You may want to name someone else as a backup or successor custodian.

If you become concerned that your child may fritter away the money once he or she attains the age of majority, you can stop adding to the account and start spending the account down for needs you would have funded out of your own assets.

When the minor attains the age of majority, the UGMA/UTMA wholly belongs to the child outside of the custodian's control, and the account should be re-registered in the sole name of the new adult.

Not all states have adopted laws permitting UTMA Accounts. Your tax advisor can tell you which account is available in your state.

The UGMA or UTMA has lots of flexibility. You, as a custodian, can direct the assets, change the investment structure, and use the money for the needs of the child, other than basic survival responsibilities that any parent would shoulder. You may not, however, fund a family trip to the Bahamas, purchase a new car for yourself or attempt to convince your 6 year old that a 25-foot cabin cruiser would make Daddy very happy at Christmas. You must use all money solely for the child's needs. A car for your child is perfectly legal, although perhaps not advisable for other reasons. Unusual medical expenses and other child related costs are also permitted.

If, however, gifting money to your child makes you nervous, parents can start college funding in a joint tenant account with each other, and mentally earmark the investment as a college fund. Though you may pay more taxes on an annual basis, you have the comfort of knowing you own the account and can use those funds for your own use, if necessary.

(I have received inquiries asking whether a parent's psychiatric fees are deductible during the teenage years since they are solely attributable to the child. This is pushing it. It is better to start your own mental health fund while your child is small and have it fully funded by adolescence.)

Family Values

No one can put a price tag on the joy of a new baby. But the new child credit gives new cause for parents to smile.

The child credit, $400 per child in 1998 and $500 per child in later years, is available for each child *under* age 17 whom you claim as a dependent. The credit is phased out (reduced) as adjusted gross income (income before subtracting tax exemptions and deductions) rises above $110,000 on a joint return and above $75,000 on an individual one.

The credit, which reduces your bottom line tax liability dollar for dollar, is in addition to the savings from claiming the child as a dependent and any child care credit you may reap as a working parent.

A qualifying child includes a child or descendant of a child, a stepchild, or an eligible foster child.

U.S. Savings Bonds

These are widely used as a gift giving vehicle for children. Savings Bonds are convenient to purchase and seem like a larger gift for the money spent because they are bought for half of their maturity face value. A bond costing $50 has a face value of $100.

Their major drawback: they won't keep up with the spiraling costs of college, even if they are tax-free for certain post-secondary education expenses. You can't chase today's college education tuition, rising at 8 percent, 10 percent or 12 percent per year with a 4-percent or 5-percent investment vehicle, even with some tax advantages. You need better inflation fighters to turbo-charge your college savings fund. A $25 bond with a face value of $50 will be worth approximately $22 in purchasing power at maturity. You must find better performers with greater potential for growth to fund your financial challenges. Growth oriented mutual funds are ideal college funding investments.

You can start a mutual fund with as little $25 and add to it. In addition, this investment can be a powerful financial education. Your children can track their account values in the newspaper and monthly statements. With a mutual fund, there is *learning* power as well as earning power.

At holiday or birthday time, parents or grandparents can add small gifts to the college fund, helping it compound even faster. Mutual funding is far superior to the usual gifts children receive: clothes left hanging in closets because they don't fit or toys broken a short time after received.

Series EE Bonds issued after 1989

These are eligible for college tuition and related expenses and are tax exempt as the result of tax legislation TAMRA 1988. An education minded Administration offers these as a method to help parents save for college and receive tax benefits. Actually, your government has a vested interest, long term loans from you for its current budgets.

You can exclude from income (part or all) of the bond interest when used for college tuition and related fees (not for room and board or football expenses). The bond must be a Series EE issued after Dec. 31, 1989, purchased in your name or that of your spouse (no grandparents allowed). The purchaser must be age 24 or older before the bond was issued.

If your family income is above a certain figure at the time of redemption (indexed for inflation), you will not qualify for this perk, even though you may have bought the bonds when under the income limit.

Weigh the purported tax benefits of savings bonds against inflation fighting mutual funds sheltered by the UGMA or UTMA with current annual tax free benefits. The lower the return you receive each year, the farther behind your money will lag as time passes. Hence, the more money you will have to focus toward college funding. Tax planning comes with an expensive price tag. Keep track of bond redemptions on IRS Tax Forms 8815 or 8818.

Stop pumping iron and pick up that broom

If you have a business, and think you can stand more closeness, you may be able to hire your child to do simple clerical, janitorial or other work. This tax advantage is sometimes abused, and when your child is supposedly working to earn money from your business he or she had better not be in the Galapagos Islands. In addition, you must pay your child normal labor wages for the job being done.

There can be minor problems and potential expenses with this strategy. If your teenager joins your home construction or clerical crew, worker's compensation, payroll taxes, unemployment taxes and other expenses may be applicable. Ask your accountant if this arrangement would still be profitable for you. If you are a sole proprietorship, the Social Security tax (FICA) does not have to be paid on a child under 18 (although your spouse is not exempt). This makes hiring your children over your spouse more attractive.

Your child can earn up to the standard deduction without paying federal income taxes. All amounts above that are subject to taxes at the child's rates.

Your child can use the dependent exemption, but you can probably make better use of it at your current tax bracket. Only one exemption to a customer today. (Parents can continue to claim the child as a dependent as long as they contribute more than half of the child's support, and the child is under age 25.)

Under an S Corporation, the child's wages can be charged as expenses and reduce the pass-through income to the parent (subject to FICA and FUTA). If you understand this, your life is complicated enough to get some advice from your tax adviser. Your children can "pay themselves first" by investing part (or all, up to $2,000 per year) of their earnings into a retirement IRA account.

Gifting securities

You may gift a child appreciated stock (worth more now than when you bought it) or other securities. The tax strategy is to buy something that produces little income (dividends and interest) and majors in growth (like IBM used to). Opting for the tax strategy, however, will likely result in riskier investments. I would give up some tax advantages to get better quality long term investments.

You gift the security to your child, and he or she sells the security, paying taxes in a lower tax bracket, probably 15 percent.

Taxes are due on profits above your original cost, not on the difference between the price when gifted and the sale price.

The parent may also owe a gift tax if the gift (the profit or net appreciation in the value of the stock) exceeds the gift tax exclusion amount ($10,000 per year, $20,000 per both parents). Tax planning should be second to more important criteria.

IRA gifts

This is a low cost way to give younger family members a head start on financial security. If the minor has enough earned income to make an IRA contribution, the contribution does not have to be made with that same money. Thus, a child with $2,000 of income from a first job can receive a $2,000 gift to fund an IRA.

Since the child will likely earn less than $30,000 per year, the gift can reduce the child's tax bill by being contributed tax deductible to the IRA Account.

A child who earns less than the standard deduction for paying income taxes can actually receive earned income and an IRA totally tax free.

Education and medical costs

These can be paid without incurring any gift tax as long as the gifted amount is paid directly to the educational or medical institution. Otherwise, gift taxes apply if paid to an individual who then remits it to an institution.

Of mice, men and child landlords

There is a current interest in funding college primarily on the real estate management talents of your college student. You buy a property near campus, convert it to a rental (with depreciation benefits) and pay your child to manage the property, for which you can take a deduction and pay her or him for services, such as negotiating student rentals, managing the property in your absence, painting, mowing the lawn and doing light maintenance.

After graduation, parents can sell the house, pay some income taxes on the gain, and feel clever that they have outwitted the taxman. This technique has been recommended by some money gurus as a great method of paying for a college education. The tuition supposedly comes from the monthly rent from other students.

Still, the average 18 year old is hardly equipped to negotiate with other taller and more intimidating college students, some who have signed up as the football team linebacker or *Partying 101* along with other studies. The condo could turn into a commune with freeloaders and loud Saturday nights (are you hearing the word "liability"?), excuses for nonpayment of rent and a big job when your student should be studying long hours for outstanding grades.

The resale value of the rental after only four years would probably be disappointing. It would have practically no equity, create maintenance expenses, while interest and other expenses would not be worked off during this short time frame.

You may have raised the most thoughtful, precocious, sensitive and mature semi-adult on campus. But if you have visited campus dorms during rush or homecoming season, you will understand that the National Guard is more equipped for this task than a young student. This avenue is highly suspect as a good college funding vehicle.

The childcare credit

If you pay for eligible childcare while working, you may deduct this cost from your taxes. A tax credit is more valuable than a tax deduction because a credit comes off your taxes at the end of the calculation. A tax deduction is worth 28 cents on your tax dollar, more if you are in a higher marginal tax bracket. A credit is worth $1 for each $1 of final taxable income you are expected to pay.

If you pay your baby sitter under the table, you will be turning him or her in to the IRS when you claim the childcare credit. The IRS is already suspicious of folks earning this kind of income. To protect its tax coffers, you must disclose whom you paid and include his or her Social Security numbers. The IRS can match these up in its mega-computers and send nasty letters to the individuals who did not report this income.

Check with your tax advisor to determine how helpful this tax break may be. The more income you earn, the less credit you can use. Check out alternative plans such as pretax flexible benefit plans at work, which may offer greater tax savings for childcare expenses. More companies are adding this employee benefit as working mothers join the labor market in greater numbers.

Trusts and other strategies

There are other more complicated tax strategies for parents with closely held businesses or corporations. Folks with oodles of money and, therefore, oodles of tax advisors (and names like Getty, Gallo and Rockefeller), can implement more complicated strategies. There are trust vehicles (GRITS, GRATS, Crummey trusts, minor trusts, generation skipping trusts, and other snooty and very expensive methods of tax reduction and passing assets to your progeny). But if you are among the yachtless, those outlined here should suffice. Beyond these basics, consult tax attorneys who specialize in these areas.

One caveat: In general, the more control you exert over your assets, the more encumbered they tend to become. Do not paint yourself into a tax corner that can be changed by Congress tomorrow. Consider how much control you will give up for tax planning before implementing a certain strategy. Weigh all aspects of a tax technique before committing your hard-fought-for financial resources.

One final word of advice: Never have children to make money. Instead, purchase a mink farm, horse breeding ranch or orange grove. At least you can claim the losses on your tax return!

Chapter 12

The hassle of the tassel

Mary Margaret is only six months old, but already she is worth a small fortune. In addition to the costs of clothing, feeding, educating and entertaining her for the next 18 years, her parents will spend approximately $158,000 for her four year, ivy-covered college experience.

When your student parades down the aisle on college graduation day, you will beam with pride. You may even forget your sacrifices to make this memorable event come true. And, if you are a middle income parent, you may also forget what steak tastes like, what a new car smells like and what your doctor and dentist look like. Welcome to the "Do I look like a savings and loan?" years.

This chapter is primarily written for parents who are willing to sacrifice their own self-interest to provide their children with the tools and skills they desperately need in today's highly technological world. It also has a message for children who would rather their parents not go bankrupt in the process and retire as wards of the state, or move in with them.

Surviving your child's college years is the ultimate trial by fire. I promise you that the cost of your child's chosen *alma mater* will be inversely proportional to the size of your existing college fund.

No matter how lonely you may feel waving good-bye to your college freshman, reminding him or her to call home often, you will learn to dread the ring of your telephone. Why? Because many conversations from campus to home sound a lot like this (what your student says is translated into what he or she really *means*):

"*Hi, Mom. I miss you.*" (I just spent my last $5 and have tapped everyone else I know for a loan.)

"*How are you feeling?*" (What kind of mood are you in?)

"*I've been so busy studying, I even forgot your birthday.*" (I remembered you the instant I ran out of cash.)

"*The food here isn't fit to eat, and they serve such small portions.*" (I spent $50 in 10 days on pizza and junk food.)

"*But don't worry. There's a grocery store close by.*" (My mother would never allow me to starve—she spent my whole childhood making me clean my plate.)

"*I've been hoping to join a fraternity/sorority because I really miss home, but I can't afford to.*" (I could become a social outcast. Wouldn't the annual dues be cheaper than all that guilt?)

"I would really love to come home for Thanksgiving, but I don't have the bus/train/plane money." (Would you be able to eat even one bite of turkey knowing I was the only human on campus?)

"Boy, are books and supplies expensive! I wanted to start this research project, but the lab fees cost a bundle." (Wouldn't it be nice to sit in the audience when I won the Nobel prize?)

"I sent you a birthday card because I was too poor to call." (I'll send you a card as soon as I finish this call.)

"I can't talk long because I'm on a friend's phone." (I could call home more often if I had money for my own phone. Maybe we could arrange to include my calls on your regular bill like the others here do.)

"The weather is getting colder, but I think I can manage with my old jacket if I wear enough sweaters underneath." (Everyone else bought a neat leather school jacket.)

"I have to go now. I need lots of sleep for my exam tomorrow." (The dorm party has already started.)

"The other moms have sent goody boxes so I don't need anything from you." (More guilt before setting up the punch line.)

"I almost forgot. Could you spare a few dollars—for the research project—remember?" (No translation needed.)

At some point during your parenting years you will have chauffeured approximately 145,000 miles, a one way distance to Mars, without receiving even one frequent flyer award. You will cut, paste, paint, glue, hold, blow dry and repair more scout, 4-H, Junior Achievement and school science fair projects than you thought possible for one child to enroll in.

The older your children gets, the more menial and minimum wage-type tasks they will need from you: message taking, refrigerator closing, car waiting, button sewing, jeans washing (one item per load), forgotten things delivering, broken heart repairing, drain unclogging, and zit checking.

One day you will emerge from the temporary driver's license phase and the pimple stage. You will believe you have been through it all—until you arrive at the high school financial aid meeting for parents of college bound students.

This is as good a time as any to buy your personal bumper sticker that will keep you going through four or more years of hamburger surprise, macaroni and whatever-is-leftover, and gluing together the soles of your shoes—one more time.

"Just wait until you have kids of your own."

The current cost of an in-state, four year public university education is approximately $36,048 ($8,000 per year and an 8-percent (8%) inflation cost increase each anniversary). That's tuition, basic room and board, and minimal supplies and miscellaneous fees. There is no "fat" in this figure—no pizzas, entertainment, no airline tickets home, no car on campus, no trip money for graduate school interviews, no clothing expenditures, and no health insurance, gasoline or telephone bills. And that's at a school that doesn't even win at checkers, let alone in the football stadium.

For that price you would think they could name a dorm after you. Note that it is also a public government subsidized facility, not a private institution.

If you are currently planning a new addition to your family, you will need between $144,000 and $150,000 to fund the same education 18 years from now. That jump is due to inflation, the enemy of long term financial dreams.

The further away your college years, the more money you will ultimately need. But as long as your college fund is regularly outpacing the higher costs of education, your goals will become more reachable. You must choose inflation fighting investment vehicles that will race faster than inflation to preserve your long term purchasing power.

Schools of higher learning live within the same price pressures you do. There are utilities, overhead, salaries, costs for expansion and equipment to remain competitive with other institutions. All these internal capital expenses cost big bucks.

What does this mean in terms of future costs to you? The following chart shows what you can expect to pay for a four year school if your son or daughter is ready for college some time during the next 20 years. The figures reflect three possible levels of inflation: 6 percent, 8 percent and 10 percent.

Year	6%	8%	10%
1998	$36,048	$36,048	$36,048
2003	$48,241	$52,967	$58,057
2008	$64,558	$77,826	$93,501
2013	$86,393	$114,353	$150,584
2018	$115,613	$168,021	$242,518

Remember, these are costs for a state supported university or college. If you and your student are considering a private school or specialized institution, double or triple these figures.

Parents tend to make similar mistakes when planning for their children's higher education:

1. Waiting too long to start saving.
2. Underestimating how much tuition will be needed.
3. Waiting for a child to decide on a career.
4. Diverting savings opportunities into spending for a child's comfort needs.
5. Thinking scholarships and grants (or some stranger) will fund most college tuition bills.
6. Directing too many dollars to current consumption expenses instead of savings.
7. Allowing children to believe financial resources are unlimited.
8. Denying children partial financial responsibility for their own education.
9. Believing that debt is the total answer, therefore, hurting future retirement reserves.
10. Funding the entire college bill instead of saving for retirement.
11. Using inferior investment vehicles that don't keep pace with inflation.

This financial burden can take on nightmare proportions unless planning starts well in advance. Financial planning today to meet tomorrow's challenges is essential. Runaway costs, tax changes and competition for grant and loan dollars will challenge your efforts.

Now, the good news

The most valuable gift you can give to your new pink or blue bundle is $25 or $50 per month in a high quality, growth oriented mutual fund. Funding your child's college education is a mutual problem. Why not use a mutual solution?

Many parents choose (or are sold) the wrong type of investment vehicle and wind up on the steps of Ivy U. many dollars short. By investing in fixed income products like zero coupon bonds, bank deposits, savings bonds, U.S. Government notes or, even worse, insurance policies or annuities, they eliminate the potential for growth vital to stay ahead of rising college costs.

You won't catch inflation napping with annual increases of 8 percent, 10 percent or 12 percent per year. How can a 5-percent U.S. savings bond, even with tax free advantages, catch up?

Insurance policies or annuities solicited by agents for college funding should be illegal, given the real inside rate of return inside the products. A 6-percent illustration on a policy illustration translates into 6 percent of what's left *after* they take out their share, much less than you may have been promised.

The tuition funds inside the insurance policy must be borrowed from the company, leaving you with less death benefit (see Chapter 7 for insurance concepts). Unless you have extra cash value built up in the policy's cash value, your death benefit reduces one dollar for each dollar withdrawn.

Insurance annuities sold as college saving vehicles may require surrender charges and a 10-percent withdrawal penalty before the age of 59½. Their rates of return are lackluster when compared to real mutual funds, and if the insurance company becomes insolvent, your savings could be withheld, perhaps for years.

Now is the time to assess your financial priorities and your responsibilities as a parent. Your *children* might want designer jeans, outrageously expensive tennis shoes and the latest computer game, but your *students* need money for college or other higher forms of education. If you yield to their demands today for immediate comforts, how will you tell them tomorrow they will be pumping gas after graduation? You will find a college planning worksheet in the Appendix.

The ABCs of financial aid

After countless hours of tests, essays, interviews, and occasionally prayer, your student has been accepted to Ivy U. Now comes the hard part: paying the bills.

Does your student need financial aid? Every parent I know can respond with an honest and resounding "YES!" But if you are counting on a mixed menu of grants, scholarships, loans and tax incentives to expand your small amount of personal savings, dream on.

In a nutshell, financial aid is the mixture of grants, scholarships, loans, and often jobs on campus defray schooling costs.

Grants and scholarships are more attractive because they don't have to be paid back; with interest. They are free money.

But unless your child is valedictorian of a large school where scholarships abound, does exceptionally well on the SAT or ACT, is a national or regional top athlete, or the family income and financial statement are minimal, scholarships may be small and relatively few. The affluent and the indigent have the best chance to attend the college of their choice.

Being accepted for admission doesn't mean your student is being considered for financial aid. You must complete the Department of Education's Application for Federal Student Aid (FAFSA) after January 1 of the senior year. Family income profiles are sent to the schools you request. Many colleges have financial aid forms of their own.

Most of your tangible, real estate and personal assets will be factored into a complex formula when you request financial aid. In essence, the more responsibly you have lead your life (the more savings you have and the less debt you have built up), the more you will be penalized by the current financial aid system.

After pumping your FAFSA data through a confusing federally sanctioned formula, your expected family contribution (EFC) is calculated.

A middle income family may be expected to shoulder most of the cost. A family income of $100,000 or more and a moderate net worth may separate you from most college entitlement programs and federal and state grant programs. Depending on your family size and the number of children attending college at the same time, your share may decrease some...but not enough to forestall a dash to the medicine cabinet.

Given the rapid escalation in college costs expected over the next 20 years, the most serious mistake is waiting too long to start investing. The more time your college fund has to compound, the greater the accumulated funds and the less money you will need to make it grow.

Don't be seduced by promoters and marketers who claim they can ferret out unclaimed scholarships or magically show you methods of using the equity in your home or some other method (often insurance) of sending your child to school. These schemes may involve leveraging your home, taking on large amounts of debt at high interest levels or purchasing questionable and inferior products.

Seek out a financial planning professional (who does not sell investment products) to calculate future costs and the general rate of return you need (after taxes) to earn.

Do not seek advice from a marketer, insurance agent or a stockbroker for this important problem. Their job is to make a sale and get your signature on the bottom line of their product application, not to dispense objective and competent expert advice regarding college funding costs. If you cannot seem to part with a few dollars to seek paid advice, use the calculations in my book that show you how to do the mathematics by yourself.

No risk is too risky

There is no such thing as "safe" or "risk free." No matter how you invest, you will have to take some risk. The solution is to learn how to manage risk: in one word, learn to *diversify*.

The optimum solution for long term college investing is to let compound interest do most of the work.

Read the chapter on mutual funds to find those right for your future college fund. A combination of equity income types and/or balanced types offer a powerful tool for lump sum investing. Be careful not to take too much risk. Aggressive growth, growth or global varieties are better suited for retirement needs.

You may be able to invest more aggressively in stock mutual funds through a systematic monthly strategy called dollar-cost averaging. A regular weekly or monthly investing program over time can turn small monthly contributions into a sizable nest egg. Dollar-cost averaging is explained in Chapter 22 along with a list of mutual fund categories appropriate for this strategy.

What about prepaid tuition plans?

Wouldn't it be great for someone to take the risk out of college funding? That's what prepaid tuition plans and similar programs promise. The proposed benefits sound ideal: You lock in credits toward a four year education ahead of time while the trust or investment company sweats over how to keep up with rising college costs.

States as well as colleges and universities are feeling pressure to address the serious problem of rising tuition and are joining forces for a solution.

Under most prepaid tuition plans (either state or privately endowed), a parent or grandparent can contribute payments that will supposedly guarantee a certain amount of education plus room and board. The college fund (usually a trust) manages the assets until they are withdrawn and used at college time.

Most such plans have been dismal failures because they are trying to accomplish the impossible: outpace inflation, pay generous management fees and invest safely. By the time they pay for outside management (which may not perform well) and pay other fixed costs, most cannot keep their promises.

Bottom line: they are promising the public too much for too little. Costs for most guaranteed future tuition costs are so optimistic that in order to guarantee your student a chair at Ivy U., their pool of assets must produce returns way beyond what the normal mutual fund (with its large economies of scale, top quality management, and low management expenses) could offer. Though they are generally part of the non-profit, apolitical landscape, their appearance (on radio, TV, and at a high school cafeteria near you) is no guarantee that their programs will work. Their written by-laws have a default plan, in case of failure. Where is your escape plan for rescuing the money if they become financially troubled?

Common sense should trigger some skeptical questions. What if their projections are too optimistic? What if the strangers who manage the money lose some of it? How can someone manage your money safely and achieve 15% or better high returns at the same time? Are they willing to add funds to make up the difference if they are long on promises and short on results?

"Sorry, we tried," won't send a tuition check to the college registrar's office. What if your child (or some other family member) needs those funds in the meantime? If your proposed student joins the military instead of enrolling in college, can you get an early refund? What accountants and regulators will be watching day and night to see that assets are properly managed to meet future costs?

The list of disadvantages grows longer. What if your child is not admitted to a school in your state? Even if your state's guarantee works, you have no price guarantee in any other state. If the trust funds result in taxable income, you may be left with less money.

You have no control over the funds. If the fund becomes financially troubled, can you redeem your money quickly? Perhaps your student will not go to college. Then who does the money belong to? And how long will it take to refund it?

If the fund becomes insolvent, how long will it take to receive your money back? In such an event, after auditors and other conservators have been paid, how much will be refunded?

A better alternative would be to start a mutual fund savings program under a tax shelter called a Uniform Gift to Minors or Uniform Transfer to Minors statute in your state. (See Chapter 11 for more detail.) Though there are drawbacks to every college funding alternative, this method keeps the control where it belongs (in your hands), provides tax advantages on an annual basis, and immediate access if your child needs the funds for another purpose.

There is always Hope

If you have college bound children or grandchildren and time is on your side, the Taxpayer Relief Act of 1997 makes paying for higher education easier.

The **Hope Scholarship Credit** is available for qualified tuition and related costs paid to cover a student's first two years of higher education at an eligible institution.

For each student, the tax credit covers the first $1,000 and fifty percent of the next $1,000 in educational expenses incurred in the first and second years of college or other qualified post secondary education.

The credit is phased out (reduced and then eliminated) for singles with a modified adjusted gross income between $40,000 and $50,000 and for joint tax filers with a modified gross income of $80,000- $100,000.

To qualify, the student must be enrolled on at least a half-time basis and attend an accredited college, university or vocational school leading to a bachelor's degree, an associate's degree, or another recognized post secondary credential.

Congress cares even more

The law also creates a **Lifetime Learning Credit** for students taking courses to acquire or improve job skills.

The 20-percent credit on up to $5,000 of tuition and fees can be used for any year of education after the first two years.

It has the same income reduction and elimination limits as the Hope Scholarship tax credit. The Lifetime Learning credit is available from July 1, 1998 on.

IRAs for education?

Parents, grandparents, other relatives, and friends alike can contribute to an **education IRA** plan designed to ease the burden of college funding. The account grows tax deferred until withdrawn tax free to pay for tuition, fees, room and board, and equipment such as computers.

Non-deductible contributions of $500 per year can be made to an education IRA for youngsters under age eighteen.

All funds must be withdrawn before the child reaches age thirty. However, this IRA can be rolled over to another eligible family child in need of an ivy-covered experience. If used for purposes other than qualified education expenses, however, earnings are taxed as income in the year withdrawn and are subject to an additional ten percent tax penalty.

The $500 contribution is phased out for taxpayers with modified adjusted gross incomes over $150,000 on joint tax returns and over $95,000 on single returns.

No contribution is possible if modified adjusted gross income on a joint return is $160,000 or $110,000 for single filers.

The new law prohibits funding an education IRA in the same year you contribute to a state sponsored pre-paid tuition program. Each year you tap an education IRA for college expenses, you forfeit the opportunity to take a Hope Scholarship credit (worth up to $1,500 per year in the first two years of college) or a Lifetime Learning credit (worth up to $1,000 per year for each additional year of post secondary education through the year 2002 and $2,000 per year thereafter).

In addition, under present financial aid formulas the account could be considered the child's asset. Planning is important to accommodate the most efficient combination of college funding opportunities. You may want to use all education IRA assets on one year's educational costs so you can take the tax credits in other years.

The youngster cannot be the beneficiary of multiple tax free education IRAs totaling over $500 per year. More than one account is allowed, and you can invest the IRA contribution in more than one place.

More help from Washington

The above law allows taxpayers who have to take out loans to pay for higher education either for themselves, spouses, or dependents, to deduct interest paid during the first sixty months in which interest payments are required on the loan.

This deduction is phased out for higher income taxpayers starting at $40,000 of modified adjusted income on a single tax returns and $60,000 on a joint return.

The deduction is fully phased out at $55,000 for single returns and $75,000 for joint returns.

Old IRAs are softies too

The ten percent penalty that applies to most **traditional IRA** withdrawals before the owner reaches age 59½ no longer applies to withdrawals taken for qualified higher education expenses for the taxpayer, his or her spouse, children, or grandchildren. This option is probably the least attractive as you are robbing your retirement fund for current needs. Robbing Peter to pay Paul solves one problem but creates another in the future.

Roth and roll for college

If you will have a child in college when you reach age 59½, you may want to fund a **Roth IRA** for college savings. You can contribute up to $2,000 per year, and once the account has been open for at least five years **and** you are age 59½ or older, you can withdraw as much as you want tax free and penalty free.

This idea is especially appealing if you have other tax sheltered retirement savings, such as a 401(k) plan or Keogh plan.

Younger parents can withdraw Roth contributions (principal) tax free and penalty free for college expenses (or for any other purpose). But if they dip into earnings, that amount will be taxed. At any age, though, as long as the money is used for college bills, the ten percent early withdrawal penalty does not apply.

Cash for college

If college is less than three years away and you have not accumulated sufficient college tuition funds, your funding options are limited. Stick with securities that protect your principal and investments that carry no investment fees, no surrender charges, no annual fees or other distribution or management expenses. This list includes short term bank deposits, money market mutual funds, Treasury bills or short term U.S. Government notes with two to three years to maturity.

Safety of principal is your first priority. Promises of higher yields may mean greater risk to your principal. Don't be tempted by sales brochures or fancy written illustrations.

Companies prey on parents' fear at this time, promising crisis aid. Their plans are suspect, often involve mortgaging your homestead or buying strange investments. With so little time left, you cannot take risky approaches to secure those tuition bills.

There are some short term methods you There are short term methods you can employ. Each comes at a price:

1. Borrowing on the equity in your home is often recommended because the interest can be deducted from your tax return. This is dangerous. You are risking your home, perhaps putting it on the auction block.

Equity lines of credit are generally adjustable demand loans written with an impaired risk clause (if your financial picture changes during the loan period, the institution can demand the money back pronto). If interest rates rise, in a few years your payments could be priced above your budget.

With home equity borrowing you are spreading out repayments over a longer time, creating a large debt to pay back. You are purchasing a long term mortgage collateralized by your home.

Use this solution sparingly. Most parents do not have many years to plan for retirement after paying for college. They should be stashing retirement savings away instead of paying for college indebtedness.

2. National Direct Student Loans (NDSL), offer a limited amount of borrowing power and seem more viable because the student can ultimately take on the repayment responsibility.

The Stafford loan is the most common since it is federally guaranteed and almost any student qualifies. Borrowing is subsidized by the government picking up the interest during the student's school years. Warning: defaulting on these loans is no longer tolerated.

3. Guaranteed Student Loans (GSL) are granted through individual lending institutions. Limits vary and specific borrowing conditions must be discussed. Give yourself enough time for loan processing If possible, apply several months before the funds are needed. The first application process will be the most confusing. After that, forms will be easier to complete.

Also, consider looking into Parent Loans to Undergraduate Students (PLUS).

4. Cash value life insurance policies can be borrowed against for such an emergency. But for every dollar you borrow, your death benefit decreases by the same amount at a time when your liabilities may actually be increasing. In addition, you are taking out another loan. You are sinking deeper into debt.

If you are healthy, purchase cheap term insurance, then surrender your cash value (whole life, adjustable life, universal life or variable life) insurance policy, and use your money for your own benefit for a change. During college, invest the extra money you save with cheaper insurance premiums (the difference between whole life and term costs) for your next impending goal (crisis), retirement.

If you purchase inexpensive term insurance while your family is growing, you can invest your savings budget into a mutual fund. Then you won't need to borrow from an insurance company and pay interest on the (your) money until you pay the loan back to them. (Cash value insurance is great for an agent's pocketbook but a lousy way for you to invest!) When your investments are not attached to your death insurance, you can access them without losing valuable death protection in the process.

5. Refinancing a home mortgage may be helpful *only* if interest rates have significantly decreased. The goal is to lower your monthly payment and free up more cash for college *without lengthening the mortgage debt period.*

Refinancing is generally beneficial when interest rates have moved down at least two percentage points and your monthly payment over the same time period is less.

6. Borrowing from an employer retirement plan may be allowed, but the government may become stingier in the future. By the time you need college money, there may be no method of extricating such funds. Don't expect to tap this option far into the future.

If your job should terminate, most 401(k) plans want the borrowed funds back or you will be taxed for an early distribution with extra penalties at a time you cannot afford it.

You are robbing your retirement fund and will have to replace whatever money you borrowed, *plus interest.* You are obligating yourself to more debt, usually not the most prudent solution.

7. Terminating an employee retirement fund or an IRA fund is even less attractive. In the previous example, though you are borrowing money, you must pay it back. This option has no automatic payroll deduction method of recouping those lost funds for the future. Unless you possess great financial discipline, this option is not recommended, even though you don't need to pay back the money you withdraw. There may be nasty penalties for early withdrawal and all taxes are due and payable in the year you liquidate your account. The dollars you can use after taxes and penalties may be small in contrast to the damage you do to your retirement nest egg.

8. Borrowing against securities can be effective, but if you have stocks and bonds laying around, why not just sell them? Liquidate savings bonds paying only four percent per year.

This solution may be more appropriate for the corporate executive than for the average college parents considering selling off the family pet to save the weekly cost of dog food.

9. The military (all three branches) have attractive programs to fund an education. These are popular, but there are service stipulations attached to each. A student should explore the various options. Some education benefits allow full education prior to enlisting. Others accumulate a college fund credit program to be utilized after discharge.

10. Cooperative education can solve an otherwise impossible funding problem. The benefit lies in the self-funding style of the education. The student works part time and attends class part time. The work is coordinated with the study curriculum, so sufficient income can be generated to maintain the costs of attending school.

A company can hire a fully trained employee after graduation. The student's advantage is obvious. This arrangement generates a dependable cash flow for tuition.

The disadvantage of cooperative education is the length of time to graduation. A typical four- or five-year course is often stretched to six years or longer. A student must be dedicated enough to pursue the longer time frame. But for a persistent student with few other avenues, this option can work out nicely.

11. Some companies offer tuition-paid college courses to high school graduates/employees as an incentive to improve employee productivity and performance. Classes may even be conducted during working hours. The company may, however, stipulate some type of reciprocal agreement, such as the student's promise to work for the company for a certain time period after graduation.

12. Commuting to a local college may limit the social experience, but from a purely financial aspect, it should be considered. There are hidden costs to consider: a car, gasoline, parking fees, auto insurance, lunches and the cost of maintaining a student at home. These should be compared to the cost of room and board on campus.

Students must be sure that all credits transfer if they later decide to attend a college away from home. If transferring at a later date causes extra time and tuition, this option may not be so cheap.

Commuting offers a hidden advantage. Perhaps your student cannot currently handle the freedom and lack of structure in a campus college environment. It is far better to successfully complete the first year of college in a community setting than to fail far from home.

All of the preceding programs and emergency measures have disadvantages and should be researched before proceeding. Call the financial aid offices of the universities you are interested in and the College Board (1-800-874-9390) for additional information regarding financial aid packages.

Double trouble

Many parents face a double edged sword: funding college and retirement goals at the same time. The answer? Transfer as much debt to your student as possible.

Though this sounds cruel, ask your students if they would rather pay back student loans after college or take you in when you are old *and* poor?

Upon graduation, the only debts they will shoulder is a car payment and a monthly rent bill. They have one advantage you don't: time on their side.

From ivy league to big league

Some parents want their student to start their working career debt free. Your kind intentions, however, may be hazardous to your retirement years and to your child's character. A student who has partially funded his or her own education may place greater value on the experience.

Many parents sacrifice their own comforts during the education years. And I believe that education is one of the most valuable investments you can make. But while we train highly skilled young adults, they often enter the working world with hardly a clue how to manage the small fortunes they will eventually earn.

Pegged as targets of credit card vendors and other tempters who will convince them that living life on the installment plan is a contemporary approach to having it all now, they will control your child's financial destiny.

Even if you have funded another child's education in the past, don't feel compelled to do likewise today if your retirement fund is at risk. Guilt can move you from the penthouse into the poorhouse.

Don't protect your most precious asset from the realities of the outside world. Financial opportunities may not be limited, but financial resources certainly are And your kids should know this before they are taught tough lessons from the school of hard knocks. Teaching them financial responsibility in this instant gratification age may be their only training ground to live a financially successful life.

Hand over that baby-sitting money

I have encountered both types of parents—those determined to fund the entire cost of higher education for their children and those not willing to contribute 39 cents to their child's schooling. My philosophy is somewhere in the middle. A child with little or no responsibility for the sacrifices involved in funding his or her college years may view your sacrifices less reverently.

Encourage (or require) your child to work before college and during summers away from school, to work between semesters, to participate in work study campus programs during the school year (unless grades are at risk) and to handle the responsibility for repaying student loans after graduation.

Your student's higher education will not be guaranteed by throwing some money toward the goal and hoping things will work out. It takes "X" amount of money working at "Y" rate of return, compounded for "Z" years, to create the significant funds needed.

You must know the amount of seed dollars necessary to create your goal, the combined rate of return needed annually to reach the required amount of money and the average inflation rate you are attempting to outpace.

Settling for any less preparation is akin to getting in your car and starting for New York or Los Angeles with no map, half a tank full of gas and no particular route in mind. If you get there at all, it will be because of sheer luck. And you will likely be very late for the party.

Chapter 13

The perils of partnerships: not married

The original family portrait was designed in Hollywood. Families were always neatly dressed. Dad sat down to discuss family problems while Mom made dinner in a dress. Everyone smiled a lot.

The most serious family crisis was solved within twenty-five TV minutes. Conversations on a higher plane became moral lessons. No one swore, yelled (for very long) or pouted for weeks. No teenage zits were allowed on stage. There were enough bathrooms to go around. Even the family dog had manners enough to doo doo behind the bushes where the TV camera couldn't zoom in.

The Donna Reed syndrome has faded. Contemporary values have evolved into variations on a family theme. Yours, mine, ours and the kid next door who is always here for dinner, are more the rule; not the exception.

There is greater acceptance of non-traditional living arrangements, as well. But non-married couples enjoy fewer protections under the law than their married counterparts. In addition to some leftover reproach from the conservative sector, they face unique financial issues and greater legal perils to their assets.

Unmarried roommates, regardless of their sexual orientation, deal with many of the same daily living and household financial issues that married couples do. Risk exposures, combined financial arrangements, legal protection for each member of the twosome and protection of assets upon disability or death are applicable to any set of roommates. But intimate heterosexual and homosexual couples planning emotional as well as financial futures together face greater obstacles, given today's legal system and family mores and values.

To clarify which financial areas are indigenous to each type of binding unit, the terms "housemate" and "roommate" apply to all non-married couples or units, while "partner" and "domestic partner" refer primarily to couples living and loving together.

Two in one kitchen

Adults living together should discuss financial roles before habit gradually shapes their savings and spending patterns. Otherwise, who pays for what, how both fixed and variable expenses are allotted and what assets are maintained separately could become sensitive, perhaps explosive issues later. Married couples can enjoy separate careers, recreational lifestyles and, sometimes, separate financial lives. It should be expected that singles may want autonomy and freedom as well. Financial disagreements can lead to incompatibility. So money concerns should be discussed and housekeeping rules implemented without one partner feeling intimidated, manipulated, victimized or resentful.

Budgetary and household expenses ordinarily are a combined effort. A session at the kitchen table with a list of monthly expenses should cover who pays for what, and which expenses are the sole obligation of the party making the purchase. Items such as appliances may be common purchases. Or one person could buy the vacuum cleaner and another the microwave. The latter may be a better solution. In the event of separation, both will have some appliances with which to set up separate households.

A joint checking account for household expenses may be helpful for convenience. Be sure you are comfortable with this arrangement as either account holder may liquidate the entire account value without the other's knowledge or permission. If both parties are dependable, you may want to pay for expenses directly from your separate accounts, or deposit into a joint checking account just enough to pay expected monthly bills.

Personal loans between partners should be conducted strictly as business deals with a promissory note outlining repayment provisions. Business matters should remain separate from relationship issues.

Credit cards should be maintained in solo names. It is too easy for excess charging to occur. Partners and roommates should not borrow each other's credit cards for any reason, though short term cash crunches may tempt one person to ask for an advance in this manner. Any charge to your credit card, even if you don't create it, is the legal responsibility of the cardholder. If one person temporarily needs a tideover, a cash loan is a better option.

It's important to separate financial issues from caring ones. A joint bank account or a single name on the property deed does not necessarily indicate greater dedication to a relationship or a lack of commitment. Individuals can have separate financial affairs and still enjoy a deep feeling of companionship. Surrendering financial separateness does not guarantee surrender of the heart.

If one partner wants separate savings, checking and investment accounts, this is not a sure sign that the relationship is weak or in trouble. Today's couples have a strong sense of individuality. Paychecks, investment income and personal wealth are trappings of personal success. And combining financial resources should not become a prerequisite for emotional security. A relationship that demands this type of surrender for overall unity may signal disturbing, underlying issues.

If one roommate has greater earned income than the other, the poorer partner can feel less valid, financially dependent or manipulated. If one partner is a saver while money burns a hole in the other partner's pocket, resentment over wasteful spending or miserly money management can fester. If these symptoms appear, it may be time to examine the basic relationship and clear the air while the issue is manageable.

Setting up house

When a domestic partner moves in with his or her housemate who has already established quarters, lease agreements, utility bill accounts and post office addresses should be modified to reflect both names. When two names appear on the apartment lease, neither party can be evicted (even for nonpayment of his or her share of the rent). Both need written housing protection and legal access to a roof over their head. A tactical plan of action should be established beforehand in case one leasee stops paying his or her portion of household expenses.

Request a clause in the lease agreement to allow subletting in case one renter moves out, leaving the other with higher monthly payments than affordable. If the lease is written to allow subletting to another roommate (at least until the end of the lease agreement period), someone else can share the associated costs.

Utility bills should also be set up in both names. If one partner moves, the current gas, electric and phone service can be maintained and a new deposit (and new number) will not be required. Utility bills, such as long distance telephone charges can become bones of contention. Keep a pad by the phone as a log to record all names and calling numbers. This helps recall who called whom, when the bill comes.

There are lots of convenient variations for housekeeping rules that work as long as each person respects the basic rights of his or her partner.

Neither partner should sign a housemate's name on any financial or other legal documents, even for convenience sake. This may be later construed as forgery. The casual check signing that married couples occasionally perform for each other is a different matter. Don't allow intimacy to blur financial demarcation lines and definite no-nos.

Insurance issues

While cars should not be co-titled in both names, an important issue to consider is whether your roommate is covered if he or she occasionally drives your vehicle. Check with your insurance company, and get it in writing that this is allowed. Even if you don't typically lend your car, in an emergency the other party may need to drive it. *Never waive the right to drive each other's autos.* If, for example, you weren't covered on your roommate's policy and you were involved in an auto accident in which you were driving his or her car, both of your assets may be in jeopardy.

Find an insurance company that will insure both of you for driving either car. Check the contract to be sure both of you are included when you receive your policy. If you must have separate policies because one of you has a poor driving record, be sure each driver is a named additional insured on the other's contract.

More insurance companies are writing this kind of business, and they will overlap the coverage to protect both drivers no matter whose car is involved in an accident. This may be a tougher sale for an insurance agent, however, so be sure to get it in writing and check for both names on the written policy when it comes.

The same principle applies for renter's (or homeowner's) insurance coverage. Renters should request a policy to cover all personal property with one policy. It is nearly impossible to pick through the remains of a fire, flood or theft trying to remember who owned what. Since you are one basic insurance risk unit, find a policy that will wrap around both of you.

A renter's insurance policy should include guaranteed replacement on personal contents and a large helping of liability protection to boot. Two roommates, two sets of friends and two families can double the chances of someone getting injured on your property.

An extra personal liability umbrella of at least $1 million should be considered in case an injured guest sues either (or both) of you. Your courtroom adversary may look toward two deep pockets of financial gain. Two professionals with two substantial incomes may motivate a larger claim and a request for higher damages.

Shop for renter's/homeowner's and auto insurance coverage from the same company so that you have an airtight policy around both of you no matter what peril you may be exposed to or regardless of who is blamed. Fragmented coverage from different companies may leave gaps in your overall protection.

Homeowner's insurance requires more detail than can be fully discussed here. Remember to request guaranteed replacement on your dwelling as well as guaranteed replacement of its personal contents. Add the extra layers of liability protection above your basic coverage for bodily injury liabilities as well.

Insurance companies often neglect to offer you excess auto uninsured/ underinsured coverage when you request bodily injury umbrella coverage, because they don't want to assume the extra risk for a small annual premium. That alone should tip you off as to how important this extra layer of legal protection really is. Depending on your current or potential career earnings, or financial net worth, you may want more than $1 million of personal liability protection.

Don't risk a lot for a little. The primary purpose for insurance is to cover catastrophic events that you cannot recover from by yourself. Chapter 7 will teach you how to get the most insurance bang for your consumer buck.

Health and life insurance

If each partner has adequate health insurance at work, danger of illness and injuries should be covered. If, however, one partner loses his or her job, coverage can sometimes be purchased for your partner under a non-spouse employer health benefit plan. If such benefits are available, don't automatically cancel individual health coverage because you believe it is redundant. The future of health care benefits is uncertain. So it may be wise to maintain both forms of coverage. If one of you leaves the relationship, the joint health coverage may vanish too. Disability insurance is also a must. If you can't purchase it through your employer and are healthy, buy an individual disability income policy with a long elimination period to keep the premium as low as possible. In most instances, consider yourselves as separate units for health and life insurance purposes.

Are there contingent plans if one partner becomes seriously ill or leaves the relationship? Or is relocated? Do either of you have the capability and financial resources (and legal authority) to care for each other in case of illness or injury? What alternative arrangements could be made for living quarters, hospitalization, family involvement and visitation? Secondary issues stemming from such an event should be examined.

A hospital may allow visitation by family members but not friends, even intimate ones. A power of attorney naming the partner to take charge of medical or financial affairs may help. But there may be extenuating factors that would reduce its effectiveness.

All attention is usually directed toward the ill person. Occasionally the sick or injured person's family becomes vindictive, creating further tension and complications. Who will provide support for the isolated unintended victim—the healthy partner?

Home sweet home

Purchasing real estate is precarious enough when married couples buy their American dream. With two singles, differing income levels, separate financial lives and the possibility that one may leave the other with monthly mortgage payments, buying your money pit becomes even more complex. If the current relationship sours for any reason, how do you divide one piece of real estate in half (or in any other proportion depending on the percentage of ownership)? The house may have a higher fair market value in the future. One will have to buy out the other, or settle for an agreement of payments for a specific period of years. But this leads to other risks. Can the remaining co-owner get such a large loan or refinance alone? Payments could stop if the remaining owner becomes sick or loses a job. The part owner wanting an exit may need his or her share immediately to purchase new housing. The third option is to sell the property outright, liquidating the entire asset, but that could take months—and leave the other partner without housing.

If incomes are significantly different and down payment accounts are uneven, structuring the deal gets more convoluted. If the higher earner puts down 20 percent while the lower wage earner pays a greater share of the monthly payment or household expenses, the deal begins to look more like an octopus instead of a commonplace property transaction.

There are few simplistic resolutions when singles purchase real estate together. The most practical solution is to rent until financial issues become more solid. This may also be the best economic solution. Homes are virtual money pits, not great investments.

Many justify the purchase of real estate as an investment. Chapter 9 on home ownership should convince you otherwise. This gigantic money eating machine will absorb oodles of after tax, hard earned, paycheck dollars that could be used for other financial goals. A house can sop up so much discretionary income that renting may be cheaper in the long run.

The perils of partnerships: not married

Homes are illiquid stores of value that can't be tapped like savings accounts, bank CDs or mutual funds. A home may be the largest cooperative purchase the two of you ever make, but it probably won't qualify as one of the best.

If, however, you proceed with your home search, finding a willing lender may not be easy. Banks are, by nature, stodgy, and they may view your joint request as less than serious. With two dependable incomes and two strong credit ratings, you should qualify as strong candidates. If you sense real discrimination, though, bring up the issue to the lender. This may promote a more positive discussion regarding purely financial issues. Banks, by law, must be equal opportunity lenders. This means they must concentrate on only one thing, the color of your money.

How will the deed be structured? If you title property in both names, should you request a warranty, a survivorship or a tenancy in common (if allowed) title? Would you want your share of the asset passed directly through a deed to your domestic partner or to some family member through your will? With a warranty or survivorship deed, no matter who paid what percentage of the down payment or monthly mortgage debt, co-owning the property in this fashion will make both of you equal homeowners. Tenancy in common, however, recognizes how much interest each of you have in the property. Your portion will pass through the will (and through probate) with tenancy in common as well as with a general warranty deed. If you want your partner to receive your property interest directly, these ownership forms are not the cheapest or most direct method. If you desire, however, for a family member to own your share through your will, tenancy in common or joint deeds will accomplish that.

Joint and survivorship deeds revert the title to the survivor after the death of one co-owner. Alternatively, through a fee simple warranty deed, each partner owns half of the real estate, and her or his share passes through her or his will at the time of death. Wills attract probate, expenses, disagreements that could result in contests, and time constraints. If you intend to bequeath the house to your partner (and vice versa), a survivorship deed will make a direct transfer to your co-owner outside your will.

If a family contest erupts, no method may be fail safe. But survivorship deeds are more difficult to set aside in a court of law. It's vital to keep careful records of down payments, receipts for improvements and monthly mortgage payments in the likelihood of a contest.

Since joint and survivorship deeds pass your portion of the real estate to your surviving partner, you need enough death insurance to pay off the total outstanding mortgage balance, not just your half of the debt. Without two incomes, maintaining home expenses may be too expensive for just one person.

Purchase (cheap) term insurance to cover the liability. You can designate your partner as the only beneficiary, or you can name both your partner and a family member, each receiving a certain percentage or dollar amount of the death proceeds. Maintain the ownership of your own policies.

Avoid credit life insurance at lending institutions if you are healthy and insurable on your own. It is a high cost product that constantly reduces the death benefit.

You can buy inexpensive level term insurance from an outside company. If you are uninsurable, however, credit life may be the only method of getting death protection to pay off the outstanding mortgage balance. As long as there is no medical underwriting (medical investigation), this option is better than having no coverage. The beneficiary on credit life is your banker. So don't expect any death proceeds left over for other financial expenses.

You may want to purchase individual term insurance to cover the mortgage and any other outstanding debts, such as car loans, final medical expenses and other liabilities your partner will be left with. Debt collateralized by your home, if not paid, will be attached to the home, potentially forcing a sale if the survivor can't come up with enough cash of their own to pay off a lien.

An insurance policy offers a choice of primary beneficiaries and contingent (backup) beneficiaries. You can designate death proceeds sent to more than one person. Insurance policy death benefits can avoid your will and costly probate by naming the beneficiaries you choose.

Real estate ownership deeds

Type	Ownership equity	How passed to heirs
Sole Owner	Single ownership	Through will and probate
Warranty	Both own equally	Through will and probate
Joint and Survivorship	Both own equally	Outside will through deed title
Tenancy in Common	According to what proportion of market value each contributed	Proportionally passed through will and probate
Tenants by the Entirety	Not available: only granted to legally married spouses	

**Some ownership titles are not available in all states

Estate planning

An effective estate plan involves more than buying term insurance to fund bills you leave behind. Individuals should have a full set of estate documents: a will, a power of attorney for financial directives, and a living will and/or medical health care directive (if appropriate in your state). You can name a close family member or your partner to administrate your estate or to manage your medical decisions and financial affairs if you can't because of illness, injury, disability or incompetence.

Powers of attorney are used during your lifetime if you are not able to make your own financial and medical wishes known, while a will (or titling assets in joint ownership or joint and survivorship) direct them after you pass on.

Assets transferred through your will generally enter into probate. Though everything you own at your death is considered part of your gross estate, many financial assets (insurance policies, investments and even real estate) can be set up to transfer by title or beneficiary designations outside your will and away from probate problems and will contests.

Many assets are easy to pass to heirs outside of probate. In addition to insurance death benefits (at work and those individually owned), employer retirement pension accounts and supplemental pension plans such as 401(k)s, thrift savings plans and profit sharing plans also qualify for beneficiary designations. Company stock plans (ESOPs) may often be transferred. Or at least if the stock must be sold back by the company, the money can be directed to your beneficiary choice. You can name multiple beneficiaries so that your assets can be directed to more than one person.

Insurance laws state that an insurance beneficiary should have an insurable interest in the insured (the person whose life is insured). This means that there should be a financial hardship stemming from the death of the insured person. If not, the insurance company may question why your partner has been named as a beneficiary. A business partner, a spouse and family dependents are easily labeled with an insurable interest. You may need to spotlight any financial relationship you and your partner share. A family member could contest this aspect as well.

Check with the insurance company you are considering regarding its policy on this issue. Get a promise in writing that your beneficiary choices will be honored as designated. Often, there are true financial concerns such as jointly owned real estate, combined liabilities or paying off estate debts. A net worth statement might be valuable to include with your insurance application when you apply for coverage.

Since employer benefit policies are traditionally structured first to the spouse, you must be sure they know your wishes and that these will be carried out as you request. Put everything in writing.

Although estate laws and statutes vary in every state, if you wish to maintain assets separately from your partner but would like to transfer them directly to your partner as beneficiary in the case of your death, there are solutions. A *payable on death* designation on bank savings, checking and credit union accounts acts similar to a beneficiary and liquidates the money outside your will. Other investments, such as mutual funds, stocks and bonds, can use a *transfer on death*. These are easy to institute and require the completion of simple forms.

Don't overlook other death benefits from professional societies, credit card companies and outside vendors. You may have death or accidental death coverage. Often these companies give you a small free benefit, hoping you will sign up for more later.

Joint investing

When the tie that binds is not marriage, investing requires careful planning and forethought. If one partner is sued for any reason, the combined assets may be at risk in a litigation battle.

Joint (either/or) and survivor banking accounts with rights of survivorship designate a divided interest in the account value.

Joint tenants with rights of survivorship (JTWROS) on mutual funds and other securities gives an undivided interest in the entire account to each owner and, unlike a bank deposit account, gives both owners full interest in all proceeds. Assets go to the surviving owner in case of death. Easy to set up, this financial bond is nearly impossible to unwind unless both parties agree to separate the account.

Under joint tenants with rights of survivorship (JTWROS), companies will liquidate proceeds to all owners together unless a signature guarantee is presented to the investment company. Any checks from such an account are sent in the name of both joint tenants. Any accountholder can liquidate a savings account. Not so with joint and survivorship investment registrations. You must have written permission from all owners to liquidate funds from a joint tenant account. This joint title is not simple to reverse once in place. Though more difficult to separate once established, they are a stronger form of joint ownership and a stronger defense against estate contests.

You can pass investments to a partner after death by naming them as a beneficiary (transfer on death) in states where this registration is allowed.

Adding your partner to your real estate deed transfers half of the property value to the new owner. If over the amount of $10,000 per year, this transfer of ownership may gift tax under IRS rules. In addition, once recorded, such ownership cannot be reversed without consent from the new owner. Combine assets only after advice from competent legal and accounting experts.

Be sure you understand all implications of joint accounts before they are set up. Your state's laws may vary. Folks change names on their money pots as casually as they change their socks. Each time you add a name to your account, you are making a transfer to another person. In other words, you are *gifting,* and the IRS has an interest in such a transaction.

If the gift is more than $10,000 per year (joint ownership in a home might gift more than the allowable annual amount), you are subject to a gift tax and must complete and file with the IRS a gift tax Form 709. Though the tax does not have to be paid now, it will be deducted from your unified credit against your estate at your death. The law may have changed by then, so look to the basic economics of the transfer before making a final decision.

If, instead, you want to maintain separate ownership of your own assets but want access to them by your partner if you are disabled, a power of attorney can be used, which names your partner as your personal representative to conduct your financial business when you are not able.

As you can see, combining assets outside of marriage should be considered carefully.

Some states recognize common law marriage between heterosexuals after a period of conducting a financial and sexual relationship. Others do not. Understand what state statutes apply in any state in which you have a property interest or an investment holding.

Protecting your partner through your will

If you use a will to pass real or personal property to heirs or to anyone outside your immediate family, be sure your intent is in crystal clear language in the document. Contact a lawyer who is knowledgeable in this area, and who will understand your concerns and your unique position.

Since a will can be contested by anyone who disagrees with the provisions you have outlined, discuss the use of will substitutes, such as joint and survivorship or beneficiary designations.

Bequeathing personal property after death is a touchy issue since family members may believe the possessions of their loved one should belong to them. Guaranteed replacement of personal contents on your renter's or homeowner's insurance will take care of vandalism, fire or theft. But for estate planning protection, you should save receipts and mark any gifts with the donee's name on the invoice.

You can also add a *personal property addendum or memorandum* to your will. This will lend additional credence to your intent to direct your personal belongings in the manner you put in writing. Check with your state to determine requirements to affect such a change.

Since most debts are not collateralized by any security (your house or car), they can't be collected by repossessing a home or auto. Don't allow anyone to pressure you into paying medical, hospital, funeral, auto, credit card or other unsecured obligations belonging to your deceased or relocated partner unless you voluntarily desire to, have insurance proceeds for such purposes or have the personal financial means to do so and are so inclined.

If you are advised to place all of your assets into a trust as a foolproof solution, don't believe that a trust is fail safe regarding contests by disgruntled heirs, ex-spouses or past significant others. Even if the trust prevails, the costs for defending such an action are steep.

Serious illness or the death of a family member can bring out the best (and the worst) in human beings. Don't assume everyone is as pleased as you with your current affections and lifestyle choices. Like other financial planning areas, a strong defense is the best offense.

Relationships are challenging enough without complex agendas. Although this is the '90s, families form their own sets of mores and behavior requirements. So discuss a unified plan of action with your partner beforehand.

Tax strategies

You still have all rights to contribute to employer retirement plans as any single would and to make annual IRA contributions (even if they are nondeductible). Separate ownership of assets creates separate tax consequences. Combined joint tenants with rights of survivorship accounts may produce only one Form 1099 tax report. Such tax due can be divided equally. Call your investment company for its policy regarding the division of the tax liability.

Mortgage interest can be deducted as paid by each property owner. There is no marriage tax (married couples receive a smaller deduction than two singles living together filing separate returns). The earned income credit may be at risk if there are children involved and one partner makes a much higher income. Child support and other financial commitments outside your present relationship have to be factored into your tax plan.

Seek a tax advisor familiar with more than a cookie cutter approach to tax preparation. You need a strategist. In a few cases, you may come out ahead of marrieds by filing separately.

Until non-married housekeeping couples and domestic partners have greater legal protection regarding asset ownership and estate transfers, they must examine financial planning issues with a balanced perspective in mind.

Prenuptial agreements

Though it may sound cold to have your bride/groom-to-be sign a waiver as a condition of marriage, if you have children from a prior marriage, are unsure whether you want your own personal assets held separately, or have other reasons to keep "his and hers" separated, a prenuptial agreement may be considered.

A prenuptial agreement is a written contract signed without coercion or duress that states which assets will be considered separate from marital property, and which assets shall be combined. This may include personal inheritances or prior marriage settlements earmarked for other reasons than combined needs.

Consult an attorney familiar with such contracts because they may be invalidated if not drafted properly or if they indicate involuntary coercion. The longer the contract date before the actual marriage the clearer the document may appear.

State and federal laws change quickly. Such an agreement should be reviewed every few years regarding new case law, state statutes and precedence in the courts.

This relatively new aspect of law is not perfected, but a written contract is strong evidence of intent in a case where emotions may run high. Good contracts make good fences—and good fences make good neighbors.

Chapter 14

When you are alone

Eat your carrots. Pick up your toys. Be home by midnight. Pick up the shirts at the cleaners. Don't forget to buy milk on your way home.

Much of your life you may have lived by the rules of significant others—your parents or a spouse. Then, suddenly, you're on your own—completely in charge of your financial well being. Or perhaps you've been living alone for years, dutifully working and handling your financial affairs as necessary, but putting off any major decisions, such as buying a house or saving for retirement. After all, what if you "meet someone" tomorrow?

Whether "suddenly single" because of divorce, death of a spouse or recent emergence from college or your parents' home; even if you've been single for much of your adult life and need to jump start your financial future, refuse those offering you freedom from managing your own financial life. No one should know more about your money than you do. No one will watch over it as carefully as you will. If you have a friend, a loved one or a colleague adjusting to a new lifestyle of self-dependence, you can offer supportive strategies.

Though you will probably never win the lottery, you will hopefully earn enough money to sustain you for a lifetime. Some weeks may seem like two steps forward and a giant leap backward. But your financial independence will grow and, with your new money skills, you will take bigger steps forward and smaller (and fewer) in reverse.

Will that be a charge?

While credit is all too easy for many Americans to secure, singles can have trouble establishing credit or obtaining even the most fundamental credit. Those suddenly single through divorce or the death of a spouse might find themselves for the first time unable to qualify for the credit they might need to purchase a new home, a car, or a new outfit. Young people setting up their own residences, small businesses, or just starting their careers will not have an employment history they can take to the bank.

In our society, even those who are not in the habit of using credit can find it difficult to get along without a credit history. Getting a credit card under your own name—without relying on a spouse's income on your application—can be the first step in developing a credit history.

Find the best card for your money

You will want to obtain one or more bank credit cards. While they might be easier to obtain, department store credit cards do not carry the same clout as major credit card standing.

Compare rates and terms available from various banks, using the credit card checklist in Chapter 6. Visa and MasterCard credit cards are offered through individual banking contracts, with each institution setting its own qualifications, rules and interest rates. If you are turned down at one institution, try another.

If you have difficulty qualifying for a credit card, obtain a collateralized card. These look like the "real thing" but require a deposit beforehand (the collateral), which is placed into an interest bearing checking account. The issuer will give you a line of credit (a card) with a limit equal to the money you have deposited with it. If you have no other alternative, collateralized cards can provide that credit history you need to become a good credit prospect in the future.

Don't give up too easily

If you are repeatedly denied credit, and feel you have been discriminated against, continue your fight for credit. Document all telephone conversations, the names of people you speak to and copies of all written letters you send. If necessary, bring documentation of all assets to a local lending institution with your request.

After all, you are not asking for the moon, just a small credit line of, say, $250. If you're not satisfied with how you're treated, threaten to remove savings or stop other business which you conduct there.

This is not a "for-women-only" issue. While we traditionally perceive that women confront this problem, I know husbands who don't sign their own paychecks or monthly pension checks for fear of being indicted for fraudulent check signing—their wives have taken care of all the financial matters throughout their married lives.

The faces of divorce

The term "suddenly single" refers to a life change brought about when a "significant other" is no longer in your life. There are two major causes for sudden singlehood in modern America—divorce and death.

There are three elements to each and every divorce: 1) the legal ramifications; 2) the financial consequences; and 3) the emotional arena.

Don't expect your attorney to assist you with more than the legal portion. Although the legal aspects tend to overshadow the others, they may be the simplest areas to deal with. The psychological and financial aspects may be long lasting—you may need advice from a psychologist and a divorce financial planner to help formulate your future.

In negotiating any divorce settlement, the parties must consider both hard dollars and soft dollars. Real estate values are considered soft dollars because the actual fair market value can vary so widely and fluctuate so much over time.

However, while the house's current market value is being bandied about like a pawn, no thought might be given to the fact that the future owner will pay real estate commissions, closing costs, and capital gains before netting a profit on the sale of the asset.

The wife usually receives the home in divorce settlements, perhaps with little thought as to whether she will be able to maintain it financially. Of what value is this kind of settlement if you need income? Before committing to continuing monthly mortgage payments, maintenance, taxes, insurance and other associated expenses, singles should complete the budget page in the Appendix to be sure they can afford the hefty financial costs for a lengthy period of time.

Securing the pension piggy bank

Although state laws vary, generally the divorcing couple will share those benefits accrued during the life of the marriage. For example, if the husband has a pension from his work and the employer's plan allows it, the couple can arrange to split the pension as they—and their lawyers—agree to.

It can get tricky, though. What if the ex-husband dies before retirement age? What if he elects not to retire at 65? What if he quits for some other reason and does not collect retirement benefits at all?

These risks can be hedged or at least reduced. To eliminate loss of pension payments if an ex-spouse dies, a term insurance policy can be purchased on his or her life for the future value of the retirement benefits. The future payee ex-spouse can be named the irrevocable beneficiary or, better yet, the policy's new owner. (Term insurance is preferable to whole life and other types of policies since the benefit is needed only until retirement age.)

Typically, it would be the ex-spouse, or the working ex-spouse, who pays the premium. But if the payer lets the policy lapse, the beneficiary/owner has the right to continue to pay premiums and can exercise all control over the contract.

The risks to the pension benefits if the working spouse were disabled can be reduced through the purchase of a waiver-of-premium rider on the term insurance policy. This ensures that the policy can continue in force without further premium payments should the insured become disabled.

If there is an insurance policy already in force, the ex-spouse can be added as a collateral or irrevocable beneficiary (one that can't be removed) or can become the new owner.

More important than wealth

Health benefits can be another great concern during divorce proceedings. An older or ill individual (currently covered on a spouse's group plan) may worry about the difficulty of finding adequate coverage for a reasonable cost. But an HMO is not the only option these people have. Fortunately, the Consolidated Omnibus Budget Reconciliation Act (COBRA) allows ex-spouses to continue to receive coverage under their former spouse's group health plan for a period of time (typically, 18 months), though the non-employee ex-spouse will now be responsible for the payments previously made by the employer.

If you are healthy, you may find a better value by shopping around for a less expensive carrier. Typically, the premiums on the COBRA insurance increase significantly when the individual starts paying them because he or she is paying the entire premium without the employer's contribution.

Health care benefits for children, can also be an important issue in a divorce settlement. Fortunately, many companies allow workers to continue health coverage for minor children after a divorce. If you are a custodial parent and your ex's group plan is covering the kids, be sure benefits are secured either by collateral assignment or by company authorization to garnish a salary, if necessary, to keep them flowing.

Insurance is also important in ensuring that child support payments will be made even if the breadwinner meets an untimely demise. In fact, the divorce decree should state that the major breadwinner or each parent must maintain a life insurance policy at least until the children are 18 years of age.

ERISA (Employee Retirement Income Security Act), a set of complicated government regulations that provide some protection benefits for singles and their children), may also offer some help. You may not always know all the answers, but you must know enough to ask: What am I entitled to? And how can I apply?

Complications

The above issues plus tax considerations of property transfers, alimony (tax deductible by the payer and taxable to the recipient), and child support (neither tax deductible nor taxable to either party) mean that working out a final divorce agreement may be difficult.

Since there is always risk of not getting payments in the future, I favor taking all available assets now... in cold hard cash lump sums or close substitutes. Even if future payments would be greater, the risk always exists that these promised arrangements, for one reason or another, might not materialize.

Social insecurity

A divorced spouse might have the same right as a married spouse to Social Security benefits. Even if the insured worker (ex-spouse) has remarried, the divorced spouse should investigate this option.

Ordinarily, a divorced spouse loses Social Security rights when he or she remarries. But benefits may continue without any reduction for a widow or widower who remarries after age 60 or for a disabled widow or widower who remarries after age 50.

When a worker starts collecting retirement or disability payments, the divorced spouse may receive benefits if: (1) he or she is age 62 or older; (2) he or she does not qualify for benefits that equal or exceed one half of the worker's full amount; and (3) the divorced spouse was married to the worker for at least 10 years.

Consult your Social Security office for details, as changes in the law continually affect benefit provisions. Discuss your individual circumstances (and request the English translation of the jargon you just read).

A divorce checklist

As King Solomon demonstrated, there's nothing fair about a 50-50 split. Attorneys and judges may try to chalk a line right down the middle, but there's more justice in an equitable, not equal, dissolution.

Divvying up decades worth of accumulated belongings is not an easy task. Assets could include one or more homes, retirement plans, insurance, securities, and family businesses, not to mention the "sentimental stuff."

According to the NCWRR, fewer than half of all women awarded child support ever get the full amount to which they are entitled. The result: the typical woman's standard of living dives 27% in the first year after a divorce, while the average man's jumps 10%, says the Social Science Research Center in New York.

Here are some other matters you should not overlook:

- You may receive stocks or bonds as part of a divorce settlement. When you sell the stock (since there was no tax on the transfer at the time of the divorce), you will pay taxes on the full difference between the original purchase price and the fair market value at the time of the sale. In other words, you will owe taxes on all of your profits from the date you and/or your ex-spouse purchased it, not from the date you received it as a settlement asset.
- Creditors usually are satisfied at the time of the divorce. If a new one surfaces and expects payment from you, contact your attorney. Even if you have been indemnified by the settlement agreement, you may need legal counsel.
- Credit ratings can suffer in a messy divorce. Rebuild credit as soon as possible. A good employment record, consistent income and good savings and checking habits are signs that you can handle credit, though your past history may indicate otherwise. Place 100 words in each credit report from the major credit rating services, explaining clearly why previous payments were delayed and how you can maintain a constant income flow to manage your credit card in the future.
- Change all insurance policies to reflect your current beneficiary wishes and all employer group death and retirement plans. Ask the personnel or benefits department for original application or beneficiary change forms so you can see that any changes have been processed.
- If you are reassuming your maiden name, review all important documents like your Social Security card, retirement plan accounts, other employer group benefits, individual insurance (life, health and disability) policies, banking accounts, and keep all documented changes or insurance policy endorsements.

- Get advice on how to file next year's tax returns (Form 1040). For example, if you have dependent children, you get a better tax shake by claiming "head of household" status than "single with children."
- Be sure you have severed all financial or property ties with your former spouse on safety deposit boxes, car titles, new locks on the home, storage units, or titles of other personal property.
- Have your personal belongings insured separately under your own homeowner's insurance policy. Reassess your auto insurance as you may now qualify for better rates as a single person. Your sex, age and a good driving record may help.
- Be sure you have current and proper titles to all property you now own, including that transferred during the divorce settlement.
- Prepare yourself for a flurry of paperwork in the weeks and months after your divorce becomes final. Certainly you will need to change all beneficiary designations on any life insurance policies and retirement plans in your name.
- Re-register all assets in your name with beneficiary designations, at least for the time being. This includes joint bank and credit card accounts. Revise your will, naming new heirs and, if appropriate, a new guardian for your children
- You will also want to update your health insurance coverage, particularly if you were covered by your partner's health plan. You can switch to your employer's health plan or pony up for your own policy.
- Don't ignore the risk of disability. Without the benefit of a second income to fall back on if something happens to you, you will need disability coverage. Review the insurance chapter to learn how to purchase a policy with value and a competitive premium.

Widows and widowers

The abrupt immersion into singlehood brought on by either divorce or death of a spouse can result in overwhelming stress and anxiety. Losing a spouse, with the accompanying grief and feelings of loss, can prove paralyzing to the surviving partner. Particularly when the grieving spouse was not the financial decision maker during the marriage. These individuals, most often older women, may find themselves in the depths of financial crisis, unable and ill equipped to make even the simplest financial decisions.

According to a report by the General Accounting Office, widows are hard pressed to maintain their lifestyles. Roughly 80% now living in poverty were not poor before their husbands died. But with some careful planning, a slow but steady approach, judicious budgeting and keen attention to your most pressing financial needs, you can emerge with your financial security intact.

Widows and widowers may face decisions for which they are not prepared—receipt of insurance company death benefits, company pension plans, retirement fund checks, disability benefits or even Social Security (fully insured workers' spouses are entitled to a one time $255 death benefit sum) as well as other types of unexpected money.

This will trigger another coincidental event: lines of creditors, financial "advisors," insurance agents (even the agent who delivers death benefits to you), bankers, pension consultants, senior citizen or "elder care" specialists, investment "advisors" and "counselors"—a traffic jam on your front lawn.

This entourage bears a striking resemblance to circling vultures following a thirsty man across a desert. Although you may initially feel grateful that an "expert" has come to your aid, this frenzied pack of "advisors" may be more interested in lifting your wallet or pocketbook than your bottom line.

You will also receive well intentioned financial advice from relatives. Ignore everyone right now. Buying on the advice of others (even those you love) is ill advised. They may have no idea of what they are really investing in (most folks don't).

This is not the time to make lasting and perhaps irrevocable financial decisions. Put incoming settlement or death benefit checks into short term CDs at several banks, separated into three different accounts:

1. A bank account or money market mutual fund account for all *pre-tax* IRA accounts, 403(b)s, 401(k)s or other voluntary supplemental retirement money that can remain tax deferred;.
2. An account containing all *pre-tax* pension rollovers that can remain tax deferred and can be transferred (rolled over) to your name, either as a beneficiary or through a spousal rollover. Ask the company benefit staff person sending the checks which money can be rolled over into an IRA account for continued tax deferral.
3. A temporary CD account for all *after-tax* miscellaneous money—death and disability benefits, alimony settlements, property settlements and other dollars—that cannot be tax deferred and will earn taxable income.

Do not commingle these funds or you may create adverse tax consequences. As you deposit the qualified money (pension benefits, 401(k)s, profit sharing, and IRA money), label those accounts as IRA rollovers. Eventually, you can make a final transfer of these tax deferred assets to other investment vehicles. But these short term comfort stations for your funds will allow you time to learn, research and ease into your new role as money manager. Allow the CDs to roll over for as long as you wish. There is no immediate need to rush into any investment until you are ready.

If you do not feel comfortable permanently allocating your funds after a few months give yourself more breathing space and more time. Make learning how to invest a higher priority on your schedule.

Do not deposit all your CD money into just one banking institution (despite the supposed backing of the FDIC). If a bank is taken over by the Resolution Trust Corporation, there may be some disruption regarding access to your account.

Managing money solo

There are many faces of investing for one. Now, you will need the financial cram course of your life. Stay away from public seminars and don't call insurance agents, stockbrokers, financial advisors or even bank trust or estate planning departments. These all represent vested interests. Pigs will fly before you can be sure you have received objective financial advice.

Do not expect your accountant or attorney to direct you or to provide investment advice. This is not their bailiwick, and there is the possibility that there may be an ongoing business relationship between your legal or accounting professional and a financial institution in your community. You are perfectly capable of finding your own materials and interviewing your own money experts.

As you feel more comfortable repositioning your assets, keep the allocations simple, flexible and manageable. Read, listen and ask probing questions.

Above all, diversify, diversify, diversify. Don't place all your assets into one or two investments, no matter how good the sales presentation. If any investment product is of true long term quality, it will still be available in a few months or next year when you add to your account.

Your choice of short term storage pots is limited because you need liquidity (the ability to get to your money fast). Therefore, you will be relegated to lower interest vehicles such as bank CDs and money market mutual funds backed by U.S. Government bills and quality agency paper. These low returns are only temporary. You are purchasing something right now more comforting than high yields—time to learn and research.

Don't be so concerned with the yield on this short term money that you forget about bank solvency. Be prepared to sacrifice a few dollars in interest for the peace of mind of keeping your money in the strongest, safest banks you can find.

Life goes on...so can you

Pile all important looking papers (including homeowner's and auto insurance declarations, utility bills and other monthly bill commitments) on the kitchen table and sort through them. Buy inexpensive files for each category. Purchase a large desk calendar with adequate blank spaces and record all incoming monthly money (such as paychecks, Social Security, insurance annuities or pension checks) in green and all outgoing bills (fixed and variable payments) in red. Plan for one month at a time, biting off small goals at first in two week increments.

This tracking will require less real thinking and will save time. Check your desk calendar each week to see which bills must be paid. Write out those checks and move on to other, more pleasant activities.

Continue to pay regular living expenses like the mortgage or rent, utilities, credit cards, car payments, storage units, and insurance premiums—no matter how uninspired. Your credit rating is at risk here, and billing departments worry about their own solvency. Don't use plastic solutions for psychological short term fulfillment. Loading up on credit cards will cause another problem months later.

A suddenly single individual may find him- or herself in new territory regarding checking accounts or ongoing investment programs. Get help from someone (your banker, a friend or a consumer community agency) who will teach you some basics about handling day-to-day money matters. Don't be afraid to ask for help. Be smart, realizing that it's not important to know every answer, just where to find the answers.

Consolidate checking or savings accounts. Frequently, spouses have separate financial lives, and you may have inherited another system of money managing. Call several institutions and check on their current rates of savings passbooks, interest bearing checking accounts, money market demand accounts or senior citizen products. Pool your dollars as follows: one savings account, one money market, one checking account, etc.

Keep most of your funds liquid. Being alone may require higher immediate income needs. Don't purchase income investments alone, such as bonds, tax free mutual funds, insurance annuities, muni-bonds or limited partnerships. All of these are inappropriate as short term investment vehicles. You can get all the income you need from your checking, money market or savings accounts.

Do not take on any major financial projects now. No remodeling, no children's financial problems and no long term financial decisions. Don't co-sign or otherwise lend any of your new assets to relatives or children. You may need them later, and the promised repayments may not materialize.

As tax time rolls around, get to an accountant to help you through the first tax year. Major tax service companies offer current tax preparation courses. Community colleges may also offer short courses. Don't let money concepts, columns of figures or new financial experiences intimidate you.

Be careful of tax professionals who also want to invest your assets. Most tax professionals frown on those who also sell products. You are there for one thing only—tax advice and assistance.

Some folks think that $100,000 or $150,000 in hand at one time makes them rich. Don't be lulled into taking life easy, spending and gifting away future dollars that you will need. Consider staying employed or get retrained for a career you would enjoy. This is healthful for you physically and mentally and will get you back into the mainstream and out of isolation faster.

Some spouses have been secured behind the walls of homemaking for so many years that they are terrified to start a new lifestyle. Get career counseling, some support counseling and find supportive friends.

Apply for grants that may subsidize your education. Take a practical course you can benefit from and some fun classes that will help you resume a well rounded lifestyle.

A large inviting and vacant home (yours) may be very attractive to grown children, other relatives or co-workers with a streak of bad luck. Don't get involved. You are not the Red Cross. You are one person taking your time to get your act together. You can do that best with your own space and on your own terms. You need fewer pressures now...and no additional costs.

Change the beneficiaries on all life insurance policies at work and on your individual insurance contracts. Don't let any insurance agent use fear to talk you into a life insurance or nursing home policy. Think this out. If you have few bills, own your own home and have some retirement savings or investments, why do you need death insurance? Unless you have dependent children (or parents) to support, your current challenge is living too long, not dying too soon. You need every dollar for daily living. Your estate will satisfy your bills with whatever assets you have remaining.

If you are still responsible for raising children, you need a bundle of cheap term insurance. Save your money for your own needs, not for the commission needs of an insurance salesperson.

Check on spousal health and pension benefits under ERISA or COBRA, and Social Security benefits. Request specimen contracts, and compare several policies with competing insurance companies before purchasing your final selection.

A widow's and widower's checklist

- If you've inherited stocks, bonds or other investments, don't make changes until you have read this book. Too many vendors use this vulnerable opportunity to sell financial products. When making lasting financial decisions, you should have a clear head.
- Many investments can be transferred into your name without income taxes. Estate tax rules differ among states. So seek expert advice to determine which assets you have inherited tax free.
- Check with your tax advisor regarding how each security should be titled and the tax ramifications of such transfers. When assets are transferred to spouses and other heirs due to death of the original owner, a *step up* in value can eliminate all income taxes. Estate taxes are a separate issue.
- Credit ratings should be checked. Women especially need to charge to maintain current credit account status with credit card providers. Do not pay creditors unless they can prove that the bill is a legal obligation of your deceased spouse. If bills are substantial, get assistance in deciding when to pay what without reducing your current income or other assets you may desperately need in the future.
- Use a tax advisor to understand how taxes apply to your assets or take a tax class in your community. Learning about your money will help you take greater command of your financial life.
- Review your auto, home, vacation home, and/or business insurance. Revise your insurance plan according to your current needs. You may not receive expert assistance in this area because insurance agents are paid by their companies to cut down risk for the company, not for their customers. The insurance chapter in this book will assist you how to properly insure your life.
- Review your personal belongings and have valuables insured separately under a special personal property floater policy. Jewelry, silverware, collectibles, and other valuables must be insured on a different policy than the ordinary personal assets inside your home.

- Transfer all real estate interests into your name and under your control. Include any properties outside your state or any interests you may have inherited from your partner's side of the family.

- If you are dependent on earned income for future financial support, consider disability insurance in case of sickness or an accident. Today's group policies at work tend to cover only short term calamities. You may need supplemental coverage through an individual disability policy. Research carefully before purchasing any insurance policy, as your understanding and the company's definition of a disabled policy owner may differ greatly. Read your contracts, no matter what financial product you anticipate buying.

- Transfer your property deed and car title(s) to your name. Then check all individual and group work policies to update the beneficiary designations. Continue to update all bank accounts, investment accounts, and other assets you own.

- Request several death certificates from the funeral director to collect various death benefits.

- Understand the various forms of ownership for savings accounts, CDs, securities and real estate. Consider the best compromises for you.

- Contact the benefits departments of the following: 1) your spouse's employer; 2) Social Security; 3) any insurance companies for which payment receipts have been discovered. Sometimes even a small premium payment receipt will generate a death benefit that otherwise might have been overlooked. **Don't leave free money on the table**. Check employee benefits booklets as well.

- Notify banks, postal authorities and those who may have a general power of appointment or a remainder interest in the estate of the deceased (anyone who has a legal right to notification).

Chicken soup advice

Solicit support in the personal areas of your life. My clients who have survived the trauma of divorce or death of a spouse have compiled these chestnuts of wisdom that comforted them until they felt both feet touching solid earth again:

Blame someone else. Your tendency right now may be to blame yourself, which can be devastating to your self-esteem. It is far better to blame others. Government bureaucrats have fine tuned this technique into an art. It can work for you, too.

Start watching soap operas. Just by comparison, your life will look brighter.

Don't feel you have to "put on a happy face" for others. You have a right to "wallow" for awhile. There is no one more important right now to impress than yourself. If your close friends do not understand, this is a good time to write them out of your will.

Don't let your grown children control your life (or move in with you or even convince you to move in with them) to protect you from the outside world. This will stifle your independent growth. They have merely forgotten who protected them years ago.

FIDO: forget it, drive on

Don't live in denial. Finding yourself on your own following the death or divorce of a partner means you're in charge now. Empower yourself with the education and inspiration to take charge of your financial destiny.

Never give control of your money to someone else, even if the financial salesperson has been recommended by a friend or family member. Your financial resources are too precious.

Pay yourself first while you have the chance. Apart from saving for retirement, there will be unexpected costs to bear. Financial promises made to you (by your company or even by the government) may not materialize.

Aggressively pursue ways to get back on your financial feet. Do the homework in this book, attend a class by an expert who doesn't sell financial products, and get involved with managing your own investment portfolio. Don't let monthly statements pile up, or file them away without understanding what you are investing in and how each security works under a variety of market conditions.

Never put all your eggs into one basket. Learn to diversify using the methods in this book and keep your options simple and understandable. Any single who can make a living in this cantankerous world can learn to prudently invest her or his own money. Any single who has raised children able to challenge this skeptical, uncertain world has the money genes to learn winning rules of the money game. Any single....yes, any single.

Chapter 15

On a clear day you can see retirement

You've probably never seen it marked on a calendar. No one's ever declared it a holiday. But it's a day that can cost you a lot of money. It's called **tomorrow**.

That's when most folks say they'll think about planning for retirement. After the bills are paid. After the children have finished college. After other personal financial commitments are met. After taxes. After inflation.

Tomorrow. Or maybe the day after Someday. There's still time, isn't there? You know the answer to that question all too well.

The penthouse or the poorhouse?

"I'm spending my child's inheritance now" and "If I had known my grandkids were so much fun, I would have had them first" were popular bumper stickers seen on the back of RVs as retirees inside them traveled down the sunny road to their golden years, relatively comfortable with secure monthly pension checks, Social Security and other retirement savings such as IRA accounts.

But today, the rising cost of staying healthy and the even faster rising costs of staying *alive* are eroding those savings opportunities so much that some retirees are finding it difficult to afford the bumper stickers, let alone the RV.

In the desert they call something that disappears the closer you come to it, a mirage. Next thing you know, they'll be calling it Social Security.

The golden years: why they are tarnishing

Years ago, our government had a clever idea: create a system in which workers would be taxed just a bit, and those taxes would be paid out to the elderly (who, it was assumed, wouldn't live very long anyway). These Social Security benefits wouldn't have to be much because they would only supplement pensions and other retirement savings. A family breadwinner could be confident, then, that after working for a company for 45 years or so, he and his wife could retire on a comfortable nest egg. And particularly if a retiring couple had owned its home, the place could sell for such a profit that it would fund a new condo in Sun City.

Medical science now has the ability to control many of the effects of aging. If only outliving your retirement money were one of them. As America grows older and grayer, the retirement picture is changing significantly. Retirees are living longer, growing poorer and requiring more expensive medical care. One study states that two out of three people who have ever inhabited our planet are still alive today. That's a lot of hungry mouths to feed and aging bodies to care for.

In addition, workers appear to be retiring earlier—whether they like it or not. With more companies downsizing and restructuring, no one is immune to forced early retirement. And early retirement means fewer years to build up the pension and nest egg, and more years of non-working life that have to be supplemented by your personal retirement investments.

Vital retirement funds will come from your company pension (if it is still healthy), subsidized by Social Security (if it is available to the middle class).

With these changes in the work force, the changing health picture of aging Americans and an uncertain economy, you must take responsibility for your retirement nest egg—and not count on your employer or the government or your children to take care of you in your old age. A combination of your own personal investments had better be working harder than inflation. Like Alice in Wonderland, your money has to grow faster and faster just to stay in the same place over time.

Retirement myths hazardous to your financial health

In the next twenty years, your grown children will have braces, college tuition and at least one wedding to pay for. Do you really want them to add a nursing home to the list? There is no great insight to retirement planning. If you spend everything today, you will have nothing left for tomorrow. If you owe it all to yourself now, you may retire in an appliance carton on a suburban curbstone. If you protect your image and foster the illusion of wealth by living *above* your means, you and your money will stray so far apart that you might as well be strangers.

Test your retirement IQ. The following statements are as hazardous to your retirement wealth as smoking is to your physical health:

1. **"Conservation of principal should be my top priority."** Dangerously false. The most critical element of any long term investment plan must be to protect your *purchasing power*. If you are planning to live for more than three years, you have an inflation challenge bigger than the potential threat of loss of principal. The two primary themes throughout this book are the time value of money (how powerful money can be when you are working it in your own interest) and how dangerous inflation can be when ignored.

    You may be earning 10 percent on a bank deposit, but if inflation is galloping along at 12 percent, you are losing financial ground. Always manage some of your money for growth.

2. **"What happened to my parents won't happen to me."** Don't bet on it. Your parents weren't spendthrifts who mismanaged their paychecks. They were very much like you—immersed in daily demands, trusting, perhaps intimidated by money, leaving basic financial decisions up to strangers who called themselves experts.

They were not taught what inflation would do to their savings over time or what they could accomplish if they worked their own savings. Instead, they loaned out their meager savings to banks and insurance companies who made astonishing profits over time at their expense.

The only retirees who will be financially comfortable and independent may be those who manage their own money, using inflation fighting investment strategies.

3. **"I will need less money after retirement."** The closer retirement appears, the more ludicrous this myth appears. The only bills that will stop are today's mortgage payments and the excruciating college tuition checks. Inflation won't stop, though your current paycheck will, replaced by a smaller monthly pension with little or no cost-of-living increases. Your dentist won't fill cavities but, instead, will present you with a full and expensive set of teeth. Income, property, school, gasoline and other federal, state, local and user taxes will continue upward. Health care increases are sure to appear. The cost of groceries, medical prescriptions, treatments and other senior services will escalate as well.

You will live longer, perhaps long enough to outlive your retirement nest egg. Like an older home, you will need more upkeep. To live comfortably, plan on 100 percent of today's income, increasing at 6 percent to 10 percent per year. Assess your retirement readiness with the **Total Compensation Benefits Checklist** in the Appendix.

4. **"I will pay fewer income taxes after retirement."** To pay for the large social bills, future costs of health care and social entitlements, the price of government (taxes) will increase. If you intend to be in a lower income tax bracket than today, you will be living on less money than you are now. Therefore, you will be in worse financial shape. Stop starving yourself for tax purposes, attempting to earn slightly less than the Social Security earned income penalty limits. You had better not be paying less in taxes, or you will be dieting, involuntarily.

5. **"I have Social Security and my company pension to depend on."** Maybe not. As the largest demographic group in history—the baby boomers—gropes toward retirement, not even our government may be able to find a way to tax our children enough to subsidize those in retirement, those who are disabled or those who are indigent.

Companies are finding more ways to unlock retirees from promised benefits as well. Corporations are terminating older workers, cutting costs of those who produce no direct benefit to the company's bottom line.

Your retirement security will come from a company pension (if the company is still in business) and some Social Security (if your children can afford you with their payments). The rest of your macaroni-and-cheese and Laundromat money is up to you. Complete the **Retirement Benefits** page in the Appendix to examine your progress.

6. **"It will be easier to save for retirement in a few years."** The fallacy here is the belief that you can isolate future income that will not be needed as disposable living dollars, college tuition, a larger home, raising more children, buying more expensive cars and funding an increased standard of living. If you

can't find the small contributions today with time on your side, how will you earmark even greater sums in five or 10 years when drains on your income leave you in even worse financial shape?

7. **"I'm young, so I have plenty of time."** Time is money, and compound interest works better the longer the time period. If it takes $30,000 today after taxes to keep your financial house humming, 12 years from now (at 6-percent annual inflation), you will need $60,000. If your budget is $40,000 a year, in 24 years you will need $160,000 in today's dollars just to maintain the same lifestyle. Where will you get that kind of money unless you start today on a regular retirement savings program?

8. **"There will only be the two of us."** Don't be too sure. Today's "boomerang" children are moving back home (often with their own children) because of divorce or the death of a spouse, or as a single parent with a child. They are also waiting longer (on *your* paycheck) to marry and set up independent households.

9. **"My home is my retirement fund."** This and other real estate fairy tales were exposed during the last real estate recession when disappointed homeowners discovered that real estate can depreciate. At best, your primary residence will keep pace with inflation.

   When your other retirement assets are consumed, how will you eat? By selling off a bedroom or bathroom? In addition to a comfortable roof over your head, you will need a comfortable feeling in your stomach from eating three meals per day. Think of your home as a nest to raise your family, a lifestyle decision, not as a shrewd retirement investment.

10. **"I'm enjoying my money now. What if I die tomorrow?"** If you save 10 percent of today's income for tomorrow, you'll have 90 percent left over for life's adventures. If you can't live comfortably on 90 percent of your take-home pay, how will you feel if you *don't* die and have only the bygone memories of purchases to keep you fed, warm and healthy in your old age?

    Saving and spending are not conflicting goals. Saving is merely not spending right now, today, so that you can have more to spend tomorrow.

Retiring too early

Our retirement system is not designed for early retirement. Company pensions, Social Security, Medicare and increased longevity are challenging public and private systems. As Americans live longer than ever, monthly pension payments may be expected for as long as 30 to 40 years!

Industry is worried too. Many are offering early retirement to get workers off health care and pension benefit roles. You may not be able (or be healthy enough) to find part-time supplementary work. Workplace age discrimination thwarts such plans.

If you are planning to retire early (before age 65), get realistic projections from a real financial planner, not a financial product salesperson who might tell you anything to get a product commission, to be sure you don't leave a dependable paycheck too soon. The sooner you leave the work force, the sooner you start eating up your retirement nest egg. The healthier you are, the longer you will need that money.

If you retire, become disabled, change employment or are downsized, you may have the option to leave your pension fund with your company *or* take your pension savings and roll it over to an IRA you manage yourself. Take the lump sum and manage it yourself.

Use an IRA to roll over the funds into a money market mutual fund and leave it in cold storage until you learn the fundamentals in this book.

Ultimately you can diversify your pension fund into a combination of bank deposits, a money market mutual fund, and those dull, boring and stodgy mutual fund "turtles" discussed in Chapter 22. You can add a small percentage to a global mutual fund. Simple to manage, easy to monitor, this combination provides some growth as a hedge against inflation and conservation of principal. No money manager could do better.

You can learn to invest like the pros—perhaps better. Use the **Portfolio Planning Worksheet** in the Appendix to get a picture of how you stand today.

Pension confusion

Planning to receive an early distribution from your retirement pension? You must understand the law regarding pension rollovers. Lump sum payouts for basic pensions, 401(k) assets, profit sharing funds, thrift saving plans; nonprofit, tax deferred annuities (TSAs, TDAs) and other types of qualified retirement plans are affected in this manner.

The law does *not* apply to IRA accounts you have set up before January 1, 1993, even the funds previously came from a pension fund.

If you receive your retirement funds in a check made payable to you (constructive receipt), you will automatically trigger a 20-percent tax withholding penalty on the entire distribution. Though this money will be returned after tax time next year, if you do not replace the missing 20 percent from your own funds, that amount will be considered an early distribution of pension funds, subject to all taxes and penalties if applicable.

The same tax penalty applies to receiving any series of payments for less than 10 years and is in addition to any penalties for early withdrawal before age 59½ or age 55 if you are retiring early.

This tax trap is easy to avoid. Your employer can send your funds directly to the IRA investment account you have opened or send the check to your address made payable to your new IRA investment for your benefit.

Choose a money market mutual fund for the IRA Rollover as a short term comfort station. Learn how to manage the funds before determining a final resting place. Be sure your pension direct IRA rollover account is labeled correctly and the funds, when finally allocated to a combination of several banks and mutual funds, are sent as a trustee-to-trustee transfer and labeled as IRA rollovers.

To max or not to max? That is the pension!

In your retirement benefit options, you may have the following choices:

1. A lump sum distribution to continue tax deferred if rolled over into an IRA-labeled account. Some after tax money may also be sent from after tax contributions to a pension plan.
2. A monthly pension check for the rest of *your* life only—*not* for the life of your spouse if he or she lives longer than you. (This is a single life annuity.)
3. A smaller monthly pension check for the lives of both you and your spouse (or another beneficiary) with a variety of percentages allowed for monthly payments.
4. Any of the above.

Beware the insurance agent

Just when you thought it was safe to go back into the financial water, those persistent insurance agents you have been avoiding for so long will pester you with a list of new and improved suggestions for retirement income and investing.

Beware! Insurance solutions have major drawbacks, large commissions for their agents, high surrender fees, hefty internal charges, and are not cost efficient at delivering either monthly income or growth on your retirement funds.

What's the right choice for your pension dilemma? Though this may pose a difficult decision to you, your neighborhood insurance agent already knows which option you should choose. They will probably recommend that you take the larger single life monthly pension payout (leaving your spouse with no payments if you should die first) and purchase an insurance policy with the difference between the larger single life monthly check and the smaller check for the joint and survivor annuity. The policy is supposed to provide your spouse with monthly payments for life should you die and, therefore, your monthly pension check stop. A win-win situation for you: the larger check to you each month (no one mentions that it will shrink because you send the insurance premiums to the insurer) and a lump sum death benefit for your spouse as well.

The agent will present attractive (and possibly deceptive) ledger sheets that are meaningless. You may purchase "designer insurance," a policy that offers affordable premiums because the illustration sheets are structured to calculate the highest interest rate scenarios possible to get you to sign the insurance application. (See Chapter 7 for this inside story.)

If the policy self-destructs, your agent will be in the Boca Raton sun, while you will be in a major financial pickle, unable to pay the increasing premiums necessary to keep coverage in effect for your spouse. If you can afford the premium, the death benefit recommended by the agent may be too small to properly replace the lifetime payments your spouse would have received had you chosen a joint and survivorship pension option.

Decline the insurance agent's offer to fund his or her retirement off your pension plan and call several agents to get "real" premiums on guaranteed premium term insurance, a cheaper way to fund a death benefit. You need accurate calculations to be sure the face amount you purchase is enough to provide your spouse with similar monthly survivor payments for their life.

The IRA alternative

You might be told by an "investment advisor" that smart investors are finding innovative ways to hide retirement funds and sock away much more money than an IRA Account will allow. Or an insurance agent may introduce you to the "private retirement pension plan," now coming to a living room near you. The benefits seem astonishing: tax deferred growth on your investment capital, no limits to what you can contribute, no penalty for distributions before age 59½, a guaranteed monthly income you cannot outlive, no reduction in Social Security payments, no matter how much growth your investment produces, **and** tax free income when you decide to take your money and run. Oh, one more benefit: a guaranteed principal, to boot.

The sizzle is so attractive that most customers never realize the steak they have really purchased is the same whole life insurance policy their parents bought years ago that kept them from making a decent return on their investments through the years, but which make the insurance companies (and their agents) filthy rich.

Ledger illustration sheets are meaningless. An insurance agent can put anything down on paper, depending on how trusting (gullible) you are. Same old duck, brand new living room presentation feathers.

Unfortunately, you can't afford to fund any more Boca Raton mortgage payments for a stranger. You need all the money you can preserve for your own retirement kitty. As the saying goes, just say no!

Lump sums offer the most control

If the lump sum option is large enough to replace the monthly annuity payments at a reasonable rate of interest per year, you can receive the entire pot of money and invest it yourself. Then you have access to your nest egg at all times.

Choosing the monthly income option is an irrevocable election. You can't change your mind later when you realize that today's nest egg will hardly purchase tomorrow's birdhouse. It also represents a lower standard of living as the years pass. What if you need medical care your health insurance won't cover? How will you buy a car when it costs twice today's price? How will you handle a large unexpected financial crisis? How will you pay for groceries at tomorrow's prices with the same monthly income check? Or none at all if your company is gone? Inflation is the most deadly money killer over time. How will you combat inflation with a fixed monthly check?

With projected health care costs at astronomical levels, you will need the flexibility to take your money as you see fit, when you need it.

What will happen if your company disappears during your retirement? How will you cope if the promises made to retirees and their families become greater than pension assets can produce? As more workers consider longer retirements, long term pension promises are tremendous risks, especially since you have no seat on the company's board of directors and no golden executive parachute.

Occasionally, a company's lump sum offer is so paltry compared to the monthly income option, that you have little choice but to take the payments. In that case, you have fewer options.

If monthly pension survivor options are your only choice, consider an option that pays your spouse the largest future benefit when inflation will be the worst and take less money today while you can better afford your retirement expenses.

Winning the lottery

I advise my clients to wager one dollar when the super lotto jackpot is enormous. Then I remind them to call me—even at 2 a.m.—if they win. As partners, we will have a long term relationship together.

Do not depend on lottery mentality to fund your retirement. But if you *do* win, apply the lessons learned about pensions to determine the best way to receive your fortune.

Calculate the future value of both the lump sum and the annual payment stream with a compound interest calculator. Which payment option is more powerful over the time period? It makes no difference whether you would buy a home for each relative, travel to Alaska to watch the humpback whales, or purchase friends. Though state rules vary regarding regulations, here are some general guidelines.

If $1 million were invested at 8 percent per year for 10 years, the total account would be worth (minus taxes) $2,158,925. If, instead, you chose the annual payment schedule of ten $150,000 payments, you would accumulate $2,346,823, more real dollars than the lump sum could produce. Though the lump sum looks larger, the series of payments may actually be more powerful. You would probably pay fewer taxes if you structured your payout into payments instead of opting for the one time lump sum payment. The annual series of payments looks like a better option from a tax angle as well.

So far we have used research to conclude our optimum decision. But common sense may be worth more than a compound interest calculator in this scenario. Since you do not actually win the lottery but, instead, receive a series of payments from an insurance company annuity the lottery purchases for your benefit, what happens if the insurance company falls apart? I'll bet the state's contract with the insurance company has discussed that aspect (and excluded itself from any future liability for payments if the insurance company goes out of business). If the state does back up its lottery promise, will you receive prompt attention when state budgets are tight and lines of poorer citizens are between you and your annual lottery payment?

A bird in hand is worth two flying overhead. Grab the money and run, pay your taxes and avoid the greatest risk of all on money—time.

Social insecurity

Social Security is based on the principle that part of the responsibility for the loss of an individual's income because of retirement, disability, death or medical needs should be born by society as a whole.

Supported through employee-employer payroll taxes, it is a pay-as-you-go program, with current workers paying benefits to those now receiving monthly payments. Controversies over how well the program is funded should caution future retirees not to depend on this or any social program for their total retirement financial comfort.

Retirement benefits are figured on covered work credits and are related to career employment earnings. A weighted formula is applied for each retiring worker's record. Participation during most employees' lives is compulsory.

Benefits are not directly based on the amount the individual contributes to the system. Benefits are not meant to totally replace a worker's wages, and are meant to be supplemented through other sources of retirement income.

Beware of single disease and accident policies

So-called "dread disease" insurance policies covering cancer or Alzheimer's disease, for example, offer relatively limited coverage. Why? Because no company that expects to make a profit on the sale of its policies would isolate the most dangerous health risks, then sell generous coverage to individuals at affordable prices.

Medicare Part A and Part B, your current company health insurance or an individual catastrophic health insurance policy, and one Medigap or other broad supplemental health policy, will suffice. Examine benefits for specific treatments before you buy.

Think before prepaying death expenses

Guaranteeing future costs of a funeral and associated expenses sound appealing. But unless there are overriding reasons (such as qualifying for Medicaid) for paying final expenses early, don't prepay funeral expenses based on today's guarantees.

The funeral director will invest your money to "guarantee" today's costs. You could do the same. What if the money is mismanaged? What if the funeral home closes down or the owner dies? What if the business is sold to someone who will not buy the existing contracts of previous customers? You might decide to move to Arizona.

Given a choice between paying for your funeral now and keeping that money to live on, arrange to pay funeral expenses out of your estate once you are gone.

Long term care and medicare supplements

If you think picking a winner on Derby Day is difficult, try ferreting through the fine print, risks, exclusions and limitations to find dependable long term care insurance and supplemental health coverage. Medicare, Medicaid and Medigap coverage can be confusing, deceptively sold by insurance agents, and unable to keep up with today's benefits at tomorrow's prices.

Policies have become more standardized. You can purchase "qualified" contracts and deduct the insurance premiums on your tax return. "non-qualified" contracts provide no tax write off but offer greater benefits. Sales abuse is rampant. So do NOT purchase an agent's sales pitch. No winged avengers will protect you from purchasing a defective product. (Read further in Chapter 7.)

Rocking chair: a piece of furniture, not a state of mind

It's not the years in your life but the life in your years that makes retirement fulfilling. Your body parts, however, may remind you that they need fewer lawn mowing and weeding chores, or more time to travel. You may consider moving into an assisted living facility or other planned residential complex.

Some facilities provide only assisted living help, and if your health deteriorates, you must find other medical care arrangements. Other systems provide several levels of step-up care so you can stay with them, whatever your future health. They vary in price, and some have steep initial residential fees plus a monthly association fee that will increase over time.

It may be comforting to believe that higher taxes, increased health care costs and other expenses can be someone else's problem. But your upkeep costs will increase over time. So will the expenses of the facility. In addition, costs for greater health expenses by some residents may be spread over the group, similar to insurance risk management. If you remain healthy, you may be expected to pay part of the costs for others that the facility has promised respite to. If your health deteriorates, you will increase the general cost of the facility.

If the organization becomes financially troubled, how will it continue to take care of you? You are its main source of funds (and those with government subsidies may be at greater risk when funds are reduced). If costs soar above expected levels, it can't create money from thin air. If it shuts down in the future for any reason—say, a highway goes through the living room—where will you go and how much of your original deposit will you retrieve?

A better alternative might be to rent in a facility close to medical assistance so you can move when you want and keep your own money for your future living assistance needs. Be aware of all the financial detours you may be facing—from early or forced retirement, rising inflation, pension problems and costly health and long term care issues. For more on saving for retirement, read Chapter 16.

Medicaid programs

Medicaid is a last resort health subsidy funded by a combination of state and federal money. It is designed for the financially impoverished. Its regulations are restrictive—to qualify, applicants must have few financial reserves or other forms of property.

How do people with significant assets still manage to qualify for Medicaid? A common strategy is to purchase a long term care nursing home policy that will self-pay from the time they transfer their assets out of their name to the date they qualify for their state Medicaid program.

As more qualified entrants fill Medicaid rolls, the rules will likely be changed and exclude those who could pay but, through such strategies, manage to qualify for a program designed primarily for the indigent. Medicaid, in addition to being an extremely complex issue, is also constantly changing, and regulations vary from state to state. Be sure you're getting the right information before pursuing benefits.

Will you have time for everything, yet money for less? Use every opportunity to provide for retirement as if it was coming tomorrow. Assess your retirement acumen below and test how well you have learned the concepts in this chapter.

Test Your Retirement I.Q.

1. ____Safety of principal should be the foundation of my retirement plan.
2. ____During retirement, creating income should be my main objective.
3. ____I will pay fewer taxes in my retirement years.
4. ____My living expenses will go down after I retire.
5. ____If I have few assets, I don't need an estate plan.
6. ____Nursing home care will be paid by Medicare.
7. ____My pension is safe, guaranteed by my company.
8. ____All retirement pensions are guaranteed by the U.S. Government.
9. ____I need more life insurance now because I have more assets to protect.
10. ____I can safely purchase financial products sold by consumer groups.
11. ____When shopping for health care supplements, price is the most important criteria.
12. ____If Alzheimer's or cancer run in my family, I need special policies for these risks.
13. ____My company pension, Social Security and Medicare are all I need.
14. ____I can't contribute to an IRA even if I take a part time job after retirement.
15. ____Medicare will take over as soon as I retire.
16. ____Social Security payments are indexed for inflation and will keep up with my increased cost of living.
17. ____My company's health benefits are guaranteed in retirement.
18. ____Professionals can manage my retirement funds better than I.
19. ____The equity in my home is my retirement fund.
20. ____There will only be the two of us.

Your retirement planning checklist

1. Determine when you are eligible to retire.
2. Identify the factors that affect your pension computation.
3. Make a decision regarding the survivor election annuity for your spouse (different options may be available such as a lump sum, life income for you only or life income for both you and your spouse).
4. Analyze your supplemental retirement savings plans.
5. Make decisions regarding health and death insurance.
6. Determine your Social Security benefits. (Send in a request for earnings to determine estimated benefits and check the accuracy of all earnings credits.)
7. Estimate your monthly retirement needs.
8. Determine the monthly retirement income needed.
9. Adjust your investment portfolio for comfort, not for speed.
10. Determine the monthly income shortfall (gap).
11. Calculate the annual savings necessary to subsidize your monthly income.
12. Apply for Social Security benefits three months before eligible.
13. Apply for Medicare Part A three months before age 65.
14. Evaluate whether to enroll in Medicare Part B.
15. Follow additional steps to ensure a comfortable retirement.

Chapter 16

Retirement: pensions, profits and pitfalls

What do IRA accounts (IRAs), Roth IRAs, Simplified Employee Pension plans (SEPs), Tax sheltered Annuities (TSAs/TDAs), KEOGHs, money purchase plans, profit sharing plans, employer SIMPLE plans, and employee stock ownership programs (ESOPs) have in common?

They are all tax sheltered umbrellas, turbo-charging your underlying retirement investment. The tax label, stamped over your choice of investment vehicles, enhances the power of the underlying securities.

How to keep up with the Joneses and the KEOGHs, and the 401(k)s, and the TSAs?

There are two basic types of pension plans: **defined contribution** and **defined benefit**.

Under a **defined contribution plan**, an individual or a corporation (or both) contribute up to a maximum limit per year for each eligible worker. This plan does **not** provide a fixed guaranteed monthly benefit upon retirement. Examples are 401(k)s, profit sharing, TSAs/TDAs, and money purchase.

The **defined benefit pension** offers a traditional guaranteed monthly income for a vested employee who retires with full service years. Because these plans are currently under pressure to provide greater dollars for more retirees, they are being replaced by cheaper (for the company) defined contribution plans, where the worker carries the risk of investing, the company does not have to make up any losses each year, and workers end up providing most of the funds invested for retirement.

Tax considerations are the **third** leg of your investment stool. Many folks mistakenly see tax planning as an end unto itself and as their most crucial objective, purchasing mediocre or downright inferior investments because they are sold on the tax benefit sales pitch.

Insurance products are sold as tax shelters. But they offer diluted returns due to large internal costs. Municipal bonds are heavily peddled for tax free income. But their returns are often well below the rate of inflation, and a triple-A bond today could deteriorate tomorrow. Investors may own thin air if their bond defaults. And bonds generally incur a long term loss of purchasing power.

The quality of the investment vehicle is more important than any tax advantage. Consider tax benefits only as a final criterion in your investment planning.

A simple pension

While Americans brace for another round of corporate downsizing and smaller employee benefit packages, more individuals are starting small businesses or exploring second incomes. Developing strategies for legally hiding income from Uncle Sam may not be as hopeless as you think.

If you own a small business or are self-employed, retirement plans can offer tax favored savings as well as precious future nest egg dollars. But associated expenses and administrative fees may gobble up precious investment capital. Take heart. Here is a pension plan that's easy to administer, convenient to install and maintain, and tax deductible with tax deferred compounding on annual earnings.

Whether you are incorporated or you operate as an individual (sole proprietorship), a **Simplified Employee Pension** (SEP) plan may satisfy your pension needs.

Employers make tax deductible contributions for themselves **and** for each additional eligible employee. All earnings are tax deferred until withdrawn after age 59½. Payments are deductible as an employer business expense, and all contributions are immediately vested.

SEPs are portable and can be transferred, rolled over to an IRA account, or liquidated completely when a worker leaves. There are no time consuming annual ERISA, IRS or Department of Labor reports, which explains why SEPs are popular pension plans for small businesses. Underlying investments in growth oriented mutual funds can enhance SEP accounts to help outpace the ravages of inflation.

Annual contributions can be maximized (up to 15 percent of each employee's compensation and 13.04 percent for self-employed persons). Business owners cannot play favorites, however, and must contribute equally for all eligible employees.

Payments are not required each year, and contributions can be changed yearly or even skipped from year to year.

Mandatory distributions from a SEP agree with those for an IRA or other qualified pension plan.

Like all financial opportunities, a SEP is not for everyone. But for a small business owner it can increase a retirement account faster than taxable investing.

SARSEPs

Salary reduction simplified employee pension plans (SARSEPs) are no longer sanctioned by the government. However, existing SARSEPs are reserved for employers with 25 or fewer employees. Workers request a salary reduction to their retirement account, and contributions to the SARSEP are not included in their gross salary for tax purposes. All earnings are tax deferred until retirement.

The basic advantage of the SARSEP over more complicated plans such as 401(k) and profit sharing plans is their simplicity of reporting, therefore, reduced costs and time consuming paperwork. Contributions of fifteen percent of gross compensation are generally permitted, indexed in future years for inflation.

Company owners, officers and certain highly paid employees may contribute up to 125 percent of the average deferral percentage other employees contribute. Therefore, this type of small business pension plan has appealed to small business owners.

Tax consequences are similar to IRA accounts, with a 10-percent penalty for early withdrawal except for death, disability or a lifetime annuity based on life expectancy. Withdrawals must start after age 70½.

SARSEPs are more confusing and a bit more complicated than ordinary SEP plans. A SARSEP A SARSEP can be rolled over to another type of employer pension plan with expert assistance from companies who specialize in such issues.

Who says nice guys finish last?

Employees of non-profit institutions such as hospitals, service organizations, and schools serve altruistic and charitable goals. But charity can also begin at home.

Tax sheltered annuities {TDAs, TSAs, technically known as 403(b)(7)s} are basic or supplemental retirement plans designed specifically for employees of educational, service, or social service agencies. TSA contributions are made on a pre-tax basis. In addition to reducing current salary and, therefore, current income taxes, any value in a TDA plan will compound tax deferred, sheltered from federal income taxes until retirement or other withdrawal time.

Withdrawals prior to age 59½ (unless special rules apply) result in a ten percent federal tax penalty. Surrender charges may apply to annuity contracts.

You determine how much of your salary (up to a certain limit) to contribute and how often (for example, at each payday). By signing a salary reduction agreement with your employer at enrollment time, the contribution can be conveniently deducted from your paycheck and sent by your employer to your chosen investment company.

You may change your contribution amount or choice of underlying investment vehicles at least once per year. You can stop your contributions at any time, though your specific plan may have penalties restricting how soon you can again begin contributing to the plan in the future.

Most TDA plans have attractive features that allow loans prior to retirement time. The loans must generally be repaid in equal payments within five years. The loan principal and interest are both reinvested back into your own plan. Therefore, you are really borrowing from yourself and paying interest to yourself. This may be a more attractive option than borrowing from a commercial lender.

But remember that you are liquidating your retirement account which may perform well above the rate of return at which you are replacing the funds you borrowed (usually the prime rate plus a small increase).

You are always 100% vested in your own contributions, though an employer's matching may vest over a period of several years.

If you change jobs, you can usually roll over your TDA into another TDA plan, an IRA Account, or leave your TDA with your original investment company. You can even defer taxes after retirement with an automatic withdrawal payout option on a monthly, quarterly or annual payout basis and still have control of your plan.

Do *not* confuse this type of employer plan with a private insurance company annuity that anyone can purchase. This supplemental retirement opportunity is available only to employees of certain non-profit institutions.

The greater earning potential of mutual funds makes them popular TDA investment choices. Although past performance is no guarantee of future results, there are many high quality mutual funds which have averaged well above the annual inflation rate.

Do not confuse brand name **insurance company sub-accounts** with real mutual funds. When the wrapper comes from an insurance company, you are paying unnecessary freight charges inside an already tax deductible, tax deferred investment.

Many insurance agents sell variable annuity products inside TSAs because the commissions are larger. You have no obligation to fund a stranger's retirement years, only your own.

Never annuitize (sign away your principal) in exchange for monthly lifetime payments. The insurance company then owns your funds for life.

Congress grandfathered pre-January 1, 1987 money. Owners don't have to withdraw this "old" money until age 75 if the plan permits and it has been kept separate.

401(k)s sell like hotcakes

To retire on $40,000 a year at age 65, you must start saving $4,818 a year at age 40. Where do you stand?

Everybody loves the **401(k):** employees, companies, and money managers.

The sizzle is appealing: tax deductible contributions (limit $10,000 for 1998), matching employer contributions, earnings tax deferred until retirement, portability upon termination, a choice of investment vehicles and tax favored status at retirement time through an IRA rollover. What more could you ask for?

Many 401(k) plans now have hardship distribution or loan provisions where you can borrow up to 50% of your account and pay back the funds with interest to your own 401(k) account if you need the money early. There are no credit checks or lengthy applications to complete.

401(k)s are popular with employers because companies don't have to guarantee any monthly retirement payments. What your account makes, you get. They are cheaper for your company, which is off the hook for a monthly income and mismanagement if the investment later goes sour.

Employees with one year of service, 1,000 hours of work in a year, and age 18 or older may be eligible to participate. The boss may match contributions up to a certain level. At separation of service, a worker may roll over his or her account into an IRA, further deferring tax consequences until after retirement.

Employees usually grab for the tax benefits, considering the investments inside as secondary issues. If the investment options are full of hidden fees, up-front commissions, annual commissions year after year, and life insurance costs, you may do better over time **outside** the 401(k), despite the obvious tax shelter assistance.

There is a more ominous aspect to maximizing these pension plans: under the rules of ERISA (who ultimately controls qualified retirement plans), distributions from your account can be restricted until normal retirement age, currently 65. As baby-boomers become part of the retirement landscape, Uncle Sam may "share" your funds for its budget program needs.

If this happens, you will eat fewer meals, travel to cheaper vacation spots and have less to spend on your medical care.

Avoiding 401(k) fraud

Most of the nation's 401(k) plans are fraud free. But if you spot any of the following danger signs noted below, request an explanation from your employee benefits office:
- your quarterly statement consistently arrives late or at odd intervals; find out when the statement is due from the investment company;
- a significant drop in your account balance that cannot be explained by normal market fluctuations;
- former employees are having trouble getting their benefits;
- you are missing contributions or they don't match your year-to-date pay stub;
- investments are not invested in the accounts you originally chose;
- frequent and unexplained changes in investment managers;
- the account statement shows inaccuracies.

If your benefits department cannot satisfy your questions, contact the Pension and Welfare Benefits Administration's nearest regional office.

Don't maximize pension contributions at the expense of your annual IRA account and other outside investment vehicles. I value control of my money above current tax savings, even matching employer contributions. With the future of Social Security uncertain, your pension funds may look tempting to Washington any day now.

Profit sharing plans

Employers control most **profit sharing** contributions and how the assets are managed and invested. There is no requirement that a company contribute every year. Most companies wait until year end to decide whether the bottom line was profitable enough to reward workers.

From a worker's perspective, no benefits are guaranteed, no annual employer contributions are required, and the employer chooses the investment manager.

Bottom line, if your employer can choose excellent managers and is generous with the working troops, this kind of pension can help with your retirement needs. Unfortunately, employers frequently know how to produce widgets, not benefit plans. So they tend to purchase the sales pitch instead of the steak.

Defense strategy: give your CEO a copy of this book and mark those chapters which will teach the boss how to distinguish between the fact and the fiction. Sales presentations, "doing lunch," clients of the firm, and relatives are a common source of choosing a money management team for these types of plans.

ESOPs

Employee stock option plans (ESOPs) are a loose variety of stock employee benefits, but they generally offer company stock. Owning a piece of the company you work for may motivate you to work harder, but if the company is unhealthy when you retire, you may have a pension *and* its stock price at risk.

Companies often match retirement plans with stock instead of money. If the stock is so great, why is the company offering it to employees? Maybe money is more dear to them. You can't spend shares of stock—you will need money. I would rather receive matching dollars to add to my retirement account instead of in-house pieces of paper.

Your company personally benefits from giving (or selling cheaply) to employees shares of stock. If the shares are already in the company treasury, it gets a full deduction for their current market value and deduct those phantom costs off the corporate tax return. It also gets a free loan from the employees to fund future growth or other costs without incurring additional debt.

With more stock in "friendly hands," there is less chance of a hostile take-over and the new owners putting in their own management team. So current management remains employed. And companies often view stock as a cheaper giveaway than money.

In addition, by transferring stock to workers, the shares may rise in price.

In summary. the company gives pieces of ownership and its inherent risk to workers who, in turn, refund part of their salaries, reducing bottom line employee costs.

The company CEO is happy because the stock price is going up, worker costs are going down, and the employees think that they are a favored group like the guys in the board room meetings. It is even possible that the company CEO is selling stock at the same time the employee is buying.

The major job of your company CEO is to raise the price of the corporate stock. Companies that nurture employees at the expense of shareholder value are rare.

By increasing your company stock holdings at the expense of diversification, you may be taking too much risk: your job depends on the economic health of your company; any guaranteed pension also depends on the profitability of the company; and, adding individual stock of the same company enhances the total risk, not necessarily the future reward. Don't look only at the positive aspects of owning stock, ignoring risks you could easily avoid.

It is possible that by not purchasing the company stock, you may give up a high flier. But by diversifying, you will cushion any losses attached to the fortunes of your company.

The IRA alternative

You might be told that "smart" investors are finding innovative ways to hide retirement funds from the taxman and sock away much more money tax deferred than an IRA Account will allow.

An insurance agent may introduce the **"private retirement pension plan,"** now coming to a living room near you.

The benefits seem astonishing: tax deferred growth on your investment capital, guaranteed rates of return or various tax deferred mutual funds to choose from, no limits on how much you can contribute each year, no penalty for distributions before age 59½. a guaranteed monthly retirement income you cannot outlive, no reduction in Social Security payments no matter how much your earnings grow, and tax free income when you decide to take your money and run.

More benefits: zero percent loans if you want to borrow from your account and no probate when your heirs inherit your account tax free.

The sizzle is so attractive that most customers never realize the steak they have purchased is a whole life cash value insurance policy like their parents bought years ago that kept them from making a decent return on their money over the long term. This product is the same old insurance "duck" dressed up in a new set of feathers with the same high commissions (which your premiums pay for), inflexibility, high annual internal charges (which your cash value account pays for), and which works so little like a real investment, that the death benefit goes to your heirs tax free and makes insurance companies and their agents filthy rich.

Ledger illustrations are meaningless. An insurance agent can put anything down on paper, depending on how trusting (gullible) you are. Same old bird, new costume, brand new living room revivalist agent presentation.

KEOGHs

There are two basic types of **KEOGH** pension plans. The most popular (and the easiest to administrate) is a **defined contribution** plan, which limits the percentage of annual contribution to 15 percent of income (actually 13.04 percent after the complex formula is computed).

The other KEOGH prototype is a **defined benefit** plan, a more confusing prototype administered at greater expense. But this plan allows greater annual funding to as much as 100 percent of your annual income at retirement time (within certain limits and after complex computations).

Employees must receive a proportional contribution, though there are methods of skewing greater dollars to the most highly compensated personnel, usually the company's owner. All contributions are tax deductible in the year they are made, and earnings are tax deferred like other qualified retirement pension plans.

Penalties are similar to those for IRAs and, in addition, both employees and the owner may have an outside IRA account as well, though it may not be tax deductible, depending on their adjusted gross income.

KEOGHs are more complicated than other small business retirement alternatives. Unless a significant amount of funds can be invested to make the extra expenses and additional tax rules worth the trouble, the SEP may be a more attractive choice. A clerical employee can handle SEP requirements, while a KEOGH needs the administration of an outside firm and comes with a higher price tag.

When Congress decides to assert its tax muscles in the area of KEOGHs, money purchase, and profit sharing plans, they can reverse previous rules, change past assumptions which plans have been using for their valuations and contributions, and cause upheaval. When the IRS changes the rules, more expense is needed to bring these pensions into compliance with new tax laws.

Therefore, some small businesses are abandoning KEOGHs in favor of cheaper and simpler pension programs.

Since KEOGHs may favor older and more highly compensated employees (including the boss), these remain attractive to high income earners despite their inherent problems of valuation and tax compliance issues. They are, however, less flexible for companies with uneven cash flows during years of reduced gross revenues.

A new KEOGH plan must be opened by December 31 of the calendar year in which it starts, but contributions to an existing KEOGH may be made until tax time or April 15 of the following year, including extensions. Since this is a complex retirement plan, expert advice should be sought so as not to run afoul of tax or contribution rules.

For small businesses with large sums to invest, this qualified retirement plan may allow you to stash more money than simpler pension plan alternatives.

Money purchase pensions

Guaranteed traditional pensions, defined benefit types, are giving way to cheaper methods for companies to provide benefits for their workers.

A money purchase contribution plan of ten percent (which must be contributed to annually, no matter what profits are left) per year of employee gross income coupled with a profit sharing plan up to fifteen percent (based on annual profits) per year may prove a viable combination of flexibility. The money purchase plan is expected to be funded on an annual basis, while the profit sharing plan can be funded in years when profits will allow.

Deferred compensation plans

Called Section 457 plans, these cover many public employees. Contributions are tax deductible because of a **substantial risk of forfeiture to the worker in the future.**

Contrary to public belief, they are **not owned or vested** by the employees themselves but, instead, are the general property of the government agency the employees work for.

The funds can be used to pay creditors or for any other budget purpose. They are risky future promises!

They are not protected by any pension agency, are informally funded, and pose a risk to your retirement health if they are used for other reasons.

Flexible spending accounts

Section 125 plans are widely used in the public employment sector. They allow certain expenses to be deducted before taxation but reduce your wages for other employee and retirement benefits.

Pension pitfalls

If you are thinking of taking a loan from your 401(k) or a similar retirement plan at work, there are a few things you may not know.

Although funds are intended for retirement, you can often borrow up to fifty percent of your vested account for excessive medical expenses, a college education, a new home, or the loss of a principal residence.

Loan payments are generally deducted from your paycheck until the loan is paid off, generally within five years, unless the funds are used for a home, when this limit does not apply.

While you are re-paying the account at a market interest rate, your account could be earning much more, invested in growth securities. In addition, you are robbing your nest egg. Instead of re-paying funds back into your account, you could be funding another future goal. A loan is a loan, even if you are the banker as well as the customer.

What if you lose your job and can't repay your loan? The unpaid balance is considered an early distribution (if under the age of 59½) and all income taxes and a ten percent penalty will be due in the year you "took" your money.

You may also be able to make special hardship withdrawals from your plan for excessive medical bills above 7.5% of your gross income, for college tuition, or for the potential loss of your home. Again, income taxes and a possible ten percent penalty may apply.

If you change jobs and take possession of your retirement money, you will be automatically assessed a twenty percent withholding tax and possibly an additional ten percpt tax for early withdrawal unless you come up with the extra twenty percent from outside sources. You can claim this money back on your next tax return if you roll over 100% of your original retirement account balance within sixty days. Otherwise, the twenty percent withholding is considered an early distribution along with the ten percent penalty for early withdrawal.

Be careful that the check is made out to the transferring custodian for your benefit, not to you personally.

If your account balance is less than $5,000, employers can cash out your plan, sending a check to you without permission.

If you retire at age 55 and need immediate income, you may want to leave some funds in your employer plan, as these can usually be tapped at age 55, while an IRA Account generally cannot be withdrawn before age 59½ without penalty.

If you receive after tax money that can be spent without income taxes, you can feel more comfortable rolling your entire balance into an IRA Rollover Account.

There are ways to tap an IRA without tears before age 59½. These are explained further in Chapter 17.

How healthy is your pension plan? Since a **guaranteed pension** is tied to your company's financial health and other plans may be temporarily stuck in case of insolvency or a sale, read your employer's annual report. Even if your company is healthy, consider a notice of pension under-funding a reminder that you must beef up other investments for retirement.

WHEN WILL YOUR SAVINGS RUN OUT?

The chart on below can help you estimate the number of years your current savings may last. Plot the number of years remaining by picking your savings growth rate and your rate of withdrawal (the chart assumes that you do not add to your savings). The number at the intersection of these two rates is how many years may be left until your savings are depleted.

For example, if your savings grow three percent annually, and you withdraw your original principal amount at a rate of ten percent annually, your savings may last roughly twelve years.

(This chart is intended as educational material about savings and investing and does not predict or depict the rate of return on any mutual fund. Consult an investment professional for a more specific and detailed analysis of your personal financial situation.)

	2%	3%	4%	5%	6%	7%	8%	9%	10%	11%	12%	13%	14%	15%	16%
15%															20
14%														21	16
13%													22	16	14
12%												23	17	14	12
11%											24	18	15	13	11
10%										25	19	15	13	12	10
9%									27	20	16	14	12	11	10
8%								29	21	17	14	12	11	10	9
7%							31	22	18	15	13	11	10	9	9
6%						33	24	19	16	14	12	11	10	9	8
5%					37	26	20	17	14	12	11	10	9	8	8
4%				41	28	22	18	15	13	12	10	9	9	8	7
3%			47	31	23	19	16	14	12	11	10	9	8	8	7
2%		55	35	26	20	17	15	13	11	10	9	8	8	7	7
1%	70	41	29	22	18	15	13	12	11	10	9	8	7	7	6

Withdrawal Rate

Chapter 17

IRAs: new and improved

An IRA is not a specific investment like a stock, a bond or a bank CD. It is a special retirement tax shelter set up by Congress for individual retirement savings. You can choose a variety of underlying investments and add the IRA tax shelter label. All earnings in an IRA account are tax deferred until withdrawn.

Even if your company has a pension and you will receive Social Security benefits, you should create additional retirement funds. Company pensions collapse and, as more workers retire earlier and live longer, many plans will be expected to pay out larger and longer benefits. We already know what pressures our social insurance system will face.

Anyone under age 70½ by the end of the year who earns a paycheck or collects alimony can contribute $2,000 per year or 100% of earned income (whichever is less) to a traditional IRA. It doesn't matter how long you have worked, whether your company has a retirement plan, or how many other employers you have worked for during the years. Rents, royalties and investment income do not qualify as earned income for IRA purposes.

Finally Congress agrees: being a homemaker and/or a mom is a full time job. A worker and a non-working spouse can each contribute the maximum to an IRA account, providing the working spouse earns at least $4,000. Single wage-earning couples can contribute up to $4,000 per couple when only one spouse works and even if the working spouse has a pension plan at work. No individual can contribute more than $2,000.

Since the rules don't specify what "non-working" spouse means, it could include unemployed, never employed, or even retired with a working spouse. Thanks to unintended loopholes, many retirees previously unable to deduct IRA contributions in the past can make fully deductible contributions to traditional IRA accounts.

Many folks believe if they have a pension they are prohibited from investing in an IRA. Not true. Such workers can still contribute the maximum contribution. Whether the IRA contribution can be deducted on your 1040 tax return is another matter.

New tax rules make it easier to qualify for a tax deduction. If your company has no retirement pension or if you are not yet eligible to join for a year or more, you can deduct your total contribution, regardless of how much "bacon" you bring home during the year.

Even if you have an employer retirement plan, you may still qualify for a deductible IRA, depending on your income. Single with an annual income of less than $30,000? You can deduct the full contribution. As your income rises, the deductible amount reduces (phases out), and you lose the total deduction when your income rises to $40,000.

For married couples, things become a bit more complex. If neither you nor your spouse has a pension, you can each deduct a full IRA contribution, regardless of your individual or combined income. If one or both of you are covered by a pension plan, but your adjusted gross income (before the IRA is deducted) is under $50,000, you can each contribute and deduct the full IRA. Above that amount, the immediate tax deduction reduces and disappears at $60,000, adjusted in future years for inflation.

If only one spouse is covered by a pension plan, the uncovered spouse can deduct the full IRA amount, even if that spouse has no income, as long as the couple's joint income does not exceed $150,000. (Remember, however, the working spouse with a pension doesn't qualify for a totally deductible IRA if his or her joint income rises to $50,000.)

You can contribute to a variety of deductible and/or non-deductible IRAs (provided you qualify for all types), including the Roth IRA. The total combination of your IRA contributions, however, cannot exceed $2,000 per person per year.

Since the primary goal of long term funds must be guaranteeing future purchasing power, IRA investments should be chosen for growth potential. Variable annuities are a waste of money because you are paying extra for an unnecessary tax free insurance wrapper. The IRA label already offers protection from annual taxation.

Mutual funds are ideal IRA vehicles. Search for those which offer prudent growth opportunities while creating wealth slowly but surely.

Old IRAs just got better

The 10% penalty that applies to most IRA withdrawals before the owner reaches age 59½ no longer applies to withdrawals taken for qualified higher education expenses for the taxpayer, spouse, children, or grandchildren. Nor to withdrawals up to $10,000 for qualified, first time home purchases used within 120 days to buy, build, or rebuild a first home which is the principal residence of the taxpayer, spouse, child, grandchild, or ancestor of the taxpayer or their spouse. These distributions are limited to $10,000 during the taxpayer's lifetime.

Penalties are also waived for withdrawals due to excessive medical expenses or for health insurance premiums if the IRA owner is unemployed and collecting unemployment benefits for at least twelve consecutive weeks.

IRAs accumulated during a marriage may be considered marital property even though the account is in one name only. A divorce may not affect the tax deferred status of an IRA account. By transferring part or all of an IRA to an ex-spouse as a property settlement, the IRA can remain tax deferred and continue compounding as though it belonged to the new owner from the beginning. No taxes or early withdrawal penalties may be due in that case.

Gadzooks! Another IRA?

Under the tax rules for the **Roth IRA** there are no tax deductions for contributions. But you can pull out the money tax free under certain conditions. And workers can contribute after age 70½ even if they are taking minimum distributions from traditional IRA accounts.

More excitement. Though contributions are limited to a maximum of $2,000 per person per year, millions of taxpayers who don't qualify for tax deductions under the traditional IRA may now reap tax benefits.

Only two of the following requirements must be met to take a "qualified" tax free, penalty-free distribution: after the account is open for five years from the first tax year the Roth IRA is opened; **AND** either 1) distributions are made for first time home buyer expenses up to $10,000 maximum; 2) distributions are made due to the IRA owner's disability or death; or 3) withdrawals are made after the age of 59½.

IRA owners can also make "non-qualified" withdrawals of their after tax contributions (principal) free and without a 10% pre-age 59½ penalty even if the above requirements are not met. With Roth IRAs, taxpayers aren't required to make withdrawals when they reach age 70½.

New Roth IRAs offer even bigger possibilities for retirees. Put in a nondeductible contribution of $2,000 per person a year, pay no taxes on the earnings and enjoy tax free withdrawals. Unlike money in traditional IRAs, all contributions to Roth IRAs can be pulled out tax free and penalty free at any time. And earnings are even tax free as long as the account has been open for five years as long as you are over age 59½.

Your adjusted gross income must be less than $95,000 for a full contribution as a single tax filer and below $150,000 for spouses filing together for a full Roth IRA contribution. Eligibility is eliminated for singles at $110,000 or above and for joint filers at $160,000 or more.

Beneficiaries inherit the assets income tax free if the Roth IRA owner dies. So retirees can now use the new tax rules to pass hundreds of thousands of dollars to heirs, tax free. Surviving spouses can roll over a deceased spouse's Roth account into their own Roth. Other beneficiaries can leave the money in the Roth for up to five years after the original owner's death. Or they can take distributions from the inherited Roth over their own lifetime if distributions are begun within a year after the owner's death.

Time to Roth and Roll?

Workers earning $100,000 or less adjusted gross income can convert traditional IRAs to Roth IRAs (except for married taxpayers filing a separate return). Although not subject to the 10% premature withdrawal penalty, ordinary income taxes will be applied to any assets previously considered "deductible." In other words, any contributions and earnings that were not previously taxed will be when converted.

The good news is that for conversions completed in 1998, all amounts subject to income tax will be included in income as if withdrawn over four tax years (1998 through 2001).

When a traditional IRA is converted to a Roth IRA, the five year holding period begins with the tax year that the conversion was made. Since the conversion is actually a "rollover," the conversion must be completed within sixty days of distribution from the traditional IRA.

If you convert to a Roth IRA and use alternate taxable funds to pay the taxes, the full account value can continue to compound tax free inside the Roth IRA and still be distributed tax free, according to the new rules.

You may want to time your conversion(s) to coincide with losses from other investments or convert in a year when your income drops. If you have several IRAs, you may convert one or more. You also have the option of converting only part of an IRA Account.

Please note that the amount you convert *does not count* toward the $100,000 income limit to qualify for the conversion. If, for example your income is $90,000, you can convert more than $10,000. The amount you convert, however, *does count* toward income limits for qualifying for a *deductible* IRA, though you can still make deductible contributions to IRAs under the income limits if you also have a Roth IRA.

The longer an IRA account has to compound before withdrawals are made, the more sense a Roth IRA makes. Qualified withdrawals are tax free once the account has been opened for at least five years, a better alternative for young taxpayers in a higher tax bracket when they retire.

Future retirees expecting to remain in the same tax bracket may also pay less tax by converting to a Roth IRA now. Retirees with a lot of money in IRAs that they otherwise would have to start taking out at age 70½ are also candidates for a Roth IRA conversion.

To Roth or not to Roth: that is the confusion

Converting to a Roth IRA is not a "no brainer" because the tax bill for the conversion may be substantial, even without penalties. Once switched, assets can't be converted back. The conversion may result in a higher tax bracket now.

In addition, there is one big unwritten concern: will the U.S. Government restrict Roth IRA tax free withdrawal benefits in the future when taxing hundreds of billions of dollars in Roth IRAs can provide significant revenues for social projects and general budget needs?

This windfall looks too good to be true.

Employer IRAs

Small companies may create simplified pensions with *Super IRA* accounts. Employers can contribute to a plan for their employees who can also contribute for themselves through a payroll deduction plan. Each worker has a separate account and all benefits of a regular IRA account. These plans have been generally replaced by more popular choices for small employers.

Simple IRA Plans

SIMPLE IRAs are employer pension plans, a combination of employee before-tax salary deferrals and required employer contributions. Employees may contribute up to 100% of their income to the plan but not more than $6,000 per year, indexed for inflation in future years.

Employers must make contributions in one of the following ways: either match eligible employees' contributions dollar for dollar to a maximum of 3% of each employee's compensation; or reduce the matching contribution to 1% in any two out of the last five years, including the current year the employer desires to reduce the match.

The SIMPLE IRA is anything but! Do NOT try this at home without supervision. Employers should seek expert advice so they do not trip over the complex tax rules and regulations.

Taking care of (IRA) business

Some folks believe they must purchase an IRA at their neighborhood banking institution or credit union. Banks originally popularized the IRA phenomenon when interest rates were high, but they actually sell CDs and add the IRA label onto the CD account. You can purchase numerous underlying investments such as mutual funds, stocks, bonds, insurance annuities, even certain gold or platinum coins. Then add the IRA stamp to alert Uncle Sam this money is tax deferred until withdrawal time.

You can use any source of funds (savings, a loan or a gift) for your contribution. You must have earned at least that much income during the year (unless you are a non-working spouse).

You don't need to invest a full $2,000 per year. Put away what you can, whether a single lump sum or payments on a weekly or monthly basis. You can invest portions of your IRA in more than one place.

The more time your money has to work, the more powerful it becomes. Investing on January 1st of each year is ideal, but many folks don't recover from holiday bills until Spring.

If you invest $166.66 on a monthly basis starting in January, you will have the full $2,000 contributed by the end of the year. Making your IRA investment at the last minute (at tax time) is better than not at all. But the longer you wait to invest, the harder your money has to work to make up for lost compounding time.

You can invest your IRA contribution in more than one place. I often recommend at least two mutual funds with different investment objectives. That way you can diversify and accommodate a larger investment menu. If you don't contribute the full amount one year, you cannot accrue or carry over that amount and add to your next year's contribution.

Whether you have a 401(k), 403(b) (TSA/TDA), profit sharing plan at work, or are self-employed and have a SEP or a KEOGH, you may also contribute to an IRA account, though it may not be tax deductible. If you have the money, start an IRA, too. The more money that can be tax deferred in one way or another, the better.

If you inadvertently contribute too much in any year, remove the excess (and any earnings on those funds) before you file your tax return. If you are too late, the excess can be transferred to next year's account. However, you will be taxed six percent per year on the excess funds in the meantime. Watch your investment statement(s) to monitor how much money you have invested.

If you are sending your IRA to more than one investment company, monitor all statements so you don't contribute more than allowed in one year.

You can designate a primary beneficiary(ies) and backup beneficiary(ies). In this manner, your IRA account will avoid probate.

Robbing Peter to pay Paul

You may not borrow from your IRA. You can, however, take receipt of IRA funds (in your hands) once per year for a period of 60 days or less. But if Uncle Sam catches you borrowing those funds, the event is considered an immediate distribution of IRA funds, and taxes will be due on all before-tax money (plus a 10-percent early withdrawal penalty if you are under age 59½).

Simple estate planning

The simplest method of passing an IRA account to your heirs is to name a primary beneficiary and a backup contingent beneficiary as well. You may name several beneficiaries if the investment institution agrees in order to direct your IRA account to your heirs outside probate.

Education IRAs

This brand new IRA can reduce the hassle of the tassel. Parents, grandparents, other relatives, and friends alike can contribute up to $500 per year for future college expenses per student under age 18.

Although there are no up-front tax write-offs on these funds, the account grows tax-deferred until withdrawn tax free to pay for tuition, fees, room and board, and equipment such as computers.

All funds must be withdrawn before the child reaches age 30. However, this IRA can be rolled over to another eligible family child in need of an ivy-covered experience. If used for purposes other than qualified educational expenses, however, earnings are taxed as income in the year withdrawn and are subject to an additional 10% tax penalty.

Single taxpayers earning less than $95,000 and couples filing jointly, earning less than $150,000, are eligible to make full contributions annually. Above such earned income limits, contributions are reduced, then totally eliminated. What a great place to put that next tax refund!

Beware. The new law prohibits funding an education IRA in the same year you contribute to a state sponsored, prepaid tuition program. Worse, each year you tap an education IRA for college expenses, you forfeit the opportunity to take a Hope Scholarship credit (worth up to $1,500 per year in the first two years of college) or a Lifetime Learning credit (worth up to $1,000 per year for each additional year of post secondary education through the year 2002 and $2,000 per year thereafter).

In addition, under present financial aid formulas the account could be considered the child's assets while attempting to market your student as a poor church mouse. You may want to use all education IRA assets on one year's educational costs so you can take the tax credits in other years.

Be careful you don't contribute more than the law allows, especially if Grandma and Aunt Harriet are both gifting funds for the education IRA account. You can invest contributions in more than one place.

Roll over Rover

Even after age 70½ when IRA mandatory distributions must begin, you can transfer your IRA account from investment to investment company 365 days per year, by directing it trustee-to-trustee and directly from one IRA custodian to another. But unless the IRA rollover came from a pension distributed to you on Jan. 1, 1993 or later, you can also receive the check in your hand once a year and manually send it to the next IRA custodian within sixty days of the date you receive the IRA check. Tax law allows you to receive your account only once each 365 days. To transfer more often than that, request a direct trustee transfer of funds to the new IRA investment company custodian.

You only have sixty days to get your IRA account to the next custodian. If you miss your transfer deadline, you will lose the IRA tax deferral benefit, and all money will become taxable as ordinary income in that year.

Keep IRA rollover accounts separate from other mutual fund money and from new IRA contributions. When rolling over a pension plan to an IRA, keep those funds separate from any other IRA Rollover accounts, even if you are investing in the same mutual fund.

A bank CD labeled as an IRA account can be moved as well. You may want to wait until the CD matures to avoid an early withdrawal penalty. Many lending institutions offer penalty free withdrawals for depositors over the age of 59½. Ask your bank about withdrawal privileges and penalties.

An insurance annuity is similar to an IRA account, and it can be transferred as well. If you are told you will incur surrender charges by moving, realize that any such charges are the investment commissions the agent received when your money was originally invested. That money is already gone, into the pocket of the insurance agent who sold you the product. Don't let fear of loss keep you from moving to a better performing and more diversified investment, like real mutual funds. You opted for the free lunch, believing someone would invest your money free, and these internal charges are coming back to haunt you.

The $50,000 mistake

If you are not putting money into a traditional IRA because it is not deductible from your gross income *you could be making a terrible mistake!!!*

Unfortunately, Congress lets no good deal go unpunished for very long. So the tax deduction that felt so good and erased a maximum of $2,000 per worker from the gross earnings of all wage earners was maimed by the 1986 Tax Act. But the Tax Relief Act of 1997 has breathed life back into this retirement vehicle. The death of the IRA is greatly exaggerated.

Before you throw away a silver bullet that Congress still allows, consider the following:

Suppose a taxpayer makes an annual $2,000 **totally nondeductible** contribution each year as opposed to merely investing $2,000 per year in a taxable investment. Both the nondeductible IRA and the taxable investment funds are invested in the same vehicle averaging 10 percent per year.

The following is the result of each investment at the end of 20 and 30 years:

At the end of:	Nondeductible IRA	Taxable Investment*
20 years	$126,005	$84,272
30 years	$361,887	$189,588

* The taxpayer is in the 28-percent tax bracket, plus 5-percent state and local income tax.

The tax *deferred power* of IRA earnings inside the IRA account over time is far more powerful than any immediate tax deduction. Even if you cannot deduct any portion of your annual IRA contribution, your earnings grow tax deferred until you take them out.

The longer the period of time that money can compound, the larger the gap and the difference between the tax deferred IRA account and the fully taxable investment.

Remember, the IRA account shown above has no tax deduction advantages. Only the benefits of tax deferred compounding are seen here. If any portion of the IRA account can be deducted, the advantages over time will be even greater.

Considering the current uncertain economic outlook and highly valued stock market, is it prudent to invest now for the long term?

Do you believe your government can continue to bail out banks, savings and loans and insurance companies, pay off mounting deficit debt, support increasingly sagging and under-funded pension funds, increase social insurance and entitlement payments to an aging population, institute a national system for health care, subsidize foreign countries' debt fiascoes, prepare for baby boomer retirement needs, fill favored sacred cow coffers to buy election votes, and have anything left over for your old age? Right! Put in that IRA, tax deductible or not!

Tapping IRAs without tears

Generally, you can withdraw from your IRA without penalty after age 59½. If you don't need the money, let it continue to compound even though you are of age. Use other investments for supplemental income, if needed. The *longer* your dollars work inside the tax umbrella, the *harder* they work.

You can withdraw your money in a traditional IRA at anytime. But, if you withdraw funds before you reach the age of 59½ (for other than death or disability), you may incur a 10-percent penalty for early withdrawal *plus* all taxes due on the amount you withdraw. Today there are several ways to tap an IRA without tears before the age of 59½.

You can withdraw money from your IRA early without penalty if you take the money out in the form of an annuity, a substantially equal series of payments based on your life expectancy or over the lives of you and your beneficiary combined together. There are several methods which can be used and which offer different annual withdrawal amounts.

This is called a 72T withdrawal and distributions must continue at least annually for five years or to the age of 59½, whichever period is longer. The remainder of your IRA account is not harmed in any way as long as you follow the early withdrawal annuity rules. This method is available under Section 72T of the IRS tax code.

You can separate your IRA accounts and withdraw from some, leaving the others to compound until after age 59½. Seek expert assistance before implementing this withdrawal method, as the tax penalties for mistakes in calculations are significant.

Taxing matters

When you withdraw from your IRA, all tax deferred earnings and tax deductible contributions will be treated like interest from a CD, or as ordinary income. You pay taxes only on the amount you withdraw (unless the law requires you to withdraw more after age 70½). The remainder of your IRA account continues tax deferred until you withdraw it.

Keep all IRA records for the rest of your life or eternity, whichever period is longer. The forms you fill out when you set up an IRA may be needed decades later to determine how the IRA should be distributed and taxed. Especially save every tax form #8606 you completed for partially or totally non-deductible IRA contributions.

Copy everything for your files, including the IRA application, the original checks and end-of-the-year account statements from your investment company(ies). These records will provide a clear paper trail if the IRS should ever examine your IRA history. Send important documentation via certified mail.

Oh, no! I'm 70½!

Fear grips some retirees when they reach age 70½ and must withdraw their first mandatory minimum IRA distribution. The IRA investor must decide which system to use for his or her systematic IRA withdrawals.

Mandatory required withdrawals must start by April 1 of the year **after** you turn age 70½, though the first IRA distribution actually counts for the year you turn age 70½, even if you take your first withdrawal in the subsequent year.

If you defer your initial IRA withdrawal until April 1st of the year after your 70½ birthday, you will have to take **two** distributions that year. Two withdrawals in the same year could put you in a higher tax bracket. To avoid this problem, the initial withdrawal can be made by December 31st of the year you turn age 70½. If you plan to be in a lower tax bracket, however, postponing the first withdrawal until the year following your 70½ birthday may lower your overall tax bite. Such decisions should be made carefully and with expert tax advice. You may always withdraw more than the law allows, just not less. Distributions may be taken as one lump sum annually or in any number of systematic payments over the year, as long as the total mandatory distribution is withdrawn by December 31st of each year you must make a withdrawal.

Distribution options

Which of many ways to take distributions depends on several factors, including your marital or family status, whether you want to minimize your payout, and your estate planning objectives.

- Single Life means the payment rate will be based on the life expectancy of the IRA owner only, with no beneficiary life expectancy included.
- Joint Life can be used when there is a spouse beneficiary (of any age) or a non-spouse beneficiary who is not ten or more years younger than the IRA owner.
- Minimum Distribution Incidental Benefit (MDIB) is utilized when the beneficiary is not a spouse and is ten or more years younger than the IRA owner.

Calculation Methods

Term Certain with No Annual Recalculation is the easiest method. If this method is chosen, the life expectancy factor calculation is locked in. The factor you choose from the life expectancy tables in the first distribution year are found in *IRS Publication #590* and subsequently reduced by the number 1 each year thereafter. So if you start with a Single Life factor of 16.1 in the first year, you will use 15.1 in the second year, 14.1 in the third, and so on.

Annual Recalculation is the method which ordinarily produces smaller annual required distributions than the term certain method. If this method is chosen, the minimum distribution is recalculated each year by using the life expectancy tables corresponding to your current age.

Divide the fair market value of ***all*** IRA and pension accounts (except 403(b) account values accumulated before January 1, 1987*) on December 31 of the previous year by the divisor you have chosen. Your answer is the amount which must be withdrawn before the end of the year. You can also request a fixed dollar amount each year or payments over a fixed number of years as long as the method chosen doesn't exceed your life expectancy.

You may name any beneficiary you wish, even a grandchild. With a younger beneficiary, your combined life expectancy will likely be lower than using your age alone. When you name multiple non-spouse beneficiaries, you must calculate the divisor using the age of the oldest beneficiary. However, if the beneficiary is not a spouse and is ten or more years younger, then the IRA owner must limit the age difference to ten years for calculation purposes.

The "recalculation" method may be wiser if you believe you'll live longer than the current tables illustrate. Then your IRA cannot be depleted in your lifetime. For some reason, the longer you live, the longer each year's life expectancy table shows you will live. However, the rules for minimum distributions after death differ, depending on whether the IRA owner died before or after minimum distributions were already started.

With the "term certain" method, your IRA will be depleted after you reach the original life expectancy age, even if you are still living. You could divide your IRAs to name several beneficiaries in this manner. But once you choose an IRA distribution method, you must continue the same method every year thereafter and with all IRA accounts.

The mandatory withdrawal amount can be taken from any IRA account, preferably from the investment providing the lowest return.

Seek expert advice on all aspects of IRA distributions because the penalties for withdrawing too much are the loss of tax deferred funds, the methods you choose may also determine how your beneficiaries must continue to take distributions, and the IRS penalty for withdrawing too little is 50 percent of the amount you failed to withdraw but should have.

For more information about IRAs, contact mutual fund service departments or shareholder services. You can also request *IRS Publication #590*, which explains more about IRA accounts.

When Congress restricted the tax deductibility of IRAs, it sent the wrong message to consumers. Despite the fact that some people can no longer deduct their IRA contribution, IRA accounts remain one of the best long term retirement investments you can make—provided, of course, they are invested in inflation fighting investment vehicles that preserve future purchasing power.

*403(b) (TSA/TDA) account values accumulated before January 1, 1987 operate under different mandatory distribution tax rules. Please contact your tax advisor or 403(b) provider for specific distribution instructions.

Chapter 18

Estate planning: You can't take it with you

It probably doesn't occur to most of you—whose "mansion" may be overmortgaged and whose "vaults" look curiously like piggies—that anyone, including your immediate family, would be interested in attending a reading of your will.

Why would you want to be around when an accounting of remaining debts determines who is responsible for coming up with the cash needed to pay final expenses, fend off a line of creditors and face the banker?

Most of you probably feel your estate could be handled simply, considering the limited personal assets to be disbursed. In fact, *your* will might look something like this:

Last Will and Testament

I leave my overstuffed TV chair to Rover, who, through 10 years of adverse possession, probably already has legal claim to it.

The assorted tools I have managed to rubber band and glue back together, I leave to my son, with the stipulation that he be forced to use them in their present condition.

To my daughter, I give, devise and bequeath a life estate in the bathroom where she spent the majority of her teenage years.

The list of unfinished chores, as well as the boards for the fence, the wire for the dog run and the paint for the house, I give to anyone willing to haul them away and sweep up.

To my grandson I leave my pool table, along with every divot, Popsicle stain and torn piece of felt from his visits.

To the colony of wasps under the eaves that I could never convince to relocate, I leave my collection of pesticides and bug bombs. Because you have evolved into a super race impervious to everything, I believe your survival instinct should be rewarded.

Finally, my touring bike, like new because I had so little time to ride it, I give to absolutely no one because it's mine, mine, mine!

Why you need estate planning

Estate planning for the yachtless is a vital part of every financial plan if:

1. You are married or have remarried.
2. You are divorced.
3. You are widowed.
4. You have children or other dependents.
5. You own tangible assets (cars, home, personal property).
6. You owe debts or financial obligations.
7. You own liquid assets (CDs, bank accounts, etc.).
8. You have financial assets (securities, bonds, etc.).
9. You have a company pension plan.
10. You have recently bought or sold a substantial asset.
11. You own property or personal assets in another state.
12. Your financial circumstances have changed.
13. Your health has recently changed.
14. You have a disabled spouse or child.
15. Your personal life has significantly changed.
16. You intend to disinherit any of your family.
17. You may become disabled or mentally incompetent.
18. Your plan has not been updated for several years, especially since 1981.
19. Estate tax laws have changed.
20. You care who gets your property after you are gone.
21. You will eventually die.

After reading through this list, I think you'll agree that it covers just about everyone. And, indeed, people should consider their ultimate mortality when putting together their financial plan. The specifics of your estate planning, however, depend upon your unique circumstances, and the vehicles you will use will vary according to them.

A competent attorney should spend enough time with you to outline options and explore will alternatives for property ownership and distribution. There are many will substitutes, ways to title your assets, that provide a detour to the cumbersome and expensive process of probate. Be sure an attorney provides a list of methods by which you can pass your belongings to your heirs without passing them through a will.

Where there's a will, there's a way

No matter how little you own, dying intestate (without a will), creates difficulties and expenses for those you leave behind. Without instructions to the contrary, state laws will determine who gets your possessions, who raises your children, how your assets will be divided and who your executor/executrix will be.

In addition, dying intestate gives tacit approval for your relatives to haggle over your belongings (at your expense) and over your children, who might be attractive if they come attached to a large insurance policy naming them as principal beneficiaries.

A well thought out estate plan, using will substitute titles whenever possible with a will to catch those assets that don't have a direct transfer plan, can provide a fair and equitable solution of your possessions, establish limitations on creditors and help you distribute your property as you wish.

Since wills can be contested, are not cheap to administer and can become bogged down, you may want to keep assets out of your will.

Unless you have a reason to protect your will from your family, consider keeping your estate planning documents stored safely in a fireproof box at home, not a bank safety deposit box or at the attorney's office. Bank safety boxes are generally locked upon the death of any owner, and documents can be lost or misplaced by a legal entity. You can provide others with a copy for their information and their safekeeping.

Don't assume any document blessed by a legal office must be competent and solve all of your estate planning objectives. A will should be your *last* line of defense, not your first. Try the KISS (keep it simple, stupid) method of estate planning before wrapping your assets so tight that they may remain knotted long after you are gone.

When you die, assets that have a built-in transfer plan such as a beneficiary or joint owner, can avoid the will and, therefore, the probate process. If your estate is relatively simple, most, if not all, your possessions can be passed directly, efficiently and inexpensively this way.

Mutual funds, bank and insurance IRAs, annuities and pensions, joint bank, checking and money market accounts, and death (life) insurance proceeds are a simple matter of designating a beneficiary or a co-owner. Real estate owned by more than one person can be structured so it will go to the surviving owner(s) and not into the will. The following checklist suggests will substitutes, ownership and estate designations that you can use:

- **Banking, CDs, checking, credit union, bank money market accounts and savings bonds.** Joint ownership with rights of survivorship, *or* individual or joint ownership with a beneficiary title called *payable on death* (POD) transfer to the named persons.

- **Securities such as stocks, bonds and mutual funds.** Joint tenants with rights of survivorship, or sole owner accounts with a *transfer on death* (TOD) transfer to the beneficiary.
- **Insurance proceeds.** With primary beneficiaries and contingent (backup) beneficiaries, you can designate certain percentages for each heir you choose. For the benefit of minor children, you can name an adult who will receive the money as a fiduciary on behalf of the children until they reach the age of majority. (See a further discussion of insurance in the section following in this chapter.)
- **Real estate.** Tenancy by the entireties between husband and wife, if allowed in your state, will transfer the home directly to the surviving spouse. A joint-and-survivorship deed keeps the property in both names during your lifetime, then transfers to the survivor after the death of one owner. Warranty deeds can have multiple owners, but each person's share goes to his or her named heirs through the will after death. Tenancy in common allows the proportional ownership of each to transfer through his or her wills depending on the percentage each individual has purchased or currently owns.
- **Auto titles, RVs or watercraft.** Joint titles allow this type of property to go directly to the survivor.
- **Pensions, 401(k)s, IRAs, SEPs, KEOGHs, tax sheltered annuities and regular insurance annuities.** These vehicles have beneficiary options that bypass the will.

Death insurance proceeds

Death benefits are so often misdirected that they should be more fully discussed. The greatest advantage of a life insurance beneficiary clause is that the death benefit passes directly and quickly to the beneficiaries outside the will and away from any and all creditors. If, however, life insurance policies are included in a will, they are part of the probate assets contingent to the claims of creditors and contests by unhappy heirs.

In a will, if the estate is sued for any reason (an auto accident in which someone is injured), and a claim eventually prevails, those insurance dollars could go to some stranger instead of your family.

Check beneficiary listings on all insurance policies (including your employer's). A first spouse won't hand over a death benefit check to your new spouse if you forgot to change the beneficiary after the divorce. Your mother may not like your choice of spouse, either. Whenever major events occur in your financial, personal or medical life, you should examine all beneficiary and ownership titles to keep them current with your wishes.

The primary beneficiary is usually a spouse, a parent or a child. But if the insured and the primary beneficiary die in a common accident, the insurance proceeds pass to the contingent beneficiary.

Young children under the age of majority are legally incompetent, so no insurance company is going to write out a fat insurance check to a 3 year old. Naming an adult trustee for their benefit keeps the insurance money out of probate and away from creditors or court action. If a contingent beneficiary has not been named, the death benefit goes to the decedent's estate and into the will.

Who gets the kids—and control of their money?

When putting together your will, don't forget about the care of your minor children—what could simultaneously be considered your most valuable assets and your most expensive liabilities. You might safely assume that, upon your death, your spouse would continue to care for and raise your children.

But what if you and your spouse are killed in a common accident? What if you are divorced and feel your ex-spouse would not be a good money manager of your children's inheritance? What if your children's only other living relatives are your aging parents? What if the solutions to your children's future well being and financial health aren't so simple?

In the case of divorce, the courts will typically award custody of children to the living parent, whether that would be your preference or not. In cases in which both parents are killed, guardianship will most often go to a close relative—your parents, brothers or sisters or perhaps a stepparent. You are advised to make your requests for guardianship in your will, but often the courts are guided by existing precedents.

You do, however, have a little more control over who controls your children's money. If you are currently married to the parent of your minor children, you may want to set up a testamentary trust within your will in case both of you are killed in a common accident. This backup plan names an adult to manage the children's money.

Another option, particularly for parents who want someone other than the likely guardian of their children, is to set up a testamentary trust (which kicks in after your death.) Most parents want their children to receive funds for maintenance, support, medical and education expenses, yet not open the door for frivolous expenses. A *trustee* can manage the estate under the guidelines you set up in the trust, even if someone else is raising the children. For example, you may indicate a certain amount of money should go to the monthly maintenance of your children's needs; you may set aside an amount for their education; you may indicate how your children receive the remainder of your estate, if any, upon their reaching the age of majority.

Whatever you choose to do, it's important to take your children's financial needs—throughout their childhood and even into adulthood—into consideration. Guardians suddenly responsible for raising your offspring with a $50,000 death insurance policy will struggle to make ends meet feeding, clothing, educating and entertaining your children. Your death insurance must be sufficient to pay off all of your liabilities plus support your children to adulthood and perhaps through college.

What if I become disabled?

Create a *durable power of attorney* for financial matters so that someone you trust can make financial decisions if you are unable to. Taxes, Social Security benefits, disability, pensions, license plates, mailing, selling securities and paying taxes are just a sample of financial tasks that must be carried out for you. You can also designate a backup if your first choice should be unable, unwilling or otherwise fail to qualify as attorney-in-fact. The document must continue through any disability to remain valid.

The *medical power of attorney* or *health care directive* is becoming an important addition to today's estate plan. It performs a similar function as the above, only in the area of medical decisions. You can name a trusted family member or friend to act in your stead and a contingent person in case the first is not able to qualify.

A living will

The *living will* allows you to provide a written intent regarding withdrawing or maintaining life sustaining medical care if you are terminally ill or permanently unconscious. Individual states vary in their approaches to this sensitive issue. Some states advise both a living will and a durable power of attorney to cover health care contingencies. Contact the bar association in your state or county to see what forms the courts will accept and if it has prototypes you can use at little or no cost.

Trust me on this

Trust-mania is rampant, with some lawyers soliciting needless documents you may not understand. While there are advantages to trusts in some cases, carefully consider why you need a trust when there are so many simpler methods to direct your personal and real property outside of probate.

Trusts are broadly categorized according to when they take effect and whether they can be changed. A testamentary trust takes effect at death, according to instructions set down in a will. A living trust, or *inter vivos* trust, takes effect as soon as it is established and is administered outside a will.

Living trusts are further classified as either revocable, subject to change until the death of the grantor or irrevocable, not subject to change once they are signed into effect. (*All* trusts, however, become irrevocable upon the death of the grantor.) The revocable trust is clearly not well advised for everyone. Each person's estate planning goals and needs are unique and must be considered in light of both the benefits and burdens inherent in estate planning strategies available today.

Keep in mind the following: A trust document represents change in the control of your assets (no matter what the seminar speaker states) before and after your death. Trust laws change and current language may be a future impediment to the execution of your trust. Some drafters purchase software with a "one size fits all" approach. Trusts may even set up your assets better for creditors, and trusts can be contested like wills.

If, however, you've decided that establishing a trust is in your best interests, think twice before naming a banking institution as your trustee. What if the bank or savings and loan becomes insolvent? What if the person you trusted moves, retires or dies? What if the bank merges with another institution? What if the bank loses the documents or mismanages the funds?

The most common reason for trust management is prudent investing of the entrusted assets. Bank performance in this arena has been less than stellar. Perhaps a trusted family member will do better with some cash equivalents and conservative mutual funds. Taxes, trust management fees, accounting expenses and inflexibility are just a few concerns. There are no clear cut answers regarding the best way to set up a trust. But you must thoroughly investigate all your options before you commit to anything.

Facts to consider before creating a trust

1. Can probate be avoided in a simpler manner?
2. Should probate be avoided?
3. Are estate tax savings available other than through a trust?
4. Divorce does not revoke a former spouse's interest in some trusts.
5. Creditor rights are not defeated through a revocable trust.
6. When do creditor rights end? Probate often has a deadline.
7. Trusts may be challenged by heirs.
8. Surviving spouses may have elective rights against trust assets.
9. Taxes may be greater inside a trust.
10. States and entitlement programs may attack a trust to pay for nursing home and disability benefits.
11. Who pays to defend the trust?
12. Probate administration doesn't always tie up assets for a long time. Will substitutes (titling assets) also avoid probate.
13. Revocable trusts may jeopardize Medicaid qualifications.
14. Interpretation of trust language may be uncertain.
15. Trusts may be improperly drafted.
16. Trust law changes may render a document ineffective or harmful in the future.
17. Trusts are expensive compared with simpler estate planning techniques.
18. State homestead property tax exemptions may be at risk.
19. Transfers made within three years of a grantor's death may be able to be included in the grantor's estate anyway.
20. A life insurance trust may be vulnerable to creditors.

21. A durable power of attorney directs financial affairs in case you become disabled, not a trust.

The taxman may not cometh

Most of you do not have to worry about federal estate taxes. Surviving spouses enjoy an unlimited marital deduction. State laws often provide tax relief for married couples. Federal estate laws currently exempt transfers to heirs other than your spouse of $600,000.

'Tis better to gift

Singles can avoid paying taxes for estates of more than $600,000 by gifting assets away before they appreciate further. You can transfer (or gift) an estate up to $600,000 without paying federal estate taxes on the property.

If you gift more than $10,000 per year ($20,000 if your spouse also agrees to the transfer), you must file a Form 709. This tells the government to reduce your unified credit/gift tax account of $600,000 by the amount over the annual limit.

Gifting during your lifetime is the easiest method to disburse your property as you wish. Be sure, however, you will not need that money later. A well intentioned gift could mean the loss of much more at a future date because that money will never again compound for you.

Estate planning measures such as Personal Residence Trusts (QPRITS), Grantor Retained Income Trusts (GRITS), Q-Tip Trusts, Spendthrift (minor) trusts and the more common A/B (Marital Bypass, Credit Shelter) Trusts are complicated estate strategies. Before committing to a major change in your life, interview several legal advisers to separate the sizzle from the steak.

The executor/administrator

If you become the executor or personal administrator of an estate, interview several attorneys (if needed) for estimates of legal fees. Do not automatically use the lawyer who drew up the deceased person's will. Get prices beforehand and a written estimate. Since this is a new experience for most folks, take your time and ask questions throughout the process.

Executors may list assets, inventory contents of safety deposit boxes and locate the decedent's property. They can admit the will into probate and advertise for creditors. They pay final expenses and estate debts, analyze business interests, prepare and file a final estate tax return.

They may request insurance death benefits and send notification of death to concerned business interests and financial companies. After administering the estate's needs, they turn over the assets to the beneficiaries or trustees to manage.

Executors have a fiduciary responsibility to beneficiaries and to legitimate creditors. Do not make any long term investments that could lose principal or distribute estate assets before you are sure all debts have been paid. You could be personally responsible for paying such bills if you cannot retrieve money given to heirs before all legal creditors have been satisfied.

Insurance companies fail, stocks go down, bonds default and salespeople occasionally take advantage of ignorance and naiveté. You must constantly remind yourself of the prudent disposition of the money under your care.

The most dangerous estate planning mistake is "default" planning—doing nothing. Though not a pleasant activity, planning for the distribution of your assets should help you sleep better so you can move on to living successfully and *creating* your wealth.

Chapter 19

Myths, legends and truths of investing

GRITS, GRATS, GRUTS, RIPS, SPLITS, STRIPS, LYONS, TIGRS, PIGS, CATS, ILITS, REITS, RELPS, SLOBS, PYGMYS, MIDGETS, GNOMES and LPs.

Encyclopedia entries under "dress making" or "zoology?" A waiter's abbreviations for the daily specials? A second grader's first spelling test?

No, believe it or not, this is a typical list of current investment possibilities. With simple to understand terms like this, no wonder you're confused.

And this is only the beginning. I could go on for days with MECs, SPDAs, SPWLs, ULs, VULs, TSAs, TDAs, ee-i-ee-i-oh!

Add some devious sales techniques and the vested interest of those in the financial industry (whom we could label, BUFONS, TICOONS, CRKS, SCHNKS, WMPS, SHRMPS and SCAMS), and it's perfectly understandable why some of you would prefer to roll over and go back to sleep rather than dedicate yourself to learning about investing.

Money managers aren't born with a special talent for predicting the future. In fact, many of them lose significant investor money when their strategies fail.

Whether the top-down approach, the bottom-up fundamental strategy, the efficient market reality or the whatever-my-neighbors-and-friends-are-buying method of investing, money managing strategies that you hear about can be colorful, varied and often diametrically opposed.

You may have heard the best mutual fund is the one that made the highest returns in the past, that the more risk you take, the more money you will eventually make, that no-load mutual funds are free, that paper losses don't count because you don't lose any money until you sell and that a losing investment can come back.

The punch line, of course, is that none of these things are true.

We expect novice investors to be naive, but some highly educated folks are staunch advocates of such nonsense, as well. Not only have many forgotten what they should remember, but they have remembered what they should have forgotten. With time, facts fade. But myths, and that includes legends sacred to the investing world, seem immortal. Let's explode some fiction and uncover some investment *truths* you can build upon.

Can you repeat the following without the Rs?

Richard and Robert purchased a retriever.

Instead of tripping over your tongue in order to duplicate *exactly what I said*, step back and look at the implication of the phrase, the theme. What does it mean? It tells us that Dick and Bob bought a dog. Simple? Of course, and so is managing your money.

Most books tell you how to make money. This one tells you how not to lose it. Stop investing for greed and learn how to manage risk. Develop a real and rational fear of losing investment principal. You cannot escape risk totally. But you can learn to manage various risks through fundamental skills of investing and true diversification of your assets.

Folks invest for the following reasons:

1. **Convenience.** The easier it is to sign up, the better.
2. **Communication.** The company sends periodic statements rattling off gross returns that may bear little resemblance to your net performance. You believe the company must be safe because a return address is stamped on the letterhead.
3. **The actual return on your money.** Instead, the order of investing criteria should be:
    - The net return on your money.
    - The verifiable net return on your money (doing the calculations yourself).
    - The "what have you done for me lately" final return on your money.

Determine your time horizon

If you have money ready to invest now, decide what the money will be used for. This has a bearing on when the money will be needed. Short term money (short-stop) savings are funds you will need within a three-year time horizon. Long term (marathon) money will work for three years or more. Short term investments should guarantee your principal. Long term funds must guarantee future purchasing power. Never forget the difference. Using fixed income investments alone will be the undoing of long term investing. You must always manage some of your funds for growth.

Determine your risk tolerance

Imagine sailing off to some exotic island for a few years. Since you know about the time value of money and inflation forces, you decide to take your investment funds with you.

On this island there are only two industries to invest in: a suntan lotion corporation and an umbrella factory. Thankfully, you have information to assist your final investment choice: the sun shines 50% of the time, while it rains the other half of the year. Like your local TV weatherperson, you can't predict when the sunny days will appear.

How will you invest your precious funds?

Most investors would choose a 50/50 split of each company's stock. Which proves the following point: given the limited bits of real investment information available regarding tomorrow's investment headlines, most folks are risk adverse.

They would rather net lower profits and conserve their investment principal than speculate on higher returns and risk greater losses. On this precept we can build healthy prudent investment portfolios for a successful financial future.

Determine the optimum investment

Consider the period of time your money has to compound before it is needed. Since short investment time frames demand guaranteed principal, your options are fairly limited: bank savings and other interest bearing accounts, bank CDs, credit union accounts, savings bonds and conservative money market mutual funds.

Money you can tie up for a longer investment period (longer than three years) dictates a completely different strategy to stay ahead of inflation. I generally recommend mutual funds as the optimum investment for such long term capital. Mutual funds will diversify your portfolio like a millionaire, allow you to monitor your assets at all times, cut through financial intermediaries for a greater share of profits and allow access to your funds at all times (often when they are inside tax sheltered umbrellas).

My word is my bond

A bond is an IOU, a promise to pay. It can be issued by your government, a private corporation, a nonprofit social entity or for a public purpose. This security promises to pay the holder at scheduled intervals a certain yield (rate of interest) or to increase the value of the investment principal at certain times (a zero coupon or discounted bond), and to repay its principal value at a specific date in the future. Bonds are fixed income vehicles.

There are five common types of bonds:

1. **U.S. Government securities.** Issued or backed by the government, they have safety from default but not from loss of value during periods of rising interest rates.
2. **Corporate bonds.** Issued by private industry, they can vary widely in yield, maturity and credit quality; they can default as well as lose value when interest rates rise around them.
3. **Municipal bonds.** Issued and backed by local and state governments, public revenue projects or general obligations of regional or county agencies, they pay investors lower yields because their income is free from federal taxes and, in some cases, exempted from state and local taxes as well. They may default and will lose more principal (because they carry a lower yield) than either government or corporate bonds when interest rates rise.

4. **Foreign bonds.** Issued by foreign entities (corporations, governments or financial intermediaries), they trade overseas and may be denominated in a foreign currency. They have volatility because of political and economic fluctuations of the country in which they are issued and risk from currency movements in the global markets.
5. **High yield (junk) bonds.** Issued by lower rated companies with poorer credit ratings, they are considered speculative, not appropriate in large doses for high quality investing. They carry a higher degree of default risk.
6. **Zero coupon (discount) bonds.** Issued at a deep discount from their final face value, these bonds make no payments of interest. The bondholder does not receive any payments until maturity, though they may be taxed on the accrued interest annually. They carry the highest interest rate risk when interest rates climb. They also gain the most appreciation as interest rates fall. We are more interested, however, in not losing money than getting rich quick. So they pose high risk to principal over time. If held to maturity, they will accrue to their final face value. They are Wall Street creations, backed by bonds held by the companies that design these securities.

All investments involve risk, the chance that the result might differ from your original expectations. Bond risks can be categorized as follows:

1. *Market risk* is the chance that the bond will fall in value based on market demand for the specific security. When inflation is low, bond buyers may increase. When stocks are moving, bonds may be overlooked.
2. *Credit risk* implies the bond issuer won't be able to make interest payments or repay the principal when originally promised. Rating agencies analyze credit ratings, but a bond issuer could deteriorate tomorrow. Therefore, a bond that looks secure today may become unhealthy in the future.
3. *Inflation risk* is the danger that investors won't keep pace with inflation over long periods of time. This is why a well diversified investment portfolio must include some stocks as well as bonds and cash.
4. *Re-investment risk* is the opportunity lost when interest rates decline as your bond matures, forcing you to re-invest your principal at a new lower rate than before. When interest rates are high investors lock in longer years of higher annual returns. When interest rates are climbing, short term bonds allow investors to re-invest their principal at higher interest rates because bond yields rise with the general direction of interest rates in the economy.
5. *Interest rate risk* occurs when bond investors learn the hard way that bond prices go down as interest rates climb. Each time market interest rises, the price of a bond held by an investor loses some actual value. Unless the bond is held to maturity (which could be 10 or 20 years away), the investor loses money, though he or she believed the security was safe from loss of principal. As interest rates rose in 1994, bond investors lost significant investment principal.

The direct correlation between bonds and interest rates is not difficult to understand. Suppose you locked into a 2-percent bond for 30 years (I know you are too smart for that) and interest rates climbed to 4 percent the following year. You would be stuck with less interest than everyone else could receive on new bonds at 4 percent. What's worse, this 2-percent lock-in would last for 30 years! If you sold your bond before maturity, no smart investor would pay you full price for a 2-percent return. The investor might buy it from you—but at a discounted price from what you originally paid.

Bond prices move inversely to the direction of interest rates. Sound complicated? Here's an example. Assume that I make the computer sales presentation of my life and convince you that my system is not only top of the line, but also will hold its value for years to come. You purchase the computer system.

Next month, my company introduces a new version with more bells and whistles and a faster response time. What just happened to the resale value of your computer?

When your bond produces higher annual interest than those your government is currently selling, your bond may even sell for more than you originally paid. But when the government sells bonds with higher interest rates than the security you own, your investment loses value. A savvy customer will not pay you full price for yours. It is salable, but at a discount, depending on how your interest rate compares with others competing in the bond arena for buyers.

Since higher bond yields tend to reflect higher inflation, when interest rates rise, bondholders lose in two ways: lower locked-in rates and a real loss of value.

6. *Default risk* means that corporate or municipal bonds could default altogether, leaving you with no yield and no principal. The penalty for municipalities and other public debtors defaulting today is *nothing*. The temptation to stiff investors may be great as state and local budgets become tighter.

As you can see, bonds are every bit as dangerous to investors as stocks. For most investors, bonds should be purchased only through mutual funds where such risks can be reduced through true diversification. If you hold two bonds and one defaults, you have lost half of your savings.

If, however, you hold 100 bonds through a mutual fund, and that single bond should fall off the face of the earth, you are still in the bond business with 99 other issues. Because interest rates constantly move up and down, short term or intermediate term bond mutual funds with objectives of total return (a return *on* the money and a return *of* the money) may give you less yield during the bond booms, but tend to hold their principal together better when interest rates rise.

Stocks and blondes

Stocks move up and down with even fewer correlations than bonds. They have a mind of their own, and sometimes based on the confidence that rock-'n-roll will never die or that Elvis has finally left the building, they find new strength for a rally or languish for lack of support.

There are no safe stocks. Those who bought IBM—"Big Blue"—at $150 per share, then watched it plummet by half in a short time, soon discovered that they had purchased "Big Black-'n-Blue."

Many dynamics shape markets that drive stock prices. Cinderella stories are headlined, and rags to riches (and vice versa) soap operas cause gossip column excitement in the world of finance.

Stock picking isn't really a financial exercise. It is a game of master psychology. Instead of poring over financial reports, listening to money gurus or analyzing dividend growth earnings models for clues to tomorrow's winners, you should be psychologically analyzing how a large group of investors will respond to major events (or lack of them) that have not yet happened! No wonder you can't predict the future! No one can.

The brokerage business has been so battered by the crash of '87, the junk bond debacle, scandals, derivative worries, plus decreased merger activity that its numbers have dwindled, and those left are pressured to produce larger gross commissions from their account activities.

In general, trading should be reserved for those who can afford to lose money. I always tell clients who want individual issues that I will recommend companies for them if they realize (and sign that they understand) they can lose all their money, they know what a monetary loss really is, and they have lost previous money in an adult manner without tears and violence. Otherwise, I recommend mutual funds. There is an argument for single issues (individual stocks or bonds), but, in my opinion, not in the beginning portfolio of the small investor with limited financial resources.

The large, mature, blue chip companies (the AT&Ts of the world), went down the most during the 1987 market crunch. Growth companies are the movers and shakers, full of vigor (and stumbling blocks). The really big money is made in the small capitalization companies (small caps) because these are the IBMs and Microsofts of tomorrow. They are also the financial fiascoes of tomorrow, often flying by the seat of their financial pants.

Sometimes only one category of stock moves up and down. Under those conditions, diversifying into large, medium and small company issues and purchasing numerous industries (or sectors) may reduce your risk to principal. But often, all stocks move up and down in sync with each other without warning investors.

Most investors should avoid single stocks and bonds and choose mutual funds where they can diversify like a millionaire without the million dollar stake. Unless you can afford to lose principal (even the greats lose large chunks of other folks' money), avoid the uncertainties of financial markets, and reduce your risk to principal through the world of mutual funds.

Myth: "Trust me. I'm the expert."

The financial industry's mission is to help itself. To do that, sales forces have to convince you that their product benefits outweigh the cost of the investment.

Institutions spend billions of advertising dollars annually to access your wallet, and sales forces are trained, pressured, brainwashed and highly motivated by lucrative commissions to sell, sell, sell!

"Looking for income? Here is income out your ears!"

"Need safety? The words "U.S. Government" are printed 51 times in this prospectus."

"Want growth? I think this could be the next Worldcom."

"Hate taxes as much as we think you should? Your IRS worries are over."

"Searching for higher yields? This is as high as the numbers go."

"You say you want safety, growth and high yield income...tax free? I'll just bet we can find it."

Would any sane car dealer send you across the street after a better overall value? Would any banker voluntarily offer you information regarding better interest rates at another bank? Would a gas station owner suggest you buy gasoline cheaper at the station next door?

Of course not. Agents, representatives and other salespeople make money only when you buy...from them. That is their job—to get your signature on their product agreement. Your job, on the other hand, is to ferret your way through all the gimmicks, hype, sales pitches, promises and misinformation to protect your pocketbook and your paycheck dollars.

If someone is a "stock market expert," why are they selling investment advice instead of buying stocks? If they are successful in their careers, why is that so? Is it because they do so well for their clients that they have so many customers? The best salesman is not who you want. You are looking for the best financial advisor.

In addition, you should beware of family, friends and co-workers who advise you which stocks or other investments are really "hot." Well intentioned incompetents create as much portfolio havoc as any self-interested vendor.

Myth: "Who cares what it is? It will save you taxes."

Tax deferred, tax deductible and tax exempt are wildly successful marketing strategies which direct billions of dollars into the coffers of insurance companies, state projects and municipalities. People will do almost anything to avoid paying taxes, even lose money.

They will make poor financial decisions in the light of more important criteria. They will encumber their assets and limit future flexibility to reposition their dollars over time. They will limit access to their money and incur severe penalties. They will ignore the necessity of outpacing the devastating effects of inflation.

A sales pitch to solve your tax problem might also lighten your pocketbook or even alert the IRS. In the early 1980s, doctors, attorneys and other professionals were induced to purchase tax favored, limited partnerships. They didn't care whether they were investing in real estate in Antarctica, pygmy bonds or horse feathers. All they heard was the guarantee to solve their tax burdens. When TAMRA (the tax law) was passed in 1986, the IRS began to investigate abusive write-off deals. Not only did investors lose their tax benefits, but many also eventually incurred huge IRA tax penalties.

The quality of the investment is always more important than the tax advantage. Never let the tax tail wag the investment dog. Tax planning at all costs may leave you with inferior underlying investments, little flexibility, no visibility to watch your money, large surrender charges, and other fees when you decide to exit.

Since there is no such thing as a perfect investment (no one mentions that during the passion of a sales presentation), you must invariably make compromises to fit your individual financial circumstances. Rarely will a single investment fit all your goals. When you make important financial decisions, give up a tax advantage before compromising more important criteria on your investment shopping list.

Often the tax pitch alone will clinch a sale. You feel smug because you beat the taxman, and the sales agent has made a fat commission.

It makes a big difference whether you are investing in gunrunning, bootlegging, goldfish breeding, saving the whales, junk bonds, rare coins, speculative real estate, insurance products or limited partnerships. In the next few years, pensions will see pressures and fallout like never before. You had better know where your money is invested. And if you are not comfortable, move it. Even if you have to give up some tax icing. The Pension Benefit Guarantee Corporation cannot guarantee every pension plan failure. You have to protect your own money.

Learn to separate the tax shelter from the underlying investment vehicle. Stocks, bonds, savings accounts, CDs, insurance annuities, guaranteed investment accounts, company stock, collectible coins, international bonds, and mutual funds are investment products. The *ways to the means*—401(k)s, 403(b)s, TSAs/ (TDAs), IRAs, SEPs and UGMAs—are the tax shelter wrapping around your investment choice. Pitching tax advantages work for marketers. Taming the tax beast is not as important as finding the best investment portfolio that will provide growth without undue investment risk.

The recurring question you must ask is: Why would a stranger include you on the ground floor of anything? Why would anyone call a random citizen in another city or state, and share the secret to instant and permanent wealth? Why isn't he or she investing every dime of his or her own and keeping the magic formula a secret?

Whether it's a dirt pile gold scheme out west, a limited partnership that must be bought today or a newsletter money guru who, for a small subscription price, will tell you how to become a millionaire without leaving your overstuffed chair, the only proven method of accumulating wealth is working smart and then carefully diversifying into investments you can understand and control.

Dialing for dollars

Boilerplate operations, consisting of rented office rooms filled with paid phone operators, solicit consumers day and night. This is a numbers game. The more calls one makes, the more suckers can be found. An illegitimate company targets an area, sets up its backroom shop with rented furniture and starts dialing for dollars. After a few weeks, the company moves and begins a similar scheme somewhere else.

Never purchase anything over the phone that is solicited without your prior inquiry. Even if you have previously sent for information, don't buy investment products or items from unknown persons. Any solid business opportunity can be found at a reputable investment company in your area...and it'll still be there next month.

Never give your Social Security number, credit card account or other personal private information over the phone. You have no idea to whom you are talking. If the company is legitimate, it will send you literature so you can check it out through state agencies and other means.

Do not purchase securities, Certificates of Deposit or insurance products from credit card offers, monthly statements, TV, or radio solicitations. If people unknown to you tell you that you have won a trip or any other type of prize, request that they send it and pay all shipping and handling costs themselves. Reputable contests don't expect their winners to pay for shipping and other expenses. The money you send may be worth more than the prize when it finally arrives...if it ever does.

Whether offered a windfall in diamonds, silver, stamps or security, apply the common sense sniff test: If it sounds too good to be true, just say no.

The laws of investing

Law #1: You are a moving target. Financial companies spend billions of dollars to stalk you (it's called prospecting)—to discover your secret desires, your hot buttons, your vulnerabilities and your weaknesses. You are classified as young, mid-age, pre-retired or retired; by income level; by zip code; by number of children and their ages; by gender and race; by home ownership; even by sucker lists. You are being statistically followed, tagged and ticketed like some form of wildlife to be sold to someone's telephone, seminar or direct mail list.

If you bought a new home, several insurance companies know—they buy the mortgage recording lists from your local area or state. If you take out a personal loan, other vendors are notified. If you recently lost a spouse, every salesperson in town has learned it from the newspaper obituary. If you were recently married, you have been erased off some lists and added to others. A new baby or a college graduate notice will bring out the car, yacht, insurance and credit card mailings. There are major retailers whose cash registers will not open unless you, the customer, provide your zip code or your telephone number.

My favorite slogan came from a TV advertisement: "We want your business so badly that we are willing to lose a little on each sale and make it up in volume." (Think about it!)

Why would you believe for one nanosecond that any of these salespeople would show you any glitch or negative that might talk you out of the sale they have sweated and worked so diligently to talk you into?

Law #2: Where you are on the road to financial success is not as important as which direction you are moving. Even if you start now, it is possible to fall short of your financial goals. But if you never start, you are doomed from the beginning. Time is money (or the loss of it).

There will never be a better time, a cheaper time or a more important time to start—than today.

Law #3: The best defense is a good offense. It doesn't take a rocket scientist to control and manage your financial life and destiny. It does, however, take some common sense, thought, a skeptical, investigative mind and more than 15 minutes a year to develop a working plan you can understand and stick with.

The inventor of financial planning was the ant who worked through the summer gathering up stores of food so he would be secure when winter arrived. The grasshopper, however, thought this type of goal setting a complete waste of perfectly good recreational time. He spent his summer and fall eating, lounging on wild aster plants and having tobacco spitting contests with his neighbors. He didn't notice the shortening days and the meadow plants losing their leaves and color as the fall nights became colder and colder.

When the first snow hit without warning, the grasshopper immediately jumped into action and scurried to the ant's home. He pleaded for shelter, but there was no response. Then he demanded refuge from the storm's onslaught and some of the bread he could smell baking in the ant's oven. Again he was ignored.

In desperation, he battered in the anthill's front entranceway, taking his destiny into his own hands. But he was so fat from dining on milkweed and grain pods all season that he could not slip down through the corridor. There he stuck, somewhere between salvation and certain death.

This is a prime example of poor planning—consuming everything today and saving nothing for tomorrow. It is exactly this kind of tragedy that financial planning was designed to avoid.

Law #4: Learn to think like the rich. The middle class has developed a demeaned concept of a dollar. To it, a dollar represents a cup of coffee, a pair of shoelaces or a lottery ticket. They see little reason to ferociously protect it.

The affluent, however, view a dollar as the means of making more money. The rich have well trained mercenary instincts (or well paid consultants or both), knowing that if that dollar keeps turning over and over, it will create $2, $4, $8 and even $16, given enough time.

To be successful, you have to think like the rich and value every dollar for what it can eventually become.

Law #5: Every potential sale is inherently an adversarial situation. Not every financial salesperson is a crook, and not all of the honest ones are incompetent. But how can you, a novice, tell the difference? Don't let personal relationships or friendly conversations interfere with your thinking processes regarding which options may be in your best interests. Successful salespeople anticipate what you are looking for. Many of them focus pitches on products with large commission checks attached.

You must separate the emotional appeal—the sizzle—from the real overall value—the steak—and, after taking your time to research and compare, determine your own financial bottom line.

Law #6: With accurate information, money will follow. Financial planning is not only for the rich. The truth is that the less money you have to manage, the more important it is to use it wisely and get objective and competent advice.

Like the bus driver who constantly complains that he can't meet his scheduled timetable because he has to keep stopping to pick up passengers, you must not defeat your own purposes by spending so much time earning your dollars that you have no time left to manage them.

Law #7: It's what you make on your money after inflation that really matters. Inflation will never go away. No one taught your parents about its ravages, and too many of them learned the hard way—they became its victims. People worry about lung cancer from contact smoke, cholesterol in their eggs, nuclear radiation from power plants and x-rays, while this insidious erosion quietly eats away at your financial futures, destroying your comfortable retirement and your children's college education.

Never forget that the return on investment is less important than your return after inflation.

Law #8: Preserving your long term purchasing power is more important than preserving your investment principal. Ignoring inflation is financial suicide. If inflation averages 6 percent per year, you must yield 6 percent (after taxes) on your money just to stay in the same place you were at the beginning of the year. If inflation is greater than 6 percent, you must receive an even higher return just to continue treading water. You must net more on your money than inflation eats away in order to make real progress. Fixed income vehicles like bank accounts, CDs, and insurance annuities have not kept pace with inflation.

Law #9: "Safe" is a four letter word...and a big lie. The risk most feared by investors is loss of principal. In fact, folks tend to concentrate so heavily on securing their investment principal that they actually guarantee the very risks they so intensely seek to avoid.

With insurance products, you own pieces of paper with lifetime guarantees based on the lifetime of the insurance company, not your lifetime. Guarantees don't work when the company making the promises can't keep them. Insurance companies can close their doors.

By diversifying, you will learn to differentiate between various types of risks and plan for them. Resist the dangerous urge to hide your head in the sand and believe promises of "safe" and "guaranteed."

Law #10: Diversify, diversify, diversify. Whether you own a neophyte or a mature investment portfolio, you need to separate your money into many investment baskets. If you invest in 90 companies, but all 90 sell dining room furniture, you are not really diversified. When the tide goes out, all boats in the same harbor go down. If that single industry slumps, so do all your investments.

Successful financial planning and money management fundamentals don't change. There will be boom and then the bust, the defiance of gravity and then the sobering reality that enduring laws may be found in science but not on Wall Street.

Law #11: A paper loss is a real loss. Your investment fundamentals should be strong, and your specific investment choices should be boring, dull and passive. Don't seek excitement with your important money. A three-year return of +10 percent, +10 percent and +8 percent is better than +20 percent, +20 percent, and -10 percent. If you lose significant investment capital, it will take time to re-build your assets back to where they were. In the meantime you will have lost from inflation and from not making money in an alternative security which didn't lose its financial shirt.

Brokers recommend you don't sell after a loss because you only have a "paper loss" until you sell. This may sound comforting, but it is also a lie.

Did you have paper profits before you had losses? Your broker or mutual fund was bragging about its top notch performance. So you must have had real money then. Now you have less money. That money is gone forever. That money will not come back. You can only make or lose future money.

If you bought a home and its price doubled, would you believe you had made an astute purchase and a healthy profit? If the toxic waste dump later moved in next door, could I convince your money genes you had suffered only a "paper loss?"

The concept of a paper loss is as bogus as labeling crashes or mini-crashes "corrections" or market adjustments or obstetricians telling women going into labor they will experience "some discomfort." No matter what the bedside manner, "paper losses" are painful events to be avoided.

Law #12: There is no such thing as a free lunch. There are also few sexy, intelligent and sensitive men who iron. (But that's another book.)

No one will ever invest your money for nothing, and claims to the contrary should make you think twice. No one will ever offer you a greater return than necessary to induce you to hand over your dollars—not the banking industry, insurance corporations, private institutions or even your federal government.

There is no safe 20-percent, 15-percent or even 10-percent return. Anyone who tells you there is, will profit from your greed and naiveté. There are no secret formulas to riches that you will be offered at rock bottom prices.

Law #13: Investment performance is determined by p-r-o-f-i-t-s, not p-r-o-p-h-e-t-s. How can one predict investor reactions and future markets created by events that haven't happened yet? Who can predict a war, a famine or even a recession accurately?

Small investors are often wrong. They get in at the peak of someone else's profits because they have spent time watching others make money and now they feel safe. Then they turn and run away at the first sign of trouble or decline. Small investors work primarily on greed and fear.

Develop a long term investment attitude by choosing quality for your investment challenges and diversifying the heck out of your money. Once your solid portfolio is constructed, make only annual re-balancing adjustments.

If you are looking for a winning formula or for secrets to financial success, your best answers are not around you. They are *within* you. The world is not full of wisdom. It is populated with sheep, followers, cunning marketers and fools. Follow your own common sense, and seek answers through logical and clear thought processes.

Law #14: It's not what they say, it's what you *sign*. When you receive an insurance or securities contract, take the time to read it carefully. Request a specimen contract **before** you purchase. If you cannot, at least read your contract carefully through after you receive it. Never take only an agent's word that you are insured or that your money has been properly delivered to its investment destination.

Law #15: There are no fair or friendly contracts. Why would a company design contracts with printing so small that you need an amoebae who speaks English to translate it, if the company didn't intend to hide the contents from you? Why would it waste profits on so much ink?

Because the consumer protection laws insist on vendors telling you certain disclosure information, but they don't regulate how readable that information must be. When I see print that small, I know it's important.

I am never impressed by a sales pitch or shiny advertising materials. Instead, I scour the written contract for risks, limitations and exclusions. *Follow the asterisk.* You could find some "nasty" hidden in the contract language that may invalidate the original sales claim. I have seen fine print which waived every benefit proposed in the large print.

Pleading total ignorance (or insanity) of what you signed will be no excuse and no defense. You paid your money, and you took your chances. You should have read your contract.

Law #16: Never invest out of greed or fear. Making money should be boring, boring, boring! People have locked into the idea that successful financiers and money moguls are the celebrities we see publicized in the tabloids, making their daily rounds to pick up a large check at one stop, sacks of dollars at another, and reproducing their megamillions because they take huge risks.

Structure your portfolio for comfort, not for speed. If you need some excitement, get it through your bowling night or golf game. Let your assets slowly compound over time.

Large investors, the kind that don't wince at buying $10 million of something at one time, spend more time than we have researching, have greater access to timely information and can implement more clever investment strategies than we know. And sometimes they lose big. It is the nature of this arena. This is serious business to the pros. Don't attempt to match wits with the experts with only your monthly mutual fund magazine as your investment guide.

You can't beat the markets. So don't try. Do what you do well—make the investment dollars with your skills (on the job), then manage your investments simply and conservatively.

Risky business

Years ago the state of Michigan upgraded its pheasant raise and release program. Managing pheasant farms had been grossly time consuming because workers tended and fed the birds at numerous substations around the grasslands. It made sense (to those in charge) to cut down labor costs, optimize operations and centralize work at one main location.

By the end of the third year, however, profits were down, not up. Bird deaths (mortality) and morbidity (sickness) increased. The problem? Before mechanization the workers walked most of the land, tending to daily fencing and maintenance chores, supervising as they worked and walked. Once the efficiency program was in place, they had no method of detecting problems that were not in close range. Unchecked, such enemies as fox, bear, pests and viruses were able to capture a stronghold on the flocks, weakening future strains as well. When finally discovered, serious measures were needed to bring the flocks back to their original vitality.

The same thing happens when you let your money tend to itself. You may have to put your financial life on auto-pilot because you have little time to actively manage it. Believing the financial community's claim of expertise, you may have turned over the reins of decision making to strangers in return for quarterly reports. Organize where your assets are, what short term and long term plans you have made, and how well they are performing. Please complete the **Portfolio Planning Worksheet** in the Appendix.

Charting your course

All investments carry some type of risk, even those "safe" ones we gravitate to in times of uncertainty. There are simply no totally safe harbors. If you try too hard to protect your investment principal you will, over time, guarantee the very losses you sought so hard to avoid through earning less than the rate of inflation. If, on the other hand, you take too much capital risk, you can lose significant investment principal as well.

Since risk is everywhere, the trick is to learn how to manage it. Through true diversification of many asset classes and negative correlation (we'll explain that one later), you may reduce your risk to principal and outpace inflation to conserve future purchasing power.

Diversification is better than a chicken

You've learned to pay yourself first, to use "OPM," and to read the fine print. But the chicken theory of investing?

Let's assume you and I decided to start an enterprise, a poultry business. After all, chickens have many uses. They lay eggs, win prize money at country fairs, and make good broth and meat for the table and stew pot. But we would be foolish indeed if we pooled our life savings together and invested it all in one giant, fluffy white chicken, or even a large flock of the same type of poultry.

What do chickens have to do with investing? You don't have to be a chicken to recognize an egg. But you do to lay one! And you will lay a giant goose egg by putting all of your investment eggs into one basket.

Diversification reduces risk to investment principal. How come the "experts" don't teach this theory so investors won't lose their savings? Because diversification isn't designed to help you "get rich quick" like today's money gurus advise. Diversification techniques will help you *not* to lose your savings.

To become an advocate of diversification you must be willing to give up some occasional lofty returns for consistent and steady progress. You need to avoid the rabbits and choose the turtles—those all-weather, dull and stodgy investment portfolios that perform in any kind of economic weather.

Real diversification goes beyond the idea of purchasing many things with your savings. The individual assets that make up your investment portfolio must come from various types of securities, separating your nest egg into many different kinds of baskets.

When one market or part of the economy sours (your chicken gets sick or, worse, dies), you are still in the investment business with the rest of your nest egg. If, on the other hand, you purchase many securities within the same asset class (such as stocks, stocks and more stocks), when the stock market takes a tumble, you can lose a large part of your savings.

Long term investing: benefits your investment plan should offer

Simplicity. It should be easy to understand and contain only basic and elementary investment vehicles. No fads, no new and innovative products and no sophisticated strategies.

Easy management. This plan should not have to be monitored or altered on a regular basis. Once the basic asset allocations are set, individual investments should be allowed to work as designed. Only triggering events like enormous market swings, distressed economic conditions or life plan changes should cause your investment policy to significantly change.

Total accessibility. Every investment should be marketable in a crisis situation, and investment policies should not shrink dollars through surrender charges when the money is recalled.

Window of observation. The design of the investment should offer the ability to see changes, to follow performance and to check up on rates of return and security holdings as often as desired.

Cost effective expenses. Investment choices should reduce or eliminate costly expenses such as lending institution partners, extra management fees, brokers and insurance companies. Go directly to the investment vehicle whenever possible.

Flexibility to change investments. Avoid investments that may take a number of years to develop returns (insurance products) or that charge surrender fees if you want your investment pot early.

Tax advantages whenever prudent. Do not grab for the tax gimmick before opting for the best investment vehicle. But whenever possible, use tax shelters commonly available. In a 401(k) or a 403(b) tax sheltered annuity, go directly to the investment vehicle instead of an insurance product that will charge extra for the insurance wrapping. Your returns will be better if you cut out more intermediaries.

Diversification. No clairvoyance or forecasting abilities should be employed. Use real common sense diversification to combine investment vehicles that avoid a domino effect and have demonstrated autonomy. Use lots of baskets and different types of baskets for your investment nest egg.

Favorable risk-to-return ratio. Establish an efficient portfolio, maximizing the return, minimizing the risk. In today's precarious investment arena, you rarely get paid for extra risk to principal.

Inflation protection. Long term money must constantly seek to outpace the ravages of inflation. So a portion of the portfolio must seek some growth. This means some equities (stocks)—and that means careful selection using mutual funds for lower volatility than single stock selection.

No insurance products. Investment and savings insurance policies and annuities are an expensive way to provide death benefits and investment performance. Purchase term insurance and separate your living and dying needs. Insurance products generate high commissions to insurance agents but are costly to investors, can succumb to inflation, offer less observation ability, accumulate wealth too slowly, suffer high surrender charges for many years, are frequently managed in-house and are not as accessible as mutual funds. Insurance companies can also close their doors.

A portfolio structured for comfort, not speed. Lower the risk of loss of principal and diversify over vehicles that have lower risk characteristics. This may give slightly lower returns. So let time accumulate compounded returns. Avoid aggressive strategies.

Separate investment accounts. Investments that are held in the general accounts of institutions such as insurance companies (fixed annuities and most insurance policies) pose risks if the company should become insolvent or shut its doors. You should have a separate investment account that the company cannot tap if it runs into financial trouble. Mutual funds and most variable annuities promise this type of protection.

Quality investment vehicles. Use only the finest investments, those that consistently produce returns. Avoid in-house investments sold by financial companies. All mutual funds are not created equal, and all money markets are not equally sound. Steer clear of brand new products that have not weathered the test of time.

Estate planning options. Designate beneficiaries on qualified or tax sheltered investments such as IRA accounts, employer group insurance, other compensation or supplementary voluntary programs such as 401(k)s or 403(b)s. Tax deferred annuities should allow for a primary beneficiary and contingent (secondary) beneficiary. Taxable and general investment dollars may be titled with joint ownership and/or transfer on death designations for ease of estate transfer and avoidance of probate.

The truths of investing

Every expert has a different formula or theory for successful investing. How can a novice find the truth?

Good money management hasn't changed much in the last fifty years, though the financial community grinds out new products as often as new and improved soap powders.

These fundamental principles are straightforward and hold true in both good and poor economic weather:

1. All investments go up and down, including those inside insurance companies, credit unions and banking institutions.
2. Most small investors do the wrong thing at the wrong time.
3. Diversification is the major key to reducing risk.
4. Savings accounts and bank CDs alone will not make you rich. They cannot outpace the ravages on your savings brought about by inflation. You must learn how to protect your purchasing power as well as your investment principal.
5. Uncertainty creates risk, not opportunity.

6. No one knows the future, not even so-called money gurus who try to convince you otherwise.
7. Markets tend to overreact. Never invest out of greed or fear. Never say *never*. In today's financial markets, anything can happen.
8. Bulls (investors who believe that the stock market is going up) make money and so do the bears (those who fear that the stock market will fall) in bad times. But the piggies (those who invest out of greed) get slaughtered. If you remove all the animals from your investing equation, you will have a lot less manure to wade through.

Chapter 20

Turning investment-ese into investment-ease

Economic lingo rules the financial world—and our lives! To become a savvy consumer, you must understand how hem lines, power lines, picket lines, and gasoline lines affect markets and, therefore, your financial success. What follows is a lighthearted investigation of common economic terms and their real meaning for the average consumer.

Learning the lingo of the pros

Recession: A slowdown or slump in the nation's leading indicators for more than two consecutive quarters. Examples of leading indicators are the consumer price index, interest rates, home starts and the sale of retail goods and services.

Depression: A prolonged period of recession marked by massive unemployment, a major reduction in business production and a great number of personal and corporate bankruptcies. Consumer confidence is low, and spending has slowed considerably.

Translation: A *recession* is when someone you know is out of work. A *depression* is when you are out of work.

Upswing in the economy: Corporate profits are on the rise, and business is borrowing money for expansion. Leading indicators are up, unemployment is down. Overtime checks are plentiful.

Translation: Your paycheck rises enough to add one more monthly installment payment.

Government fiscal policy: The government's taxing and spending programs and their impact on the economy at large manipulate certain driving forces. This creates momentum during recessions or curtails periods of high inflation. Supply and demand are artificially stimulated or reduced like a car is harnessed by cruise control.

Translation: You must work even harder to maintain your normal standard of living. Tax freedom day moves back even further. Middle class fiscal policy often dictates another summer vacation at Motel 6 and a promise to visit Mouseland next year.

Governmental monetary policy: Bureaucratic policies and federal programs ease or restrict the money supply and assist smooth transitions through the various stages of the business cycle.

Translation: Monetary policy should not be confused with fiscal policy, as your government has no money to make policy with except yours (which it systematically takes). Monetary policy in any one direction rarely lasts more than 90 days, the time period between popularity polls.

Tight money or easy money policy: A concerted effort is made by the Federal Reserve to hold down interest rates and promote borrowing to stimulate an economic recovery. As expansion develops into full blown prosperity, credit is purposely restricted, reducing the money supply, driving up interest rates and staving off inflationary pressures.

Translation: *Tight money* is a well known middle class phenomenon, revealing there is more month left at the end of the money. *Easy money* is what your teenagers think you are made of. Most families primarily practice tight money policies (at least until all the kids are out college).

Supply and demand curve: Capitalism creates goods for the marketplace, and workers offer their labor for hire so they can purchase those goods. If goods are priced too high, the prices will decrease and wages will reduce until all goods are sold and all labor is employed. (Economists earn healthy salaries, pension benefits and international prizes for theories like this!)

Translation: No matter how many extra Rolls Royces or Lexuses are produced or what sale price is announced, pigs will fly before a luxury car ends up in most middle class driveways.

Discount rate: The price that large lenders pay for money, which they then sell to their customers. When this rate is low, lenders' costs decrease so they can, in turn, pass on that good news to their shareholders in the form of higher profits and lower costs to customers.

Translation: The banking industry didn't memorize the part that says they are supposed to pass on reductions in their costs to consumers. If CDs and savings accounts duck much lower, I intend to donate my money and take a charitable deduction off my taxes. Today's bank deposit rates give new meaning to the words "get rich slow."

Prime rate: The prevailing interest rate at which money is loaned out to a lender's best customers.

Translation: Your name is not on that preferred customer list. You are the little guy, the loyal customer who keeps lenders in business, paying your mortgages quietly and dependably when the big customers like AT&T and Microsoft are not hanging around the bank CEO's office. The prime rate has little real meaning for the average customer (except when it raises monthly home equity loan payments).

Winning the Money Game

The cost of money: The prevailing interest rate is the price of money. This cost fluctuates according to the laws of supply and demand. When these natural forces don't work properly, the Fed (Federal Reserve) tampers by buying or selling securities to lenders, thereby increasing or reducing bank reserves. This process adds to or reduces an institution's ability to lend. (No wonder I slept through high school economics class.)

Translation: Buying money is like purchasing a lawn mower or a toaster—it comes at different prices, and you should shop for it just as you buy soap and poultry at your supermarket. When you are loaning yours to others, seek the highest prudent returns. When borrowing theirs, negotiate for the cheapest rate you can find.

Confidence factor: This yardstick measures consumer spending necessary to keep the economy rolling along.

Translation: Another front page news headline probes into a check overdraft scheme, political scandal, personal diversion of public funds or ethics violation of yet another political figure. This confidence factor slumps each time a voter swears under his or her breath to throw the bum out at election time.

Total gross compensation: The sum total of all wages and benefits a worker receives, including health care, disability insurance, pension plans and vacation or sick leave, the economic cost of an employee.

Translation: You never see your gross pay. It's a meaningless number, what your boss tries to convince you the company is shelling out for you. You never see gross, you can't spend gross and you don't manage gross. Only take-home pay is meaningful—that's what you have to spend.

Inflation: Too many dollars chasing too few goods is the standard definition. When demand exceeds supply at current prices, product prices are bid up.

Translation: Your last car cost more than your first house. Motel 6, now "Motel $32.95," may be "Motel $75" by the time you retire.

Consumer price index (CPI): The CPI represents a mythical basket of goods and services designed to compare relative price changes over time. Many benefits, such as pension cost-of-living raises, Social Security increases and entitlement programs, are linked to the CPI.

Translation: Mythical is right on! Whoever makes up this universal basket of expenses you are supposedly purchasing isn't checking out your grocery receipts, last month's electric bills, the cost of your health care insurance or your student's tuition invoices. Plan for inflation hikes of close to 6 percent, not the comforting figures propagandists are publishing.

High level of credit: A generous amount of credit in the economy for consuming is compared with the money supply directed toward investing purposes.

Translation: You don't know how much you owe and you are afraid to add it up. You pay minimum payments or less each month. You purchase your life on the installment plan.

Treasury bills (T-bills): Short term investments (debt obligations) are issued by the U.S. Treasury on a discount basis (you pay a little less than their face value of $10,000). Treasury bills constitute a large portion of our national debt, and this huge dollar volume is considered the bellwether of short term interest throughout the economy. The most frequent reason for purchasing T-bills is to earn short term interest on idle cash.

Translation: The most likely "T-bills" we may see are those nasty IRS notices with a penalty attached arriving one to three years after you've filed your Form 1040 tax return. Most consumers have such limited idle funds that purchasing one security at a price of $10,000 per bill is as likely for them as placing in the Kentucky Derby without the aid of a horse.

National budget deficit: The accounting shortfall resulting from the government spending (borrowing) more than it takes in through taxes and interest on outstanding loans.

Translation: When numbers get that large, we lose all track of their impact and horror. We also lose confidence to tackle such a mountain of debt and get back into the black, to run our government the way we must run our own budgets. If we, as taxpayers, want our government to live only for today, our children and their children will pay for it tomorrow...and tomorrow...and tomorrow.

Downsizing/rightsizing/restructuring/re-engineering: Corporate America is becoming lean and mean, cutting excess costs, beefing up technology and trimming financial fat. Companies are reducing inefficiencies in an effort to boost profit margins.

Translation: This is "dumbsizing," a kinder, gentler term for throwing a hard working employee out in the street after 20 or more years of loyalty to the company. Unemployed workers don't purchase cars, homes and other products vital to keep our economy moving. Jobless folks increase entitlement and other subsidy roles in exchange for increases in company stock prices and greater shareholder profits.

Leading economic indicators: Analysts use signs to predict changes in the business cycle, like a meteorologist uses a barometer. Examples include first time unemployment claims, manufacturers' new orders for goods and materials, new building permits and the money supply.

Translation: The middle class has its own set of omens: The paycheck doesn't go as far as it used to, the emergency fund is shrinking, savings are decreasing, overtime is being cut down or the second family income has collapsed. During good economic times, the reverse may be temporarily true.

Business cycle: A continual transition from trough (recession) to recovery through expansion and back to trough again.

Translation: No worker is immune to the risk of unemployment or early retirement from job elimination.

Prospectus: A document that provides information about a mutual fund or new investment offering to potential buyers.

Translation: @%(&*^%. If you can thoughtfully analyze a prospectus, you don't need one. The investing public would do as well translating German codes sent during WW II.

I figure if the mutual fund company wanted folks to know what was happening to their money they would print the darned things in plain English. Any similarity to terms you learned in high school will be immediately deleted if the investment company finds out you are beginning to catch on.

Odd lot theory: Small investors purchase stocks in odd lots (less than 100 shares). They are unsophisticated and often wrong. The rich invest in the opposite manner because they feel the little guy is always in the wrong place at the wrong time.

Translation: This long standing theory hasn't weathered the test of time for lack of supporting data.

Sinking fund: A pool of money that provides for the orderly retirement of a bond issue during its life.

Translation: Last year's top performing mutual fund that you purchased at its high and has been slowly losing investment principal since.

Bull market: An extended period of time when the stock market rises sharply. It is traditionally accompanied by investor optimism and confidence, easy credit and economic recovery. During this period, the quality of securities is secondary to the momentum and direction of the market in general. Investors snap up lower quality issues, often bidding them up to unrealistic prices.

Translation: The bulls aren't the only ones stampeding. The piggies forget the fundamentals of diversified investing and liquidate lower risk (and lower yielding securities) in favor of stock market rewards. Following every boom comes a bust. Greed has its price.

Bear market: A period when the stock market declines rapidly with no relief in sight. Historically, bear markets have lasted as long as 18 months. Most issues suffer price deterioration, and even defensive stocks (those too stubborn to lie down at first) finally lose value.

Translation: After the thrill of victory comes the agony of defeat. Driven by fear, novices flee to the safety of banks and money markets. Safety becomes more important than long term investing objectives, and the investor is painfully absent from the next stock market rally.

Blue chip stocks: These are stocks in companies with long records of earnings, dividends and competent management, mature corporations with stable earnings histories that are household names. Investors tend to pay higher prices for these companies, which symbolize greater safety of investment capital.

Translation: During the crash of 1987, these stalwart veterans lost more value than "riskier" types of stocks. After the debacle there was a "22-percent off" sale on such gems as GE, AT&T and Eastman Kodak. <u>There is no safe stock.</u>

Bonds: Long term debt represents a contractual obligation by the issuer to pay interest and/or principal. Bonds can be issued by the federal government, by private corporations, even by cities, states and revenue projects (such as toll roads, airports and public works). Some bonds are taxable; others may be partially or totally tax free.

Translation: The only "safe" bond you can purchase is one issued by your own insolvent, defunct, deficit ridden (broke) government. Bonds are believed to be safer than stocks, which some investors fear more than the bad cholesterol. All bonds, even those marked "U.S. Government," move up and down daily according to how market interest rates are moving.

Total return: The total profit (or loss) for a given time period, including both yield and the gain or loss of principal. It may be stated as a cumulative figure or a compound rate of return.

Translation: There are two elements to every investment: the yield and the change to investment principal. Too many fixed income vehicles provide yield at the expense of shrinking principal. If that price per share goes down, you are losing investment capital. Be sure you are getting a return *of* your money as well as a return *on* your money.

Dow Jones industrial average: The best known index, it has little relation to the stock market as a whole. It tracks the stock movements of 30 industrial companies that have changed composition greatly since the Dow's inception.

Translation: Discussing the Dow will ingratiate you at cocktail parties and give the impression that you are an astute financial mind, worthy of attracting a small group of onlookers and information seekers. As a tool to understanding financial markets, however, it is relatively inane, as it bounces up and down according to a small segment of the total stock market.

Standard and Poor's 500 composite index: This average tracks 500 companies, a broader base for visualizing stock market trends. It is weighted for size and for stock splits. Its individual companies produce everything from ant poison to zippers. Therefore, it reflects a broader picture of what's happening to industry.

Translation: This index gives a larger scope of where the stock market has been, though not where it is going tomorrow.

NASDAQ composite index: The average price of approximately 5,000 over the counter issues, mostly newer, riskier companies with a small capitalization but a bright future.

Translation: This is the "Now you see it, now you don't" index. As dangerous as shark infested waters, this is no place for the uninitiated. Even the experts lose big with these high fliers.

Certificate of Deposit (CD): A bank time deposit savings account that pays a fixed yield over the specific period of time the money must be left with the lender. Most CDs are protected by the Federal Deposit Insurance Corporation (FDIC) against loss of principal. There is usually a significant penalty for withdrawing a CD before its maturity date.

Translation: A CD is also a certificate of *depreciation*. Of all the guarantees lenders offer, the one they fail to disclose is the guaranteed loss of real principal over time due to inflation. If you put all your assets into CDs, you may go broke...safely.

Risk: The chance that the actual return on an investment will be different from the expected return.

Translation: Risk is a term the small investor does not understand. Lured by fat double digit returns (from prior-year performances), investors often unknowingly choose high risk investments. The major difference between a paranoid and a realist is that the paranoid thinks the world is after him, while the realist knows it!

Try to reduce risk in all aspects of your investment portfolio. Occasionally, risk reduction techniques produce a "free lunch" and increase your overall rate of return.

Tax shelters: Some investments can create either tax deductible benefits, tax deferred profits, tax free income or all of the above for their owners.

Translation: Folks will do nearly anything to avoid paying taxes, even lose money. Tax-advantaged investments can be inferior vehicles and far from safe. Tax planning should be the last investment consideration, not a primary investment objective.

Translation of this entire chapter: Don't listen to the economists and the pundits. Use your common sense and get a good financial education. Then, go and manage your investments yourself.

Getting salt on the annual report

The Beardstown ladies' success proved that women and investing is a powerful combination. Whether it's guys, girls or a mixed group, investment clubs can teach while you earn.

To organize a new investment club, call the National Association of Investment Clubs. Or structure the club format from the American Association of Individual Investors instruction booklet. For greatest flexibility and informality, set up your own, enroll an attorney and an accountant to take care of the paperwork (by-laws and annual K-1 IRS forms).

The art of stock picking is risky. So use only funds you don't need. Be sure the goal of your club is social: a night out with companions (and a hearty meal) with the hope of a profit. For a substitute to bridge or bowling night, these clubs can provide some financial food for thought.

Chapter 21

Investing strategies: short-stop vs. marathon money

Genetic engineering, subatomic physics, quantum mechanics, investing for today's consumer. One of these doesn't have to be rocket science.

Before sending remnants of the Pacific Fleet to the defense of Midway Island in 1942, Admiral Nimitz's instructions to Task Force commanders were simple but powerful: "Be governed by the principle of calculated risk, which you shall interpret to mean the avoidance of exposure of your force to superior enemy forces without good prospects of inflicting...greater damage on the enemy." Change a few words and you have an investment policy statement!

Devise different strategies for your short term (short-stop) savings to guarantee the principal, and another method for long term (marathon) funds to guarantee future purchasing power. Every household should establish a rainy day money fund for emergencies. A breadwinner could become unemployed, a medical emergency could occur, most furnaces are programmed to shut down in December, or the car's water pump, the refrigerator and your youngest son could all need repairs at the same time, all before payday.

Short term funds are savings you will need within three years. This could include your emergency fund rainy day account, next Christmas, a cruise vacation, new car, romantic honeymoon, or real estate taxes.

Short term money can include large financial goals less than three years away. College, lurking over the horizon, retirement around the corner, or changing employment plans.

The nature of the goal is not as important as the time frame. Once you isolate short term goals from long term objectives, you will be better able to choose investment vehicles that are suitable, considering the various time periods.

In addition, a cash foundation underneath your investment portfolio can act as a cushion or shock absorber when other securities markets are on the decline or become volatile. The purpose of cash, whether for short term or long term goals, is safety, not yield.

Cash equivalents are short term, interest earning instruments with high liquidity. They are easily converted to cash with little or no risk to your principal. Liquidity and marketability are not the same. A *marketable* investment can be quickly sold for cash like a stock or bond. A *liquid* security implies that, in addition to gaining access to cash fast, every dollar originally invested can be retrieved without a loss of principal.

Cash equivalents are an ideal temporary storage spot while you research potential investments. They can be available 24 hours a day through check writing privileges. Generally, bank Certificates of Deposit, money market mutual funds, and credit union share accounts yield more than a regular bank savings account. Cash equivalents provide safety of principal but are victims of inflation.

Short term bond mutual funds are *not* cash equivalents. They can lose principal when interest rates rise. They are not necessarily smarter banking.

I would avoid money markets investing in mortgage securities, though you may be told they are backed by the government. They have interest rate risk, and some are more complex than sales vendors disclose. They can include collateralized mortgage obligations (CMOs) and adjustable rate mortgage mutual funds. Designed for higher yields, they buy securities with greater risk to principal.

Derivatives are too complex for discussion here. Since they move according to the underlying investments they represent, they are undependable when interest rates are volatile. Request a mutual fund's statement of investments to determine how much of their assets may be invested in these issues.

If the yield on a particular investment looks more attractive than on alternatives, be suspicious. Higher yields usually mean higher risk to principal.

Time is a risk where money is concerned, and many cash equivalents maintain their price stability by limiting the time until repayment of the IOUs they purchase.

Certificates of Deposit (CDs)

These are individual time deposit agreements made with your lender. You are usually paid higher returns the longer you allow a lending institution to keep your money.

Don't deposit all your funds in one institution, despite FDIC insurance. If FDIC reserves should became dangerously low, or if your lender ever shut its doors, cash transactions may be temporarily disrupted. The chances of two institutions in the same neighborhood going under at the same time are less.

The FDIC is an agency of the U.S. Government. It is technically not "the" U.S. Government. Some day that distinction could become important.

CD deposits are issued with different maturities. Don't be lured into locking up long term rates unless the yield is worth it. You could be locked in at lower interest rates when future rates have risen and banks are issuing higher yields than yours.

It pays to shop around for cash equivalents. Search for solvent banking institutions first, then higher yields. Smiles on the faces of employees and ATM machines located in every neighborhood are a last priority.

Credit unions

Though credit unions are not backed by the federal government, they often have insurance of their own. However, back-up default plans are no substitute for solvency.

Credit unions may offer better interest rates on their share-draft accounts and lower interest auto and personal loans. As part of your cash foundation, they can provide diversification and competitive rates of return. As a member you can benefit from loan sales.

Credit unions, however, can suffer from adverse selection. Since they offer better benefits than many banks, they have less profit to invest for their own bottom line. All customers must have a common bond (other than getting rich) to qualify as a member. Therefore, everyone could be losing their job at the same time, stressing liquidity of the organization.

Sweep accounts

With a brokerage company you can purchase an interest bearing checking and savings account all in one.

Such an account offers a range of services bundled together—checking, investing, borrowing and short term storage for funds. Excess (uncollected) funds are automatically "swept" into short term securities on a daily basis, similar to a money market mutual fund. This product is **NOT** backed by the FDIC or any other government agency. You may pay internal charges and annual fees.

It is unlikely that a small investor would reap enough benefits to justify the fees. However, for a business, a large investor who trades frequently, or for those who need the status, this type of banking may be attractive.

Be careful that opening a sweep account does not signal the nod to a stockbroker who may want to introduce your money to a different investment world.

Money market mutual funds

A money market mutual fund is a large pool of investor money managed by an investment company. It seeks short term interest and conservation of the investment principal (i.e., higher yields than bank savings accounts without losing your investment principal).

Large corporations, the government, and state and local municipalities borrow large sums for short periods. Their short term IOUs are considered low risk because of their short duration and the credit worthiness of the entities. Loans may mature overnight, last for a week or up to one year. Money market mutual funds purchase only short term maturities, averaging 30 to 60 days.

The U.S. government borrows by issuing Treasury bills (T-bills) and federal agency notes. Private companies issue IOUs called commercial paper. Cities, states and public projects sell TANs, RANs and BANs based on future tax collections. Money market instruments are short term. So their yields are relatively low. These mutual funds may purchase only one kind of IOU or a variety of terms, issuers and quality of paper.

U.S. Government T-bills are almost $10,000 a pop, while jumbo CDs are packaged at $100,000 or more. With a large pool of investor funds mutual fund companies can buy expensive securities, enabling small investors to purchase shares of the total investor pool.

Money market funds offer daily interest. Their yields vary compared with bank savings accounts and short term bank deposits. Not all money markets are created equal. So you can't compare them intelligently by merely shopping for the highest returns.

Like all mutual funds, money markets are *not* guaranteed by the FDIC nor any agency of the government, even if they invest only in U.S. Government issued paper.

Securities Investor Protection Corporation (SIPC) guarantees investor funds up to $500,000 total value ($100,000 in cash) if the brokerage should close its doors or suffer financial troubles. But this does not protect an investor from problems associated with an investment **inside** the money market mutual fund, even when you read the words "U.S. Government" stamped inside the prospectus 72 times.

Money market mischief

U.S. Government money markets invest only in government Treasuries, or U.S. agencies, or both.

Worldwide money market funds have currency risk as foreign currencies move up and down in relation to American money. They are also vulnerable to risk of default

Tax exempt money markets offer tax free income but come with lower yields. Those not backed by insurance companies (premiums which you pay for) have the potential for default.

Double tax exempt money funds contain "munis" issued only in your state. You receive tax free income from both federal and state income taxes but increase default risk since all obligations are issued in the same geographical area.

Higher but riskier yields may be achieved by investing in derivatives, options or asset backed issues. These tend to lose value when interest rates rise.

The price of a money market fund is stabilized at $1 per share. Instead of the principal (net asset value) moving up and down, the investment yields rise and fall on a daily basis. Some money market funds have dropped below $1 per share because issues defaulted. Though the fund management companies made up the difference in the past, there is no guarantee that they will so in the future.

The primary purpose of a money market is safety of principal, not return. So choose wisely. Be sure your return isn't much lower than comparable money market funds and be wary of funds that offer higher yields.

The money market fund you choose should also offer free transactions, unlimited check writing and all services of the mutual fund family. Buy funds with low minimum check amounts and low management fees.

You can open a money market fund with as little as $1,000, sometimes even less. Some offer an automatic monthly investment plan with as little as $25 per month.

Since the funds are invested in short term issues, the yields are relatively low and succumb to inflation over time. They are useful to diversify your short term savings or to provide a foundation of safety beneath your remaining investment portfolio.

Investors in high tax brackets often compare the yields on tax free money markets to their taxable counterparts. By dividing the tax exempt yield by {1 minus your federal tax bracket}, you can see how much you would have to net from a taxable money market to break even after paying taxes. For example, a tax exempt bond paying 4 percent would yield the same percent after taxes (to a taxpayer in the 28-percent bracket) as a 5.556 percent taxable bond {4 percent divided by (1 minus 28 percent) equals 5.556 percent}.

However, there is a compelling argument against tax free (municipal bond) money markets. The underlying securities are not backed by the federal government nor any of its agencies but, rather, by cities, counties, states, hospitals, schools, revenue projects, foreign issues and public institutions vulnerable to public sentiment voting and cutbacks in federal and state funding.

How safe is your money market?

All money market mutual funds are not created equal. Some take more risk with your investment principal for potentially higher yields. Below are some rules to remember:

1. Don't pick a fund simply because it advertises a high seven-day (or annual) return. The fund manager may be taking extra risks to obtain a higher yield.

2. Pick a sizable (but not too large) fund. While bigger isn't necessarily better, a larger fund with a significant asset base may be more diversified, better able to cover losses from default.

3. Be wary of those funds that attempt to compete by promising to lower expenses, perhaps squeezing their profit margins. A mutual fund must be profitable to the investment company to stay in business over the long term.

4. Avoid money market funds that invest in foreign debt. Are you comfortable with your liquid assets invested in a Hong Kong bank, an Australian waterworks project or a Philippine railroad? Probably not.

5. Examine credit ratings and favor those with Treasury bills and US agency issues to decrease default risk. Avoid any fund that allows trading of securities before their maturity.

6. Call the mutual fund you are considering (or you are already invested with) and ask what percentage of its holdings are invested in CMOs, inverse floaters and other interest sensitive securities that can increase risk.

7. Analyze maturity averages. The shorter the time period to maturity, the better the opportunity to profit from interest rate spikes, and the less vulnerable a fund may be to risk of default.

If you open the money market in multiple names, you will have a joint ownership relationship with all other owners on the account. This is called *joint tenancy with rights of survivorship* and is a bit different than a traditional bank survivorship account. Each joint tenant owns a 100-percent undivided interest in the entire account.

Your college student, spouse, or brother-in-law could go on a spending spree without your knowledge until the monthly statement came.

To protect against unauthorized withdrawals, you can require that every owner's signature appear on every withdrawal request, whether by check, letter or telephone.

Savings bonds

Sold by financial institutions at a discount to their final face value, they have a double life: the time it takes the bonds to double in value; and the subsequent interest rate to their end of maturity. The interest rate is variable and adjusted every six months depending on the overall level of interest rates.

Savings bonds do not expire when they reach face value but keep on paying interest for at least thirty years. The interest collected when the bonds are redeemed is subject to federal income tax but not to state and local income tax.

Here are the top ten reasons to invest in Savings Bonds.

1. **Convenient.** Easy to buy at work through payroll savings or where you bank.

2 **Guaranteed principal**. Backed by the full faith, credit and taxing power of the U.S.

3. **Competitive yield.** Earn market-based interest rates.

4. **No-load investing.** You pay no commissions to buy or sell and no annual fees.

5. **Tax free compounding.** Interest is exempt from all state and local taxes and bonds purchased for college by parents with incomes below certain limits are

6. **Tax free bond exchange.** EE Savings Bonds can be exchanged for HH bonds with only the interest income taxed annually.

7. **Replaceable.** If lost, stolen or destroyed, they can be replaced even with the Bond.

8. **Liquid.** Can be cashed in anytime after six months from date of purchase.

9. **Diversification.** As a cash equivalent they diversify and reduce risk in portfolios.

10. **Affordable.** A Savings Bonds can be purchased for as little as $50.00.

Beware: They attract inflation and are not generally recommended for long term investing. Mutual funds are better for goals such as college or retirement. Bonds already purchased, however, as long as they are still earning competitive interest rates, can be used as part of your cash reserves.

Campus crisis

A jointly owned money market fund between parent and student, with one signature required for withdrawal, can produce instant cash for tuition, books and living expenses. The parent sends appropriate checks to the fund. The child redeems what is needed by writing checks on the share balance. (Sounds just like home again, doesn't it?)

Parents can maintain some control over the account by limiting the amount they deposit. Some funds offer overnight wire transfers. You can quickly wire money from your local bank or credit union for the occasional campus crisis call.

Copy cat bank money markets

Money market mutual funds originally generated so much appeal that banks started offering accounts bearing the same name to capture assets disappearing to mutual fund companies. A bank money market demand account has little in common with a money market mutual fund. When you purchase bank products you loan the institution your money. Mutual funds are owned by the shareholders (investors). Bank products are insured by the FDIC; mutual funds are not.

Money market funds follow the same general operating and regulatory policies as other mutual funds. A money market fund offers an investment prospectus, outlining all pertinent data—very dry stuff, but helpful once you decipher what foreign language it is written in. Request the statement of investments to determine what kinds of securities the funds is holding.

Read the prospectus and investment statement carefully before sending money to a money market, for that matter, to any mutual fund company. (How to use a mutual fund prospectus is explained in Chapter 22.)

Long term marathon money

In 1963 a pound of ground beef cost 33 cents. In 1974 one could purchase a full sized car for $3,200. In 1980 health care was an item in the family budget, not a major purchase.

Today, however, your next car could cost more than your first home. With more companies downsizing, rightsizing, restructuring employee payrolls, no one is immune to forced early retirement or termination.

Inflation is in your refrigerator, lurking in your heating ducts, hiding in your car's gas tank and cunningly waiting in your next tax bill. Inflation is the deadliest money killer over time, perhaps more dangerous that any other loss of principal.

The primary goal of long term investing must be conservation of your **purchasing power.** The biggest mistake a retiree can make is to gather their assets around them like they had six months to live and invest solely for safety and monthly income. Their nest egg will lag behind inflation with their dollars at risk over time primarily because they tried too hard to preserve capital.

Investing strategies: short-stop vs. marathon money

How much risk to principal is enough to sustain growth and stay ahead of inflation? How much is too much? Some investors currently feel immortal because recent stock market returns have nearly doubled their original investment capital. They bravely buy emerging markets, small company new issues, and jam lots of stocks and other volatile investments into their retirement plans. They are led to believe the greater the risk the greater the ultimate wealth over the long run. However, tomorrow's stock market couldn't care less what **they** think.

Other investors are terrified to venture outside banks, Treasury Direct, or insurance companies for fear of any loss of principal. Both investor types are taking too much risk. I believe there is a prudent middle ground to strike a balance between conservation of **principal** and conservation of **purchasing power.**

The long run is really a series of short steps

If you don't create profits over the short term, how can you become successful over the long term? Riding investment roller coasters can make you poorer over the short term, perhaps even in the long term. Ignoring either risk to principal or the insidious effects of inflation is hazardous to your future financial wealth.

If I placed a narrow plank on the floor I could probably convince you to walk its length for $5. Would you walk that same thin plank perched ten feet above ground for $50? For $500 would you take your chances 100 feet up? When the real risk is understood, the potential rewards don't always look as appealing.

Focus on the prudent fundamentals of successful investing. You can stay ahead of inflation **and** remain risk adverse through the diversification strategies in this book, the long term natural upward bias of the equity markets, and patience.

Defensive investing

Building a long term bullet-proof portfolio from today's menu of investment products is a book in itself. But with a combination of guaranteed accounts and the optimum mutual funds discussed in the next chapter, you can invest like a millionaire without the millions. You can also provide enough diversification to reduce your risk to principal **AND** unleash enough investment power to outpace inflation. By utilizing a technique called "negative correlation" to design a defensive portfolio, you may reduce overall volatility, perhaps even raise your total investment return as well.

No pain, more gain

High returns won't help if you consistently lose principal during stock or bond market declines.

From an original $10,000 investment compare the following investment returns after three years:

Investment	1st Year	2nd Year	3rd Year
A	+20%	+20%	-20%
B	+20%	+20%	-10%
C	+10%	+10%	+8%

Which What to do investment made money the fastest?

Answer: Portfolio A accumulated $11,520.
Portfolio B was worth more, $12,960.
Portfolio C gained the most, $13,068.

In this example heavy losses in the final year in Portfolios A and B outweighed the add benefits of much higher returns in previous years.

Why are you rushing? Greater risk to principal does not guarantee greater returns, even over longer periods of time. **Create your wealth slowly but surely.**

The right way to invest

We don't see things the way they are; we see them the way we are. The stock market has an occasional upset stomach, bonds can dance the macarena when interest rates are on the rise, and international markets are unreliable. Where can you find solid ground when the landmarks keep moving?

- Insist on excellent, long term performance. Returns should not be measured by short term market changes or past annual results (except when poor performance repeats itself).
- Have a stated objective. Don't change your investment policy every time market winds change direction. Maintain the discipline and confidence to stick to your plan.
- Embrace a disciplined approach to investing. Invest regularly, not just when past performances motivate you toward fast dollars. Never invest out of greed or fear. Eventually, your greed will exact a stiff price: loss of principal.
- Know the difference between **risk** and **risky.** Though there are no safe harbors, no wealth without some risk, portfolio volatility can be managed and controlled. Develop your wealth slowly but surely over time using the magic and miracle of compounded interest.

- Always purchase quality products. Don't shop with a priority on price tags. You deserve the best, not the cheapest investment. Would you hire the cheapest doctor in town? Maybe you don't want the cheapest money manager either.
- Search for independent financial planning. Don't expect salespeople to provide objective financial advice. Learn the fundamentals of solid investing **before** you invest. Your investment portfolio should contain all four investment building blocks (stocks, bonds, cash, and global) to perform in any kind of economic weather.
- Investing in mutual funds should be easy. Communications, services, and reporting should be understandable, forthright, and timely.

Don't settle for nothing

When comparing how well your investment portfolio is running in the race against time and inflation, re-visit your investment philosophy and avoid the following losing strategies:

The do nothing theory

Perhaps you have made a lot of money in an aggressive mutual fund or high flying stock over the last few years. You know it is volatile (or maybe you own too many shares because of re-investment programs) but you can't bring yourself to part with it because you will owe taxes on the sale. Perhaps you have decided to sell and accept some tax consequences in return for lower risk and a sounder night's sleep, but you haven't gotten around to reapportioning your money into a more diversified asset allocation.

The pay nothing theory

You believe if you can't see the investment charges, internal fees or other expenses, they don't exist. Would you invest some stranger's money for free?

Not all charges associated with an investment or its distribution may be disclosed. Some investment advisors may pay vendors for distribution of their products, though such disclosure is not mandatory under current SEC laws, even in the fine print.

Some investors who would never rely on the cheapest doctor in town or feed their families only the cheapest food nevertheless are so price conscious that they will focus on cheap management of their money. Choose your investments as carefully as your friends, insisting on quality first at a fair price.

The know nothing theory

These investors are too busy earning money to spend time managing their financial lives. Is your investment portfolio stuck on auto-pilot?

If so, make a commitment to watch over your precious investment capital more consciously, to protect it from others, and to understand how the underlying securities perform inside the shiny brand name labels folks tend to feel secure with. Know all potential risks as well as the potential rewards.

Collecting brand name financial products may not make your wealthy. Consider carefully building your financial house using all of the investment blocks (cash, stocks, bonds, and global) in moderation. Through real diversification you may guard your portfolio in all types of investment weather, stock market rain or shine.

The something for nothing theory

Relying on the advice of so-called "money gurus," the media, financial publications, or using the "whatever-my-friends-and-neighbors-are-buying" method of investing is generally unproductive. If these "experts" are smarter than you, why are they selling , even giving away for free, advice instead of secretly buying their favorite picks for themselves?

What to do with $25 a month?

With as little as $25 per month, you can become financially successful. With time as your friend and compound interest on your side even small amounts of money are powerful. Start today. Invest today for tomorrow's returns.

1. Pay off your credit cards as soon as possible. This is a guaranteed, double digit return: no risk, just pure gain. What mutual funds could promise such results?
2. Start an emergency fund. Use only guaranteed accounts.
3. Start an IRA account. Even $25 per month invested into a high quality mutual fund can turn into a significant nest egg. IRAs are long term plans. Aim to outpace inflation.
4. Start a 401(k) employer plan. These supplementary pension plans may offer matching funds from employers that turbo-charger your account.
5. Start a tax sheltered annuity if you work for a non-profit organization. This is further explained in Chapter 16.
6. Begin a college fund. Start while your children are young to put time on your side.
7. Start a down payment savings for your home.
8. Start a vacation fund.
9. Start a Christmas savings.
10. Create your own business capital, so you can realize your dream of starting your own business.
11. Match your teenager's IRA account. This motivates them to invest.

12. Start a self-determined project fund.

For goals less than three years away, limit your investing to bank CDs, credit unions or money market mutual funds. If your goal is longer than three years, fight inflation with mutual funds.

Chapter 22

Mutual fund-amentals

"Do not gamble, take all of your savings and buy some stock and hold on to it till it goes up, then sell it. If it don't go up, don't buy it."

—Will Rogers

Unless you have dollars to lose, don't major in individual stocks, bonds or any other single product. You can't build a sturdy home with only five or ten boards. Similarly, you can't build a bulletproof, defensive investment portfolio with only a few securities. You must diversify as though you were a millionaire, even if you don't own a million!

Investing used to be simple. Consumers would deposit their savings into a banking institution, a credit union, an insurance company, or purchase U.S. savings bonds, Treasury bills or long term government bonds. With all these investments, they'd "leave the driving to others."

As a result, financial institutions have grown richer at the expense of savers who, today, fight for their financial lives against mismanagement of assets and inflation, the deadliest money killer over long periods of time.

The world of mutual funds

But that was yesterday. Today, opportunities for the small consumer abound. The "little guy" can literally diversify like a millionaire, hire top money managers, have access to assets at all time, control how funds are invested, and maintain the freedom and flexibility to change investment vehicles as financial goals change.

And what makes this possible? Mutual funds. What are these wildly popular investments, how do they work and are they right for you?

Mutual funds have made it possible for ordinary folks to invest in the same instruments as the rich and famous, simply by lowering the ante for getting into the game. Before the mutual fund era, only the rich could play the investing game because the price to play was so stiff. A single U.S. Treasury bill (T-bill) cost nearly $10,000, and a middle class investor had to find a friend to in order to purchase one.

Today, the small investor can easily own a portion of 100 or more T-bills and other U.S. Government agency issues for as little as $25 per month, or with an initial investment of $1,000 or less.

Mutual fund investing is basically a method of managing money. The term "investing" should not frighten consumers because savers have been investing most of their lives, whether they realize it or not. Bank savings accounts, bank CDs, savings bonds, insurance policies and annuities, credit unions and employee pension plans are all forms of investing.

With mutual funds, investors are pooling their assets and hiring top professional money managers to manage their portfolios. What's more, companies that offer mutual funds continually are introducing new services and benefits.

Mutual fund companies manage pools of investor dollars and act as a temporary holding center until investors request their account dollars (shares) back. The companies can keep only expenses and fees that they disclose beforehand. All surplus profits (or losses) pass directly to you, the shareholder. If your mutual fund has a good year, so do you.

Specifically, a mutual fund is a large pool of money from investors seeking similar investment objectives. The fund's investment policy decides what securities can be purchased, what types of risk or investment strategies will be allowed and what policies will be employed to produce profits. Some mutual funds invest wholly in stocks of private companies (and I recommend that you pass those by except under certain circumstances). But many other types of mutual funds invest totally in U.S. Government bonds, U.S. Treasury bills and notes, Ginnie Mae (GNMA) mortgages, corporate bonds or a wide range of all these instruments, avoiding entirely any association whatsoever with the stock market.

All investments contain some type of risk, even those "safe" ones we tend to gravitate to in times of uncertainty. There simply are no "safe" investments. If you try too hard to protect your principal you will, over time, guarantee the very losses you worked so hard to avoid through the ravages of inflation. If you take too much capital risk, you can lose significant principal as well. Since risk is everywhere, the trick is to learn how to manage it.

Through a system of mutual fund investing, you can purchase many types of investments at one time and, through diversification, reduce your risk to principal. Mutual funds can also help to outpace inflation to conserve future purchasing power.

Whether you intend to invest your company year-end bonus, your retirement lump sum pension rollover or an extra $25 per month rescued from your limited budget, there is a mutual fund combination right for nearly every investor.

A mutual understanding

Assume that you and I pooled our money together to purchase more securities than we could individually afford. We would share proportionally (depending on how much each of us invested) in all profits (distributions), expenses and any future losses. But by pooling our assets together we could benefit from economies of scale such as volume discounts on purchases and liquidations, reduced costs of management fees and other fixed costs that tend to decrease as the size of any money pool increases. The value of our investment pool (fund) would be its ***total asset value.***

Each of us would own a part of every security in the investment pool proportional to the money invested. But we would be equal partners, entitled to the basic privileges of ownership regarding many benefits explained in our written agreement with each other and with the investment manager—the ***prospectus***. We would have the right to change investment managers periodically and the ability to vote on any fundamental changes of investment strategy our money managers may suggest.

To invest our money together we would need similar investment philosophies and objectives. If you wanted to purchase gold or other precious metals, for example, while I was intent on buying only U.S. Government bonds, our investment partnership would not work very well. We would need compatible investment objectives in our cooperative venture.

Are mutual funds safe?

Because we are realistic investors, we would understand that any type of investment carries risk of loss of principal as well as the hope of significant future profits. Since investment returns depend on ***profits,*** not ***prophets,*** we would need to understand the inherent risks and limitations of the securities we chose as various markets adjusted over time and the economic environment changed. Various phases of the business cycle, the direction of interest rates, the general health of the economy, political forces, and international issues all affect the faces of investing. Diversification would be our motto along with patience and realistic expectations for future returns. We would structure our investment mix for comfort, not speed.

Dividends, interest and/or ***capital gains,*** called ***distributions,*** would be apportioned to all shareholders, on a monthly, quarterly or annual basis, depending on the appropriate accounting procedures. **When distributions were made, the price of our mutual fund would decrease because it was no longer trading with the distribution just transferred to their shareholders.**

You could choose to reinvest your distributions back into our fund and purchase additional new shares, while I could request the cash **dividend** or **capital gain** and either spend the money or reinvest it into another investment.

Eventually, we might be investing alongside several types of investors: working folks, retirees, parents saving for college, high school and college grads investing for the first time and young married folks building a nest egg to buy a home. No matter how little each invested, each would share the basic privileges that our mutual fund offered.

The major advantage of purchasing mutual funds is that through diversification (pooling investors' assets to purchase more securities than one could afford alone) they help you **not to lose money!** Money market mutual funds are available for short term (short-stop) money, while a combination of conservative mutual funds providing some growth can keep your long term (marathon) money working as hard as you do.

When you purchase an investment product backed by the solvency of a single company, such as an insurance company annuity or a bond issued by a private corporation, if the company fails, you can lose all your investment principal.

If a single company inside a diversified mutual fund disappears, you have many other securities remaining in your investment portfolio. This spreads the risk of loss and reduces your overall risk to loss of principal.

Remember this old camp song, "99 bottles of pop on the wall"? *If one of those bottles should happen to fall, 98 bottles are still on the wall.* Mutual funds were created with the same concept in mind. Look on mutual funds as a method of prudently managing your money, not a way to "get rich quick."

Mutual funds are ideal for a variety of tax advantaged plans such as retirement IRAs, SEPs, KEOGHs, profit sharing and 401(k) pension plans. They can be utilized as custodial accounts for minors as college funds and for nonprofit institution tax deferred annuity programs.

Mutual benefits

As you become more familiar with this system of diversifying your investment assets, you will discover many benefits mutual funds can offer the average financial consumer. Service and customer benefits include:

1. Professional money management.
2. Economies of scale for cost efficiency.
3. Diversification of investment capital.
4. Wide range of investment choices.
5. Public newspaper/media reporting.
6. Direct wire transfers to and from your local savings institution or checking account.
7. 24-hour telephone access to account information and pricing data.
8. Check writing privileges for instant access to your funds.
9. Convenient transfers (exchanges) between funds in the same mutual fund family.
10. Automatic monthly income checks sent to your home or bank.
11. Account link-ups with the banking institution you choose.
12. Detailed and understandable account statements and timely earnings updates.
13. Prompt distribution of dividends, interest and capital gains.
14. Automatic re-investing and systematic withdrawal plans.
15. Reduced sales charges for larger investors.
16. Availability for IRA accounts and other tax sheltered retirement programs.
17. Tax advantaged college savings programs like UGMAs.
18. Automatic monthly investment programs.
19. Payroll deduction plan options.

20. Telephone transfers to other affiliated funds.
21. Simple record-keeping and tax information statements.
22. Simplified tax preparation.
23. Full investor privileges regardless of your account value.
24. Optional Certificates of Ownership, like issued on stocks.
25. Simple and convenient investing methods.
26. Prompt telephone liquidation of account funds.
27. A ready buyer when you want to sell your shares.
28. Joint, trust and custodial ownership registrations.
29. Reader friendly periodic statements and reports.

In today's fast paced society, conveniences and services save time. But select them *only* after you have chosen a high quality mutual fund portfolio. Today's mutual funds are truly service oriented.

Mutual fund investing offers diversification of investment capital, professional management, the potential for higher investment profits, access to your money when you want it, and a simple method of monitoring your progress. There is a mutual fund that's right for nearly every type of investor.

31+ flavors to choose

The last thing the world needs is another mutual fund. A better way to choose one, however, would be helpful. There are nearly as many categories of mutual funds as there are types of investors. They can be grouped according to their investment strategies and goals and the securities they purchase:

1. High risk stock funds

- Aggressive growth funds seek maximum capital gains and invest in higher risk companies that aim for higher returns than the stock market in general.
- Small company growth types are comprised primarily of stocks of companies worth less than $500 million.
- Growth funds mainly include medium sized company stocks expected to grow faster than average.
- Large capitalization funds major in large "blue chip" stocks of major U.S. corporations that have consistently increased profits over the years and usually pay consistent dividends.
- Defensive stock funds usually include utility and other companies which tend to hold up well in price during downturns in the economy until higher interest rates drive them down.
- International funds specialize in stocks of companies outside the United States. Though only 65% of their assets must be invested abroad, they seek aggressive returns and may take large stock positions in one or two countries at a time.

- Precious metals funds buy stocks of gold, silver or platinum **mining companies** and trade like stocks. Few actually hold metals as core investments.
- Sector funds buy securities from only one industry or market niche, attempting to enhance returns when that sector is in favor, while increasing risk to principal when that market is out of favor.
- Social awareness funds invest in socially responsible companies (when managers can find some) and are generally invested in stocks. The marketing is attractive but performances are usually lackluster.

A stock mutual fund is typically geared for long term growth Conservation of principal is usually not an objective. Your return is primarily dependent on appreciation (or growth) if stock market prices increase. Current income may come from dividends on companies chosen by the money manager.

2. Medium risk stock mutual funds
- Balanced funds generally have a three part objective to conserve investment principal, to pay current income, and long term growth of both the principal and income. They aim to achieve this through common and preferred stocks and bonds, typically 60-percent stocks and 40-percent bonds.
- Growth and income funds are made up of high dividend, mature stock companies, a few bonds and some cash
- Equity income funds invest primarily in stocks with high dividend pay outs for current income. They tend to be less risky than stock funds which invest primarily for growth. Equity income funds should contain many types of securities including stocks, U.S. bonds, corporate bonds, and cash equivalents.
- Asset allocation funds may change investment mixes, moving between stocks, bonds, cash and even gold. Their composition may change depending on the manager's outlook of market conditions.
- Option income funds are out of favor types that invest in blue chip stocks with options to boost the income yield.
- Global stock funds tend to diversify among more countries, betting less on the fortunes of a single foreign market. They are generally under less pressure to produce stellar short term returns and can better hedge against risk to any one foreign economy or currency. Portfolios vary.

Balancing current income, growth, and conservation of principal may lower these returns when the stock market is in full swing. But they can hedge against stock market downturns with bonds and cash they hold.

3. High risk bond funds
- High yield (junk) corporates are issued by lower quality credit corporations.
- High yield (junk) municipals are lower rated municipal bonds issued by cities, states, counties and revenue or public projects with impaired credit ratings.

- International bond funds are portfolios of foreign debt and carry economic and currency risk of the country where they are issued.
- Income funds seek a high level of current income for shareholders by investing in high yielding stocks or high yield bonds, or both. They may seek income at the expense of their investment principal if interest rates rise, or may invest in lower quality issues that pay high dividends or interest rates.
- National municipal bond funds (tax free munis) contain long term, tax exempt bonds of states, revenue projects, hospitals, nursing homes, schools, highways and other public projects. Though income is not federally taxed, these funds are vulnerable to interest rate hikes and defaults, many riding on the future of health care and public sentiment.
- State municipal bond funds (double tax frees) are issued solely by public projects within your own state of residence. Often tax exempt from both federal and state income taxes, they intensify risk to principal because they are not geographically diversified. If state budgets contract or industry leaves, municipal revenue can dry up fast and they may default.
- Mortgage backed securities funds contain mortgage obligations packaged by brokerages, but may also invest in complex derivatives that fluctuate wildly when interest rates move quickly. They may be more risky than they look when interest rates become volatile.
- Target funds buy bonds that mature in specific years. They may hold corporate or government, municipal or zero coupon (zero) obligations. Prices fluctuate with interest rates and the longer maturities are very sensitive to interest rate risk (loss of principal when interest rates rise). Managers promise to redeem both principal and interest at maturity of the portfolio (they said that, not me).

4. Medium risk bond funds

- Ginnie Mae (GNMA) funds seek high levels of income by investing in mortgage securities backed by the government. They are safe from default but not from loss of principal like other funds. They self-liquidate during falling interest rates as the mortgages producing the higher returns disappear when folks pay back their home loans. As interest rates rise, they struggle, similar to bonds, to preserve principal.
- High grade corporates are higher quality private corporation debt, which lose less principal than government bonds during periods of rising interest because their yields are higher. Unlike U.S. bonds, they can default.
- High grade tax exempts are higher quality municipal debt that may be insured and hold up better against default, but suffer more in rising interest rate markets.
- U.S. Government bonds are protected from default but not from loss of principal from rising interest rates. Depending on the length of time to maturity, these bonds can suffer as much as a 10-percent loss of principal when the prevailing interest rate rises 1 percent.

- Triple bond funds (strategic income types) combine several types of bonds such as U.S. Government, higher yield corporates and global bonds to protect against the loss of principal during rising interest rates. When one class zigs, hopefully the other classes will zag, maintaining a stable principal when interest rates are troublesome.

5. Lower risk bonds funds

- Short term taxable funds have two- to five-year corporate debt obligations, which makes them less vulnerable to rising interest rates.
- Short term tax exempts contain shorter maturity municipal bonds that, due to shorter durations, lose less principal when interest rates are on the climb. In addition, they may be less likely to default because time is one of the greater risks on IOU promises.

A bond fund invests for current income and often pays dividends on a monthly basis. The risk level and potential return can vary depending on the type of bonds within the fund's portfolio. Bonds have offered less long term growth potential than stocks.

6. Money market funds

- Treasury money markets invest only in U.S. Treasury issues, but may have derivatives inside to boost yields. Check the underlying securities for principal risk.
- U.S. Government agency funds are not all T-bills as some securities are issued by federal agencies, not technically backed by the government itself. They can also contain volatile derivatives in their mix.
- Taxable money markets without specific descriptions usually invest in IOUs (commercial paper) issued by private corporations and are backed only by the creditworthiness of the company issuing the short term debt.
- Tax exempt money markets use short term municipal and/or foreign debt instruments to increase yields; these can offer currency and global risks as well as the vagaries of the municipal bond market. They are attractive for their tax exempt income on a federal basis, occasionally also some state and local tax relief but are not appropriate as guaranteed cash equivalents.

Most money market funds are designed to provide income and stability of principal. Although no money market fund is insured or guaranteed by the U.S. Government, risk is minimal.

Subsequently, you tend to earn less interest income than on other fixed income investments. Money market mutual funds are often temporary comfort stops for funds looking for a more permanent home.

Clean money

Socially responsible investing is popular today, considering investors can put their money where their hearts are. But to date, such funds have not fared as well as their siblings, partly because funding for such altruistic projects is languishing, and partly because of the nature of the companies, which are not traditional money makers like industrials, pharmaceuticals and other heavy hitters that socially aware investors attempt to avoid.

Who is the mutual fund primarily socially responsible to? I believe you should optimize your investing through research and fundamentals and send those "dear to your heart" organizations cold hard cash to accomplish their missions.

It's getting harder to find companies who don't put hamsters into cages, pollute the environment, pose health hazards, or produce politically incorrect products. How they actually produce their earnings may be quite different from their annual corporate mission statement.

Avoiding the Asian flu

Ten years ago, only 30 percent of all investing opportunities were found outside the United States. Today, that fraction is nearly reversed. Economic uncertainty and currency fluctuations are evident from today's headlines. Diversifying into many parts of our planet and through different types of companies will help reduce the negative impact of economic, political or military strife in one part of the world.

International funds must invest 65 percent of their total assets in foreign issues. In addition, they tend to take large positions in emerging markets for potential stellar returns.

Global funds tend to spread their investing among many foreign sectors (and the U.S.), instead of bunching investments in only a few locales or countries. Therefore, you may reduce the risk of owning foreign securities by searching for funds which invest in as many as thirty of forty countries (and inherent currencies).

When one country catches the flu, everyone gets a cold. There is a strong correlation between the world's economies and, therefore, their stock markets. Tread carefully on foreign soil.

A global fund may benefit your portfolio more than it can hurt your total return due to diversification into many parts of the world. An international fund, on the other hand, because it concentrates in only a few countries or types of securities, offers no soft landing when instability or crisis affects foreign markets.

How risky is a bond fund?

When interest rates rise, bond prices go down. **Bond maturity** is the average time to maturity of the bonds inside the mutual fund wrapper.

The longer the bond time to maturity and the lower the yield (interest rate), the more the bond will lose in price when interest rates are on the climb.

Bond duration assumes that a bond has a shelf life of its own and which may not coincide with its maturity date. For example, a 30-year GNMA may have a reduced investing life of only two years when interest rates decline by two percent or more. Bonds can be volatile when interest rates are doing the macarena.

You can find the **duration** of a bond fund in its prospectus. The lower the number the less the fund's net asset value (principal) is expected to fall when interest rate rises. A duration of, say 2.5 indicates that the net asset value (NAV) should fall approximately 2.5% when interest rates rise by one percent. A duration of 9 means that the price of the fund may fall by as much as nine percent on an interest rate hike of one percent.

Even low duration bond funds are not substitutes for guaranteed investing. Stick to money market funds for short-stop cash equivalents.

Like all security analysis techniques, none are infallible. However, understanding how the "experts" view risk versus reward issues helps you to become better acquainted with the challenges investment advisors face when managing your money.

Decoding the prospectus

There may be stricter labeling laws on a $2 carton of cottage cheese than on a $2 billion dollar mutual fund. A mutual fund prospectus is your written contract with the mutual fund company. It outlines the investment objective(s) of the fund, the methods management intends to use to achieve their goals and the special strategies, techniques and hedging options that might be used. The prospectus can give you a general idea of how much risk the fund will tolerate, although in the past some have utilized riskier issues than they disclosed to shareholders.

Most costs are listed, fund managers and outside directors are introduced and many helpful pieces of information are enclosed, once you learn what language the prospectus is written in.

A typical prospectus might sound like this:

XYZ Company Agreement provides that the compensation of the Advisor will be reduced by the sum of its parts and divided by the number 13 (because that's my lucky number) plus the straight line depreciation of the office furniture, assuming the reinvestment of all dividends and capital gains, and unless changed by a majority vote of the shareholders, upon the receipt of all proxies (and if you don't send them in the first time we will spend more of your money to send them to you again). In accordance with the investment objective and policies of the Advisor to provide current income and growth of the brand new shrubbery at the lobby entrance, there can be no assurance that XYZ will achieve its original investment objectives (whatever they were—as defined in subsection 4-f-A2). However...

An exaggeration? Not much! Is it any wonder that consumers rely on newspapers and magazines to tell them what funds to invest in? Who wouldn't feel intimidated by such gobbledygook?

Small investors may find a mutual fund prospectus a cheap solution to insomnia. But electing *not* to read it because it's too intimidating is not advisable, although you will need some help to get started.

Most mutual funds offer toll free telephone numbers. Call information or visit your library for a complete listing. The Investment Company Institute in Washington, D.C., the fund industry's trade association, can connect you with individual fund families and can send their own generic publications to learn from.

When your prospectus arrives, be sure it is current. Then check the minimum dollar requirement to open an account.

Be sure you have received the correct prospectus. Some fund companies offer several funds with similar names. U.S. Government is a common term, and sector (single industry) funds may have several spin-offs from a basic theme like global.

The Securities and Exchange Commission (SEC) has its own disclaimer on the front cover, which states that it will not approve or recommend any securities or guarantee the truth of any prospectus statements even though it regulates mutual funds or authorized the fund when it was first organized.

This hint tells you just how far away the SEC may be if your investment stalls and you are left with one oar and a leaky investment boat. It's up to you to "approve" or "disapprove" of a particular fund.

The prospectus should highlight the risks, limitations and special concerns inherent in the type of securities the fund intends to purchase. Also included is information on how to buy and sell shares, multiple price structures (if available) and technical data about the fund's past history. Try to separate extraneous information from what you must find out: how much risk is inherent in this investment and how well it can expect to perform in the future when negative factors affect the investment allocation.

Until you are familiar with the underpinnings of a mutual fund, you are *not* ready to invest in it. Stay awake—if you snooze, you could lose.

How do I get rich?

Not all funds earn profits in the same manner. Mutual funds can distribute dividends and interest periodically, distribute capital gains profits from the securities bought and sold inside the fund portfolio, and raise the share price over time.

The investment policy is key. If you are uncomfortable with terms such as "junk," "speculative" or "lower quality," cross those selections off your research list.

If the investment policy states it seeks better than average stock returns (beating the stock market), it will employ investment methods to strive for high returns, using lots of stocks, even if they increase risk to principal.

If it states that the fund intends to stay fully invested at all times, don't expect your manager to run for the hills to preserve principal in the middle of a stock market meltdown.

A statement goal of current income might place greater emphasis on yield and add more risk to principal to get the higher rates.

Since no fund can be all things, you must learn what compromises are needed to keep your financial machine running well in bad economic weather, while profiting during those sunny seasons. A fund seeking aggressive growth struggles as the stock market declines, while one investing only in long term government bonds loses principal when interest rates are rising.

What's the sticker price?

Mutual funds may have management fees, custodian fees, transfer fees, 12b-1 distribution fees, shareholder servicing fees, accounting fees, administrative fees, legal and audit fees, reporting fees, insurance fees and printing and postage fees, not to mention interest expense for funds that borrow on margin.

Most of the fund's sticker price is listed, although there are some charges that may not show up in a prospectus. This section discusses whether an investor will pay up-front charges (a front load), or declining surrender charges (a back load), and/or annual charges (12b-1) for marketing and distribution expenses. If there are no external charges, the fund may be paying distribution fees from other sources, creating higher turnover (buying and selling a lot) or higher brokerage costs (sometimes to its own affiliated companies), paying out transaction fees to distributors or "soft dollar arrangements" not disclosed in the prospectus.

Once upon a time there were loaded (up-front sales charge) funds and no-load (sold directly to investors by the distributor) funds. Today many no-loads are converting to loaded varieties, loaded counterparts are reducing or submerging their distribution fees in the fine print, and many more are paying fees to mutual fund networks or large brokerages to sell their products through distribution systems.

No one will invest your money for free, and investors attracted to what they believe are the cheapest funds may pay more than they realize. Internal charges reduce your net return just like the external ones an investor can see.

Highly educated folks who know they can't buy a free car, a free house, a free pair of shoes, or a free college tuition may buy the delusion that some stranger will invest their money for nothing.

Who is watching my money?

You may believe that the fund's superstar is managing your money 40 hours per week, but often less experienced staff directs basic buying decisions. You couldn't single handedly cater 500 Thanksgiving meals in your dining room. Likewise, no one human can manage billions of dollars. Funds advertise their managers to bring in business. By deifying personalities, the public becomes groupies and loyal investors.

The prospectus defines the rights of each shareholder, whether they have a $25-per-month account or $1 million invested. Shareholders vote on major business matters and choose the investment advisors approximately every three years.

Retirement accounts such as IRAs often require a small annual trustee fee to the fund to report your progress to the IRS. Funds have different policy positions and occasional sales. But these are minor compared to finding permanent high quality investments to create your wealth.

One last chance

Occasionally a mutual fund will advertise its closing, so investors can flock to get in before the deadline. These performers may deteriorate because of the high volume of last minute money coming in and market conditions out of favor with the investment style. They may have a special investment style that increases risk. Our theme is *getting rich slowly*, not getting in the door just before it closes.

Don't live in the past

Consumers are often confused by the different returns quoted in the media. Magazines depend on information from various sources—which they may not check. Most likely, however, is that mutual fund returns are quoted for different time periods. While one magazine may quote a year-to-date (the performance from January 1 of that year to the date of printing), another may quote a one-year return (say, from June of last year to this June).

Past performance is no guarantee of future results. Repeat that sentence until you believe it. You don't drive your car looking in the rear view mirror. You don't live your future exactly like you did in the past, and nothing in the past will give you a clue to tomorrow's financial headlines! Ignore past returns and concentrate on building a mutual fund portfolio using investment fundamentals, scouring the additional statement of investments to see where your money will be invested. In short, lower your risk to certain markets.

What are Rights of Accumulation?

Some funds offer price discounts (breakpoint purchases) for volume purchases. For example, you might pay less per share if you invest more than $50,000. As your contributions and earnings grow to, say $50,000, through **Rights of Accumulation** you may pay less per share on future purchases. Such offers may include any combination of mutual funds the investment company offers.

What is a Letter of Intent?

A **Letter of Intent** may reduce your price per share if you are planning to invest a large sum over a period of time, the next 13 months. By signing a loose commitment to invest a certain amount, you can pay the reduced price from the beginning. If, however, you fail to reach your investment goal within the following 13 months, your price per share will be adjusted to reflect your actual total contributions during that time. In the meantime a small part of your investment is held in escrow so it cannot be liquidated until your goal is reached.

Flip to the index

Almost all mutual funds aim to beat a bellwether index for stocks, bonds, or foreign investments. Because so many funds have under-performed the various market averages in recent years, index funds have become popular.

These weighted portfolios mirror a specific index and aim to replicate the index's performance without managing the assets. Since there is no management responsibility, index funds cost less than their managed fund peers.

Indexing is a little like taking a plane ride without a pilot. The "pilot on board" ticket costs more and may not be necessary when instruments can handle the aircraft. However, when turbulence erupts, you may wish for an experienced pilot in the cockpit.

Recent stock market thrills have overshadowed the inherent risks of indexing. Since the fund represents only one investment market, there is no diversification for a soft landing should that market suddenly decline.

When the next "bear" stock market occurs, and small investors see how quickly profits can disappear, they may exit these funds, leaving remaining shareholders with even further market declines because managers redeemed assets for redemption requests while stock prices were falling.

Cruising the Barbary coast without a captain, boarding Apollo 15 without a crew, or driving around town in the back seat with your car's cruise control in place aren't worth the risk when your Titanic hits an iceberg. Markets are fickle, react quickly, and don't care how close to retirement you are.

Purchase managed mutual funds and let the manager create your wealth slowly but surely.

My superstar has everything under control

A major landmark in the debate over how money should be managed occurred with a 1986 publication by Brinson, Hood, and Beebower. Their study over a 10-year period (1974 through 1983) sought to explain how much the money manager contributed to annual return figures of pension funds.

Further studies tend to indicate similar conclusions: 92%-94% of investment returns may be more a result of asset allocation, being at the right place at the right time, than the superior security selection ability of the investment advisor. This phenomenon, not superior money management capability, may account for how well your "superstar" fares in the annual year-end mutual fund survey.

Look at historic fund results. Most winners come from the same asset selection category. One year international funds may be golden, while the next the U.S. stock market may move ahead. It's gold in January and technology stocks in December. Health care issues may be killed in March and financials may take a hike in July.

You can avoid the thrill of victory followed by the agony of defeat through the fundamentals of real diversification, instead of looking for a miracle worker money manager, who can't predict the future any better than you can.

Rating fund risk by beta

Beta is a measure of a fund's sensitivity to market movements (ups and downs). It compares the fund's movement with an index, say the S & P 500 benchmark, which is set at 1.00. A fund with a beta of 1.10 is expected to perform 10% better than the index in "up" markets and 10% worse in "down" markets.

The benchmark for equity mutual funds is the S & P 500 Stock Index. For fixed income (bond) funds, the bellwether is the Lehman Brothers Aggregate Index. The EAFE, Europe Australia, Far East Index compares international funds with their peers.

Please note: the further up or down from 1.00 that a fund's beta appears, the less correlation there may be; therefore, the less you can depend on it as a tool for measuring risk.

Alpha isn't much better

Alpha is the difference between a fund's actual returns and its expected performance, given a certain level of risk. In plain terms, it is supposed to measure a money manager against others in the same fund type of fund.

The difference between the two figures is expressed as an annualized percentage, either above or below 1.00, the expected performance. A positive alpha figure indicates the fund has performed better than the norm. In contrast, a negative alpha indicates a fund has under-performed, given the expectations established by the fund's risk level (beta).

Most funds' alphas are below the benchmark because an index often outperforms a managed fund due to the expenses of paying the manager and associated costs of portfolio turnover.

You have heard it a dozen times: read the prospectus. Here are some key points to examine:
- The date of the prospectus.
- The minimum dollar amount required to invest.
- The fund's investment policy(ies).
- Past performance.
- General investment strategies.
- The Statement of Additional Information.

- The additional Statement of Investments.
- Special techniques the investment advisor may use.
- The management team.
- General risk level.
- Special risks involved.
- Fees.
- Portfolio turnover.
- Transfer agent.
- Shareholder rights.
- Services.
- Reporting methods.
- Distributions.
- Taxes on earnings.
- How to buy shares.
- How to redeem shares.

Most newspapers publish a "Mutual Fund" section page. Find the alphabetical listing of the parent group or mutual fund family that manages the specific fund you wish to research and track. You may see an abbreviated name title (e.g. "Gwth" for growth fund, "EqInc" for equity income, or "G & I" for growth and income, etc.).

There may be other symbols beside your fund:

- (r) indicates a redemption fee might apply when you liquidate your shares. This surrender charge might decline over several years or remain fixed over the life of your investment.
- (p) indicates periodic distribution expenses may be charged after the original sale. They might be as small as ¼ percent, as large as two percent. These pay for marketing expenses and are called 12b-1 charges.
- (x) means the fund has just distributed a dividend and is trading at a lower price, without the dollar amount of the dividend it just credited to its shareholders.
- (e) signifies that the fund has just distributed a capital gain to shareholders and the price is shown without the capital gain included.
- (t) means the fund has both 12b-1 plan and back-load redemption fees.
- (NA) means the price is not available due to incomplete information, performance or cost data. The fund may not be old enough if long term performance is compared.
- (f) means only the previous day's quotation is available.
- (k) discloses that the figure has been recalculated by another rating firm, using updated data.
- (nl) stands for no-load, which does *not* mean no charges. No-load funds have no external front or back-load charges. There may be, however, other charges and expense fees to the customer.

With the information provided by the newspaper reports of your mutual fund you should be able to track:

1. The investment objective based on stated goals in the prospectus.
2. The net asset value (NAV), the per-share value, based on closing quotes from the fund itself.
3. The offer price (POP), the NAV plus any sales commissions.
4. The NAV change from the previous reporting period, usually the previous business day.
5. The total return may be shown in some major business newspapers.
6. Some publications may also show the performance calculations during certain periods such as 1-year, 3-year, 5-year or year-to-date (from January 1 to the current quote).
7. The maximum initial sales commission based on information in the prospectus.
8. The grade the news media has given the fund based on its standing against other fund performances during the same period.
9. The highest and lowest price during the latest 52-week period. This has little bearing because many funds distribute much of their profits to shareholders during the year and, therefore, do not increase in price as a primary investment objective.

The most important column is the change, if any, in the NAV, from the preceding quotation (number 4 in the preceding list). This provides the most revealing method of assessing just how fast (up and down) a fund may move when markets are correcting or fluctuating. All mutual fund prices go up and down on a daily basis and you can monitor their progress. But the less fluctuation, the more dull and stodgy the fund is likely to remain during chaotic and uncertain market periods. Like a normal blood pressure, you can search for those funds that move up and down within a smaller activity range.

The best time to view how well a fund defends itself against market pressures is to watch closely when the stock market or interest rates are volatile. How a fund reacts during crisis says a lot about how it will perform under normal conditions. Heavily diversified funds tough it out better in stormy economic weather, while performing quite admirably during the sunny periods.

Many funds provide a 24-hour information system for access to fund information and your account values. You could soak in your tub, relax by the pool or drive in your car, receiving up to the minute status reports on your investments.

Your fund manager will send account statements every time some financial activity occurs—for example, when a dividend or capital gain has been credited to your account. An end of the year statement will provide an easy to read picture of your entire year's activity.

Some funds also provide the cost basis of shares you have redeemed through the year, to make your accountant happy.

When should I buy?

To get the most shares for your money and avoid immediate taxes on your account, be mindful of the date you purchase your shares. You are better off buying on the day **after** it has declared its dividend or capital gain, usually done quarterly, or annually.

Such payment, called **ex-dividend,** reduces the net asset value of the fund's shares by the amount of the distribution, and the selling price of shares drops by that same amount. By buying in **after** the dividend is declared, you avoid paying taxes on that particular payout.

Call the fund's customer service department for the next ex-dividend date. On the day after a fund goes ex-dividend, an "**x**" appears beside the fund's net asset value in the newspaper.

How much am I making?

You can calculate exactly how much your fund account is worth on a daily basis by multiplying the total number of shares you own by the latest net asset value (NAV).

Mutual funds periodically distribute to their owners (shareholders) the dividends, interest and capital gains paid by the securities on a monthly basis, while dividends are quarterly distributions. Capital gains can be paid at the end of each year and consist of profits through the sale of securities by the fund.

You can elect to have all distributions paid to you in cash when they are distributed or have them reinvested by purchasing additional shares. Reinvestment of all distributions, whether you need income or not may benefit you most because even if you need a monthly income check you can always have your fund sell part of your account instead.

Unless you have a tax advantaged wrapping over your mutual fund such as IRA, SEP, 403(b), or other tax deferred benefit, you will pay taxes on all distributions, whether your profits are reinvested or taken in cash and sent to you.

Can you avoid paying current taxes by exchanging from one fund to another in the same mutual fund family? Unfortunately, no. Any exchange, even if you consider it to be a like exchange, is considered by the IRS as a sale and a new purchase. There may be a profit, a loss or perhaps no taxable results. But your tax advisor must know an exchange has taken place to determine whether taxes are due on the transaction.

To minimize tax consequences, sell the shares you paid the most for (specific shares). You must inform your mutual fund *before* you sell, however, or the IRS will assume you have sold those shares you purchased first. This is called FIFO (first in, first out) and is a normal method of selling other types of securities as well.

Keep your purchase and redemption records, in case the IRS questions you later. Through IRS Publication 564, you can research more details of this tax strategy. Also keep in mind that if you sell only higher cost shares as you liquidate your funds over time, you will be left with low cost shares and may incur even greater taxes in the future. You may want, instead, to sell some more expensive shares and some lower cost ones to even out your current tax liability. Your tax advisor can help in this matter.

The mutual fund must redeem the shares at a price based on the next current NAV per share that the fund computes after the shareholder's request is received. This is commonly called "forward pricing." Everyone receives the same price per share, whether they redeem $100 or $1 million.

Allow a few business days for delivery of your check. Some funds will even express deliver funds to you for a small extra charge.

A signature guarantee may be needed to request a change of account registration, a large liquidation (redemption) from your current account value, funds from a retirement account or a check payable to anyone (or any address) other than you. Take the appropriate forms to a U.S. registered securities brokerage, U.S. commercial bank or trust company, a savings association, credit union or national securities exchange or clearing agency where an officer can vouch for your signature.

Confessions of an investment chicken

Any daredevil investor will tell you that over the long term, mutual funds that put you through the rockiest ups and downs reward you with fatter returns than the turtle-like funds that crawl along, slowly but surely. So goes the theory.

From the time you were a child, you have been taught to avoid risks whenever possible. "Don't play in the street." "Don't talk to strangers." "Buckle your seatbelt." Those who cared for you warned against dangers lurking in the shadows.

Today, everyone, it seems, is discovering the world of mutual funds. But many so-called money experts advise you to take greater risks on your precious savings than may be prudent. They tout unrelated facts that over the last 20 years stocks performed better than any other one class of investments. Therefore, they conclude, invest in high risk stock funds. A little red ink shouldn't bother you. After all, it's only a paper loss!!!

Some mutual funds would have you believe that all you have to do to make money is to show up with your check. Their ads are certainly seductive and sound reassuring. "If you had invested $10,000 in our Sure Fire mutual fund, today you would be worth 50 gazillion dollars and your friends would be paying *you* for advice." The illustrative graphs and bar charts are even more appealing. By compressing all those hiccups and down years, marketing departments can produce graphs that look like the back side of Mount Everest—straight up. Then in small print comes the following disclosure: "Past performance is no guarantee of future results." And they mean it.

Diversification 'R Us

Winning The Money Game is not just the name of this book. It represents developing a different attitude about managing your money. Crashing red traffic lights is certainly not safe driving, and ignoring financial warning lights and the unforgiving laws of the investment world is downright dangerous to your financial health. Today's hot investment may quickly cool tomorrow. A top performer with stellar returns in one year can plummet in the next. It's not that shooting stars are bad, they just burn out quickly.

Every investment portfolio should have a healthy portion of cash or cash substitutes such as bank deposits, credit union accounts, money market mutual fund savings or even some previously purchased U.S. savings bonds. On that foundation you may want to add U.S. Treasury bills, some long term U.S. Government bonds, a variety of corporate bonds and a sprinkling of all three major classes of stock: small companies whose names we don't recognize, growth companies on the move and large monoliths we consider household names. For some investors, a global exposure may actually reduce the risk from other U.S. investments. But, like any cooking seasoning, just a pinch is quite enough.

You can't operate a chicken farm with only 10 chickens. The actual cost of keeping each hen would be prohibitive.

For most of us, real diversification may seem hopeless considering our limited financial reserves. But mutual funds, which invest in all of the above, can do the same job with an investment sum as small as $25 per month.

Markets move up and down in response to good news, bad news or no news at all: interest rates, inflation fears, prospects for next year's profits, consumers' increasing credit debt, the political atmosphere, international conditions, general economic conditions, unemployment, the consumer price index, new housing starts, the discount rate, public confidence and, once in a while, just the belief that "bad things come in threes."

No market is rational. The domestic cash, stock, bond, international and currency markets respond to the two most critical motives of large investors: greed and fear.

Risk cannot be totally eliminated. But through a system of mutual fund investing you can diversify like a millionaire, cut out financial middlemen for a greater share of the profits, become your own money manager and take control of your own financial destiny.

How to buy the **wrong** fund

More people choose a dog over any other pet. More people choose blue over any other color. More sports fans choose football than any other televised sport. More small investors are in the wrong investment at the wrong time, therefore, buying high then selling low.

Winning the Money Game

Mutual funds total more than $4 trillion. Over thirty percent of all households own shares in at least one fund. Mutual fund companies rival commercial banks and insurance companies in financial power.

Mutual fund investing is not about tracking down the hottest fund of the moment. It's about settling in with funds that could serve you for years to come. Wealth doesn't happen overnight. It accumulates over time.

More money has been lost searching for higher returns than at the point of a gun. Here are 22 ways to purchase the **wrong** mutual fund:

1. Grab last year's best performer. During your next library research visit, request back issues of consumer money magazines. Compare year-end results for the past few years. See how rarely top performers maintain stellar results the next year.
2. Select the most popular mutual fund category. One year it's bio-tech. The next maybe technology, then healthcare, then Asia, then anything **but** Asia. Funds on a hot streak won't guarantee scorching long term results.
3. Choose the mutual fund with the highest year-to-date (current) return. Predicting future winners on the basis of short term performance is like calling the winner of a horse race before the ponies have rounded the first turn. Look for consistency and stability, not today's boom (perhaps tomorrow's bust).
4. Use long term performance as a reliable predictor of future results. Many mutual funds that tout long term records had lots of help from bull stock markets, declining interest rates and longer runs of certain market sectors. A fund's manager may have left, its composition and investment style may have changed, its investment selection may be in favor, or it might have guessed right more often than its competitors.
5. Become seduced by sector (single industry) funds. Buying sectors like utilities, pharmaceuticals, financials or other narrowly focused markets enhance risk when that market turns sour. A performance graph of a sector fund can look like an EKG of a patient in major cardiac arrest. The main purpose of a mutual fund is to *reduce* risk by diversifying your dollars into many investment baskets.
6. Concentrate on funds that invest only in stocks or only in bonds. Choose true diversification, stocks, bonds and cash. When one type of investment is declining, sellers are buying an alternative investment, one you also own.
7. Buy funds that invest in hard assets such as real estate and precious metals. No more than one third of your assets should be in real estate, including your own home. Most investors would be better served with direct ownership of real estate.
8. Choose funds for income when you really need growth. Anyone planning to live more than three years has inflation as an enemy. Fixed income vehicles like bank CDs and bonds or bond mutual funds will not keep pace with inflation. Always invest something for growth. You can get a monthly check (in-come)

from any type of mutual fund. You need total return—a combination of income and growth.

9. Scramble for higher yields isn't smarter banking—it is courting higher risk to principal. Instead of seeking higher income investments, develop a diversified portfolio for a total return.
10. Purchase a new fund with less than a five-year track record. Would you bet part of your retirement on a horse that had never run a race? Don't bet precious money on a new product with a small asset base, a new approach to investing, a new manager at the helm, and no past performance statistics to tell where it is vulnerable during unfavorable markets?
11. Trade funds for short term returns, seeking quick profits. Mutual funds were developed for long term investing. Switching increases volatility to your portfolio. You hired a money manager. Let him or her manage.
12. Choose funds that use market timing strategies. Asset allocation or timing funds try to outguess which market will shine tomorrow. When they guess right, you profit—when wrong, you lose—sometimes big time.
13. Purchase an investment because of its popular reputation. This may guarantee quality in burgers and chicken, but not in investing. Company reputations are created by marketing departments and "word of mouth." Choose your mutual funds like you do your friends—selectively and for reasons other than their popularity.
14. Choose funds touted by newsletter or publication money gurus. These strangers are risking your money with no risk on their side (unless you don't send in your subscription check). If they are smart enough to foretell the future, why are they selling advice to strangers, when they could be secretly buying stocks for their own accounts?
15. Purchase on recommendations from consumer publications. You can't pick tomorrow's track winners with yesterday's racing form. Similarly, you can't foretell future winners by looking backward at historical data. Some things improve with age. Mutual fund track records don't.
16. Buy on the advice of friends, colleagues, co-workers or relatives. Well meaning incompetents can do as much financial damage as any vested interest. Get a competent and useful financial education.
17. Believe that "no load" always means "no charges." No one will invest your money for free. End of story. Can you think of any other product you can get without a charge? Why would you believe any investment company with large overhead to pay, managers to bonus, payroll to make, full colored ads to buy and customer postage to absorb, could invest your money for nothing? Mutual funds may charge you in ways you can't see.
18. Buy the cheapest mutual funds. Are you driving the cheapest car made today? Do you purchase the cheapest food for your family? Do you want the cheapest doctor in town? Buying on price alone may cost you more if it falls apart. Don't shop on price alone. You deserve the best—good value for every consumer dollar spent.

19. Buy without reading—and understanding—the prospectus and the Statement of Investments. The prospectus will disclose vital information.
20. Believe the biggest funds must be the best. Some are so large that they have great difficulty flexing their muscles in any direction. You can't beat the market if you *are* the market. With novice investors timing their investments, these funds can be whipsawed by greed and fear. They may also be targets for professional market timers. Funds under pressure to produce consistently outstanding returns might carry little cash on hand for mass investor exits in a quickly declining market.
21. Investing solely within the same family of funds. Investing in the "family way" allows you to move from one fund to another easily and without additional charges. But don't choose mediocre fund types just because they are offered by the same fund group.
22. Staying with a losing fund because you paid a load. You could have even greater losses tomorrow and you are paying opportunity costs by not being where the profits are now. Separate the psychological issues from the facts.

How many funds?

The answer depends on how much money you invest. If you have only a few thousand dollars, two funds with different investment objectives can give you all four investing building blocks at the same time: stocks, bonds, cash, and global.

With a much larger sum, a well diversified portfolio might contain five to six funds with different objectives.

Beyond that point, real diversification may not increase, but your return may decrease due to duplication of underlying asset allocation.

Dollar-cost averaging: You don't have to be a fat cat to invest

Discipline. What was your parents' approach? "Do it because I said so?" "If Joey jumped off the bridge, would you jump off after him?" "It's about time you grew up." "We're doing this for your own good."

They certainly commanded your attention, even if they might have been more effective through kinder and gentler means. Discipline (at least when it comes to investing) can be **very** good and **very** kind to you.

Knowing when to buy low and sell high is impossible, even for the experts. But an old investing strategy, dollar-cost averaging, may help increase your profits over the long run.

Dollar-cost averaging, in simple terms, is putting a regular systematic investment plan into action. By contributing the same amount of money each time into a mutual fund (no matter what price per share), you limit your purchases when prices are higher and purchase more shares when prices per share are lower. Over time this may yield a greater accumulation for your long term financial goals. For example:

Amount per Pay	% Return	# of Years	Accumulation Value
$50	10	10	$10,328
$50	10	15	$20,896
$50	10	20	$38,285
$50	10	25	$68,695
$50	10	30	$113,966

This automatic investment plan accomplishes several major goals:

- You pay yourself first.
- You develop a habit of disciplined long term investing.
- If you don't see the money, you will be less apt to spend it.
- You get used to various market ups and downs.
- You provide a relatively painless method to save for the future.
- You may earn greater profits per dollar invested over the time frame.

The optimum investment vehicles are stock mutual funds, which fluctuate more up and down than the dull "turtles" advised for lump sum investing. If you liquidate your account, adding it to your diversified accounts when the stock funds are high priced, you will retain your profits and keep them healthy when the next bear market comes along. By using your profits to re-balance your asset mix into the original percentages you chose, you have re-balanced your portfolio while using greater risk to make smaller investments work even harder.

A disciplined "pay yourself first" investing program accumulates wealth over time. The point is there is never a bad time to make a good investment. You send your check (or automatic deposit draft) whether you feel like it or not, rains or shine, whether you need new tires for the car or a better living room couch. Every week or month, your systematic savings plan kicks into action.

Value averaging

This new investing strategy takes the averaging concept further by focusing on the value of your investment rather than the cost.

Instead of investing a set amount of, say, $100 each month, you set an investment objective of increasing the value of your portfolio by $100 per month. At the end of the given time period, depending on the current value of your portfolio, you either invest or divest whatever amount is needed to bring the value of your portfolio to the desired level.

If your stocks have decreased in value, you put in more than the $100 to replace the lost value. But if they have increased in value, you put in less than the usual amount, perhaps even selling shares.

By reducing your investment and taking profits off the table when stock prices are high, you may achieve an even lower average cost per share than with dollar-cost averaging. However, you may also accumulate less overall money in your account because you are not consistently adding as much as possible to fund your portfolio on a regular basis. You also attract short term capital gains taxes like mad when certain markets are rapidly rising.

Mutual funds are "set and forget" money. Invest as much and as regularly as you can, re-balance your portfolio occasionally, and let simmer like a great stew on the back burner of your kitchen stove until it's time for dinner.

Your financial bicycle

Building a mutual fund portfolio with cash (and cash equivalents) as a solid foundation and shock absorber is similar to assembling a marathon bicycle for long term comfortable transportation. Here are some guidelines:

1. Bicycle tires keep close contact with the road and hug around the turns. Cash performs the same useful purpose; it cushions the bumps and potholes in the road and hugs the turns when the highway becomes dark and slippery.
2. Fenders keep the mud from splashing up on you. For diversification, and protection in case a temporary banking crisis hits your town, a money market mutual fund with check writing privileges will provide 24-hour access to funds for groceries, short term bills and other expenses. Since no mutual fund is insured, check for solvency as outlined in Chapter 21.
3. A comfortable seat is a must for long term traveling. You can travel long financial distances with a portfolio well diversified into all major asset classes: cash, stocks and bonds.
4. Handlebars help you steer and, depending on your age, a global fund or a triple bond fund for retirees may raise total return without adding much more risk to the overall mix.
5. An annual tune-up, re-balancing the elements back to their original percentages, is desired. If, for example, your global mutual fund performed much better than expected, global exposure should be reduced by exchanging some of your profits into the other asset classes.

Bearing up in bear markets

Big investors run **to** out of greed and run **from** out of fear. Their big money makes tomorrow's markets, our money just tags along.

If you structure your portfolio for comfort, buying all four basic investing blocks at the same time (stocks, bonds, cash, and global), your financial ship will weather the stormy seas, stock market rain or shine.

Taxing matters

Some "experts" recommend you keep tax efficient investments like stock shares and stock mutual funds outside of tax shelters, placing your tax magnets, like bonds and other lower yielding investments, inside your IRA and other retirement accounts.

The end result is that the low return issues get the best tax advantage, while the growth investments (stocks and stock mutual funds), get pummeled when you sell or every few years in an end of the year sell-off. Direct the inflation fighting growth oriented issues into your bulletproof tax shelters like IRA Accounts, and let Uncle Sam pound the heck out of your 5% - 8% fixed income securities.

The rap on wrap accounts

Brokerages want their share of money management fees. Today you can hire your own private money manager to look after your investment assets. This product has snob appeal. What great cocktail conversation! However, you pay extra for the right to name drop.

Brokerage fees are exorbitant, considering both the broker and the money manager get a piece of the action. You are threading your money through two financial intermediaries before your profits start. Private money managers may not perform any better than mutual fund superstars. With mutual funds, you can monitor their daily progress and know exactly how your money is doing at all times.

Discretionary accounts with brokerages who can buy and sell without your approval can be dangerous. The free rein can also cause churning, excessive buying and selling to induce commissions by the registered representative, the salesperson.

There is no status in overpaying. Mutual funds will cost you less, offer 24-hour service and provide lots of benefits to boot.

Don't give up your role as money manager and decision maker. I want someone to fuss over me for my intrinsic value, not for my investment account.

Final points to remember

- Past performance records are often a rotten guide to future results.
- Even poor quality funds may briefly rank as top performers.
- Some mutual funds are mislabeled; names can be misleading.

Winning the Money Game

- Higher yields usually mean greater risks to investment principal.
- Total return includes both a yield and the return of your principal.
- Avoiding risk is often least appreciated until you lose money.

Dull, stodgy, boring mutual fund "turtles" will help you become rich slowly but surely, allowing you to sleep tight when others are losing their peace of mind and significant investment capital.

Conclusion

The best thing you can do to help the poor is not to join its ranks. With this in mind, I close this book by offering you the following suggestions:

The five best investments for Winning the Money Game

1. Pay off your credit card debt. I can promise you a safe, guaranteed double-digit return on your money if you will stop living life on the installment plan. If necessary, put credit cards on "ice," in the freezer to provide a "cooling off" period, or use "plastic surgery"—cut them up.
2. Pay yourself first. Develop a rainy day emergency money fund through payroll deduction or automatic bank draft. If you don't see and handle that money, you will be less tempted to spend it.
3. Complete and follow a financial road map. A budget is your first step toward financial independence. A budget doesn't take time; it *saves* time. It doesn't prevent you from having what you desire; it makes your financial dreams possible.
4. Learn to live *beneath* your financial means. The most dangerous status game you can play is purchasing a home you can't really afford to impress a lot of people you don't really like.
5. Give your children *who* you are, not *what* you have. Stop buying your kids. Instead, build around them a useful structure of integrity, common sense, intelligence, and caring and teach them the meaning of those honorable four-letter words—"h-a-r-d w-o-r-k."

Appendix

Worksheets: I know it's in here somewhere

Mortgage payments. The orthodontist bills. Is your good cholesterol winning over the bad? Not another gray hair!

What's on your money mind? Keeping financial information in your head or on assorted Post-its isn't the best way to have financial records organized and easily accessible to you and to your family. I have created a variety of worksheets and forms to help you document all aspects of your financial affairs. Feel free to make multiple copies of these pages, so you can scribble, rework and update as necessary. Then, keep them together with your other important papers.

Worksheets: I know it's in here somewhere

NAME _____ DATE_____

FINANCIAL GOALS AND OBJECTIVES

RETIREMENT OBJECTIVES_____

CAREER GOALS_____
_____

FAMILY PLANS_____
_____

EDUCATION OBJECTIVES_____
_____

ESTATE COMMITMENTS_____
_____

CURRENT INCOME NEEDS_____
_____

BUSINESS PURSUITS OR SPECIAL DREAMS NOT MENTIONED ABOVE
_____
_____

ATTITUDES

How important are the following to you? Please rank 1 to 5

____ Financial provisions for family/spouse in the event of your death.
____ Educational plans.
____ Future retirement needs for yourself/spouse.
____ Current need for income.
____ Special plans/objectives.

WHAT IS YOUR RISK TOLERANCE

How much risk can you (are you willing to) tolerate?
___A lot   ___A fair amount   ___Not a little, not a lot
___A little   ___As little as possible

My risk attitude toward investing is:
___ Conservative   ___ Moderate   ___ Aggressive

I would be upset if I lost*:
___ $1 out of $10
___ $10 out of $100
___ $100 out of $1,000
___ $1,000 out of $10,000
___ $10,000 out of $100,000

*Since each of the above examples shows a 10-percent loss of principal, you may believe you are more risk tolerant than you really are. If you marked none of the above, you are an aggressive investor. The more money you are working with, the more risk, averse you tend to become. Review your answers. You may be more conservative than you believe.

Are there investments you would not consider? ___Yes ___No

If so, what? _____

Worksheets: I know it's in here somewhere

SHORT TERM FINANCIAL GOALS

	Essential	Important	Not Important
Eliminating credit card debt	___	___	___
Taxes	___	___	___
Vacation	___	___	___
Home furnishings	___	___	___
Medical expenses	___	___	___
College expenses	___	___	___
Emergency fund	___	___	___
Hobbies/collections	___	___	___
Other (please list)	___	___	___
	___	___	___
	___	___	___
	___	___	___

Short term goals are those within a time frame of one to three years. Short term money must be handled in a special manner because liquidity, flexibility and accessibility are top priorities. The tradeoff will be a decrease in yield. By concentrating on conserving the principal or the safety of the investment capital, you must give up higher potential rates of return.

Winning the Money Game

LONG TERM FINANCIAL GOALS

	Essential	Important	Not Important
Retirement funding	_____	_____	_____
New car	_____	_____	_____
New home or condo	_____	_____	_____
Vacation home	_____	_____	_____
Starting a family	_____	_____	_____
Boat/RV	_____	_____	_____
Major home improvements	_____	_____	_____
College education	_____	_____	_____
Child's wedding	_____	_____	_____
Extended vacation	_____	_____	_____
Professional studies	_____	_____	_____
Career change	_____	_____	_____
Starting a business	_____	_____	_____
Other (please list)	_____	_____	_____
	_____	_____	_____
	_____	_____	_____

The goal of long term dollars must be conservation of purchasing power, not principal. If your goals are more than three years away, inflation will loom as your deadliest adversary, and you must plan your investments to beat, or at least keep pace with, inflationary pressures each and every year. Some growth investments are essential.

Worksheets: I know it's in here somewhere

PORTFOLIO PLANNING WORKSHEET

Short term investment objective: _____

Long term investment objective: _____

SHORT TERM MONEY
1. Cash, checking accounts, emergency funds, CDs:

Where deposited	% Return	$ Value	Percentage of portfolio
TOTAL			100%

SECURITIES/LONG TERM MONEY

2. Retirement programs, college funding, vehicles for other goals:

Name of vehicle	% Return	$ Value	Percent of portfolio	Maturity Date

3. Regular investment programs (IRA, SEP, 401(k), 403(b), profit sharing, ESOP, bonds):

Name of vehicle	Amount of investment	Frequency	Present value

Worksheets: I know it's in here somewhere

DO YOU KNOW WHERE THESE DOCUMENT ARE?

1. Original birth certificate(s) (if married, for both spouses, children and other dependents); other religious (not legal) documents

2. Original Social Security card(s)

3. Legal marriage licenses

4. Military records and discharge papers

5. Divorce decree or legal separation document; death certificate of spouse (if widowed)

6. Property deed; titles of ownership to real estate in other states; rental contracts

7. Mortgage note; satisfaction of mortgage, title insurance; real estate purchase contract

8. Receipts for real estate improvements, plus buying and selling costs

9. Federal and state tax returns (for the last six years); deceased spouse estate tax return

10. Home and auto insurance; declarations and underlying contracts; automobile titles; auto leasing agreements; driver's license number(s)

11. Life insurance and annuity contracts; all current beneficiary designations (include benefits through employer)

12. Rights of interment for cemetery plot; prepaid funeral contract

13. Employer pension, retirement, health, disability and other contracts; employee handbook

14. Medical history of family members; current prescription(s); special medical instructions

15. Emergency phone numbers (police, fire, hospital, next of kin)

16. Personal and supplemental health, disability and other insurance contracts

Winning the Money Game

17. Insurance/survivor benefits and services (through professional/consumer associations, societies, credit cards)

18. Professional liability contract (if applicable)

19. Credit card (numbers and issuer's toll-free phone numbers

20. Back-up disks for business files and records

21. Location of safe deposit box (keys, passwords or security measures)

22. Location of negotiable securities (stock, bond, mutual fund certificates; savings bonds)

23. Name and location of banks, credit unions, mutual funds, other investment holdings.

24. Savings and checking account statements; IRA records; cancelled checks; current and past investment statements

25. Wills; power of attorney; living wills; trusts; promissory notes; loan agreements; other legal and estate documents

26. Names, addresses, telephone numbers of family; physicians; clergy; personal/business attorney; accountant; stockbroker; financial planner; investment advisor; employer benefits contract person; other professionals

27. Jewelry and antique appraisals and certificates of authenticity

28. Inventory of household goods and furnishings (photos or videotapes)

29. Guarantees, warranties and receipts for products purchased

Worksheets: I know it's in here somewhere

MONTHLY EXPENSE DETAIL

The left column is the recommended percentage per expense category. If any of the expenses below are based on weekly outgo, multiply by 4.3 weeks in each month for an accurate monthly figure.

MONTHLY CASH FLOW STATEMENT

10%	**Savings and investments** Company pension plans, individual retirement plans, emergency fund, savings account and general investment accounts:	
22%	**Housing costs** Monthly mortgage payment/rent:	
	Property taxes/condo fees:	
	Property insurance (per month):	
	Home equity loan payments:	
18%	**Consumer debt** Dept. store accounts:	
	Credit card accounts:	
	Bank loans:	
	Car payment(s):	
	Other time payments	
50%	**Other monthly expenses** * Child support/alimony:	
	* Electricity:	
	* Heat:	
	* Telephone:	
	* Water:	
	* Liability insurance:	
	* Auto insurance:	
	* Life insurance:	
	* Medical/dental:	
	* Medicare B/Medigap:	
	* Life, disability, long term care:	
	* Other insurance:	
	* Groceries:	
	* Gasoline/diesel:	
	* Car maintenance:	
	* Commuting/parking:	
	* Dining out:	
	* Entertainment:	

Winning the Money Game

	*	Cable TV:	
	*	Garbage collection:	
	*	Clothing:	
	*	Childcare:	
	*	Vacation:	
	*	Student loans:	
	*	School tuition:	
	*	School supplies:	
	*	Church/charity:	
	*	Organization dues:	
	*	Subscriptions:	
	*	Household items:	
	*	Home maintenance:	
	*	Holidays/gifts:	
	*	Miscellaneous:	
	*	Allowances:	
		Total	

* These items may have to be slashed to allow for savings and investments and overruns in other areas. If, on the other hand, money used for "other monthly expenses" represents *less* than 50 percent of total take-home pay, other areas can be expanded, such as purchasing a bigger home or increasing the savings and investing portion.

MONTHLY BUDGET & EXPENSES

Net take-home pay:	
Monthly expenses:	
Fritter money (take-home pay minus expenses)	

PRESENT LUMP SUM OBLIGATIONS

Mortgage balance	
Home equity	
Education	
Major debts (car loan, etc.)	
Student loan	
Credit cards	
Bank loans	
Personal loans	

WHAT ARE YOU WORTH?

Liquid Assets	DATE
Cash/liquid money	$
Checking accounts	$
Credit Union:	$
Savings accounts:	$
Savings bonds:	$
Money market funds:	$
Life insurance cash values:	$
Total Liquid Assets [a]:	$
Investment Assets	
Stocks:	$
Bonds:	$
Mutual funds:	$
Certificates of Deposit:	$
Retirement Plans	
Vested company pension/income:	$
IRA's/SEPs/KEOGHs:	$
401(k), 403(b), TDA, TSA plans:	$
Other:	$
Total Investment Assets [b]:	$
Real and Personal Assets	
Vacation home or land:	$
Rental property:	$
Jewelry/art/antiques:	$
Collections:	$
Other:	$
Total Personal Assets [c]:	$
Total Assets [a + b + c]	$

Liabilities	
Mortgage:	$
Credit card balances:	$
Home equity loan:	$
Car loans:	$
Time/personal loans:	$
Education loans:	$
Life insurance loans:	$
Other debt:	$
Total liabilities	$

YOUR NET WORTH

Total assets:	$
Minus total liabilities	- $
Your personal net work	$

ADDITIONAL LIVING ASSETS*

* Do not include these in previous net worth statement unless plan to sell a bedroom or car to pay for three meals a day!

Fair market value of home:	$
Current value of auto(s):	$
Market price of personal belongings:	$
Other:	$

Winning the Money Game

CREDIT CARD REGISTER

Card issuer	Balance owed	Card number	Phone, if lost
1.			
2.			
3.			
4.			
5.			
6.			
7.			
8.			
9.			
10.			

CREDIT CARD MANAGEMENT STRATEGY

Name of company	Balance of payoff	APR*	Minimum monthly payment	Annual fee
	Shame	**on**	**you!!**	

* Annual percentage rate. These rates can be deceptive because they lead you to believe that the interest is not compounded, while the monthly interest is compounded each and every month throughout the year on an unpaid credit balance. You will add almost two percent more interest per year to the average cost of credit borrowing in addition to the stated interest rate if you pay your credit card debts over long installments.

Worksheets: I know it's in here somewhere

HOME IMPROVEMENT

Description of work	Date
Additions (bath, breezeway, closet, deck or terrace, dormer, fence and gate, fireplace or stove, garage or carport, laundry room, patio, porch, porch enclosure, new room, room divider, hot tub, sauna, swimming pool, radiator covers)	
Air conditioners (central, wall, window if left when you sell)	
Assessments (sewers, sidewalks, streets, street lights, connections)	
Attic (bath, fan, room conversion)	
Awnings, shades, venetian blinds	
Basement (recreation room, sump pump, waterproofing)	
Built-ins (barbecue, bookcases, cabinets, furniture, stereo, shelves, TV, valances, mirrors)	
Curtains, draperies, traverse rods	
Drain pipes and dry wells	
Driveway	
Electrical (chandeliers, circuit breakers, cove lights, fuse box, lightening rod, outdoor lighting, outlets and wall switches, wiring system)	
Fire detection and security systems, locks	
Floors	
Greenhouse	
Heating system	
Hot water heater	
Insulation and weather stripping	
Kitchen (compactor, cooking range and hood, counter top, dishwasher, food freezer, garbage disposal, refrigerator, sink, ventilator, grease traps, towel racks)	
Laundry	
Lawns and landscaping (bulbs or perennials, compost bin, grading, sod, top soil, sprinkler system, trees/shrubs/bushes/vines, trellis and ornamental fixtures, mailbox, dog run)	
Locks, bells and chimes	

Modernization	
Paneling or plastering	
Play equipment (permanently installed)	
Plumbing (sinks, shower stalls and tubs)	
Retaining wall	
Roof, storm windows and doors	
Septic tank	
Siding	
Stairs	
Telephone jacks	
Tennis court	
Termite proofing	
TV antenna/satellite dish	
Walks and pathways	
Water softener	
Windows (additions and replacements, permanent treatments)	
Work shed and outbuildings	
Other (any permanent improvements left with home when sold)	

Worksheets: I know it's in here somewhere

COLLEGE PLANNING WORKSHEET

1. Estimating The Cost Of College

Enter the name and age of your child or grandchild in the space provided. In the next space, enter the estimated annual cost for tuition, fees, and room and board at the institution you'd like him or her to attend. Or, if you prefer, simply use the average cost figures for public and private colleges, which for the 1996-1997 school year were $9,649 and $20,361, respectively.

Next, look up the Estimated Future Cost Factor (based on an average annual increase of 6%, as projected by many college planning experts) on the chart below. Enter the number in the space provided. Multiply the current college cost by the Estimated Future Cost Factor and enter that number in the final space. This is the estimate of the total four-year future cost for the child's education.

Name and age of child	Current annual college cost	Estimated future cost factor	Total college costs in future dollars
	$	x	= $
	$	x	= $
	$	x	= $

2. What You'll Need To Save

Again, enter the name and age of your child or grandchild in the space provided. In the next space, enter the estimated total costs from Step 1. Next, look up the Required Savings Factor below, and enter that number in the space provided. *Multiply the estimated total cost by the Required Savings Factor and enter that number in the final space. This is the estimate of the annual savings required to accumulate enough money for the college you have selected.

Name and age of child	Total college in future dollars	Required savings factor	Annual savings required
	$	x	= $
	$	x	= $
	$	x	= $

Winning the Money Game

Age of Child	Estimated future cost factor	Required savings factor
1	11.780	.025
2	11.113	.027
3	10.484	.031
4	9.891	.034
5	9.331	.038
6	8.803	.043
7	8.304	.049
8	7.834	.056
9	7.391	.064
10	6.972	.074
11	6.578	.087
12	6.205	.104
13	5.854	.126
14	5.523	.158
15	5.210	.205
16	4.915	.285
17	4.637	.445
18	4.375	.926

*This factor assumes a hypothetical fixed average rate of return of 8%. This is not intended to depict or predict the performance of any specific investment for any period of time and does not take into account any tax obligations or changes in capital value. Since the future costs of a college education are subject to change, estimated future cost factors should be used only as estimates.

Worksheets: I know it's in here somewhere

TOTAL WORK COMPENSATION BENEFITS CHECKLIST

			YES	NO
1.	Group basic term life insurance amount	$_____	____	____
2.	Optional term or other life insurance amount	$_____	____	____
3.	Deferred compensation amount	$_____	____	____
4.	Retirement health/dental plan amount	$_____	____	____
5.	Flexible spending account (cafeteria plan) amount	$_____	____	____
6.	Retirement insurance plan amount	$_____	____	____
7.	Basic pension amount	$_____	____	____
	Employer match	____%	____	____
8.	Supplementary retirement savings	$_____	____	____
9.	Employer match Lump sum retirement option (Such as 401(k), ESOP, 403(b), TSA)	____%	____	____
9.	Thrift savings plan/profit sharing	$_____	____	____
	Employer match	____%	____	____
10.	Spouse/dependent plan: type	$_____	____	____
11.	Special benefits	$_____	____	____

Winning the Money Game

RETIREMENT BENEFITS

Type of pension benefit	Amount $	Lump sum $	Monthly benefit $	At Age	Eligible for IRA rollover? Yes No
Basic pension	_____	_____	_____	___	___ ___
401(k)	_____	_____	_____	___	___ ___
Profit sharing	_____	_____	_____	___	___ ___
Tax-sheltered annuity (TSA, 403(b), TDA)	_____	_____	_____	___	___ ___
Thrift-savings/ supplemental	_____	_____	_____	___	___ ___
ESOP/stock plan	_____	_____	_____	___	___ ___
Previous plan	_____	_____	_____	___	___ ___
Deferred compensation	_____	_____	_____	___	___ ___
Employer match (if separate)	_____	_____	_____	___	___ ___
Social Security	_____	_____	_____	___	___ ___
Other pension benefits	_____	_____	_____	___	___ ___
IRA accounts	_____	_____	_____	___	___ ___
Investments	_____	_____	_____	___	___ ___
Other	_____	_____	_____	___	___ ___
Retirement life insurance	_____ (level)	_____ (decreasing to)	_____	___	___ ___

INFLATION FACTOR TABLE FOR PROJECTING ANNUAL RETIREMENT INCOME PAYMENTS

	(Inflation rate)		
Years to Retire	3%	4%	5%
30	2.43	3.24	4.32
29	2.36	3.12	4.12
28	2.29	3.00	3.92
27	2.22	2.88	3.73
26	2.16	2.77	3.56
25	2.09	2.67	3.39
24	2.03	2.56	3.23
23	1.97	2.46	3.07
22	1.92	2.37	2.93
21	1.86	2.28	2.79
20	1.81	2.19	2.65
19	1.75	2.11	2.53
18	1.70	2.03	2.41
17	1.65	1.95	2.29
16	1.60	1.87	2.18
15	1.56	1.80	2.08
14	1.51	1.73	1.98
13	1.47	1.67	1.89
12	1.43	1.60	1.80
11	1.38	1.54	1.71
10	1.34	1.48	1.63
09	1.30	1.42	1.55
08	1.27	1.37	1.48
07	1.23	1.32	1.41
06	1.19	1.27	1.34
05	1.16	1.22	1.28
04	1.13	1.17	1.22
03	1.09	1.12	1.16
02	1.06	1.08	1.10
01	1.03	1.04	1.05

ESTATE ORGANIZER

Important names and phone numbers

Relatives	
Attorney(s)	Insurance agent(s)
Employer	
Financial planner	Employer benefits contact
Stockbroker/investment advisor	Accountant
Physician(s)	Bank/credit union
	Dentist
Other	Clergy

Worksheets: I know it's in here somewhere

CURRENT STATUS FINANCIAL GOALS AND OBJECTIVES
(Check off as review is completed)

Name: _____

Current status   **Date completed**

◊ Statement of financial position   _____
◊ Debt management   _____
◊ Emergency fund: liquidity   _____
◊ Active financial goal   _____
  ◊ short term   _____
  ◊ long term   _____

Asset allocation
Changes:

_____

_____

Risk management

◊ Home insurance   _____
◊ Auto insurance   _____
◊ Liability insurance (umbrella)   _____
◊ Death (life) insurance   _____
◊ Business liability   _____
◊ Disability   _____
◊ Health/dental   _____
◊ Nursing home care   _____
◊ Medicare B/Medigap   _____

Estate planning
◊ Current will   _____
◊ Health care directive   _____
◊ Durable power of attorney (financial)   _____
◊ Living will   _____
◊ Trusts   _____
◊ Special considerations   _____
◊ Deed ownership   _____